SAIL
the
WORLD

Everything You Need to Know
to Circumnavigate the Globe

ERICK A. REICKERT

Sail the World

Copyright ©2017 by Erick A. Reickert

For more information, pictures and detail go to: www.SVEscapade.com

ISBN 978-1-54412-143-7

Library of Congress Control Number: 2017905397

CreateSpace Independent Publishing Platform, North Charleston, SC

Edited by: Marilyn Murray Willison

Book Design and Cover by: Yellow Prelude Design, LLC

Quotes selected by Lady Susan Willis-Reickert

Dedication

*This book is dedicated to my wife and sailing
partner, Lady Susan, whose encouragement
and faith in me has been my inspiration.*

*Her belief that others will benefit from
my experiences has been unwavering.*

*It is also in memory of my late wife, Heather,
who began the grand adventure
of sailing around the world.*

Sea Fever

by Johns Masefield

I must down to the seas again, To the lonely sea and the sky,
And all I ask is a tall ship and a star to steer her by,
And the wheel's kick and the wind's song and the white sails shaking,
And a grey mist on the sea's face and a grey dawn breaking.

I must go down to the seas again, For the call of the running tide,
Is a wild call and a clear call that may not be denied;
And all I ask is a windy day with the white clouds flying,
And the flung spray and the blown spume and the seagulls crying.

I must go down to the seas again, To the vagrant gypsy life,
To the gull's way and the whale's way, Where the wind's like a whetted knife;
And all I ask is a merry yarn from a laughing fellow rover,
And a quiet sleep and a sweet dream when the long trick's over

Contents

CHAPTER 1
The World is Yours. 1

CHAPTER 2
The Implications of World Cruising 4

CHAPTER 3
The Cruising Experience 7

CHAPTER 4
Passage Making 10

CHAPTER 5
Required Skills 13

CHAPTER 6
The Crew 16

CHAPTER 7
Selecting a Blue-Water Boat 21

CHAPTER 8
Choosing Equipment, Features and Specifications. 32

CHAPTER 9
Planning the Route 39

CHAPTER 10
Passage, Plan and Log. 42

CHAPTER 11
Navigation and Communications 46

CHAPTER 12
Security and Pirates 50

CHAPTER 13
Layup 53

CHAPTER 14
Cost of Cruising. 56

CHAPTER 15
Ownership, Taxes and Insurance 60

CHAPTER 16
Governmental Requirements 64

Contents

CHAPTER 17
Maintenance 66

CHAPTER 18
Provisioning 69

CHAPTER 19
Weather and It's Implications 72

CHAPTER 20
Heavy Weather Sailing and Tactics 75

CHAPTER 21
Living Onboard 79

CHAPTER 22
Cruising Risks and Ways to Evaluate Them 81

CHAPTER 23
World Cruising Grounds 85

CHAPTER 24
Our Circumnavigation 88

CHAPTER 25
Cruising Australia and New Zealand 97

CHAPTER 26
Pirates, The Red Sea and The Suez Canal 101

CHAPTER 27
Cruising from Alaska to Maine 105

CHAPTER 28
Shipping *ESCAPADE* by Ship 111

CHAPTER 29
These are the Good Old Days *114*

CHAPTER 30
ESCAPADE Journal 2002 116

CHAPTER 31
Memories and Experiences 196

CONCLUSION 210

EXHIBITS 211

Introduction

I first started sailing on Lake Michigan with my father when I was twelve years old. It was during those times that I acquired basic skills and experiences that helped me develop an enduring passion for sailing. And, consequently, I have been an enthusiastic sailor all my life, and have always loved the sea. My retirement plan was to buy a boat and sail the world's oceans. Doing so provided an outlet for all my energy, and was a thrilling challenge—both mentally and physically.

My background includes a degree in Engineering from Northwestern University and a MBA from Harvard Business School with High Distinction. I spent 30 years in the automotive industry as a product planner and then Vice President of Export Operations at Ford in England. I convinced Henry Ford II that my concept, the Fiesta, had a major market potential in the UK and then implemented the Fiesta in Europe where it still holds a major market share. I was President and CEO of several divisions and entities at Chrysler. Lee Iacocca took me with him from Ford to Chrysler where I was President and CEO of Acustar, the parts supplier for Chrysler, and President and CEO of Chrysler Mexico.

This experience gave me strong engineering capabilities that permitted me to select and specify the type of sailboat that would be superior in circumnavigating the world. It also gave me the ability to service and maintain all of the equipment aboard the boat.

The motivation to write this book was because much of the information I sought to make decisions was not readily available or in a form that was easy to digest. The popular boating press does not handle many of the critical issues and often does not put "disaster" stories into context.

This book presents data and information not available elsewhere. For example, there is a concise analysis of boat design alternatives, a discussion of crew, a unique approach to risk analysis, tax implications, and the knowledge necessary to cruise successfully and maintain the boat.

You will find this book a refreshing new look at cruising, and everything associated with it. So if you are considering cruising or circumnavigating, this book is a must read.

CHAPTER 1

The World *is* Yours

The Rewards of World Cruising

Do just once what others say you can't do,
and you will never pay attention to their limitations again.

— CAPTAIN JAMES COOK, BRITISH ROYAL NAVY —

Do you want an adventure that very few people have ever experienced, much less imagined? Are you thrilled by travel to exotic locations with unspoiled beauty, as well as to major cities and luxurious surroundings? Do you long for new challenges that will test your own abilities, skills, and provide an unparalleled learning experience? Do you seek excitement of the highest order, as well as plenty of tranquil moments? Are you an individual who is confident when alone, and not dependent upon outside assistance? Do you admire and respect the world's oceans, and love to sail your own boat?

If so, sailing around the world is for you! This book will describe what it takes to accomplish a circumnavigation of the globe on your own boat, as well as how to do it easily and in style—with comfortable living and minimum risk. Plus, I will share with you details from several of our many experiences.

There are a variety of ways to accomplish this goal, and many choices to make, but this book will describe how to do it in a relaxed, even luxurious way. There are—of course—cheaper ways, but none that will provide a more pleasant or refined experience. Cruising does not have to be an endurance test or the complete loss of normal living standards. It can be an uplifting and pleasurable adventure, as well as a worthy lifetime accomplishment.

The rewards of global cruising are enormous, and they are both life changing and satisfying. Additionally, you can tailor your experience to your personal tastes. Some of the appealing aspects are

- Sailing, in and of itself, is enjoyable. Being on the water—with the wind propelling the boat as you manage the sea and weather conditions—is fun and challenging. Cruising—of course—also requires that you get to a destination, no matter what the wind velocity is or in which direction it is blowing.

- Cruising requires continuous and accurate navigation in unknown territory to reach your destination safely and to avoid all hazards. This generally requires stringent research prior to departure, as well as knowledge of tides, currents, traffic schemes, port restrictions, etc., etc. Observing and overcoming the legal requirements for customs, entry, emigration, departure and health can be—and often are challenging. They invariably require advance research because many countries have multiple rules and regulations, which frequently change and must be followed. This often requires months of planning in advance of arrival.

- Since you are as divorced from humanity to the greatest degree possible while on a passage, it can be a truly liberating experience. When it is just you—and those with you—on your boat, nothing else exists in the world. When land is out of sight for days on end, the whole experience should be comfortable and enjoyable. A long-distance passage is the true "get away from it all" voyage, and a truly magical experience.

- Getting there may be half the fun, but the destinations are the real goal. You can choose remote anchorages in idyllic settings that are picture perfect. Very few people can partake of this experience because cruise ships are too large, and only private boats can access the unique locations. You will often be able to interact with the local population, and meet people who are not part of the "modern" world. Two areas that I found to be especially delightful were the San Blas Islands on the northern coast of Panama and the Yasawa Islands west of Fiji. Later in the book, I will give a more thorough description of these destinations.

- Arriving at a major city in your own boat is a wonderful experience, and you often have a unique location from which to explore the city. Most cities have marinas right on the waterfront, which is generally the most desirable place to be. We have been in heart of things in Auckland, Baltimore, Lisbon, London, Miami, Monaco, Seattle, and Sydney—among others.

- Participating in water sports from your own boat can be exhilarating. Whether you like scuba diving, snorkeling, swimming—or being towed by a dinghy—your own "swim platform" is the perfect place to start.

- Cruising is generally an individual boat affair. There are, however, many opportunities for group activities that involve other boats. There are boating rallies that cross the Atlantic Ocean, go around the world, or go from the States to the Caribbean and back. There are also multi-day events organized by boat builders, sailing organizations or other groups. These all provide a good dose of camaraderie, as well as competition. By just sailing from port to port you can meet many other cruisers, and a good number of these will probably become life-long friends. Plus, you can also cruise jointly with other boats.

- Travel to many foreign countries provides an opportunity to learn about, and participate in many faraway cultures. When you are on your own boat in a port, you are actually living there, not just visiting. This experience is vastly different from being a tourist who is staying at a hotel. As a resident, you have to go to the indigenous markets, rely on nearby transportation, and become familiar—as well as involved—with local events. If the port is small, we would often rent a car and drive throughout the countryside or the island. Sometimes these side trips took a number of days, and gave us a deeper insight into the area's unique culture.

- There are plenty of "cruising grounds" scattered around the world where you can enjoy relaxed sailing and pleasant surroundings while becoming familiar with the local environment. I will cover several of these in more detail later in the book, but a few of them include the Barrier Reef of Australia, the Bay of Islands in New Zealand, the Caribbean, Chesapeake Bay, the coast of Croatia, Greek islands, Islands near Phucket, Thailand, and Long Island Sound.

We participated in all of these activities and locales, but you can select your own mix to suit your taste. Cruising is, in fact, one of the freest and most enlightening activities available today. Basically, you can depart from a port, and sail into the ocean without getting permission or informing anyone of where you are going. You might want to let some people know about your intentions for safety reasons, but there is no rule that requires it. More countries, including the United States, however, are adding requirements for arrivals so make sure you know and understand all the local legal travel requirements.

Selecting the boat and the equipment are the first—most basic—and most important decisions that must be made. The boat, of course, has a dual purpose because it is your home as well as your mode of transportation. Most of your time aboard will be in ports, and—as your domicile the boat must be both spacious and comfortable enough to make living onboard pleasant and enjoyable. This means a layout that is suitable for you, your family, the crew, as well as all the equipment—including air conditioning, communication devices, entertainment systems, freezer, heating and refrigeration. But the boat is also your transportation, which means it must be capable of handling—and surviving—the always changing conditions that will be encountered in a world cruise. It should cope with these conditions with assurance as well as a large safety margin. Bottom line, the boat should give you a surplus of confidence because you are placing your life—and those of the people with you—in its trust.

I made many decisions at the beginning of my quest, and nearly all of them turned out to be correct. I will describe all these choices, and which ones I would—with the benefit of hindsight—change. In basic terms, I advocate the selection of a well-equipped boat that has an excess of "creature comforts." In other words, the polar opposite of a "keep-it-simple" sailing philosophy. Naturally, more equipment means more maintenance and—ergo—more repairs. But I believe that the resultant comfort, pleasure, and safety are worth the added burden.

I will also address numerous topics that will help facilitate good decision-making and—hopefully—a better experience when you slip the lines and start your world cruise.

This book is based on my own cruising experience of over 73,000 nautical miles, covering a circumnavigation, and a voyage from Alaska to Maine over a span of 15 years. During that period, I lived onboard for nearly six years, and sailed the equivalent of 477 days. I entered 918 different ports around the world, visited 73 islands, 39 countries, and encountered 16 foreign languages. I used—during a total of 1300 times—all manner of securing the boat. I completed 45 passages, 63 overnights, and encountered fog, many gales, sandstorms, and one Force 10 Storm. Plus, there were plenty of other challenges that had to be met. But that is part of the appeal connected to a life-enhancing adventure.

Let's get going.

Escapade in French Polynesia
PHOTO BY CHARLIE SCOTT

CHAPTER 2

The Implications *of* World Cruising

Basic World Cruising Considerations

*By prevailing over all obstacles and distractions,
one may unfailingly arrive at his chosen destination*

CHRISTOPHER COLUMBUS

World cruising is great, but there are countless choices, and many attendant implications. First and foremost, the boat you choose must—MUST—be capable of crossing oceans, which is often called Blue Water sailing. This is true even for American sailors who just want to go to the Caribbean. The variables involved with crossing oceans are complicated, significant, and vastly different from those related to local or coastal sailing.

The basic requirement for a Blue Water Cruiser is that it can withstand and survive whatever sea conditions it may encounter. Even with modern and sophisticated weather forecasting and routing capabilities, it is still possible to get caught in severe weather conditions. On a passage between Fiji and New Zealand, two weather routers told us that it was safe to depart. But 400 miles from land, we found ourselves in a Force 10 Storm with 30 to 40 foot seas, and winds in excess of 55 knots. We had to sail in these very tough conditions for over two days, and maintain a course that would assure arrival in New Zealand rather than Antarctica. Even in normal Ocean conditions, the bigger the boat the better, and—obviously—one that has a greater displacement and is more seakindly will generally yield a better motion. Also, the boat needs to be strong and not flexible. Production boats that are flexible can result in drawers and cabinets

flying open, and the "working" of the rig (as well as the whole boat), which can lead to failures.

Another important consideration is the boat's range while motoring at cruising speed. I recommend that the minimum range should be 1,000 NM with the internal fuel tank. This is important for both crossing oceans and for cruising in remote locations where fuel can be hard to find. Some cruisers resort to jerry cans lined up—or flexible containers tied to—the deck. These are unsightly, unsecure, and definitely not a good solution. Also, bear in mind that the actual amount of motoring required while cruising is much more than most sailors would like.

Crossing oceans also requires a good deal of time. The typical distance across the Atlantic is around 2,800 NM from Las Palmas in the Canaries to St. Lucia in the Caribbean, and around 3,000 NM across the Pacific from the Galapagos to the Marquesas in French Polynesia. It took us 17 days to cross the Atlantic, and 18 days to cross the Pacific—which is on the quicker side. But you need to provision for at least a 50% longer trip than you expect to take, just to accommodate light winds or other situations. This means you must have storage, refrigerator and freezer space for more than a month's supply of food and liquids.

It is also critical to maintain electrical power while sailing. This requires a large battery bank, as well as a means to keep the battery charged. Later in the book, I will discuss this issue in more detail, but the power requirements—and a means to recharge—has far-reaching ramifications. My boat was quite power hungry because I needed electricity to charge the batteries, heat the water, make water, operate the autopilot, and run the refrigeration as well as fulfill all computer, general lighting and navigation requirements. As a result, I had a diesel generator as well as solar panels. This energy management also applies if you are in a remote anchorage for long periods of time. In summary, you must have a large battery bank—as well as the ability to keep the batteries charged—so that it meets all electrical requirements while sailing for weeks on end.

Having enough fresh water for drinking, washing and showering is important. Only when you are in the middle of an ocean do you realize how true the old saying— "Water, water everywhere but not a drop to drink"—really is. A large water tank is required, but also having a water maker is an important element for a good Blue Water boat. When we crossed the Atlantic, all six crewmembers had a hot shower every day, and when we arrived the water tank was still full. While cruising Mexico and third-world nations, we had another use for our water maker: If the local water is of questionable purity, you do not want to take on bacteria-laden water from shore, and have it contaminate your tank. My strategy was to make water while at sea, and then come into a port with a full tank of fresh water. By doing that, we never had to put local water into the tank.

Most cruisers sail westward around the globe, thus utilizing the trade winds that sailing ships have used for hundreds of years. This requires a sailing rig that is designed for downwind sailing, and can be "carried" in a wide range of sea and wind conditions during both day and night. Since cruising—unlike racing—does not usually involve constant trimming of the sails, a rig that you can just set and leave alone for days on end is important for pleasurable cruising.

Communications in the middle of the ocean requires satellite connections. That is true for data, e-mail, EPIRB, GPS, or internet. Even TV is available. This is, of course a fast-changing field, and the solutions that existed when I started cruising were different from those currently available. It all depends upon what you want to receive, and how much you want to spend. The bottom line is that, today, you can be as tied in with the "real world" as you want to be. It is no longer necessary to disappear for weeks on end, and lose all contact with your family and friends while you are cruising. While some people think that separating yourself from all the pressures of the world is a big plus for cruising, this is now a matter of choice.

It is important to determine—in advance—what areas of the world you want to cruise. Temperature, of course, is a major environmental consideration that will impact the type of equipment needed for your boat. When I started, I thought that I would only sail in warm (or hot) waters. So I equipped my boat with an air conditioning system that had reverse cycle heating for occasional heating needs. But when I decided to cruise Alaska—replete with icebergs—I installed a diesel-powered heater. This made the experience a pleasurable one, but without the heater, it would have (literally) been unbearable. Adequate ventilation is also important while maintaining security in hot, rainy and sticky climates. Make sure your boat has plenty of rain-free ventilation while in a picturesque anchorage, especially when the temperature approaches 100° F, and there is a rain shower.

Since security is of increasing importance these days, your boat should be lockable from the inside because you do not want unwanted visitors. We had the boat boarded three times while cruising, and once some of our equipment was stolen. Each time, it happened while we were sleeping. After those events, we made sure to lock up each night before retiring whenever we were in port.

One of the biggest factors when cruising in foreign countries is the difference in shore-side facilities. And the one with the most impact—outside of the US, Canada and Mexico—is electricity. Basically, the rest of the world is 240 volt, 50 Hertz AC, which differs from 120 volt, 60 Hertz in America. Of course, 50-amp service in the US is 240 volts, so that eases the problem a bit. But, be careful, because the wiring for the ROW (Rest of World) is different from what is used in the US. Also, all connectors are different shore-side. There are other additional electrical issues that exist, and I will discuss them later in the book.

Water connectors are also different, which can require specific hose fittings; these can vary greatly between countries. Also, TV and VHS standards are different, and since DVD's are protected by world region, locally-purchased DVD's will not necessarily play in your DVD player. While VHF frequencies are different in the rest of the world, most VHF radios provide a ROW option. Additionally, navigational buoys and marks are different in the ROW. For example, "Red right returning" is not correct. Chart symbols are also somewhat different, and all of these variables need to be—must be—learned and understood in advance.

In many countries, a major difference is the method of securing to a dock. In the Mediterranean, as well as other places, it is customary to use the "Med Moor" technique. This requires dropping the anchor, and then backing down to a point where you can tie stern lines to a dock or quay. The tension on the anchor line will keep the boat from hitting the dock. In some marinas, they have "laid lines" so your anchor is not necessary, because they already have either anchors or blocks—with lines attached—that are then tied to the dock. In this case, the procedure is to back down, as above, to the dock. An attendant will then hand you a line to take to the bow. In either case, to get ashore you need a gangplank off the stern. This is commonly called a "passerelle". So, you will need a passerelle, as well as the means to deploy it. Also, as you commonly back down between boats that are already Med Moored, you will need to be able to deploy the "anchor rode" from the helm, and have a crew member on each side of the boat to keep your fenders from "fowling" on the fenders of the other boats. It is a procedure that requires practice, but it results in a close packing of boats of all sizes in a limited dock space. It also has some unique advantages, like the times when we have had the end of our passerelle land only inches away from chairs at a Taverna in Greece.

These subjects will be discussed in more detail later in the book.

Escapade at Bozcaada, Turkey

NOTE PASSERELLE AND DINGHY UNDERNEATH ~ PHOTO BY ERICK REICKERT

CHAPTER 3

The *Cruising* Experience

What to Expect

The sea, once it casts its spell,
holds one in its net of wonder forever.

———— JACQUES YVES COUSTEAU ————

What is involved in cruising, and what it is like? This chapter will give some insight into what a person would experience, and what would be expected if he or she were to go cruising. In fact, I have shared this information with all perspective crew members, whether they were experienced or had never before been on a sailboat.

There are many aspects of sailing that contribute to the cruising experience. These include adventure, being out in the open with nature and the weather, excitement, new experiences, relaxation, travel, as well as the sheer exhilaration associated with sailing a large, high-performance boat. There is also, however, an element of risk because sailing—and weather complications—can sometimes be challenging. It's important to remember that—if not properly handled—there can be danger associated Blue Water cruising.

On *ESCAPADE*, we had experienced hands onboard, as well as newcomers to sailing. What we asked of those who came with us was an eagerness to learn, enjoy, and participate in the operation of the boat. Our primary priorities were the safety and comfort of the crew, as well as protection of the boat. To accomplish this, all crew—regardless of the level of their experience—participated in, and took responsibility for, their personal safety as well as

the safety of others. And this included handling lines in a manner that would avoid injuring hands as well as hurting muscles.

By design, a sailboat "heels" when under way. This can make moving about and performing tasks difficult. But since it is part of the fun and challenge of sailing, it should not be a concern. At all times, agility is required to move about on deck and to go below, but the boat will NOT "tip over".

All who come aboard should be able to swim confidently in salt water. Those who can't, will need to wear a personal flotation device (PFD) when outside of the cockpit. Under certain potentially risky conditions, all crew should wear a PFD when on deck, and sometimes all crew need to wear a harness and tether that is attached to the boat. "Man overboard" situations should be discussed and practiced, because it is everyone's responsibility to not fall into the water. Unfortunately, because once a person falls overboard, there is no assurance that they can—or will—be recovered.

Obviously, no one can enjoy sailing while seasick. And, in fact, their discomfort can diminish the enjoyment of the journey for the others who are aboard. Those who are susceptible to seasickness—or think they might be—

THE CRUISING EXPERIENCE   7

should bring seasickness remedies aboard, and use them ahead of time.

In terms of comfort, every person should have suitable clothing for a variety of cruising conditions. This will include various temperatures, the strength of the sun, and the possibility of rain.

Our boat—ESCAPADE—was a large and luxurious sailboat. She had air conditioning, a microwave, washer/dryer, TV, VCR, CD player, and DVD player (all of which could only be run under certain conditions), a large salon, two bathrooms ("heads") with separate shower areas, and generous cabins. She was beautiful inside and out, with a light oak interior and a teak deck. She was still, however, a sailboat with a limited amount of room. Spaces were small and tight by home standards, and living was in very close proximity to everyone else onboard. It was a group experience with little privacy. A good deal of "give and take" was required, and the goal was that everyone onboard would contribute to a cheerful, friendly, and helpful atmosphere.

As part of the learning—as well as the total—experience, everyone onboard was expected to participate in all aspects of running ESCAPADE. This included all the facets of sailing on deck—like docking, going about, keeping lookout, mooring, steering, tending lines, and trimming the sails, etc. Naturally, no one was asked to do anything beyond his or her capabilities or experience. This also includes domestic aspects like cleaning, cooking, keeping the boat shipshape, washing up, etc. Remember, as the boat was self-contained, there was limited water and power. Therefore, water and power conservation regimens were required. The toilet required pumping, as well as some knowledge and care. The boat had holding tanks for wastewater, but since they were limited in size, they could become full, which required a pump-out while in protected waters, or a discharge when far from land. And, it was important to remember that hatches and ports could only be opened under certain conditions. Everyone onboard was expected to adhere to these regimens and requirements. While cruising, good crew look for opportunities to be helpful, and taking part is the best way for everyone to feel involved.

Because sailing depends upon the weather, tides, seas, and other conditions outside of human control, timing simply cannot be precise. On a cruise, leaving a harbor will depend upon the projected weather and tides. Also, arrival at a certain point at a given time simply cannot be guaranteed. Everyone onboard must understand this, and be flexible. These unpredictable variables can affect your travel arrangements, and land sightseeing. We made sure to allocate time for shore visits, and let everyone participate in decision making to help determine the schedule.

Our boat was equipped with a large number of safety and navigational items, and was completely seaworthy. I believe that she was properly equipped and prepared for our planned voyages, as well as nearly any weather or navigation situation. Most of these items require expertise for operation, and correct usage of these was explained to everyone onboard. Our plan was to avoid bad weather by not leaving harbor if poor conditions are expected. If you get caught out in extreme weather, the motion of the boat can become violent, and conditions can quickly become difficult—even dangerous—both above and below deck. If this kind of situation arose, or in any other emergency or crisis, all crew knew—without question—that they had to immediately (for the safety of all aboard) obey orders from the Captain. The Captain needs to be competent and fit in order to both sail and manage the boat without a crew in any weather.

When cruising, meals onboard were based on the provisions available in foreign ports, and what was left in the pantry. Timing of meals depended upon the sailing plan. When underway, the type of food reflected the preparation requirements, and special dietary requirements or desires had to be expressed beforehand in order to be accommodated. Every person onboard had to make the Captain aware of any special medical conditions that—in the event of a medical emergency—could have arisen. A small First Aid kit was available, but it did not contain a wide variety of medications. Everyone on board should understand that —under some conditions—emergency medical help could be many hours away. Passengers were asked to bring ample medication for a period at least twice as long as the expected voyage.

Every person onboard your ship needs to have a passport, and all other legal requirements (visas, etc) for the countries through which the boat will pass. This often requires a way to leave the country, such as either an airline ticket to return home, or the cash to buy one. Note: Not all countries accept credit cards. Additionally, all persons embarking on a cruise must not bring any illegal substances, weapons, or packages from other parties onboard.

Sleeping onboard will be quite different from what you experience in your own bed at home. When in port, the boat will usually be anchored or tied up to either a dock or a pontoon. This means that even though the beds will be level, the boat may still have a rocking motion. The ports and hatches on ESCAPADE were not light tight, and—depending on where you are—temperatures can vary. Also, there will probably be many unfamiliar sounds—both inside and outside the boat. These can include possible noises from both shore and other boats, like pumps running, rigging banging, and water lapping, etc. When cruising, it's a good idea to bring eye masks and earplugs if any of these ambient conditions might bother you.

If all crew understands, accepts, and considers what is ahead of them (and what conditions might exist) that are part of the sailing and cruising experience, then they should have a delightful, memorable—even wonderful—time. On *ESCAPADE* each person had to take full responsibility for his or her decision to join the boat, and agreed—and was willing—to accept all the events that might have transpired. Crew also agreed that they would not hold the Captain (or the owner of the boat) responsible for any accident, damage, or injury that could have happened to them or a family member, or their possessions while aboard.

Escapade at anchor in Wall Bay, Turkey

THE STERN IS TIED TO SHORE ~ PHOTO BY ERICK REICKERT

CHAPTER 4

Passage Making

Aspects of Making a Passage

It does not matter how slow you go as long as you do not stop.

CONFUCIUS

A passage is a voyage that lasts more than one night, and (while sailing) allows the boat to be underway and moving 24 hours a day. This requires that someone should be on watch 24 hours a day. The watch consists of sailing the boat, which means keeping the sails in trim and properly adjusted, as well as keeping the boat heading in the desired direction. This can be assisted by an autopilot, which has the ability to maintain a constant angle with the wind, a constant direction, or a pre-specified course as desired—it can eliminate a major amount of work. The autopilot is the equivalent of an extra full-time crewmember.

Being on watch also requires monitoring the boats system's, navigation, possible contact with the outside world by radio or satellite, as well as watching for—and avoiding—other ships. Obviously, in the middle of an ocean there are fewer other ships and boats, but a passage may transverse through high-traffic areas, which requires constant lookout. Fishing boats present their own problems because they have the right of way when engaged in fishing operations. Each type of fishing boat, such as long liner, seiner, trawler, etc., has its own patterns of operation. And they are often oblivious to other boats around them, especially at night—when their own deck lights blind the crew.

Another factor to remember is that the conditions are never constant. The wind—often over a broad range—usually varies in intensity and direction. The waves and swells change in response to the winds, but if the wind switches quickly the waves are sometimes not consistent with the wind direction. Swells, which are long-period waves, come from long distances, and are often not related to local conditions. Wind waves are superimposed upon the swells. This means that the crew has to continually adjust the sails—even possibly the course—to respond to the changing wind and sea conditions. The steadiest conditions occur in the trade wind areas, which are usually just north or south of the equator. These conditions are generally quite consistent, but there are often small micro cells of weather associated with clouds that are going faster than the sailboat. These cells often contain both rain and high winds, the direction of which relates to your relative positions. These can be dangerous and—if possible—should be avoided. Many require sail reefing, or shortening, prior to their approach. Sailing in the trade winds also requires a good, stable downwind sail rig. On *ESCAPADE* we sailed wing-on-wing, which means we had the mainsail set to one side of the boat, the boom held in place by a preventer, and a polled-out Yankee foresail on the other side of the boat. Since this is a very strong setup, we could handle winds up to 22 knots true, without furling. In the

Pacific Ocean, we sailed 1,200 nautical miles in six days with this setup. This let us achieve 200 miles a day for six days, which is very good for a cruising sailboat.

All of this means that there should be an experienced sailor on watch at all times. This requires a watch schedule that allows the crew to also sleep and eat. There are many effective types of watch schedules, and they all depend upon the number of crew aboard, their skill levels, and the preferences of those involved. The one I prefer, based upon my cruising experience, is a three-watch system with three hours on and six hours off. To provide companionship—and to make sure there is always someone on deck at all times—I prefer to have two people on each watch. That way, one of them can go below to prepare food or drink, and below deck complete other chores. This watch pattern requires six persons onboard, including three experienced Watch Leaders. As Captain, I was always immediately accessible—even if I was off-watch and sleeping—in case there were any unusual situations that the watch crew might have been concerned about.

The advantages of the three-watch system include a relatively short watch of three hours. This means that during the first hour all is new and exciting, and by the third hour there is the comfort of knowing that the watch will end soon. So, essentially there is only one hour—in the middle—during which to be bored. And with six hours off watch, there is an opportunity to get at least five hours of good sleep, twice a day. With this system, fatigue is not an issue unless the sea conditions make sleeping difficult. Also, the watch moves in time each day, so no watch team is stuck with working the same hours every day.

Many boats sail with just two people aboard, and there are solo sailors as well. In my opinion, these are potentially dangerous situations that should be avoided. A major factor of sailing is the crew's ability to avoid seasickness. A person who is seasick is really not capable of handling the boat in a proper manner. I have had passages during which three members of the crew became incapacitated. Naturally this places a lot of unwanted pressure on the remaining crew. And just think of what it would be like if there were only three people onboard. Another factor is how well the boat is set up for sailing by only one or two individuals. If sail changes or reefing requires two people, and there are only two people onboard, then neither one will get any sleep during these maneuvers. Sleep deprivation can lead to major disaster if the crew makes poor decisions. During my circumnavigation, I heard of several cases where shorthanded boats went missing—and even crew were lost—as a result of poor decisions being made by an otherwise experienced (but sleep deprived) crew.

On ESCAPADE, nearly all sailing operations could be handled from inside the cockpit. This increased the safety and comfort of the crew. Going outside the cockpit,

especially at night, can be downright dangerous and even moreso in heavy seas. This maneuver requires the crew to clip on to the boat using a tether that is attached to jack lines (straps or wires that run the length of the boat). How the boat is rigged—relative to normal operations—is very important when making passages feasible with few crew.

Crossing oceans and being away from land and possible assistance many days requires a high degree of self-sufficiency. All passages should be undertaken with the attitude that no assistance (911 or Mayday) will be available. So it is wise for the Captain to have completed—in his own mind—a long list of "what if's," and to determine what the possible response to these would be. These would include issues like bad weather, engine problems, hitting a floating or submerged object, sail problems, loss of fresh water, etc., etc. Being prepared for any unwelcome eventuality is very important, and adds to everyone's confidence that the passage will be pleasurable and safe.

It is, of course, important to maintain all systems onboard at all times, even during a passage. Since we were cruising in remote areas of the world, I made sure to have—onboard—a very large selection of spare parts for all the systems on the boat. Also, I have the ability to maintain all of the systems. As a result, I was able to make necessary repairs as required—even when we were in mid-ocean. This included fixes to the autopilot, engine, fresh water system, generator, etc. so to keep ESCAPADE in top-notch condition.

A pleasant passage is one with a happy crew. And that, naturally, means plenty of food. We always took enough food for a time period that was half again as long as we expected the passage to take. Actually, there is an art to provisioning because it is not easy to store the amount of food needed by six people for 30 days or so. ESCAPADE had a good-sized refrigerator and freezer, but it wasn't that large. That's why so many food items have to be non-refrigerated—like canned ham, canned vegetables, pasta, UHT milk, unchilled eggs, etc. We made bread underway. Fresh fruit and vegetables had to be consumed early in the passage, but we always had plenty of great food. Provisioning in most parts of the world is generally easy, and grocery stores are often willing to freeze items overnight and even—sometimes—deliver them to the boat. ESCAPADE also had a water maker, so we had plenty of fresh water at all times.

A passage is a truly magical experience. I have made many of them, with the longest being 18 days sailing across the Pacific Ocean and 17 days across the Atlantic Ocean. Obviously, you are out of sight of land for the entire journey. But, after being underway for a few days, a comfortable routine sets in and there is a peaceful existence in which it seems as if the only people in the world are the ones on your own boat. It is an incredible feeling, and you join the flow of nature—the ocean, possible sea life, sunrise, sunset, the wind, etc.

When sailing west, we made sure—every three days— to change the clocks one hour in order to keep up with the time zones. Making landfall, of course, is a great feeling after so many days at sea. And, the person who sights land first gets to yell "Land-Ho". But, every time I heard those two words I couldn't help but feel sad that the passage was coming to an end...

Porpoises at play at the bow

PHOTO BY HEATHER REICKERT

CHAPTER 5

Required Skills

Necessary Knowledge for World Cruising

*Knowledge is of two kinds; we know a subject ourselves,
or we know where we can find information upon it*

SAMUEL JOHNSON

A world cruise requires significant knowledge as well as a wide variety of skills. These need to be mastered prior to departure, and should include all aspects of sailing. Here is my list of the essentials: Boat handling (especially in confined spaces and difficult conditions); Communications; First Aid; Maintaining all boat systems; Navigation; Offshore safety and Survival. In most cases, acquiring this knowledge is a learning experience, and it provides great satisfaction simply in the process of gaining these new skills and abilities.

It is not the intent of this book to provide instruction in each of these skills. Especially since there are many courses—both basic and advanced—available in all areas of the world to teach all the required sailing skills. One of the best is the RYA (Royal Yachting Association) based in the UK. There are also RYA courses taught in the Mediterranean and Caribbean, as well as in England. The courses can take a complete novice, or a person with any other level of knowledge, and raise their skills to the highest level. RYA courses include Start Yachting, Competent Crew, Day Skipper, Coastal Skipper, Yachtmaster Coastal, Yachtmaster Offshore and finally Yachtmaster Ocean. Certificates of Competence for even the Yachtmaster levels are available, and practical onboard experience is combined with shore-based courses. These

highly-recognizable and valued levels of competence are known throughout the sailing community.

Courses of a similar nature are also offered in the United States. We have some friends who—after spending a week cruising on our boat—decided to take up the sailing challenge. Over a twelve-month period, they took the necessary courses both in the Caribbean and in the US. They have now embarked on an around-the-world cruising adventure of their own.

While sailing experience in coastal conditions and protected waters is certainly an advantage, it is definitely not sufficient for setting out across an ocean. Much additional knowledge (and many new skills) are required for ocean cruising. And these really need to be acquired before you leave on such a voyage.

Many people who read this book may have been sailing for years, possibly in smaller sailboats. While the actual sailing principals are the same for both small and large sailboats, if one's experience has been gained on smaller sailboats, the major difference will be in the forces involved. And this "change" can be quite surprising—even overwhelming. For example, foresail tension is vastly greater on a large sailboat, and requires respect for all the various pressures involved. And you do not want to get your fingers caught in a winch because they could get cut off. Since the effort to crank a winch—invariably—increases greatly, electric or hydraulic winches are a great blessing.

Another example of the importance of experience is the implications of the boat's weight when approaching a dock. A small boat can be easily fended off using hands or feet. But on a large boat, most people don't have the physical strength to stop the boat's momentum. As a result, it will hit the dock unless the skipper takes appropriate action (such as putting the transmission into reverse). This scenario requires the skipper to accurately place the boat, and to then gently approach a dock and use the appropriate fenders. Finally, larger boats have larger anchors, which—in turn—require larger chains as well as larger windlass.

Today, since there are so many pieces of equipment—and especially electronic devices—onboard, it is extremely important that you take the time to learn everything possible about all aspects of each piece of equipment. And your partner or First Mate should learn them as well. This includes practice with each device, because if (or when) there is an emergency, there will be no time to pull out the manual! For example, even the VHF radio, which was once very simple, has become quite complicated. Today, its complex features include display of local time, latitude and longitude, DSC capabilities with a selection of the type of distress, dual/tri bands, International frequencies, scanning, and weather channels.

Besides learning how to operate all the equipment onboard, you must also know how to service every system, and each piece of equipment. This includes being able to fix the diesel engine, generator, refrigeration, transmission, water maker, etc. When in the middle of the ocean, in remote cruising grounds, and even in many ports there are no service people to call upon for help. And even if there is a person who is available, I recommend that you

Escapade under sail in the Strait of Georgia, BC, Canada

UNDER REFFED YANKEE ~ PHOTO BY HEATHER REICKERT

Erick fixing fresh water system

PHOTO BY SUSAN REICKERT

be very careful, as I have seen local "mechanics" damage other people's boats simply because they did not have the specialized knowledge required for complicated marine systems.

To avoid surprises, you must assume that you will be performing all the routine scheduled maintenance. It would be best if you could perform all maintenance requirements. Later in the book, I devote a whole chapter to maintenance.

While sailing consists of many different conditions, some of them never resurface. The weather is the largest variable, so it takes skill to understand as well as fully interpret weather patterns and predictions. And it also takes practice (as well as experience) to fully understand the impact that weather conditions will have on your boat and your crew. Before going to sea, it is imperative that you have experience with some heavy weather conditions at least gale level (Beaufort 8), which is 34 to 40 knot winds and seas of 18 to 25 feet. These types of conditions will be encountered frequently, and you should be able to comfortably handle them. You should also be prepared for severe weather conditions (Beaufort 9 to 11,) but do everything you can—if possible—to avoid such situations.

Planning is one basic skill that will serve you well in all aspects of sailing. Actually, planning as much in advance as possible will eliminate many unwanted problems and smooth the way so that your passage (or trip) will be genuinely enjoyable. When it comes to Blue Water cruising, nearly everything needs to be planned. Although some sailors might like to feel "free and unencumbered," without planning you will be subject to unforeseen impacts. Items to be planned should include: when and where to go, what to provision for, what crew is required, what will be the legal requirements, what service parts to take, what navigation hazards will be encountered, where you will anchor or which marina to use, and a multitude of other essential aspects.

Even with the most meticulous planning, a cruiser will always be subjecting himself to new situations and unknown conditions. Whether it is the lack of knowledge of the sea bottom when anchoring or changes in the legal entry requirements when arriving, there will be differences from what is (or was) expected. I've always tried to keep these surprises to a minimum.

As I mentioned earlier, there are many skills and much knowledge to acquire before you depart. And, in many cases—such as reading a radar display or anchoring in a variety of conditions—it takes a lot of practice as well. I strongly recommend that you take whatever courses that you require, read as many cruising publications as possible, as well as study and learn both your boat and your equipment with all due diligence.

CHAPTER 6

The *Crew*

Free or Paid–need for, number of, and where to locate

We are all tied to the ocean.
And when we go back to the sea—whether it is to sail or to watch—
we go back to whence we came.

JOHN F. KENNEDY

Crew—a problem, or a way to improve your sailing experience? While they can be both, a well-selected crew can add enjoyment, as well as make your sailing easier and safer. Although the classic image is for a couple "to sail off into the sunset" by themselves (as was our intention), extended cruising will often demand other solutions for crew requirements. Additional crew can also ease the burden on one or both partners. In fact, this is one aspect that I did not consider when I selected the boat. That was a mistake, because I would have chosen a different cabin layout if I had recognized that I would have full time crew.

The cruising couples we have met during our travels have adapted to the demands of cruising (or they wouldn't be out there). But, passage-making with only two people on board can lead to safety concerns, as well as the disadvantage of being together on the boat, but not seeing each other due to the fact one person is on watch while the other is sleeping or otherwise occupied. In rough weather conditions, both often have to be on deck at the same time. And—or if—one partner becomes incapacitated, neither person gets adequate sleep. As we all know, sleep deprivation and exhaustion open the door to bad decisions, poor judgment, and—sometimes disaster. (Once, while cruising, we were aware of at least two incidents that resulted in deaths that had been caused by

sleep deprivation and subsequent bad decisions.) Also, one of the partners on your boat may not be totally committed to the cruising lifestyle. We have often discovered that—after getting to know a cruising couple well, and they feel comfortable enough to let down their defenses—the truth often emerges that one of the pair is not totally enamored by or satisfied with various aspects of the cruising experience. Often, the dissatisfaction relates to the stresses related to watch responsibilities on passages. The solution is to have additional crew on board, even though this adds yet another interpersonal dynamic to the boat.

There are many other reasons to have additional crew aboard, such as company with friends, the addition of specialized skills, the ability for the owner to leave the boat, etc. We utilized both free and paid crew to cover the spectrum of our cruising needs. Although this advice comes from the perspective of the boat owner, it should be recognized that every crew position is an opportunity for someone who does not own a boat, but wants to have the exhilarating experience of cruising.

Whether or not to have a crew onboard—in addition to family—is a major decision in many respects. Foremost, the addition of another person or persons alters the interpersonal dynamic onboard. The relationships onboard must be harmonious because there is very little space, and you are interacting with each other nearly every minute. So, the added crew must be compatible, or else the result will be unpleasant or—worse—unbearable.

As the lowest-cost alternative, having free crew is always pleasant on the pocketbook. In fact, some owners expect their crew to contribute to the grocery kitty, which means that they essentially cover their meal costs. On *ESCAPADE*, we provided the food, but if a crewmember wanted something special then we asked him to bring it with him. Also, we expected the crew to get to and from the boat at their own expense. In remote parts of the world, this type of transport can be quite expensive. In some cases, we know that the owner has paid for half (or all) of the flight cost if the crew could not otherwise join. And on the other extreme, we know of crew working simply to obtain experience, and hoping to find a paying job the next time. Each case is different, and we have seen examples of all of them.

In summary, an owner can reasonably expect to find good crew who are willing to sail for little or no cost. With that understanding, the advantages or disadvantages of having additional crew aboard should be considered without concerns about cost. How would you utilize additional crew aboard your boat?

Overall, we split our requirements into three categories: short-term cruising (or day sailing of one or two weeks), specific passages, and long-term cruising of two to three months or more. For the shorter periods, we invited friends and family to share our experience. They did not have to know how to sail because we had the skills to handle *ESCAPADE* without them. They were, however, encouraged to actively participate to the extent they felt comfortable. Basically, we enjoyed the company for the interaction it gave. Frequently, we day sailed along a coast or between islands, and were in port every night. This permitted us to explore the cities and do land-based activities as well as enjoy the sailing. Since these are short time periods, the crew can hold down a regular job, and use their vacation time for cruising. Having friends and/ or family aboard added immeasurably to our cruising enjoyment.

As I mentioned in chapter four, one of the key elements for passages is the watch schedule because this determines the number of crew required. There are a variety of watch schedules used on boats, and there are proponents for each of them. Obviously, if one watch schedule fits your personality then that is the one for you to use. My choice was for a three-watch system that is composed of two people on each watch. This system has several advantages. Most importantly, it allows someone to be on deck at all times. The second watch person can go below to make tea, obtain food and do personal things. Two people can also keep each other awake. Also, if sail changes are

needed, the two of them can handle the situation without waking up the off watch. With the three watches the watch length is three hours while the off watch is six hours. Three hours, even in the middle of the night, is tolerable. And, with six hours off, you can usually get a good five hours of sleep twice a day, which is good for most people. Finally, with the three-watch system, the watch time moves forward each day, which means that no one is stuck with the same time every night. The three-watch system requires six people onboard, and three of them need to be of watch leader capability.

The reason for having someone on deck at all times—and scanning the horizon every 15 minutes, at least—is that a ship travelling at 20 knots or more can come up over the horizon and be within collision distance in only 15 minutes. There is a famous case when a wife—who was on watch by herself—went below to do something, and a ship hit her boat with the resulting loss of her daughter, son and husband. Although this occurred off the coast of New Zealand on a stormy and rainy night, it illustrates the need for a continuous watch. In my opinion, single-handed sailors are not safe, and they constitute a hazard for other ships around them when they are sleeping.

Six crewmembers, including the Captain, are required for the three-watch system, and *ESCAPADE* had sleeping positions for six people. In our experience, we had six crew (including myself) on the Atlantic crossing and five on the Pacific crossing. In fact, I had planned on six for the Pacific, but one backed out at the last minute due to health problems in his family. If I had planned on the minimum, I would have ended up short-handed. In any event, we had one solo watch so I rotated the watch partners to make sure that everyone had a different person to talk with during the passage. During our crossing from Fiji to New Zealand, a storm hit with over 55 knot winds. There were five crew on board, but three became seasick because we were beating into 40+ foot seas. Down to two good crew, we nevertheless kept to our modified watch schedule, and continued to sail all the time. The operating crew remained rested (as much as one can sleep under such conditions). Other cruisers around us hove-to or ran before the wind to reduce the strain on the crew.

As most passages require one to three weeks, crew must be able to take that amount of time off (plus travel time). In our experience, that means the most likely crew candidates are retired people or those with unusually flexible jobs. For example, one of our regulars was a freelance photographer, another was a lawyer with a private practice, and a third was a doctor from the UK who was taking a sabbatical. These individuals were able to adjust their work patterns to permit them to take weeks off for their passion of sailing. In any event, it is preferable to have crew who are not rigidly tied to a fixed schedule.

The long-term crewmember is similar as those just mentioned. We have had crew who has joined us for two or three months, and they view the experience as their taste of the cruising life—but without having to buy a boat. These long-term individuals provide stability among the crew, and they gain a though knowledge of the boat making them very valuable participants and watch leaders.

All crew who joined our boat were given a boat T-shirt so that we could put on our team "colors" when we went to social events, were leaving on, or arriving from a passage. This small detail helps build team spirit, and improve cohesiveness. I also hosted crew dinners ashore both before leaving and after arriving. In total—in all categories—we have had 103 people as crew. Many of them (if they were not friends already) have become good friends beyond the sailing experience. This broadened our enjoyment of cruising because the individuals came from many

countries and backgrounds. Some crew members came on *ESCAPADE* every year for six years, and genuinely enjoy sailing in various parts of the world.

You can locate free crew through a wide variety of sources. In our case, we liked to start with family and friends. After that, expand the circle to include those recommended to you, as well as people you hear about through yacht clubs and cruising organizations. We have also used two crew-matching organizations: Crewseekers in the UK, and Offshore Passage Opportunities (OPO) in the US. These are quite good sources of potential crew, and are organizations that enable people who are in search of crewing opportunities with a way to get in touch with boat owners. Since the people who are seeking to become crew have the total range of skills, from neophyte to very experienced, the onus is on the boat owner to select individuals who match his requirements.

Escapade at sea in the Pacific

WING-ON-WING-TYPICAL TRADE WIND SAIL SET-UP ~ PHOTO BY ERICK REICKERT

Speaking of skills, it has been our experience that the single most important aspect of selecting crew is to find individuals who are compatible with you—and with each other. This is even more important than sailing skill in most cases. Compatibility includes being: a non-smoker, cheerful, eager to participate, friendly, and having compatible drinking habits—among many other factors. On *ESCAPADE*, smoking was not permitted and no drinking of alcoholic beverages was allowed when underway. Since the close confines of a boat cannot stand divisiveness, it's important to choose well. We carefully screened every potential crewmember—if we could not interview them face-to-face, we would do it by telephone. We have conducted these meetings at our house, their house, pubs, boat shows, etc. Although most people tend to embellish on their sailing experience a little, we used the interview to judge the compatibility factor. Do you like the person? Do any habits bother you? Talk specifically about what they like to eat and drink. Do you look forward to being with this person in confined (and sometimes strenuous) circumstances? We have found that sailors from other countries, and specifically Britain, often have their qualification book with them, which gives a log of their sailing experience as well as the level of Royal Yachting Association (RYA) skill achieved from shore based courses, actual sea experience, and examinations.

Many people actively want to become crew, and this is true in nearly every port in the world. Young people seeking a position have approached our boat in every country asking if we need crew. In summary, it should be possible for you to fill your ship's crew requirements for little or no expense.

After you have agreed with a person for him or her to join your boat as crew, agree on a specific time and place. This can often be on the other side of the world and in places where it may be difficult to get to—and even hard to find—the boat. Lock down all the specifics well beforehand, but keep communication links open so that any last-minute changes can be accommodated. We provided new crew with a list of suggestions about what to bring, and what would not be needed (see Exhibit 11). For example, we provided all our crew with inflatable PFD's that included harnesses, tethers and lights. Make sure that all crew have passports as well as the necessary visas and immunizations for all the countries that will be visited.

Paid Crew

For dependability, you might want to choose paid crew. We had one crewmember for the complete circumnavigation of four and a half years. He made our voyage much more pleasant for my wife and me, because he handled many of the trip's routine items. This freed us up to enjoy sailing even more, and it gave us more time on land. He assisted in preparing the boat for departure, helped in sailing the boat,

and did the primary job of tying to a dock or operating the anchor. He would also do additional chores—such as preparing the dinghy or passerelle, securing the boat, and washing down the boat. He also watched *ESCAPADE* when we were not there, so his presence also gave us increased security. Finally, he also assisted in putting the boat on the hard, and commissioning it when it was put back in the water.

Many paid crew are Captains, and they can handle your boat when you are not available. One of our friends owns a boat that is on its second trip around the world. He joins the boat when and where he likes so he chooses the best segments to sail. For example, you might want your boat in the Caribbean in the winter and in the Mediterranean in the summer. A captain can deliver your boat to your desired location—when and where you want.

The crew also stayed onboard in those situations where the boat could not be left unattended. These were unique, but important places, such as at Santorini in Greece. Also, he would remain living onboard providing security when we returned home for a few weeks every quarter. Further, he was capable of skippering the boat in case I became incapacitated. Thankfully, that was never required, but my wife use to say that we had back-up strategies for all systems onboard, except for the Captain. The First Mate was my back-up!

For nearly all the years we sailed, I had a First Mate or First Mate and Chef as paid crew. With the Chef it resulted in gourmet meals even in the wilderness of Alaska. It also gave my wife much more of an "on-vacation" feel for the cruising. Other paid crewmembers can even serve as nannies if you have children aboard. And oftentimes husband and wife teams operate as joint crew.

Other friends of ours bought a new boat and—since they were unsure of their sailing skills—they hired a Captain to run the boat and teach them the skill of sailing bigger boats. When we picked up *ESCAPADE*, our owners' representative was along while we had our sea trials. He stayed with us for the first two weeks to ensure a smooth take over and proper functioning of all systems onboard.

One summer, we made an innovative use of a crew when we day sailed up the Atlantic coast of the US from Miami to Boston by hiring a college coed to drive our car from port to port. We scheduled our time at marinas a week or so in advance, so we knew where we were going. I brought my car to Miami, and she drove my car between marinas all the way north. That way, we had a car waiting for us at every stop we made. The crewmember slept onboard every night, but during the day she was free to do whatever she liked—as long as she was at the marina when we arrived. Each day, she visited the local visitor's bureau to research and learn about sightseeing possibilities. She also made sure that the marina knew we were arriving shortly. That way, as soon as we got the boat tied up, we were able to step into our own car and visit the area, much of which was beyond walking distance from the boat. It turned out to be a great summer, and we saw much more than would have ever been possible without the car. It also turned out to be a great way for her to see a lot of the US.

The costs for paid sailing crew vary greatly, and there appears to be no common pay level structure. There may be similar pay levels on mega motor yachts, but at the sailboat level all is negotiable. Often, the boat owner is one nationality, the boat is registered in another nation, the crewmember comes from a third country, and the boat may be operating in a fourth nation's waters. As a result, many crew do worry about taxes. Pay is often for twelve months, but the boat may be operated for less time than twelve months (due to it being up on the hard). The time off the boat can be considered the crews paid vacation. Besides all the meals aboard, our First Mate was invited to join us for meals ashore. In addition, we provided flights to their home county once a year. All this might be part of the package deal, as well as an annual bonus, but the salary has to be competitive. How to structure the pay package—and to agree to it with a suitable person, is up to you. Usually, from the crew's standpoint, it is great to be paid to be on a luxury yacht, and be able to do what they love to do—sail. All in all, it's not a bad job!

For *ESCAPADE*, I had an agreement for crew to sign when they joined our boat. The form that I used, which is modified from similar forms published elsewhere, is shown as Exhibit 2. This form was designed to handle some legal issues, as well as to clarify responsibilities on both sides. You will need to modify it for your own boat. Whatever you do, be sure that you both have a clear understanding of your expectations of the crew's duties and responsibilities. For example, I prepared an exhibit defining the First Mate's duties and requirements (Exhibit 21), and made sure he understood the duties before we negotiated salary. I defined the Salary Package in advance. Exhibit 22 shows the package for 2008.

Selection of paid crew is more important than selecting any crewmember. You can use the same sources mentioned earlier for locating paid crew, but there are also crew agencies—as well as referrals from your boat builder. Be sure to get references—and check them—before interviewing crew. Wait to make a decision until after you have assessed all the information.

Knowing whether or not you want crew, and how many, is important when you consider what type of boat you select. If I had known earlier that we would have paid full-time crewmembers, I probably would have selected a bigger boat, and one that separated crew and guest quarters. Think this issue through carefully, and decide on the best solution for you.

In summary, extra crew—whether paid or not—can make your cruising experience both more enjoyable and safer. Consider your goals and objectives carefully, and then select the right crew to make it happen.

Extra crew is always nice

L TO R

JACK PRYDE, ROGER KENYON, ERICK REICKERT

PHOTO BY HEATHER REICKERT

CHAPTER 7

Selecting a
Blue-Water Boat

Analysis of (and specific recommendations for) boat design

No man will succeed unless he is ready to face and overcome
difficulties and prepared to assume responsibilities.

WILLIAM J. H. BOETCKER

The selection of your Blue Water boat will be the most important decision you make prior to departure. The following is my suggested process to help you select the best boat possible. It is an uncompromising approach that starts with a "clean sheet of paper."

Boat selection is often a very emotional process that includes extremely important factors such as specific design characteristics, in addition to style and past exposure to boats. But because there are so many boats from which to choose, it is useful to try to strip away the emotional component—as much as possible—and focus on facts. To do this, a boat buyer should consider his needs, and then select from various boat designs to narrow the choice. Of course, this choice will depend upon how and where the boat will be used. So the process should begin with a serious self-appraisal of your sailing intentions. This includes, of course, the number of crew that you expect to have onboard, as well as the boat's possible operational uses. That is why I covered the issue of crew and the number of sleeping positions required first.

Since, we want to discuss Blue Water cruising boats, I will assume that the type of boat you're looking for is one that: will be making ocean crossings, leading to a circumnavigation; you will be living on for months and even years; and much of the cruising will be done in

foreign countries and/or remote areas of the world—away from both good yacht facilities, as well as the availability of parts and service. This is the most severe type of sailing activity, and it places the most demands on the choice of design.

I first focused upon the major design alternatives for mono hull sailboats in the 45 to 60 foot range, and I tried to understand the advantages and disadvantages for each design. The design alternatives that I focused on included: cockpit location, dinghy storage, foresail configuration, hull material, keel configuration, rig, rudder configuration, salon configuration, stern boarding and stern configuration. These, taken collectively, will largely define the type—and probably the make—of sailboat that is acceptable for your needs.

There is some degree of subjectivity in this analysis, but based on my experiences, the logic behind my choices holds up well in the real world. Of course, each subject could be examined in greater detail and with more quantified data, but such an analysis will probably not change the conclusions. It's essential that you insert your own experiences and knowledge into the overall analysis.

My complete decision process is presented at the end of this chapter, but in summary I concluded that the ideal

Blue Water cruiser would have a center cockpit, cutter rig, dinghy storage on davits, fiberglass construction solid below the waterline, medium-length fin keel with lead bulb, raised deck salon, and a skeg-mounted rudder, "sugar scoop" stern, and a stern passerelle.

Catamarans are not included in this analysis primarily because I do not have direct experience with them. There are proponents for cats, which do not heel, and generally have a faster sailing speed, and large living areas as well as shallow draft. Some of the disadvantages of cats for cruising are that most cruisers have huge amounts of fuel, spare parts, supplies, etc., so weight is a major issue. The cat's sailing performance is often significantly degraded when the full cruising weight is considered. They generally cannot sail as close to the wind as mono hulls, being lighter they can have undesirable motion in seas, many marinas cannot accommodate them because of their width, and you never want to tip them over—as they will not re-right themselves. In really heavy seas, a cat may suffer from extreme twisting of the structure, and racing cats have proved to be dangerous. But because, in certain situations—such as charter service in a specific geographic area, that involves mainly anchoring out where shallow draft is a big advantage—cats could be very suitable. You will have to reach your own conclusion regarding the suitability of a catamaran for your cruising needs.

In addition to those previously-mentioned characteristics, I also wanted a boat that was "seakindly." This is widely desired, but there is no real industry standard available to describe or measure it. Once you are in the ocean, however, you will immediately recognize whether or not a boat is seakindly. In broad terms, it involves the type and character of the boat's motion in a variety of sea conditions. An important ingredient is the displacement. A medium-displacement boat is probably the best compromise. While a lighter boat will accelerate faster (especially in light winds), it will also be slowed down more by hitting waves when beating to windward. A heavier boat will smooth out the effect of the waves, and give a more stable (i.e., comfortable) motion. Also, a wider boat has more form stability, which helps the keel in the righting force. Reducing weight aloft makes a boat less "tender," so that it yields less heeling with a given change in wind speed.

Another consideration is the amount a boat will "pound" when going into waves. This is related to the amount a boat will pitch in the waves, as well as the configuration of the hull forward of the keel. A boat that pounds will have jaw-dropping shuttering stops when hitting a wave. Altogether a boat that is seakindly will have a smooth, predictable motion in the sea—and one that is not perturbed by sudden changes in the wind.

The boat, of course, must be seaworthy to sail in all the oceans. That means it must be capable of sailing and maneuvering in even the most extreme conditions. I

encountered seas of 30 to 40 feet, possibly with occasional ones of 50 feet, and winds in excess of 55 knots. This is described as a Force 10 Storm. The seas were breaking at the top of the waves and the wind created spumes of foam on the face of the waves. The result was that it made the sea look white. Not quite a hurricane, but very severe. I do not want to experience that ever again. But *ESCAPADE* performed well, and we sailed into the wind for more than 48 hours before the weather conditions dropped down to a gale. The autopilot worked really well, and managed to maintain our course. In my mind, a seaworthy boat is one that is strong and will not flex in the high seas. A boat that "works" (or twists) essentially puts loads on many items that should not have them. A strong stiff boat is generally achieved by fiber glassing all interior components and bulkheads directly to the hull. That's why a production boat with a drop-in shell will not be as strong or rigid. Remember, the rig has to be super strong. And I also wanted a boat with a positive stability range of up to 125°. That is the range where the boat will still right itself. At 125°, the mast would be pointing down by 35° from the horizon. There are industry standards for calculating the positive range of stability, and responsible quality boat builders will know the number for their boats. If they don't, I would question the builder's claim that it really builds a boat for oceans.

Another consideration is the ability to sail the boat shorthanded and completely from the cockpit, except when using a spinnaker. It is simply not desirable to have to leave the cockpit at night (or in heavy conditions) to make normal sail changes. This also reduces the demands on the crew—and the number of crew needed on deck—for sail changes. This means that you must have the ability to furl the sails from the cockpit. We had roller furling on both foresails (yankee and staysail). The mainsail had electric power in-mast furling, which one person could operate up to a gale, and usually without having to point into the wind.

Additional design features can affect the choice of boat. These include vast storage capacity, with both a large lazarette and internal storage. The lazarette was always full with: an additional anchor, drogue, extra lines, extra sails, scuba and snorkel equipment, sea anchor, two folding bicycles, and water hose—among other things. The dock lines, fenders, life raft and power cables were stored elsewhere.

For safety considerations, I wanted the boat divided into at least three watertight compartments. So the foreword cabin was designed with lip seal on the door, and multiple fasteners (dogs). The limber hole (the drain slot in the bilge) had a seacock so it could be closed. The lazarette was also watertight with a seacock, and the anchor locker in the bow was separate from the forward cabin. I also added Kevlar (the material used for bulletproof vests) to

Escapade main salon, looking forward

PHOTO BY CHARLIE SCOTT

the hull build-up in the frontal crash zone forward of the mast. Since I felt that the most likely risk at sea was hitting a submerged or semi-submerged item (like a container or log), this would only impact the bow area or crash zone. Even if an object penetrated the solid fiberglass build-up aft of the chain locker (including the Kevlar), then we could close off the forward compartment. That way, *ESCAPADE* would remain afloat, although down by the bow. Emergency access to the compartment could still be achieved via the hatch over the bed.

I have already mentioned the need for a large battery bank, fuel capacity to motor 1,000 NM, and plenty of fresh water. In our case, the battery bank was 480 amp hours at 24 volts. That is equivalent to 960 amp hours at 12 volts, and was adequate for our use with the generator—as well as solar panels. The fuel tank was 1,000 liters (265 US gallons). While motoring at 7 knots in a relatively calm sea we would use 1 liter per mile, thus achieving a range under power of 1,000 NM. With modern water makers, it is not necessary to have as large a water tank as it used to be. But you still want to have sufficient capacity to survive—even though you don't shower everyday—in case the water maker breaks down. You will have to personally decide on the safety factor you are willing to accept. In our case, we had sufficient fresh water—even if the water maker failed—to cross the Pacific.

A bow thruster, which is invaluable in so many situations (and required to maneuver in tight quarters) is really essential. *ESCAPADE'S* bow thruster was 10 HP, and it had the ability to hold the bow against a cross wind of approximately 10 knots. This was generally adequate, but a few times it would have been better if I could have handled a 15-knot crosswind. This is especially true in Med mooring when—even in a crosswind—you have to back down in a straight line.

For the chefs, there should be a large refrigerator and freezer. As mentioned in chapter four, a month's supply of food is often required, so large-capacity appliances are required. Plus, they need to be efficient, handle temperatures of 100° F, and sun loads on the side of the boat. They should also be easily accessible for all foods and liquids, without spilling the contents when heeled.

The length of the boat is the most critical dimension, and is the major determinant of displacement, interior volume, price, and speed potential. Based upon my experience—with the addition of some important caveats and qualifications—the bigger the boat the better. My original specification said that I wanted a boat with a mast no taller than 64 feet above the water and a maximum keel draft of six feet. This is required to be able to go under the fixed bridges of the Intracoastal Waterway of the US

East Coast, and to recognize the Waterway's depths in many places. A 48 foot boat that I was considering met these requirements, but—for a variety of other reasons—I selected a 55 foot boat with a 72 foot air draft, and a keel draft of 7 feet. One consequence of this choice was that we had to sail "on the outside" whenever we went up and down the U.S. East Coast. Actually, it is faster to sail in the ocean than to motor in the Waterway. And although it was limiting in some ways, I believe I made the right choice. But this is the type of practical trade-off that has to be made with most requirements.

A larger boat does have a few limitations in terms of marinas because not all of them can accommodate larger boats. At 55 feet, *ESCAPADE* was too big to enter bout 20% of marinas we approached, and at those where we did dock, we were generally at the end of the dock. Sometimes, the limiting factor was the draft. There are, of course, a number of marinas that cater to super yachts, and when we arrived at those, *ESCAPADE* was on the small size.

In general, everyone would like a boat that sails and motors faster because increased speed reduces the time for a passage, and it provides more flexibility in regards to changing weather patterns. Displacement boat speeds increase with water line length, and the formula for hull speed says that maximum boat speed is related to the square root of water line length. Boats can, however, exceed hull speed if enough power—either by sail or by engine—is applied. But for increased speed, it is desirable to have more water line length. To that end, boats with less overhang perform better (and have more interior volume). Remember, for a sailing boat the real water line length is the water line that exists when the boat is heeled.

Your boat's cost will be principally determined by its size. I will discuss the cost of cruising in a later chapter, but the larger the boat the greater the fuel costs, marina fees, hull anti-fouling paint and many other costs. In spite of that, I still recommend obtaining the largest boat that makes financial sense to you. A larger boat provides more interior volume, which give you more living space as well as room for all the gear required for cruising and having fun. Based on my experience—as well as conversations with many cruisers and discussions about their experiences—I would recommend that the smallest boat be 46 feet long, and the ideal size would be 55 to 65 feet. Obviously, smaller boats have circumnavigated and crossed oceans, but we are discussing a boat—and a passage—that will be enjoyable and safe.

Prior to selecting *ESCAPADE*, I did an intensive analysis of all of all new and used boats on the market. I identified all the good features of every boat, and then combined them into a specification list. This is presented in Exhibit 1. I finally selected one boat as the one that came the closest to my requirements ("The Boat to Beat"), and

then pitted each contender against that one. I accepted the fact that to achieve a desired feature, it might be "optional" rather than "standard" equipment. This is identified in the exhibit. It was amazing to discover that many salesmen did not really know their own boats very well, and could not fill out the exhibit for the boat that they were selling. Also, many did not know their boat's range of positive stability. Finally, some manufacturers were simply not willing to make minor changes to their boats or add optional equipment to bring them up to my requirements. But on the other hand, I learned that some boat manufacturers will build a boat for you that is either custom or semi-custom, and create exactly what you want. In some cases, however, you may have to trade off some design features against others. At that point, it will be a difficult decision to decide which characteristics are particularly important to you, and which ones aren't.

When you have completed your analysis, and have developed a list of boats that meet your requirements, then pricing can be compared. In many cases, the features you really want are independent of pricing, or they may actually cost less. Hopefully, you will be able to identify the lowest cost boat that meets all your requirements. With this accomplished, you can finally let yourself become emotional. Styling is very subjective, and is often in the eye of the beholder. Many people have a very clear idea of what a boat should look like. But it is probably not good to select a boat based on style or appearance if it doesn't meet your requirements because you may regret your choice in the future. Reputation is also important relative to "build quality," possible future problems, and whether or not the builder will stand behind his product. Once all of this has been considered, you can allow yourself to "fall in love". All sailors should be in love with their boat, or—at a minimum—fully confident of their boat's strengths and virtues before they go to sea.

It was also highly informative for me to visit the manufacturing plants of each of the final contenders because the quality and internal construction techniques were readily visible. Also, the willingness of the manufacture to truly satisfy you—as the client—will become clear. If you are having the boat built to your specifications, working directly with the factory is dramatically better than dealing with a local boat dealer.

When it comes to boat manufacturers, another difference is their willingness—after the sale—to support boat owners. Some builders have an active "after sales department" that maintains records of all the equipment on a given boat, and can supply replacement parts anywhere in the world in response to an e-mail or phone call. Also, some builders hold rallies or races at various places in the world to bring together boat owners of that marque. These can be very enjoyable activities that add variety to the cruising life.

Escapade in travel lift in Portsmouth, Rhode Island, USA

PHOTO BY ERICK REICKERT

A lot of improvements—in many areas—have been made since the days when I went looking for a boat. For example, one advancement is the availability of self-storing washboards, which eliminates the need to get them out and store them each day. Also, many boats are now available that have twin steering wheels and helms. This can assist with visibility. and make it easy to walk through the cockpit. In light of these improvements, you will need to update my list of requirements (Exhibit 1) to fit your own requirements.

As the features I wanted were very specific, I selected a semi-custom boat builder, and had them construct the boat of my dreams. I was involved in all the design decisions, and visited the boat "in build" every two or three months. In between those trips, I hired an "owner's representative" to view the construction progress each month. This meant that there were absolutely no surprises when *ESCAPADE* was handed to me after commissioning. For me, the whole

decision process and build took about a year. But, based on the order bank of the builder, times can—of course—vary. I've included my spreadsheet of available boats is shown as an example (Exhibit 13).

The boat I selected was an Oyster 55 built by Oyster Marine in Ipswich, England. This boat was the one that best met my basic requirements in standard form and Oyster then built-in all the other requirements as optional equipment. That way, when I received the boat it was ready—in every regard—to sail away. In fact, our first sail was an overnight from Ipswich, England to Guernsey, in the Channel Islands across the English Channel.

The rewards of this approach became apparent during our 15 years of cruising, which included a circumnavigation. *ESCAPADE* had all the right design features and equipment to handle cruising well. And—based on observations of, (and discussions with) other cruisers—it was better suited than most other boats for the task.

Stern Configuration- Double end versus normal stern

Double end
>Presents less stern area to high following seas
>Generally used in conjunction with aft cockpit (see below)

Normal stern
>Stern has more flotation, so it rises above following seas
>More internal space for storage including possible Lazarette
>Better able to mount dinghy davits
>Can have sugar scoop stern (see below)

CONCLUSION: Normal stern wins hands down

Stern Configuration- Conventional versus "sugar scoop"

Conventional (forward or aft slant)
>Difficult to board except with side ladder, especially from the water

"Sugar Scoop" Stern
>Provides easy location for boarding from the water or dinghy (The front door "porch")
>Major safety benefit for recovery of man overboard (either solo or with assistance)
>Provides bathing and shower platform
>Unaffected by seas

Conventional stern with deploying platform or ladder
>Provides sugar scoop features if deployed
>Not useful for accidental man overboard
>Depending upon design, could be battered by heavy Seas

CONCLUSION: Sugar scoop clearly better functionally for a cruiser

Keel Configuration

Full length
>Excellent forward tracking
>Prevents lines entangling in enclosed propeller
>Large area to minimize side drift

Partial length
>Less wetted area yields less drag and faster speeds
>Better backing control
>Easier turning at lower speeds (marina maneuvering)
>Permits use of solid lead bulb to make boat stiffer with less draft
>Solid lead at bottom provides good protection during grounding
>Medium length gives good forward tracking with minimum side drift

CONCLUSION: Medium length keel best compromise; better with solid lead bulb for possible grounding (Encapsulated iron bits not recommended)

Keel attachment

Bolted to bottom of curved hull
>Strength is a major issue. Grounding and/or heavy wave action can cause the keel to break off.

Bolted to keel stub molded into hull
>The molded stub gives the opportunity to highly reinforce the hull bottom and to provide a deep bilge. This reduces the torque on the keel bolts.

CONCLUSION: The best design is the keel bolted to a keel stub molded into the Hull.

Hull Material

Fiberglass (GRP)
Easy to maintain
Possible osmosis or blistering if not built properly

Steel
Very strong against puncture
Rust issues require constant maintenance
Electrolysis and electrical grounding issues
Framing and insulation takes space inside boat
Condensation issues
Noise issues

Aluminum
Strong against puncture
Electrolysis and electrical grounding issues
Framing and insulation takes space inside boat
Condensation issues
Noise issues

CONCLUSION: Fiberglass better under normal circumstances. Steel or aluminum better for collisions. Choice dependent upon risk analysis.

GRP Hull Construction

Solid lay-up in the hull
Heavier for equal strength compared to cored construction
Better for penetration resistance
Possible to add Kevlar layer

Cored construction
Lighter for equal strength compared to solid
If outer skin is penetrated there is a major loss of strength and core will absorb water

CONCLUSION: Difficult decision. If concerned about possible penetration thensolid is better.

Cockpit Location

Aft cockpit
Location will yield more pitch and less roll motion for occupants than center cockpit
Able to see whole mainsail from cockpit
Farther from bow will yield less spray, which is more significant for shorter boats
Generally precludes large full height aft cabin
Close to following seas
Generally precludes poop deck and lazarette
Difficult to locate dinghy davits that are out of the way

Center cockpit
Location will yield less pitch and slightly more roll for occupants than aft cockpit
For larger boats (above 45') spray is not an issue,and cockpit is higher above water
Permits large aft cabin
Good salon layout; i.e. galley can be aft rather than in main salon,
Which gives 'living room' feel upon entry.
Easy to see widest part of boat when docking
Permits poop deck, lazarette, and dinghy davits
Permits better location of mainsheet and traveler aft of the cockpit
Often permits better bimini design

CONCLUSION: For boats over 45' center cockpit is better

Salon configuration

Conventional salon
- Deep and dark
- Longer companionway stairs

Raised deck salon
- Bright and airy feeling
- Easier to see out
- Able to place heavy items—such as batteries, fuel and water—under sole, farther below.

CONCLUSION: Raised deck salon is superior

Location of Master Cabin

Forward
- Better for ventilation using dorades
- Far more motion, especially in heavy seas, making the cabin unusable in many conditions
- Bow wave noises

Aft
- Usable even in extreme weather conditions, often the best location for sleeping
- Engine, propeller, and auto pilot noises can be disturbing
- Wave slap an issue depending upon hull shape
- Separated from the people in forward cabins is positive

CONCLUSION: Difficult choice that depends on your priorities

Rig

Ketch
- More sail configurations available for balanced sailing.
- Less mast height
- Can use aft sail to minimize swinging at anchor
- More lines to handle
- Harder to tack
- Harder to configure deck and cockpit

Sloop
- Easier to sail short handed
- More sail area higher so better for light winds

Sloop with cutter staysail (Cutter rig)
- Harder to go about as genoa or yankee can "hang up" in slot between the two forestays
- Better for heavy weather as staysail can be used as a storm sail with good "balance"

CONCLUSION: Sloop better overall, cutter is better yet

Foresail configuration

Jenny or genoa
- Basically a foresail that overlaps the mast, and the tack, clew and foot are at deck level
- Large sail area

Yankee
- Basically a foresail that overlaps the mast, and the foot rises to a clew above deck
- Smaller sail area, but area of loss is close to the water and maybe not critical
- Easy to see under sail
- Sail does not conflict with lifelines or items stored on deck
- Easier to use spinnaker pole to pole out yankee for downwind sailing

CONCLUSION: Yankee better for cruising

Boat Design Feature Alternatives

Dinghy storage

Dinghy davits

    Convenient, easy storage

    Dinghy can be deployed quickly

    Dinghy extending past stern can be a problem when backing down between boats

    as well as when departing docks with high obstructions

    Dinghy can be stowed or deployed easily by one person

    Can be used with hard or inflatable dinghies (inflatable more typical)

    Secure even in extremely rough seas

On deck

    Difficult and time consuming to stow; generally requires two people

    Requires lifting dinghy on deck for either deflating inflatable or dinghy tie down

    Takes up deck space, and sometimes interferes with sails

    Reduces forward visibility

Garage or forward deck compartments

    Only available for very large boats

CONCLUSION: Dinghy davits are best solution for medium-length boats

Stern boarding

Passerelle

    Required for typical stern-to docking in Europe and rest of world

    If arranged properly, dinghy can hang under passerelle from davits

No Passerelle

    Difficult or impossible situation for most of the world

CONCLUSION: Passerelle is required for world cruising

Rudder configuration

Spade

    Minimizes wetted area

    More control for size

Skeg or partial skeg

    Prevents rudder from falling out

    Reduces side loads on main rudder bearings

    Full skeg provides point of contact when grounding

CONCLUSION: For cruising, full skeg mounting is preferred

Equipment

Engine

Diesel engine either naturally aspirated or turbo powered

    Power should be suitable to motor in calm water at 9 to 10 knots,

    but fuel economy should provide 1,000 km range.

    Quiet operation is important for comfort.

    Engine access should be suitable for easy maintenance, even when at sea.

Generator

Diesel generator recommended to reduce running time on engine.

    Capacity should be sufficient to handle complete boat requirements including A/C, water heater, water
    maker, and battery charger. This could be in the 6 to 10 KW range.

    It should be brushless to minimize maintenance, and should be inside sound box to minimize noise.

    Generator access should be suitable for easy maintenance—even when at sea.

Shore voltage compatibility

240 Volt AC connection

        Suitable for Europe and rest of world
        Suitable for most of US and especially in areas where A/C use on boats is typical (50 amp service)
        Should have an isolation transformer
        Arrange for components to work with both 50 or 60 hertz for maximum flexibility
        Requires 240 Volt appliances (vacuum, toaster, etc.) unless a step-down transformer is installed.
        Can use a "reverse Y" when only 120 VAC is available 120 Volt AC Connection
        Only suitable for use in the US, Canada and Mexico

CONCLUSION: Equip boat for 240 VAC shore connection

Autopilot

Wind vane

        Uses no power
        Downwind sailing (typical in the trade winds) is not the best point of sailing for control due to reduced wind velocity on vane
        Takes space on stern, possibly precludes sugar scoop stern and dinghy storage on davits
        May preclude Passerelle
        Requires removal of in-water rudder when backing
        Not useful for motoring without wind
        Better on smaller (under 45') boats

Electric or hydraulic

        Uses power continuously, which is an issue
        Good, dependable operation under sail and power at all points of sail
        If properly sized, can handle boat even in Force 10 or greater storm conditions
        Best approach is rams acting directly on rudder stock. This provides a back-up to the normal cable steering as steering can be accomplished without the cables
        Can be used to follow desired track, or heading or wind angle
        Most reported problems can be traced to either undersize units or units using belt drive to steering wheel

CONCLUSION: Electric/ hydraulic far superior to wind vane, even considering power consumption

Fuel and water tanks

Fuel Tank
Should have sufficient capacity to motor 1,000 NM

Should be able to clean inside tank, if required

Should have device to measure level like Tank Tender without the use of a dipstick

Fuel tank should be located low in the boat, below the floorboards

Filler pipe should be located on deck at a place that can be accessed from a dock

Tanks can be made of a variety of materials, but maximum capacity can be achieved by building them into the hull and using gel coat as lining.

Water tanks
At least two tanks are recommended. The output of the water maker goes to the larger tank.

That way, if the water maker malfunctions and puts brackish water into the tank, then the smaller tank will still contain pure water.

Valves to switch between tanks should be conveniently located

Total capacity depends on number of crew, but can be less if there is a water maker. Suggest around 200 gallons.

Should have a device to measure level in tanks, or use a "water computer" that can keep track of usage as well as water added by the water maker.

Water tanks should be located low in the boat, below the floorboards.

Filler pipe(s) should be located on deck at a place that can be accessed from a dock, and not confused with the fuel filler. (Possibly on the opposite side of the boat.)

Tanks can be made of a variety of materials, but maximum capacity can be achieved by building them into the hull, and using gel coat as lining.

Holding tanks (Black water) from toilets
These should be as large as possible to avoid frequent pump-outs.

Use of Vacuflush toilets instead of hand pumped toilets reduces the amount of water required for each flush. Also they use fresh water instead of salt water so it minimizes encrustation build-up.

Tanks should be made of a non-permeable material (like stainless steel) to avoid odors.

Gray water tanks from sinks and showers
Very few boats have gray water tanks, but some countries (like Turkey) are considering laws that would require them.

Choosing Equipment, Features *and* Specifications

List of Recommended Equipment and Specifications

Every calling is great when greatly pursued.

OLIVER WENDELL HOMES

By Equipment, I mean the wide variety of items that are either loose or attached to the boat. Features are those design elements that add to the function of the boat, and Specifications are specific numeric levels for various aspects of the design.

This chapter gives you a compilation of the equipment, features and specifications of *ESCAPADE*, the boat I used in my circumnavigation. Since, in nearly all cases, my experience validated these items as necessary, I would definitely recommend them. In the few instances when items did not work or were not useful, I identified them.

There are many reasons for equipment, and these include: comfortable living, operation in foreign ports, sailing or operating the boat, and safety. Some of the items I've written about were extremely valuable, but only in specific situations.

Remember, your boat must have storage space for all your needed equipment.

On the first day that we sailed *ESCAPADE* out of the commissioning marina to an international destination, nearly all of this equipment was onboard. This required detailed planning in advance, and purchasing everything in a foreign location. A few items, which were not available overseas, were shipped from the US.

Escapade at dock in Stamford, Connecticut, USA

ALSO SHOWS OUR TWO BICYCLES
~ PHOTO BY ERICK REICKERT

As concluded in Chapter 7, I recommend the following boat characteristics:

- Monohull sailboat with length of 45 to 60 feet, or as large as possible
- Capable of one or two handed sailing
- Capable of sailing from the cockpit except when using a spinnaker
- Seaworthy and seakindly of medium displacement
- Positive stability range of up to 125°
- Interior separated into at least three watertight compartments
- Normal stern with "sugar scoop"
- Large lazarette and vast interior storage space
- Medium length keel with lead bulb. The depth of the keel should be as deep as possible for good upwind performance, but over 7 feet will limit cruising areas. (*ESCAPADE'*S draft was 7 feet.) Lead on bottom will minimize possible damage during a grounding.
- Rudder mounted with full skeg. Lowest point should be above the keel.
- Fiberglass hull with solid lay-up at least below the waterline, and Kevlar in the crash zone (No coring below the waterline.)
- Bow thruster (Capable of holding bow against at least a 10 knot cross wind.)
- Center cockpit
- Raised deck salon
- Cutter rig (A version of sloop rig) with Yankee foresail. Air height is critical only for the Eastern US waterway, which has a minimum design height of 65 feet except for a few specific bridges.
- Dinghy davits for dinghy storage
- Passerelle designed for the boat is required
- Diesel engine capable of powering the boat to 9 or 10 knots in still water
- Generator, diesel, of 6 to 10 KW in separate enclosure. Should be brushless.
- Shore power connection for 240 VAC. (See detailed analysis at the end of this chapter)
- Autopilot either electric or hydraulic. (See detailed analysis at the end of this chapter)
- Fuel tank sufficient to motor 1,000 NM at 7 knots
- Water tanks, two recommended of sufficient capacity
- Holding tanks sufficiently large to go 5 to 7 days without pumping

In addition, desirable design features for the boat include the following:

Hull

- Interior divided into at least three watertight compartments, with one forward of the mast
- Bow area separated from interior by watertight bulkhead
- Lazarette area separated from interior by watertight bulkhead
- Bulkheads and stringers fiberglassed to the hull
- Hand laid Fiberglass and Kevlar mats (not sprayed glass fibers)
- Isophthalic resin in gel coat to minimize blistering
- Hull with internal flange & bolted hull-to-deck joint, plus adhesive for maximum strength
- Hull should be "stiff" with little flexing in heavy seas
- Beam sufficient for large interior and good form stability (*ESCAPADE* was 16 feet)
- Rudder with stainless steel rudderpost
- Mast stepped on keel for maximum strength and support
- No screws or fasteners through a cored area such as the deck
- Anti-fouling paint. Should be of a type available around the world for compatibility.

Rig and sails

- Cutter rig
- Roller furling on both foresails
- In-mast furling on main- electric or hydraulic (In-boom is an alternative)
- Yankee at 130% (Must pass inner forestay easily)

- Staysail should be heavy duty, suitable for storm sail
- Asymmetrical spinnaker for reaching and downwind light air performance
- Spinnaker pole mounted on mast and pole lift rigged
- All guys, lines, sheets, etc. for spinnaker
- Color-coded halyards, lines and sheets
- Self-tailing winches
- Power winches on main and Yankee sheets, electric or hydraulic
- Rigid boom vang with downhaul
- Boom preventer operated from cockpit (After attaching outer end to toe rail)
- Stainless steel cable rigging, continuous (Easier to replace than rod rigging)
- Insulated backstay for SSB
- Manual backstay tension adjuster
- Lightening conductors connected from mast and stays to keel
- Lightening protection at masthead (bristle brush type)
- Electric windlass, with remote control at helm for both raising and lowering
- Radar reflector on mast (Firdell Blipper)

Deck and Exterior

- Double anchor roller platform for two anchors
- Anchors:
  - Primary—CQR plow (60#) with all chain rode—300 feet
  - Secondary—Bruce claw (44#) with chain and rope rode—300 feet
  - Emergency—Fortress (Danforth style) (32#) with rope rode—200 feet (kept in lazarette)
- Seats on stern pushpit
- Attachment points for jack lines at bow and stern
- Safety harness attachment points in cockpit (4)
- Aluminum toe rail for attaching lines, blocks, preventer, etc. at various places
- Cockpit table, folding
- Mug rack in cockpit
- Teak decking (Teak was trouble free, easy to take care of, and provided insulation)
- Cockpit seats with built-in backrest
- Dodger, capable of folding down. (Also zippered center section to provide airflow)
- Bimini with side curtains, clear and solid so the cockpit can be enclosed
- Hatches and ports with aluminum frames for strength and positive sealing
- Dorades for ventilation
- International running lights at deck level on stanchions (port, starboard and stern)
- Masthead tri-color light (Useful for night sailing to reduce power consumption)
- Masthead anchor light (Later converted to LED to reduce power consumption)
- Foredeck light mounted on mast
- Cockpit light
- Steering wheel covered in leather (Otherwise SS wheel can get very hot or very cold)
- Stowage compartment for life raft on deck (Preserved life raft and not unsightly)
- Large lazarette (Full width and full depth)
- Deck stowage compartment for dock lines and power cables
- Gas storage locker, vented outside, capable of storing either propane or butane bottles
- Rub rail with stainless steel striker (Striker was 1 inch in diameter)
- Single lever engine control
- Control for autopilot in cockpit and at nav station, with detachable wander lead
- Set of instruments in cockpit
- Companionway washboards that can be secured in place (In case of knock down)
- Salt-water wash-down hose at bow (For washing anchor chain and anchor)
- Granny bars- SS bars at each side of mast (For safety when working at the mast)

Accommodations and Interior

- Galley aft of companionway (I wanted to enter the "living room" rather than the "kitchen")
- High-quality joinery
- Good-looking light wood interior for brightness
- Main salon that is full width and spacious
- Folding or foldaway dining table
- Two individual lounge chairs, in addition to bench seating
- Companionway stairs capable of descending facing forward
  (I requested a change to the angle of the stairs for this)
- Large navigation station sufficient for all equipment, nav computer and personal computer. Also, storage for full-size paper charts.
- Entertainment center with TV, DVD, VCR, CD and AM/FM radio. The TV, VCR and DVD must be for international operation (SECAM, PAL, & NTSC) DVD or BluRay must be Multi-region
- Audio speakers in salon, cockpit and aft cabin, switchable
- Ultra suede seating surfaces (For non-slip surface when heeling)
- Microwave oven
- Stove, 4 burner, and self-regulating oven on pivots (gimbaled) Propane is not available in most of Europe, so the stove and oven must be capable of switching between Butane or Propane.
- Double sink
- Corian counter tops with lip around all edges
- Foot pump for fresh water at galley sink (If electric water pump fails)
- Exhaust ventilation over stove
- Water filtration system for pure water at galley sink (Seagull)
- Owners cabin with:
  - Queen size bed
  - Seating
  - Make-up table and mirror
  - Plenty of storage for clothes, including full height closet
  - Bathroom (head) in suite with separate shower area
  - Vacuflush toilet
  - Safe hidden inside closet (very useful)
- Guest cabin with:
  - Queen size bed
  - Seating
  - Storage for clothes, including full height closet
- Crew cabin with:
  - Double bunks and storage
- Forward Head (bathroom) with manual toilet
- Positive catches on all cabinets and drawers (No holes to poke fingers in)
- Fans in all areas (4), DC powered
- Lee cloths for all sleeping positions
- Washer/dryer (Not that useful, would do without)
- Good white lighting throughout—Halogen (Now should LED)
- Red lighting for nighttime running at steps, galley, nav station
- Shades and screens on all windows, ports, and hatches
- Easy and good access to engine compartment
- Floorboards screwed down where possible
- Mounting brackets for Scuba air tank in lazarette

Mechanical and electrical

- See-thru water intake strainers with manifold and separation valve for engine, generator, refrigeration and water maker. The manifold is very useful if one strainer is blocked.
- Engine drip pan to catch any oil or diesel leaks
- Central air conditioning with reverse cycle heating and digital controls (3 zones)
- Diesel heater with hot water circulation system (Added later for Alaska)
- Engine compartment lights and blower
- Sound insulated engine compartment
- Dual Racor see-thru diesel fuel filters with changeover valve (valuable many times)
- Easy access to filters and inspection items
- Engine oil change pump out system (hand operated)
- Automatic fire extinguisher in engine compartment
- Viewing port into engine compartment (to determine if a fire exists)
- Three sets of batteries—Engine start-24V; Generator start-12V; House-24V
  Engine and house battery banks should be mounted low for stability. Generator battery should be high to avoid flooding in case of high water in bilge
  Switch for VHF and GPS to permit being powered by generator battery
- House battery bank should be large—460 AH at 24 VDC, minimum
  (equivalent to 920 AH at 12 VDC)
- All batteries should be secured in battery boxes with exhaust fans. Issue of Gel cell versus lead-acid (Lead acid batteries require constant maintenance, but have greater deep-cycle capacity)
- Inverter to convert DC to AC- 2,000 W continuous, enough to power refrigeration
- Charger, smart for house batteries
- Charger, smart for generator battery
- Solar power panels on davits for supplemental power at anchor or sailing
- Large alternator on engine, additional (actually two alternators)
- Electrical outlets in all cabins, salon, nav station and galley—240 VAC
- 24 VDC outlets in cockpit, chain locker, and nav station (multiple uses)
- LVR- Line voltage regulator to accept 120 VAC 60 Hertz and variations in voltage. Also acts as isolation transformer
- Shore connection for cable TV (not really used)
- Shore connection for water in bow locker with pressure regulator and valve
- Pressurized hot and cold water system
- Hot water heated by engine and 240 VAC
- Water maker- AC powered
- Pressurized salt water system with outlet in chain locker (for wash down of anchor chain and anchor when hauling up and also decks at sea)
- Bilge pumps—Electric automatic, emergency engine driven one, hand pump in cockpit, hand pump inside, and electric emergency pump that can be dropped into any area.
- Bow thruster- Should be capable of holding bow in 10 knot cross wind (15 kts better)
- Prop shaft thrust bearing like Aquadrive
- Maxprop 3 blade propeller with rope cutter on shaft (To minimize drag when sailing)
- Refrigeration system with holding plates in both refrigerator and freezer as well as thermostats
  Refrigerator, front opening and large freezer, top opening and large compressor 240 VAC driven
  Temperature gauges for refrigerator and freezer that are visible in galley
- VHF radio at helm and nav station with DSC and connected to GPS
- SSB long range radio with isolated backstay and tuning box in lazarette
- Radar antenna mounted on mast
- Weather fax and navtex
- GPS, including readout at helm
- Chart plotter (computer) and repeater
- AIS system with readout on electronic chart (added later) Very valuable
- Integrated instrument system like Autohelm
- Folding steps at top of mast (to reach top of mast you must step out of bosun's chair)

- Forward facing sonar—This device only worked at very slow speeds, like below 2 knots. The viewing distance forward was more limited the shallower the water, but it did save us a couple of times in reef areas by indicating a reef ahead.

Loose equipment

- Docking lines, 50'- 6
- Fenders, air filled- 4
- Fenders, solid foam- 2 (Obtained after air-filled ones popped in heavy pounding)
- Shore power cable of 50 feet and extension cable of 100 feet
- Shore power "reverser" cable (short cable that changes polarity)
- Shore power "adapter" cable (to easily attach any local unique connectors)
- Shore power smart reverse Y cable (to combine two 120 V outlets to give 240 V)
- Heaving line with monkey fist
- Flag and staff
- Emergency tiller
- Cockpit cushions
- Winch handles
- Boat hook
- Snubber—A nylon line shock leader with chain hook
- Dinghy, inflatable 11.5'; with canvas cover; oars, anchor line with small anchor, SS cable with lock, detachable light for night operation, painter that floats (polypro)
- Outboard—10 HP minimum (I used a 4-stroke for its fuel economy and quietness, but the offset is that it is harder to pull start than a two-stroke)
- Emergency distress radio—406 EPIRB
- Individual EPIRB with alarm—four (The alarm was loud enough to wake sleeping off-watch crew if an EPIRB went into the water. The overboard crew could be located by signal strength)
- Emergency Life raft for six people and equipment with deep stability bags
- Passerelle with masthead lift and controlling lines
- Fender boards (2 x 4 wood boards with rubber bumpers on ends)
- Loop chains (for tying up to rough walls)
- Side boarding ladder
- Flares, smoke, dye (Had flare gun, but note it is illegal in UK)
- Binoculars—two pair (one for Captain)
- Night scope- This was VERY valuable. (You can actually spot a ship over the horizon)
- First aid kit, Offshore
- Hand-held depth finder—(This was very valuable. Used to find entrances in reefs, where to drop anchor, etc.)
- Hand operated water maker for emergency and life raft
- Wireless headsets with mikes (avoids shouting to top of mast or bow)
- Fishing gear for emergency or sport
- VHF, Handheld—two
- GPS, Handheld
- Searchlight, handheld battery operated
- Flashlights—six or more, various sizes and types (including one worn on the head)
- Bolt cutter, very large (For cutting away rigging in case of de-masting)
- Fire extinguishers—four mounted in galley, utility room, aft cabin, and forward cabin. (Must buy in the US or the US Coast Guard will not accept them)
- MOM—8 (Man Overboard Module)
- Life sling
- Horseshoe buoy
- Sea Anchor (never used)
- Drogue (never used)
- Grappling hook and line
- Chain lifter and release device (useful in Med.)

- Bosun's chair
- Funnel Filter, Baja 6" (To filter suspect diesel)
- Tapered wood plugs to match thru hulls (tied to each thru hull)
- Air Horn, hand held pressurized
- PFDs for 6 persons - inflatable with safety harness & strobe light
- PFDs for 4 persons - for use in the dinghy (as they are left with the dinghy on shore)
- Tethers—double with retracting lines for each PFD
- GO Bag with all necessary items
- Compass, hand held electronic, with memory for averaging
- Country courtesy flags for all countries to be visited
- Signal flags—two sets (For "dressing the boat overall")
- Yellow Q Flag (For quarantine when entering a new country)
- Bell (This is a legal requirement, 8" diameter minimum)
- Clock & Barometer (Clock was set to "boat time", generally local time)
- Chafe guards for docking lines- Very useful and valuable
- Portable electric bilge pump with hose (for emergencies if primary fails or is blocked)
- Bicycles, folding, marine grade- 2 (And bike equipment like locks, tire pump)
- Sail sewing kit
- Plastic storage bins for all storage locations
- Pots and pans, stackable
- Dinnerware set, good china
- Dinnerware set, plastic
- Buckets, one with glass bottom
- Diesel pump, hoses and Racor filter to "polish" fuel and to pump diesel aboard from containers

Tools and spare parts

A complete set of tools, including specialized ones (like right-angle screwdrivers, pulley puller, oil filter straps, traveler car removal carrier, etc.) is an absolute necessity. Tools for repairing and troubleshooting electrical and electronic systems such as a volt-ohm meter, soldering iron, etc. are also required. Additionally, spare parts for every system on the boat are needed. I followed the policy that if anything failed because of wear or fatigue, I would then buy two (or more) of them as the part would probably fail again. Nearly all the failures were associated with third-party equipment.

I also made sure to have a complete set of owner's and service manuals onboard for every bit of equipment.

Some items did not work well, or I did not use:

- Washer/Dryer—Will not work when the boat is underway and many harbors frown on discharging of vast qualities of soapy water. We resorted to using the washing facilities available at marinas
- Ice Maker- will not keep ice cold if it is not always on power. Removed.
- Clear plastic bottom dinghy- Leaked, and plastic got scratched on sand beaches. Became useless, so resorted to glass bottom bucket for viewing anchor set.
- Rear cabin audio system controls because I did not spend that much time in the cabin
- Foot pump on fresh water system, because I was able to keep main pump operating, but maybe still a good idea.

Items or features that I would have liked:

- Self-stowing washboards (now available)
- Twin steering wheels with cockpit walk thru (now available)
- Chain counter with display at helm (to see the amount of chain deployed)
- Cabin configuration with two heads forward so crew and guests have their own head
- Satellite system for phone, data (Internet), and TV.

A list of ESCAPADE'S safety equipment is presented in Exhibit 16.

CHAPTER 9

Planning *the* Route

How to Plan for a World Cruise, and the Timing Implications

The winds and waves are always on the side of the ablest navigators.

EDWARD GIBBON

At first, circumnavigation seems so overwhelming that it is hard to know how to start planning. I found that breaking the voyage into meaningful legs, and then focusing on each leg made everything manageable. Each leg has specific challenges and objectives that are reasonable. Overall, a circumnavigation can take as little as 18 months, but then there is no time to see much of anything. I chose, instead, to take four and a half years, and found that it was a relaxed pace—but one that meant you still had to keep moving. Other sailors have taken ten years or more.

There are four major factors that affect the overall (as well as specific) timing of your passage. When it comes to your the major ocean crossings, these must be taken into consideration:

- The best time of year to make specific ocean crossings.
- The amount of time spent on local cruising and going along a coast.
- The amount of time spent away from the boat.
- Legal and Tax requirements of the countries visited.

There are so many good cruising grounds around the world that it is hard to choose amongst them. Later in the book, I devote an entire chapter to my favorites. When I bought

my boat, my objective was to cruise the Mediterranean and Caribbean and to cross the Atlantic. Obviously, this expanded into more ambitious plans. All told, I spent four years cruising the Mediterranean, which was divided between time blocks that were both before and after the circumnavigation. Included in the circumnavigation was going up and down the East coast of the US, the San Blas Islands of Panama, Ecuador and the Galapagos, French Polynesia, Tonga, Fiji, New Zealand, Australia between Sydney and Darwin, Indonesia, Malaysia, Thailand, Maldives, and the Red Sea. My route is presented in Exhibit 10. For the more adventurous, there are plenty of alternatives—including, for example, Antarctica, Cape Horn, Japan, South America, and the Artic.

Pick your cruising grounds, and provide adequate time to explore them as thoroughly as you want. There are jewels to be found between the passages. I normally did not stay more than a day or two in each port, except prior to and immediately after a passage. As a tradeoff, some people like to spend more time once they become familiar with a port, but then go to fewer ports. Select your timing well. For example, the Mediterranean is not at all pleasant in the winter. It must be enjoyed between May and October, and Alaska is good only in July and August.

The most typical circumnavigation is around the middle of the world, just north and south of the equator. This route is all warm weather, and it utilizes the trade winds. It also goes through the Panama Canal and the Suez Canal. Due to piracy concerns, people may now go around Africa, but doing that adds significant distance, time and risks. In a later chapter, the issue of piracy will be discussed.

When it comes to planning ocean passages, the bible is Jimmy Cornell's book, World Cruising Routes. In it, he describes the best and worst times to make nearly all the most likely sailing passages. Basically, do not plan passages during hurricane or typhoon seasons. That means crossing the Atlantic between mid-November and May. Most people leave Europe early to provide as much time in the Caribbean as possible before the next hurricane season. The Pacific crossing is usually made between April and September. Again, earlier passages provide more time to cruise before the next typhoon season. On the US East Coast, it is recommended that you be as far north as the Chesapeake Bay by June 1st, and not go south before November 1st. In the Pacific, it is recommended to be either in New Zealand or in Australia (and south to at least Sydney) between December and March.

The third element is the amount of time you want to be away from the boat. I planned to be home at least once a quarter because I had business obligations, and we wanted to be at home during Christmas time in order to be with our family. That meant four trips home a year, no matter where in the world the boat happened to be. Also, once a year, *ESCAPADE* was hauled, and left on the hard for several months. This provided time to perform needed maintenance, and to paint the bottom with anti-fouling paint. By timing this with the December trip home and the winter season, it did not subtract time from good cruising time.

Obviously, this kind of schedule required that we planed airline flights and marinas to dock at well in advance. Our sailing schedule was formed around those commitments. This may seem very rigid to some sailors, but we kept to the plan for over 15 years of cruising. At no time did we ever miss a flight or a crew pickup. We built-in contingency factors to our plan so that neither weather delays nor maintenance issues would cause us to miss any key dates.

Major ocean passages can be very intimidating to first-time blue-water sailors. One alternative is to join an organized group or rally, and do the passage in the company of other boats. Examples include the ARC (Atlantic Rally for Cruisers), and the Caribbean 1500, both of which are sponsored by the World Cruising Club. They have safety standards for participating boats, daily weather briefings, daily log-ins, as well as satellite tracking so friends and family can follow your progress. Although—in the vastness of the ocean—you rarely see other boats, you do have the comfort of knowing that participating boats are relatively near, and that you are being monitored. There are also social activities both before and following the passage. There is a cost to join a rally, but many believe the friendship and security are well worth it. There are also world rallies, but they keep a very fast pace. Some permits dropping out for a season, and joining the next fleet.

For our first ocean crossing, we went with the ARC, and we enjoyed it. I would definitely recommend going with a group for your first-time passage. For our second crossing, which was of the Pacific, we went on our own. We simply pulled up the anchor in Santa Cruz Galapagos one day and sailed 3,004 NM to our next anchorage in Fatu-Hiva, Marquesas. We did the same thing when we crossed the Indian Ocean. Our circumnavigation started—as well as ended—in Antalya, Turkey. As you can see, it's possible to "close the loop" practically anywhere.

In summary, set short-term and long-term goals to create a broad outline of your plan. This will define both where and (approximately) when you will be cruising, as well as when the passages will take place. The plan, of course, can always be modified if you find a place you fall in love with and want to spend more time, or if other unforeseen events occur. After all, there's no real downside to spending another year in paradise.

Escapade Sailing near Palma, Spain

PARTICIPATING IN AN OYSTER REGATTA ~ PHOTO BY OYSTER MARINE

CHAPTER 10

Passage, Plan *and* Log
Specific Forms and Examples

The secret of success is constancy of purpose.

BENJAMIN DISRAELI

It is very important to take the time to plan out the next day's sailing—not to mention organizing everything needed for a complete passage. To do this, I created what I call a **Passage Plan Form**. This is shown in Exhibit 5. I used it for day sails, as well as for multi-day passages. I started by planning a complete route on the navigation computer, with all waypoints (which could be a marina or anchorage), from the start position to the end point. This included—as much as possible—the whole route with all waypoints related to geographical points such as SE of Buoy 10 or N of Point Able

This gave me the ability—if required—to very accurately locate waypoints quickly on a paper chart. It also gave the complete distance very accurately. Finally, knowing all the waypoints made it possible for me to navigate even if the conditions changed. This would include, for example, darkness or fog. Although it sometimes seemed like overkill to plot all the waypoints up a river or through a large port, there were many times when it proved to be extremely valuable. Large ports (like Charleston, SC), can be very confusing for the first time, especially at night when the navigation lights blend in with the background ones.

Accurately knowing the complete distance allowed me to better estimate the time it would take to complete the

journey. For *ESCAPADE*, I calculated time using 5.0, 6.0 and 7.0 knot averages. That gave me a range of expected journey times, and possible arrival times. In general, we averaged near 6.0 knots—whether under sail or motoring. You will have to determine the most likely average with your own boat, as well as the possible range of averages.

I also entered tide timing at both departure and arrival locations. Since there may be depth issues along the route, this can—at times—be critical. Sometimes this could mean that arrival at the destination—or at an intermediate waypoint—may be required by a specific time. Also, timing may be required for bridge, lock, or marina opening times—or even for meeting a pilot boat. When all of these factors had been taken into consideration, it would determine our Target Start Time. We adhered (very strictly) to the Target Start Time, and every crewmember knew that we had to depart on time. That was when the anchor was up, or when the last line was released from shore.

I entered all the waypoints into the GPS, and it was independent of the navigation computer. So—even if the computer went down—we could still complete the passage by using the GPS. And, if required, we could follow the course on a paper chart.

The navigation computer recorded the actual course traveled in real time, which made it easy to see if we were deviating from the plotted course. Most of the time, we let the autopilot do the steering of the boat, since we had it set to "Track," or to follow the plotted course. That meant that the autopilot would automatically adjust for tides, drift, currents, and any other factors that could affect the boat's course by trying to keep the Cross Track Error to zero. When sailing, we adjusted *ESCAPADE's* sails to the best possible trim for the course the autopilot was steering. If the wind was too far forward or dead astern, we sailed the best route we could toward the next waypoint. When beating into the wind, the navigation computer helped us determine when to tack, as well as which tacks were making the most ground.

Even if we deviated from the plotted course, it was reassuring to know where we should be at all times. For example, when laying out the plotted course off a point, I would determine the closest I wanted to go to that point based on the depth of the water and rocks or other hazards. That way, I knew—if we were deviating from the plotted course—we had to be to seaward of either the waypoint or plotted course, rather than inside the waypoint or plotted course. That way, I did not have to consult the chart every time we changed course.

To ensure that all of *ESCAPADE's* systems were in a proper state, I also recorded data on battery charge, engine hours, the exact time of leaving and arriving, fuel level (by using Tank Tender inches), generator hours, the GPS mileage, the log distance, and the water level (by using a water computer). Before every departure, I "zeroed" the trip data on both the log and GPS.

This procedure—as well as the form—served me well, and helped me avoid many issues before they became problems. In fact, I cannot count the number of times that thorough, proper, in-advance planning "saved the day". Even if the plan is done in advance, it should still be reviewed again when the actual weather conditions can be projected. For example, when entering many inlets to harbors or rivers from the ocean, if the wind is onshore and there is an ebb tide, there will often be large waves in the inlet. Due to the height of the waves and the depth of the inlet, this can turn into a real problem. For that reason, timing your entrance with a flood tide will make the situation much easier to handle. Therefore, it pays to plan your departure time to coincide with a flood tide for when you expect to arrive. With an offshore wind, however, there may not be a problem.

For true passages of more than one day, I developed another form called **Passage Log** *(see Exhibit 6)*. This is more detailed and more complete than many of the available printed logbooks. My Passage Log form is intended to permit dead reckoning with confidence if the GPS fails. You can use it for any time period you like, but

I chose to take readings every two hours. Consequently, we had a written record—as recent as two hours ago—of exactly where we were, what true speed and course we were making, as well the compass heading and wind conditions we faced.

The data recorded were as follows:

Time

- I used local time, but GMT could be used. I adjusted the ship's clock every three days when on a long east-west passage.
- Position- Latitude and Longitude

GPS Data

- SOG—Speed over Ground
- COG—Course over Ground
- XTE—Cross track error (distance to plotted course)
- Distance to Way Point

Trip Log

- Course steered as indicted by the Autopilot
- Course steered as indicated by the magnetic Compass
- At Helm—Who is at the helm (name; AP=Autopilot; APT=Autopilot on track)
- Wind direction
- Wind Force (I used the Beaufort scale but could be knots)
- Barometer reading
- Sea—The sea condition. Judgmental but could include wave height or description such as confused or choppy.
- Sky—Clear, cloudy, rain, fog, etc.
- Engine or sail—Includes what sails are being used.
- Fuel—This is the Tank Tender reading (Not useful at sea.)
- Amp hours—From the Battery Monitor showing amount of electrical power remaining.
- Water—Quantity—Gives indication when the water maker needs to be run.
- Notes—Anything—Sightings, sunrise, when engine turned on and off, etc.

Whoever was on watch filled in the form every two hours (at the even hours). Over a period of several days it gave a good indication of the true speed over ground as well as how the weather has changed. It was all valuable information and I definitely found it a very useful form.

Examples

Sail Plan for Crossing the Pacific (Exhibit 7)

We planned to depart from Santa Cruz in the Galapagos on March 27, 2000, heading for Hiva-Oa in the Marquesas. The total estimated miles were 3,004 NM. As you can see, we changed the destination to Fatu-Hiva. The actual passage was 3,010.0 NM, which took 433.58 Hours (18.06 days). We arrived at 1425 on April 14, local time. This gave us an average speed of 6.94 knots. We motored for 123.0 hours, primarily in the beginning in order to reach the trade winds. We ran the generator for 95.5 hours and we made 711 gallons of water.

All of the waypoints are listed, including the new ones when we changed destinations. The suggested waypoints were from Cornell's book for established trade winds. When determining waypoints for approaching an island, I would use a progressively declining distance approach. This enabled us to make sure the island was in the proper location—relative to the GPS system—by visual observations before I would trust getting too close to the island. This is especially important if landfall occurs at night.

Passage Log for the Pacific Crossing (Exhibit 8)

This log starts at 0800 on April 7, 2000 local time (-8 hours from GMT). It gives the Latitude and Longitude at that time. The SOG (speed over ground) measured by the GPS was 9.1 knots. Note that for the remainder of the entries, the SOG was generally above 8. In fact, on this passage we set our own record of 1200 NM in six straight days for an average of 200 NM per day.

Escapade Sailing in the Indian Ocean

PHOTO BY ERICK REICKERT

The COG (course over ground) was 264° and the XTE (cross track error) was zero. But the course steered by the autopilot was 257° and per the compass was 255°. The "person" at the helm was APT or Auto Pilot, Track. The wind was from the SE at Force 6. Note that for the rest of the page the wind was generally Force 6 or 7, occasionally dropping to Force 5. The barometer was 1010, and did not vary much for two days.

The sea was 6 to 10 feet. Near the bottom of the page the sea was moderate, which would be 10 to 15 feet. The sky was overcast that day but became clear the next day. We were sailing at the time. Toward the bottom of the page, we noted that the engine had been turned on for a few hours.

The amp hours recorded the state of the battery charge. We turned on the generator whenever it dropped to 360 or so. For that reason, the charge kept going up and down. The water entry recorded the gallons in the fresh water tank, and in the notes it shows how many gallons were made. In general, I ran the generator when I could do four things at once—charge the batteries, heat the water in the hot water tank, run refrigeration, and run the water maker.

In the notes column, I recorded anything of interest. The numbers around 200 (such as 203.6 in the third row) indicated the actual nautical miles we achieved during the previous 24 hours. About half way down the page, we achieved two-thirds of the way across the Pacific.

These forms and data provide interesting memories, but they would be the repository of invaluable information—at the time—if any of the systems onboard failed during the passage.

Another useful form that I developed was a Departure Check List (Exhibit 20). This guaranteed that—before getting underway—we'd made sure that everything was ready, and all systems had been checked.

CHAPTER 11

Navigation *and* Communications

Charting Strategies and Communications Options

Success is not final, failure is not fatal;
It is the courage to continue that counts.

— WINSTON CHURCHILL

Navigation

Knowing where you are going (and what to expect when you arrive) is crucial for safe cruising. This falls into two basic categories. The first is charts—both electronic and paper. I always had paper chart backup to the electronic charts, just in case, and I highly recommend using this system. The second are Pilot Books or Cruising Guides. These can be obtained for nearly every cruising area of the world, and in some cases there are actually several books available. As far as I'm concerned, these are invaluable and I purchased all that were available for the next cruising ground. They provide huge amounts of data, including anchorages, bridges, local information, and marinas. Study these books or guides carefully before arrival.

For navigation, I evolved to using an electronic charting system, which not only worked well, but was also one in which I had complete trust and confidence. After all—for me—that is the key. The navigation system you use must—MUST—be one that you believe in, in fact, one in which you will trust both your life and your boat.

Of fundamental concern is the quality of the charts that you use. For an electronic system, the first decision is either vector or raster charts. Even after considering the touted advantages of vector charts (which are primarily

smaller file size and have the ability to provide different layers) I still don't trust them. They are an interpretation of a paper chart by someone of undisclosed origin. And layering means that you will not always have all the data at every level—some of which might be critical. They are also untried over many years, and are not kept up to date with registered changes by an official organization. A friend of mine checked one of the most popular electronic vector charts of an island he knew well in the Caribbean. To his horror, he found that an important reef was not even shown on the chart. I have compared vector charts to my system in many areas of the world, and nearly every time they lacked the detail of a paper chart, as well as the necessary information for safe navigation.

In a recent case, a race boat—Team Vestas Wind—that was depending upon vector charts went onto a reef in the Indian Ocean. An expert who testified in litigation over the loss of a cruising yacht when it hit a reef, recommends that if a course is plotted on an electronic chart using vector charts, then the course should be checked on paper charts to make sure no significant issues exist that the vector chart did not show.

So, I decided to use raster charts, which are direct copies of paper charts. The issue then becomes which paper charts to use. I have found that British Admiralty charts from the United Kingdom Hydrographic Office (UKHO) are the best overall, and they cover nearly every cruising area in the world. They use colors that make them highly readable, they are very detailed, the depths are frequent in the required areas, they provide land contours, the paper is thicker, and they are generally uniform in size. Plus, they are continuously updated. As a result, I—almost exclusively—used Admiralty paper charts, except in the U.S. and in specialized situations. One example was the Yasawa islands west of Fiji. In that case, the best paper chart was from Fiji, and I determined my waypoints from it. For the U.S., I used the standard NOAA (National Oceanic and Atmospheric Administration) charts. Canada has its own Canadian Hydrographic Service.

The UKHO offers nearly all of their charts in electronic form, called ARCS (Admiralty Raster Chart Service) charts. These are exact duplicates of the paper charts, but they appear on your computer. (See their web site, www. admiralty.co.uk for more information.) The entire chart is visible—including all the tide data, notes, and survey data—and the numbers are the same. This means that you can generally find out when and by what method (lead line, sonar, swept wire, etc.) the soundings were made. The charts are contained on CDs,, and what you buy is a permit for one year to open the purchased charts. The permit can be obtained via e-mail from an Admiralty Chart supplier. As long as you have e-mail capability, you can obtain additional ARCS charts—even in remote areas. Besides the basic chart CDs, which are by region, BA also issues weekly updates. When you purchase a chart, you also get the latest update, which means the purchased chart is up to date. In fact, I have found that recently-purchased electronic charts are actually more up to date than recently-purchased paper charts. To use ARCS charts you need to have navigation software that is set up for them, and there are very few programs available—and most chart plotters cannot use ARCS charts. ARCS charts also require registration with BA, as well as the use of a dongle with the computer.

To provide a degree of redundancy, I kept the electronic charts separate from the autopilot. That way, the boat was steered by the autopilot with data from waypoints entered into the GPS, and was not solely dependent on the electronic charting system. The computer chart plotter received input from the GPS and plots the present position. Then—for future reference—I retained the tracks of all our sailing on the computer. This is very useful when departing a port or anchorage that has a complicated entrance, because—when you were on the way in—you learned that the path was acceptable.

For all trips, whether three miles or 3,000 miles, I made sure to develop a passage plan in advance. This consisted of all the courses, distances, and waypoints for the passage. Because it was easier, faster and more accurate to do so,

I created this electronically on the computer. I decided, however, to keep the passage plan on paper as well as entering it in the GPS. I also compared the courses and distances that the GPS computes from the waypoints to what was computed on the charting program in order to assure that the waypoints and courses were correct before we departed. See Chapter 10 for a full explanation of both the Passage Plan Form and the Passage Log.

The final major concern regarding charts—which applies to paper charts—as well as electronic ones, is how a specific chart relates to GPS positions. The UKHO is working to adjust all charts to WGS 84 datum, but some are not there yet. Some charts give the amount of latitude and longitude to correct for, and you can enter this into the GPS. My greatest concern about them involves landfall, when you have no prior knowledge as to the alignment of the chart, which is why I set the landfall waypoint far away from any dangers. This is followed by subsequent waypoints that are progressively closer to known objects. When we had visual or radar confirmation of our position, I determined how accurate our position was on the chart. We then proceeded accordingly relative to the chart position. Our most notable concern in this regard was the island nation of Niue. Before leaving Rarotonga, we were informed that Niue could be up to two miles SSW of the chart position. But when we got there, it was exactly where the Admiralty chart said it should be. I had set the landfall waypoint more than three miles south of the island, just in case.

When on a passage we recorded our course, position, speed, and other critical factors on paper every two hours so that we could proceed by dead reckoning if the electronics failed (it never did). To minimize the cost of charts—both electronic and paper—I used a strategy of selecting the most critical ones rather than acquiring a complete duplicate set. For example, if the cruising guide for a specific area is quite good—especially in terms of harbor approaches and entrances—then I did not purchase detailed paper charts. Instead, I got large-scale paper charts of the area to permit route planning to within the detail of the cruising guide. For electronic charts, however, I obtained the most detailed ones available for the area we were sailing, as well as for all ports that we might enter (including backup ports) and large-scale electronic charts so that I had continuous coverage from start to finish. This strategy proved itself when we were transiting the Red Sea, and decided to divert to Port Sudan because the winds had turned against us. Even though we had not intended to go into Port Sudan, I had a detailed ARCS chart of the port. As we approached, we were hit by a sand storm, and visibility dropped to less than a tenth of a mile. To enter, we had to go between reefs that were only a few hundred yards apart. And since these reefs are under water, the radar was of no help. Consequently, we had to rely solely on electronic navigation. When we could finally see, we were right in the middle of the entrance channel.

Using ARCS charts this way gives the same navigating accuracy as paper charts. Additionally, electronic chart plotting is automatic and continuous. This is especially comforting when in high tidal areas where it is easy to get off course. Finally, changing routes and establishing new waypoints is far easier and quicker when using the mouse than dividers. It is also far more accurate and less prone to error, especially when the boat is bouncing about.

This electronic/paper chart strategy is fairly expensive, but it provides superior results. With very few exceptions, electronic charting was proven to be very accurate all around the world. There are, however, exceptions—such as in tight quarters where visual observation is the only sure method. Fortunately, we have been able to navigate electronically in extremely difficult situations. For example, in Chesapeake Bay we got caught in thick fog. Steering by autopilot (based on our pre-calculated passage plan), we monitored our position by the electronic chart, as well as by radar returns on buoys, and then by visual sighting of the buoys when they were within 50 feet. The accuracy is generally good enough to not only remain in the channel, but to stay to one side. This also means that buoy positions should never be used as waypoints. Actually, our greatest concern was the possibility of other ships and we took appropriate actions to see and be seen on radar and by sound signals.

Golden Gate Bridge, San Francisco, California, USA

FIRST ENTRANCE UNDER FOG ~ PHOTO BY ERICK REICKERT

This strategy makes using electronic charts the primary navigation tool, and paper charts a backup choice. I believe this two-pronged approach is superior to former methods, and the best system currently available. We have proven it while sailing around the world, in a variety of different situations, and with many charts.

Communications

This is a fast-changing field. What is available today is far different from that available 20 years ago, and the technological advances occur each year. Basically, you can get nearly anything you want, for a price. Essentially, the question is, "What do you want?" and then, "How do you achieve that reliably at the lowest cost?"

Let's consider the requirements for a cruiser, which means that there is no permanent dockage (and, thus, no landline telephone or cable TV). Next, we need to separate the requirements for when offshore at sea (i.e., more than ten miles from shore) from those near shore or in anchorages or marinas. If you are considering remote areas of the world (and third-world countries), assume that they are the same as being offshore unless you have specific information to the contrary.

For offshore, it has to be satellite based except for an SSB exception, but let's separate normal communications from emergency requirements. For regular communications, it is now possible to receive phone (voice), data (e-mail), TV and Internet anywhere on the high seas. The phone and data connection can be made most easily by a satellite like Iridium. Other satellite services may be available, but they may not cover the entire globe. It is possible to connect to a phone and e-mail by SSB radio, but this is sometimes not reliable. I used Iridium for voice and Inmarsat C for e-mail, but now—in today's world—that is considered an old system. TV and Internet at sea require the use of a stabilized tracking system housed in a dome. Since the size of the domes has been shrinking, they can now be considered for sailboats. There are now systems that will receive US TV and European TV without the need to change the hardware. Satellite systems require a major hardware instillation (including the dome), and usually a subscription as well as possible data-usage charges. But it is available.

When close to shore, it is generally possible to use a cell phone. I used Verizon around the Americas (from Alaska to Maine), and found that there was signal nearly everywhere—including in many areas of Mexico. Obviously, there were some areas that were not covered, but overall I was pleased. With 3G and 4G coverage you can also receive data and the Internet. In the old days, I was using Wi-Fi from marinas (but we were usually at the end on the dock and the signals were very unreliable). And remember, there is no security with most Wi-Fi hotspots.

For emergency distress calling, the basic device is the 406 EPIRB. These now include an internal GPS so that it transmits the lat/lon to facilitate rescue. Individual PLB's (Personal Locator Beacons) are also available to aid recovery of a person who has been lost overboard. Many new VHF radios with DSC also have a distress capability that is useful when near shore.

You will have to research the systems that are available at the time. Hopefully, the costs will diminish (as the capabilities increase) over time. And the Internet will become available wherever you happen to be.

CHAPTER 12

Security *and* Pirates

General Security Issues and Piracy Considerations

*As a rule, what is out of sight disturbs men's minds
more seriously than what they see.*

JULIUS CAESAR

Let's separate this subject into two major categories—routine security and major pirate attacks. Unfortunately, the world seems to be getting more dangerous all the time. But that also includes your own hometown as well as all major cities. There are many metropolitan areas in your own country where you would not comfortably go walking—especially at night. This caveat applies to all areas of the world, and the problem is that in strange cities you may not know how to identify the safe areas from the unsafe areas.

An additional factor is that in many remote areas of the world—particularly ones that may be very poor—a cruising yacht represents huge wealth in the eyes of the locals. For that reason, everything on the yacht is subject to theft. The dinghy and outboard are especially vulnerable because they can be detached easily. The simple solution is to keep everything locked at all times, except when sailing. Everything on deck should be either well attached or locked. All loose items—such as winch handles, binoculars, etc.—should be stowed below. Leave nothing visible that might attract attention.

During 15 years of cruising, we were boarded three times—in France, Spain and Indonesia. In France and Spain it was by youths who came aboard in marinas, but we were sleeping below because we ate earlier than Europeans typically do and we were already back from dinner. Since we scared the kids away, neither attempt resulted in any loss. In Indonesia, we forgot to lock the lazarette and some snorkel gear was taken—including my prescription-lens mask.

Remember that boat equipment is usually of more value to other boaters than for the locals. So for this reason, don't trust anyone. Also, you should keep the companionway and hatches locked when you are sleeping, as that is the prime time for thefts. This is why need to have a boat that has adequate ventilation when everything is locked. For example, there are stainless steel bars available for the hatches that will prevent entry, but they need to be removable (or unlocked) when underway. I tried a motion detector aimed into the cockpit, but that was not satisfactory because there were too many false alarms due to things moving around as a result of wind or rocking. But it is an approach that might be successful, if properly applied.

The dinghy should be out of the water, and locked with a chain or steel cable. Dinghy davits are great. Without davits, the dinghy should be lifted on deck or put in another secure position. The outboard should be locked and chained to the dinghy. We locked the dinghy to every dock we left it at on shore—every time, everywhere. The Caribbean is an especially bad area for dinghy theft.

Unfortunately—without exception—every area of the world is subject to theft. So be vigilant and keep everything locked. Do not become lax, because that is when you will lose things. Just like never transmitting financial or sensitive data over the Internet when connected by a public Wi-Fi network, extreme caution regarding security is always required.

Piracy

Piracy of the major type is dangerous, and could affect your cruising route around the world. This is where pirates highjack ships or yachts, then take the crew prisoner before asking for ransom. The major problem areas have been the Gulf of Aden, the Indian Ocean off the Horn of Africa, and the Arabian Sea with pirates based—due to the lack of a functioning government—in Somalia. The conditions change continually, and you should assess the situation when you are at the decision point.

I went through the Gulf of Aden and up the Red Sea in 2002, which was a hot pirate area at the time, but not as dangerous as it was by 2010. By 2013, things had improved. We followed our "anti-pirate protocol," which included:

- going as fast as we could by sailing with the engine on so we were doing well over 9 knots
- maintaining a course that was 2/3 away from Somalia and 1/3 from Yemen
- no American flag
- no navigation lights at night
- no radar on
- VHF radio silence

We sailed directly to Djibouti for a stop before going into the Red Sea. Luckily, the wind was up so we were sailing well and the seas were around five feet. The state of the sea would have made it difficult for pirates to board us. Once, a local boat targeted us by altering course for an interception, but when they realized how fast we were sailing they broke off and changed course. But don't forget that pirate skiffs can often do more than 20 knots, so they can overtake any sailboat.

The issue of whether it is advisable to carry a gun onboard for pirate protection is often debated. There are strong opinions regarding this matter on both sides of the argument. I chose—for several reasons—to not carry a weapon. Firstly, it is very impractical to carry a weapon when world cruising because all countries have some type of rules pertaining to importing guns (or having guns onboard while in their territorial waters).

These rules vary dramatically between countries and can range from: obtaining a permit to have a gun onboard, requiring the gun to be surrendered to Customs people, and having the guns locked up in a proper cabinet. If the gun is surrendered, then you will probably not get it back because most cruise routes leave a country from a different port than the port of entry.

There were other practical reasons that kept me from carrying a gun. The pirates are well armed with automatic weapons—including AK-47s and rocket launchers. And there are many individuals on each pirate boat. There was no way I could conceive of winning a gun battle against such an overwhelming force. Also, if I showed them a weapon, then a gun battle could erupt. Finally, winning any gun battle assumes that you have control over the scene, as well as situational awareness. In military terms, surprise always tips the balance to those who control the situation. What happens if two pirate boats approach from opposite sides? What if they do this at night? What happens if you are off watch and sleeping and the person on watch did not detect the pirate approach until too late, and you came on deck with boarding already in progress? The aggressor nearly always has the advantage.

Another issue regarding carrying a gun is when to show or use it. After going through the Gulf of Aden and up the Red Sea, we anchored behind a sand dune island before heading up the Gulf of Suez. We were very aware of the possibility of pirates. So what do you do when a local boat approaches with several men whose faces are covered with balaclavas? Remember, we were at anchor. I had heard that some local fisherman used balaclavas to protect their faces from the hot sun, so maybe that was not a sign of aggression. My solution was to have everyone onboard—there were five of us—assemble, and spread along the deck to make us appear to be as formidable as possible. It turned out that they were, in fact, local fishermen who only wanted water, which we gladly gave them. But we kept them at a distance so their boat did not touch ours, which would have let them easily jump aboard.

In Indonesia, north of Bali, small local canoes were once aiming directly at us as they approached *ESCAPADE*. Only at the last moment would they swerve, and barely miss us. It turns out that they were attempting to get rid of their "evil spirits" by conducting such a maneuver. According to their cultural beliefs, evil spirits only go in a straight line so they can be flung off the local fishing boat onto ours. That way, the occupants increase their chances of catching fish. This belief also applies to Indonesian houses, which explains why the entrance to their yard requires going around a wall that blocks the entrance. The wall stops evil spirits from entering. But the bottom line for cruisers is that it isn't good to become trigger happy in foreign lands or in situations where you do not know local customs.

All that having been said, the decision to go through or avoid a pirate area is critical, and one that must be based on the most current facts available. Due to a number of factors, the level of piracy in the Gulf of Aden declined in 2012 and 2013, but does that reduction make it safe enough for you?

Another approach is to travel together into a convoy. I had timed my departure from the Maldives to allow me to meet up with a convoy of boats that were leaving Salalah Oman. At the last minute, I elected to not join the convoy because they were going slower, and sailing closer to Yemen than I considered safe. Plus, the convoy can only go at the speed of the slowest boat, and maintaining a close formation—especially at night—can be difficult.

In other words, the safety in a convoy is in numbers, not speed. Perhaps the best approach would be if a convoy of boats hired an armed patrol boat to accompany and protect them.

While deciding on my course of action, I did lay out a route around the southern tip of Africa. It required many more ocean miles, up to a year more in time, sailing in waters with the largest waves in the world south of Madagascar, and dodging the frontal systems that sweep from west to east around the tip of Africa. Finally, if your destination is the Mediterranean Sea, you will generally have to sail back across the North Atlantic to get there. Since there are risks inherent in either approach, you will have to decide which one you would be willing to accept.

Sunset after a day Sail

PHOTO BY ERICK REICKERT

CHAPTER 13

Layup

The Ability to Layup a Boat Around the World

My soul is full of longing for the secret of the sea,
separate on the surface but connected in the deep.

HENRY WADSWORTH LONGFELLOW

I laid up my boat on the hard every year to perform annual maintenance, and to secure her better when I returned home for extended periods of time. This also provided drying out time for the hull. Doing this around the world is more of a challenge than utilizing your home boat yard, but it is quite achievable.

I hauled *ESCAPADE* in Gibraltar (twice); Marmaris, Turkey; Savannah, GA, USA; Gulf Harbour, NZ; Phuket, Thailand; Alcudia, Mallorca, Spain; Zadar, Croatia; Richmond, BC, Canada, Portsmouth, RI, USA (twice), Palm Beach, FL, USA; and Annapolis, MD, USA.

Escapade at dock in Boston, Massachusetts, USA

ONE OF MANY CITIES VISITED ~PHOTO BY ERICK REICKERT

All of the facilities were good, and some were excellent. Language was not a problem, as all places had people who spoke English. In fact, I had good experiences in all of the boat yards.

The key is to do extensive research using cruising contacts, Cruising Guides, and sailing organizations. Also, it is desirable to make reservations well in advance because many yards fill up to capacity. In the chart below is an E-mail, I sent to prospective yards six months in advance.

Not all my requirements were met. The hardest one to achieve was finding a surfaced hard standing. Many yards had gravel. In fact, the one in Rhode Island said gravel was a legal requirement so that contaminated water would not run off into the bay.

Although I did not elect to do it, on Fiji they stored boats over the typhoon season by digging a trench the width and depth of the keel and rudder in the ground and then surrounding it with old tires on the ground. The boat

Inquiry Questions for Potential Layup Locations

Dear Sirs:

This may seem a little early, but I am now doing my planning for this fall. Thus I am writing at this time.

I am seeking a place to haul out my sailboat and store it on the hard for the 20xx/20xx winter. It is 17 meters (55 feet) long, has a beam of 4.8 meters (16 feet), and a draft of 2 meters (6'10"). The weight is 30 tons (60,000 pounds, 27,200 kg). I want to haul it out at around September 14, 20xx, and I want put it back in the water in April, 20xx. Can you accommodate ESCAPADE for this period?

In addition, can you answer the following questions:

1. *What is the cost for haul out and putting back in the water and the cost for being on the hard for x months?*

2. *What size travel lift do you have that will take at least 35 tons? What width boat will the travel lift accommodate?*

3. *How is the boat supported while on the hard? For example, is a metal cradle or are adjustable tripods used?*

4. *Is the hard standing surfaced and dust/dirt free? For example, concrete or asphalt?*

5. *Is electrical power (50 Amp- 240 Volts AC) and water available for each boat on the hard?*

6. *What type of security exists? For example, is the yard fenced, is it patrolled, are there guards, etc.? Has there been any type of theft at the yard recently?*

7. *Can you power wash the bottom at the time of haul out?*

8. *Can I have work performed on the boat while on the hard such as painting the bottom with anti-fouling, and having the topsides waxed and polished?*

9. *Are there service people available locally to do painting and waxing work?*

10. *What other types of work can be performed?*

11. *For winter, should the boat be shrink-wrapped? Who can do that?*

12. *Dockage will be necessary prior to pulling the boat out and after putting in the water. Is dockage available one week before and one week after hauling?*

was placed in the trench with the hull resting on the tires. They said this method would survive a typhoon even with the mast up. But you could remove the mast as well.

The major issue was to find a yard with enough Travelift capacity, including width, as *ESCAPADE* was especially wide. A smaller issue was to locate anti-fouling paint locally, which was compatible with what was already on *ESCAPADE*.

In general, the costs were reasonable all around the world. The haul-out time was also useful to conduct more major maintenance projects. For example, our water maker had to be rebuilt in New Zealand because the original design had dissimilar metals at a seal point, which needed repairing. I had the solar panels installed in Gibraltar. The batteries have to be replaced every three to four years due to the heavy use they receive. I took zincs with me because they were not always available locally. So I stocked up when I could. At one point, the Max Prop propeller had to be rebuilt because of wear due to the number of hours it had been used.

I had a complete checklist of everything that needed to be done when laying up the boat for the winter or for a period of time. It is attached as Exhibit 23, and it also identifies what is needed to be accomplished when launching or commissioning. The items in bold had to be done before the boat was put into the water. I checked off every item as it was accomplished, and made notes if anything additional was required. Develop a list for your own boat. I found mine invaluable, and it also helped to allocate work when a person was available to help you.

Even though I was reluctant to leave *ESCAPADE*, she was always safe and sound upon our return. Local labor was skilled for the tasks we asked of them. So, you should be able to locate a good facility to haul your boat where and when you need to.

Escapade anchored off Hope Island, Australia

PHOTO BY ERICK REICKERT

CHAPTER 14

Cost *of* Cruising
The Rewards of World Cruising

Adventure is worthwhile in itself.

——— AMELIA EARHART ———

The cost of cruising ranges dramatically and is primarily dependent upon the number of days spent cruising, the style and location of cruising, the length of the boat, and if there is a paid crewmember. But there are many other costs involved that can add up. The following is a list of the major cost elements.

Marinas including electricity and water

The charges are by the length of the boat, based on the season. Transitory costs by the night are the most expensive. Discounts can sometimes be obtained for weekly or monthly contracts, which are useful if you want to leave the boat for a period of time to either go home or explore the local countryside. Annual contract costs are the least, but if you have an annual contract you are not cruising. Most marinas charge for electricity, either a fixed cost per night or by a meter. Some places charge for water as well.

I found that some of the highest costs for marinas were in the US. Other areas of the world are much more reasonable, with the exceptions of the Island of Capri in Italy, Venice, Italy, and Porto Cervo on Sardinia. To get an idea of the costs involved you can contact various marinas, possibly using their websites, for the type of boat you own.

Marina expenses can be the largest single cost if you utilize them every night. Note that is some areas there are no suitable anchorages, so using a marina is mandatory.

Anchoring charges, buoy charges or dinghy landing charges

Anchoring is far less expensive than are marinas, but it is not necessarily free. In many places there can be charges for anchoring or securing to a local buoy. These are generally collected every evening. In some areas, to avoid damaging reefs, you may not be permitted to anchor, and even after anchoring there may be charges imposed to land your dinghy if you want to go ashore. And in the Caribbean, you may be coerced by a local "Boat Boy" (a man) to watch your dinghy so no harm comes to it. The implication being that if you don't pay for him to watch the dinghy it may not be there when you return.

Crew

Paid crew costs can vary dramatically, depending upon the agreement you have with them. See Chapter 6 on different types of crew.

Fuel, oil, and coolant

Diesel prices vary widely between countries, and vary with the price of crude oil. Some of the most expensive countries were France and Italy. Some of the cheapest were Djibouti, Gibraltar, and Mexico. Thankfully, sailboats do not use a lot of fuel compared to motorboats. The amount of motoring, however, will be far more than a sailor expects—or hopes—if you plan to keep schedules, and are in light wind areas. Based on your plans for the upcoming year, and the fuel economy of your boat, you can fairly accurately estimate the expected number of gallons of diesel that will be required.

Maintenance—scheduled and unscheduled repairs and haul out

Unscheduled repairs cannot be predicted, but can cost a lot if a major problem is encountered. It is difficult to budget for, but you know something will happen so a provision would be in order. Scheduled maintenance should be free (except for the parts), as you will be doing it. Hauling out and storage on land (see the Chapter 13) will be required and can be determined in advance.

Travel

Travel is discretionary, but can vary dramatically according to your preferences. As mentioned previously, we flew home four times a year from wherever *ESCAPADE* was. We sometimes did side trips on the way to or from the boat. For example, we visited Machu Picchu on the way to *ESCAPADE* when she was in Ecuador. These travel arrangements can be expensive, but it provides further travel experiences not directly associated with the sea.

Provisions

Buying groceries and other provisions in countries around the world can be exciting and challenging. This includes figuring out how to describe the food you want, and determining what is in a can or box. Prices vary around the world, and are often more than your local supermarket might charge back home, but the cost was never exorbitant. However, you often need to provision for multiple crew so the total bill might be higher than at home.

Eating and sightseeing ashore

We ate out nearly half the time we were in port because it gave us a better feel of the local community. Eating onboard will save money, but then there is no difference between countries or ports. We always tried to soak up the local atmosphere, and we did it in a variety of ways. For example, we had two folding bicycles onboard so if the area was relatively flat—and traveling by bicycle was safe—we found it was a nice way to get around. If we wanted to go farther afield, then we rented a car or hired a taxi. In many places around the world, the car rental companies will bring a car to the marina, which makes it very convenient. And if you negotiate well, taxies can often be hired by the day or the trip.

In terms of cost, eating and sightseeing are highly variable and really up to you. After all, you have to eat no matter where you are (even at home), so that is really not an incremental cost associated with cruising.

Clubs and organizations including towing assistance

To achieve a sense of community and to provide the ability to meet other cruisers easily, we joined several clubs. These included the Seven Seas Cruising Association (based in Ft. Lauderdale), Ocean Cruising Club (based in England), and the Cruising Association (based in London). We also joined Boat/US, which provides towing assistance at several levels for US waters. There are other clubs and groups that may be of interest to you. We met many people through these organizations, and they also provide up-to-date cruising information. The annual fees are modest, and I believe they are well worth the cost. You may also be a member of a Yacht Club back home. In some locations there were local Yacht Clubs that had reciprocal agreements with our home Yacht Club. This provided additional places to go, often at good rates.

Insurance

Insurance costs vary widely, but should be known before you depart. You will need an insurance company that will insure you all the way around the world. Besides the limitations placed on the geographic areas and time of year, there are other potential requirements pertaining to crew. But the cost will also vary based on the area you will be sailing. The most expensive was the Pacific, as distances are great and repair costs could be high. I kept moving the coverage area as we progressed. These costs can be anticipated.

Coast Guard documentation and state licenses

The costs associated with the legal requirements back home will be known in advance. To enter foreign countries will require your boat to have US Coast Guard Documentation. State licenses are not required. In fact, *ESCAPADE* did not need a state license until we quit world cruising, and spent substantial time in the US.

Charts and cruising guides

You will need a lot of charts, both paper and electronic, for your cruising plans. Also, obtain as many cruising guides as possible for each of the areas you intend to visit because each one offers a different perspective, and may prove useful. The cost of these can add up to substantial amounts.

Cruising permits, entry fees, canal fees and rally fees

Entry to most countries requires some type of permit, entry fee or other charge, which can be identified in advance. One good source of current information on entry requirements is the web site www.noonsite.com Most major canals—like Corinth, the Panama, and Suez charge fees. Some of these can reach several thousand dollars, depending upon the size of the boat. Boat rally fees are large as well.

Weather services

Sometimes it is good to hire the services of a weather router. There are many to choose from and they have a variety of rate plans. These vary from a single forecast to daily updates. In general, I found this type of service invaluable when I was sailing as a solo yacht across oceans. There are also weather services available on the Internet that may require a subscription.

Yacht Agents

Yacht agents provide a variety of services at many places around the world. Super yachts often use them to arrange for docking, provisioning, bunkering (fueling), crew-related aspects, and shore-based support. Although they charge a fee, it is sometimes much easier, quicker and possibly the only way to achieve an objective. I used agents for the Panama and Suez canals. At Suez, the canal regulations required you to use a local agent, probably as a make-work scheme. At Panama, it is possible to "do it

Nuevo Vallarta, Mexico
ESCAPADE TUCKED AWAY FOR CHRISTMAS ~ PHOTO BY ERICK REICKERT

Escapade sailing with both foresails

ERICK AT USUAL SAILING POSITION ~ PHOTO BY BARRY HEDLEY

yourself" but that can lead to frustration and delay. By using a local agent I was able to specify when I wanted to transit the canal, and he made it happen. He was also responsible for obtaining all permits and paperwork as well as for arranging the admeasure. I viewed the extra cost as good value for money. Other yachts were often sitting waiting to transit for weeks. I also used agents in Venice, Italy and Rhodes, Greece. In both cases there were special local circumstances that made the use of an agent extremely desirable. For example, in Venice an agent arranged for us to tie up alongside the main canal (Gludecca) over the weekend of the Fiesta della Redentore, a celebration to commemorate the end of the plague in 1577. There is a massive flotilla of all types of boats which is then followed by a spectacular fireworks display in the canal. We had a front row seat on *ESCAPADE*, and it would not have been possible without the agent's assistance.

Pump outs and disposal of trash

Increasing environmental regulations require you to pump out the holding tank in most coastal areas. In general, there is a charge for this service, but a few forward-thinking municipalities provide the service for free. On some remote islands, you are not permitted to leave trash on the island, or they may charge by the bag. When crossing oceans, we never dumped anything overboard that was not biodegradable. We used the dinghy, which was up on davits, to store the trash until we reached land. When more than ten miles from land, we emptied the holding tanks directly into the ocean.

Summary

I would recommend that you prepare a budget with amounts for all the above cost areas. The major cost elements are eating onshore, marinas, paid crew, travel and sightseeing and unscheduled maintenance and repair. These can be adjusted to meet your budget and lifestyle.

CHAPTER 15

Ownership, Taxes *and* Insurance

Imporant Foreign Legal Issues

*So fine was the morning except for a streak of wind here and there that the sea
and sky looked all one fabric, as if sails were stuck high up in the sky,
or the clouds had dropped down into the sea.*

VIRGINIA WOOLF

Owning a boat subjects you to a variety of duties, laws, and taxes around the globe. This is a very complex subject that requires the advice of tax professionals. I will, however, attempt to provide some ideas that may be of interest to you, and which you can pursue with proper legal advice. At every stage, I sought the advice of legal and tax professionals.

When going to foreign countries, a US boat must be Documented by the US Coast Guard. State registration is not required or accepted. A boat can be built by a foreign boat builder, and still be documented as a US boat. In fact, it does not have to ever enter US waters.

My boat was built in England. I filed for documentation when it was under construction, and the documentation number was properly carved into the structure of the boat, as required. So when it was launched, it was an American flagged vessel. I did not have to pay any US taxes or duties when it was completed as it was outside the US.

Ownership

Some lawyers advise that the ownership of a boat should be by a Corporation to separate it legally from the personal business of the owner. In my case, I established a Delaware Corporation to own the boat. It was appropriately named World Cruising Ltd. This is relatively easy to do, and

there are firms located in Delaware that can handle the necessary paperwork. The main requirement is that the Corporation has to file annual statements with Delaware, and pay a small annual corporation tax. An annual meeting of shareholders is required to elect the Corporate officers. In my case, I was the sole shareholder. The Corporation must have at least one annual business meeting to approve the financial statements. We normally did this in February or March in preparation for the Delaware filing and tax documents. This may sound complicated, but it was actually quite easy, and just required a little paperwork once a year. I also carried a document onboard stating that I, as an individual, was authorized to use the Corporation's boat.

The Corporation was designated as an S-Corporation, and had a US Federal Tax EIN number. I filed annual tax returns for the Corporation, but as it did not have any income or expenses, there was never any tax due.

Another advantage of a Corporation is that if the boat is chartered, the charter business is clearly separated, and the boat's expenses can be written off against the income. This would include costs of a hired Captain and crew, as well as all operating costs.

The final advantage for corporate ownership is that when the boat is sold, it is actually the Corporation that is sold.

As the boat owner does not change, the sale is not subject to Sales Tax in most states.

Taxes

For fifteen years, my plan for cruising was determined by taxes. This is a harsh, but true fact. Basically, if you keep moving from country to country or state to state you will be OK. Each country, and the EU (European Union), has its own rules and regulations, and you must research these well in advance of entering a country or else you may be unpleasantly surprised. The length of time you can spend in a country varies, and is dependent upon a variety of modifying factors. In addition, these rules change over time so you need to be up-to-date with your information.

The rules are also dependent upon the flag of the vessel, and the nationality of the owner and/or Captain. Finally, the rules generally prohibit chartering of a boat in their country (to protect their local chartering fleet). For the rest of this Chapter, I will be talking about an American flagged boat with an American owner and Captain who is using the boat for pleasure rather than chartering.

Fundamentally, you must clear in and clear out of every country. Failure to do so can lead to very harsh penalties. In fact, in many areas of the world you will not be permitted to clear into the next country unless you produce your exit papers from the prior county (called a Zarpe). It is general practice to fly the yellow or Q signal flag on the starboard spreader below the country's courtesy flag until the boat has been cleared for entry. Until that happens no crewmembers may leave the boat. The Captain must report to the appropriate Customs/Immigration office with the necessary documents to obtain clearance. When cleared, the Q flag is removed.

Clearance into a country always involves two things—Immigration and Customs. In addition, there may be other requirements like reporting to the local Police Station and a medical inspection. At one island, *ESCAPADE* was fumigated. You must enter at a Port of Entry (not all ports are a Port of Entry), and there are also special requirements for weapons and pets. Some ports will even inspect the boat's bottom for unwanted pests.

Immigration for a boat's crew is generally no different than other forms of entry. That is, Passports are required, and there may be Visa requirements as well as length of stay limits. One exception is that entry into the US of a non-US citizen on a private boat requires a Visa, because

Large following seas on Atlantic Crossing

PHOTO BY ERICK REICKERT

the US Border Patrol will not issue a Visa Waiver as they would if the same person arrived by plane or cruise ship. I was held responsible as Captain when I brought two UK nationals into the US without visas. (They were eventually cleared and I escaped charges.)

There are also requirements for other documents. Some examples include the original of the Documentation (issued annually by the Coast Guard), Boat Insurance Policy, Ship's Radio License, Radio Operators License for at least one crew member, and Proof of Competency of the Captain. There may be others, depending upon the country.

The main issue for the boat is Customs and their requirements. The EU, for example, allows a stay of 18 months in EU countries under Temporary Importation (TI). Other countries can be a much shorter time. For example, Thailand is 60 days, but it may be extended to six months. The penalty for staying beyond the time limit can be severe, such as paying the VAT tax on the value of the vessel (possibly 20 to 23% in the EU). In Thailand, I had to sign a paper that said they could charge 100%

of the value of the boat if it was kept beyond the allowed period of time—essentially, giving up *ESCAPADE*.

It's important to remember that as part of the clearance process, some countries require Cruising Permits. These are essentially revenue generators for the country involved. Some countries—such as Indonesia and the Galapagos Islands—require advance approval and impose strict requirements. For others—like Croatia—it is just a matter of paying the fee (they gave a discount on the second visit).

When I was sailing in Europe, the rule was a limit to stay of six months out of any twelve-month rolling period. But even before I could begin cruising, I had to export the new boat out of the EU or else the builder would require a security deposit that would be equivalent to the UK VAT tax. So, after I took possession of the boat in Ipswich (England), I had to clear out of the UK and the EU. So for my first sail, I chose—for tax purposes—to go to Guernsey in the Channel Islands because it is outside the EU tax wise. I was then able to return to England as "a visiting US-flagged boat." We cruised England,

Escapade at Annapolis, Maryland, USA

PHOTO BY WALCZAK BROKERAGE

France, Spain and Portugal. For that winter, I chose to have the boat hauled in Gibraltar because it is also outside the EU. My next sail was to Malta (also outside the EU), before cruising Greece and then Turkey. I hauled the boat in Turkey—which, again, is outside the EU.

This type of entering and leaving the EU, with hauling over winter outside the EU, kept me "legal," and I never overstayed the maximum time. Even under the current laws, I believe that you can "reset" the 18-month limit by going outside the EU for a period of time. (There is, however, some debate on how much time.)

We did not enter the US (for the first time) directly. Instead, I first entered St. John, then St. Thomas in the US Virgin islands, and then Puerto Rico. After cruising the Dominican Republic, Jamaica, Cayman Islands and Mexico, we finally entered the US. By that time, we had nothing to declare and *ESCAPADE* was over three years old. We cruised up to Boston and back down to Savannah, but never stayed longer than 60 days in any one state. We then continued our circumnavigation—always keeping within the time limits for every country, even including hauling in New Zealand and Thailand. We spent another two years in the Mediterranean, going in and out of the EU. After shipping the boat to Vancouver (Canada), we learned that we could not haul the boat in Washington State because we would exceed their time limit. Fortunately, Canada would allow us to haul for the winter if the boat was kept at a recognized boat yard, and money was spent on the boat. The boat yard took care of reporting to Customs.

When we did enter the US for an extended time we were faced with having to register the boat in a State. Naturally, all the States have different requirements, which also differ if the owner happens to be a non-resident. Most States have some type of time limit for visiting boats before registration is required. For example, Maine is 60 days; Florida and Virginia are 90 days, and Maryland in "most of the calendar year". Most states require paying of a Use tax, which would be the difference between the already-paid Sales tax on the boat, and their Sales tax in order to register it. This is addition to the registration fees. The exception to this is Rhode Island, which repealed Sales and Use taxes on boats in 1993, as a way to encourage the local boat industry. As we had never paid Sales tax on *ESCAPADE*, we chose to first register her in Rhode Island. If fact, we put her up on the hard in Rhode Island for two years so the local boat industry did benefit. While in Rhode Island, Susan was able to be the curator at the Belmont Castle Museum in Newport. We then registered *ESCAPADE* in Florida. In Florida, because Use tax is exempted for boats that: have been owned for more than six months; have been in use in a taxing jurisdiction of another state for over six months; and were not intended for Florida use when first purchased. So we were able to register our boat in Florida without paying a Use tax.

As a result, we were able—totally legally—to avoid paying a VAT or Sales tax on *ESCAPADE*. But doing so required a lot of effort and consultation with tax experts. Our plan for where to cruise, where to haul, and how long to stay in any country, State, or the EU was carefully—meticulously—planned in advance.

Insurance

Another major determinant of cruising is insurance. It may be difficult to find an insurance company that will insure your boat all the way around the world. Even if you do, the rates will vary depending upon the part of world where the boat is located. So I kept changing the coverage area every six months as we progressed. Ironically, the German/UK insurance company that covered us for the circumnavigation did not want to cover us in the USA because the US is so litigious.

Insurance companies have many possible requirements that will affect cruising plans. On the East Coast of the US, most insurance companies will not cover boats south of the Chesapeake Bay before November 1st because of the possibility of hurricanes. This leads to an annual mass southward exodus around November 1. The same kind of timing constraints will apply to other parts of the world that are prone to hurricanes or cyclones. If you want to keep a boat South during hurricane season the insurance company may impose special requirements like the ability to haul if a hurricane is predicted. This requires reservation of space in advance, as well as a firm commitment from a Captain who will be responsible for moving the boat.

Certain geographical areas may be excluded as well. The major concern today is piracy. You will have to determine if your insurance company will permit sailing through the Gulf of Aden and the Red Sea. If you are unwilling to take the risk, and/or if your insurance company will not cover such a trip, that may mean your route around the world will need to be altered to go around the southern tip of Africa. When I sailed up the Red Sea, my insurance company requested that we do it non-stop. So we did not plan on any stops, but in the event—as a result of bad weather—we had to put into Port Sudan. But, as directed, we did not cruise up the coast. The insurance company also designated several Central American countries as "off limits." Insurance companies may also require a proof of competence on the part of the Captain and/or crew.

With a paid crewmember, special insurance coverage may be required. Additionally, dinghy and outboard insurance may be separate from the main boat. It pays to research insurance alternatives thoroughly, as there can be a large variance between insurance companies.

In summary, tax and insurance considerations will probably determine your route, the places you visit, and the timing for all your stops.

CHAPTER 16

Governmental Requirements

Important Foreign Legal Issues

There is something healthy and invigorating about direct action.

HENRY MILLER

In addition to Customs and Immigration, many countries have other legal requirements. These can be wide-ranging, often confusing, and continuously changing. In addition, in many cases the rules and regulations are not uniformly enforced throughout the country at various ports.

All issues related to cruising should be followed closely, and be sure to obtain the very latest situation. One of the best sources is the Internet website www.noonsite.com, which claims to be the global site for cruising sailors. I found it to the best source.

The most common requirement is for a cruising permit. These vary considerably in terms of cost, length of time and conditions, and some require advance approval. Some countries or islands prohibit anchoring in specific areas—generally on reefs or coral areas. This is to prevent damage to the coral.

There may also be requirements for specific equipment onboard boats entering or leaving a country. For example New Zealand (a country that was tired of rescuing boaters in the ocean), passed Clause 21 of the Maritime Safety Act, which required a Safety Certificate before a boat departed. This legislation was very controversial, and has now been repealed. But other countries may have a variety of requirements such as, for example, AIS.

Most countries require black water holding tanks. Turkey is proposing to also have grey water holding tanks. Very few boats have that capability, so it is unclear what will happen. This issue is changing and evolving over time.

Some islands have strict rules regarding solid waste and its disposal. The Galapagos has specific rules, and a variety of other islands do as well. Charges are sometimes levied for every bag of trash left.

In the EU, the diesel that is sold (with the tax already paid) is clear. So if any tax-free diesel—which is colored red—is put in the tank it will be evident, even after many fill ups. This issue becomes imperative when a boat that has visited England (where they only sell red diesel, even if the tax has been paid) travels to the continent. For a while French authorities would not accept the rationale that the tax had already been paid in England. There is a recent report that suggests the French authorities will now accept it if a receipt can be produced to show the tax has been paid. All of this is a very confusing (and exasperating) issue that continues to evolve. I actually saw—first hand—customs people in France dip a tube into boat fuel tanks to determine the color of the fuel.

There may also be proficiency requirements in certain countries for the Captain. In late 2013, Mexico impounded 338 boats for infractions of their rules. A Temporary Import

Permit (TIP) has been required for years, but there was a new push by Customs officials—accompanied by armed marines—to check paperwork. If no one was onboard (or if some mistakes in the paperwork were found) the boat was immediately put in "precautionary embargo," and not allowed to leave the dock. The marinas, of course, are required by law to report any departures. This issue had not been resolved when I wrote this.

Visiting the Galapagos is quite complicated. Basically, it requires a cruising permit, as well as stops in only a few designated ports on inhabited islands. An agent may be required. A private boat is not allowed to visit other islands without an official guide onboard, and a permit that has been obtained well in advance. Ultimately, it is easier for cruisers to visit the other islands by using a local tour service and small cruise ships, which is what we did. It becomes even more complicated if you visit Ecuador before the Galapagos.

In a recent report, I learned that the Galapagos now inspects the bottoms of boats for unwanted marine organisms. If any are found, the boat must go out to sea—at least ten miles away—and have a local diver clean the bottom of it in the middle of the ocean. This can, understandably, be both costly and time consuming.

Since medical requirements also vary between countries, it is desirable to make sure that you and your crew have all the recommended pills, shots and vaccines for all the areas you intend to visit. Don't forget that this may include malaria pills for the duration of your visit to certain areas.

Again, be sure to investigate all the requirements for visiting a country well in advance, and then prepare for them. These regulations keep changing, so only a current analysis is of value. Six to nine months in advance of every departure, I created a folder for every country. I reviewed each and every requirement—starting with the ports of entry—and planned our cruising appropriately. An example of the entry requirements for several different countries is shown on Exhibit 14.

Escapade at dock in Seattle, Washington, USA
PHOTO BY ERICK REICKERT

CHAPTER 17

Maintenance

Maintenance Strategies — Including Record-Keeping Forms

Success is where preparation and opportunity meet.

BOBBY UNSER

Maintenance is one of the most important and critical activities that is required to keep a boat in a safe and seaworthy condition. World cruising puts a whole different perspective on maintenance because it is something the Captain or crew must be prepared to do without outside assistance. When sailing from a homeport, the owner can request his local mechanic to go to the boat to sort out the problem or issue prior to his next sail. But when underway—especially in remote areas of the world, and with many days offshore—the Captain must be able to perform the maintenance himself. And, often, he must do this when the boat is underway.

This scenario requires that the Captain, or a member of the crew, must have the knowledge and skills to do the maintenance and repairs to any system on the boat. This type of situation, in turn, requires an understanding of the major boat systems—such as the electrical, electronic, engine, fuel, generator, instruments, outboard, propeller, refrigeration, steering, toilet, transmission, bow thruster, and water maker systems, as well as winches. The ability to troubleshoot or identify problems in any system is critical.

It's essential to have owner's manuals for all the equipment and systems onboard the boat. Even better, it pays to have service manuals, diagrams, and the ability to identify

part numbers for all the components of every system. This is particularly useful if a replacement part is needed because—by using the exact part number—a precise part can be ordered. A wiring diagram for the boat—which should identify the location of all fuses and circuit breakers—is also essential. My boat builder had assembled all of *ESCAPADE'S* manuals into large binders so they were always readily available.

If the Captain has no previous mechanical experience, then it is recommended that courses on diesel engines and electrical maintenance be taken. The person doing the servicing must be comfortable with working on all systems, and must also be able to troubleshoot all types of problems. This requires enough knowledge to safely work on a variety of systems. For example, since the 240 AC system can kill if not properly respected, it is highly desirable that the maintenance person has an engineering or handyman background.

The proper equipment and tools are also required. For example, a Volt/Ohm multimeter and soldering iron are required for electrical systems. Additionally, a complete tool kit with all types and sizes of hammers, screwdrivers, wrenches and C-clamps, is required—as well as any "special tools" required by the boat's various systems.

To provide both familiarity and practice, I recommend that you perform all the routine scheduled maintenance. This process helps you get "down and dirty" and intimate with all the systems. To determine the maintenance required, I reviewed the operating manuals for every piece of equipment, and then listed every periodic maintenance operation, as well as the recommended frequency (hours of operation, days, weeks, years, etc.). For *ESCAPADE'S* engine, this list included the following:

Engine	Frequency
Oil and coolant levels—Check and top up	daily
Record hours	daily
Raw salt-water strainer—Clean	weekly or as necessary
Racor fuel filter—Check for water and contaminants	weekly
Belts—Check and tighten as required	2 weeks
Zinc—Check condition	2 weeks
Racor fuel filter—Replace	4 months or 250 hours
Air filter—Clean	4 months or 250 hours
Oil and oil filter—Change	4 months or 250 hours
Engine fuel filter—Replace and bleed air	4 months or 250 hours
Water impeller—Check	yearly
Exhaust system—Check for leaks, tighten clips	yearly
Engine mounts—Check	yearly
Coolant—Confirm anti-freeze solution	yearly

Exhibit 3 is the list for my boat. I then assembled these recommended operations into time periods to provide an overall a Maintenance Schedule, which is shown as Exhibit 4. I then created a Maintenance Log Form so I could record the dates that each operation was performed. That way, with a quick glance I would know the status of every recommended maintenance item. This is Exhibit 18, and I followed this schedule rigorously. By doing this, you may also catch or observe other possible issues prior to them becoming a crisis.

Not only should you have the confidence to perform all these procedures yourself, but you also need to have all the spare parts and expendables (like coolant, filters and oil) onboard. Additionally, you need a way to store used oil until you can get to a proper disposal facility.

Some service procedures—like bleeding the engine fuel lines of air after filter replacement—require two people working together. This generally requires turning the engine over while the injectors are loose in their sockets. This means that one person operates the engine start button, while the other tightens the injectors when fuel squirts out.

I highly recommend that all scheduled maintenance procedures be practiced prior to leaving on a world cruise. This will identify any gaps in either knowledge or tools. Also, since some maintenance operations may require the removal or disassembly of other parts or equipment for access, practice is required.

The service of items in case of failure or breakdown can be more complicated, and require more skill. First, this requires the ability to troubleshoot so as to determine the exact problem or failure. For example— the engine will not start, or will not run, or looses power. There are several potential causes for each of these issues. It will be necessary to identify the specific cause for the problem before a repair can be made. Also for electrical circuits, it is necessary to identify "shorts" or "opens" in order to locate the source of the problem. Identifying the exact problem or the failed part is often the hardest part of the task. Fortunately, some service manuals have a troubleshooting section, which can be very helpful.

If you are not confident of your own ability to diagnose and repair all systems on the boat, then one recommendation is to identify experts that you could consult for advice. Prior to leaving home, recruit friends or mechanics who are expert on various systems for consultation later. Then, if you are not sure what to do, you can contact your experts by e-mail or phone. They can provide you with valuable advice, assistance and ideas. These arrangements could even include agreeing to pay for the advice when dealing with professional mechanics. This type of help and assistance has worked for some cruisers, and it can give you a heightened sense of confidence.

One of the key decisions to make before departing, is what spares to take with you. I asked the advice of the boat builder, and referred to owner's manuals for all the equipment. In addition, I learned that anything that moved—or had areas of wear—was susceptible to breakage. Essentially, all fans, impellors, motors, pumps, springs, toilet parts, etc. are subject to breakage. I followed the rule that if a part failed, I bought at least two replacement parts because I fully expected the part to fail again. That proved to be a good policy, and if the part did fail a second time I would immediately obtain a stock of the parts. After cruising for several years, I had many (many) spare parts. Some people (erroneously) claimed that I could probably build another boat with all of my spare parts. *ESCAPADE'S* Spares List is presented as Exhibit 15.

But if a part does fail, and you have no spare, that can become a major problem. Even if you can identify the part required (possibly by a part number), and you have the builder or a friend obtain it for you, then getting the part in your hand can often be difficult. Overnight shipment is not "overnight" in most areas of the world. And Customs will often hold up shipments for payment of duties (even if the boat and the part will be leaving the country). That's why getting a part delivered within a week is often the best that you can do. And that unanticipated week can put a crimp into both your schedule and your sailing enjoyment.

Getting replacement parts to (and on) the boat can be a major challenge. I had various crew bring parts with them when they came to join *ESCAPADE*. This system is far easier than shipping parts because it avoids Customs. In fact, I once actually carried a new windlass to Tahiti in my luggage. I had to do a lot of talking to get it past the X-ray inspection at the airport, because it looked very strange. Also, since it was not a direct replacement, I had to also bring along the special tools necessary to install it.

Unfortunately, even with the best intentions and skill, it is not always possible to make the necessary repairs yourself. Sometimes, it may take expert service people—who have proper facilities—to make the repair. In this event, you must simply work around the issue until you can get to a satisfactory repair facility. For example, one time *ESCAPADE'S* transmission failed, and would not engage in reverse. To fix it required removing the transmission from the boat and then having it rebuilt in a shop--to extremely fine tolerances—with a new thrust washer. The first time this happened, we were in Australia and—luckily—I located an excellent authorized transmission dealer to do the repair. In another example, the engine was running hot (the weather was hot as well). The problem turned out to be that the heat exchanger was calcified. Since rebuilding is best done in a shop, I bought a new heat exchanger (for installation), had the old one re-built, and I kept it as a spare so that—if necessary—the next time I could swap the heat exchangers myself.

In order to cruise in both comfort and safety, maintenance is clearly a major issue that must be addressed. It—absolutely, positively—cannot be ignored, so it should be approached as a challenging intellectual activity rather than as an annoying chore. I present *ESCAPADE'S* complete Repair History as Exhibit 12, which shows the bad, ugly, and trivial things that happened over many years. I include it only to show that—with cruising as in life—"things happen," as well as the frequency and variety of problems. You will, of course, have a different range of experiences, but they are guaranteed to be similarly challenging.

Erick at the top of Escapade's mast in Nelson, New Zealand
PHOTO BY HEATHER REICKERT

CHAPTER 18

Provisioning

Procuring Strategies in World Ports

For a man seldom thinks with more earnestness of anything than he does of his dinner.

SAMUEL JOHNSON

Provisioning is both an art and science, but it's one that must be mastered for safe and comfortable cruising. In this chapter, we will mainly deal with foodstuffs, but in the broadest sense of the word. After all, provisioning includes a variety of other items—such as charts, clothes, pilot books (cruising guides), prescription medicines, and spare parts. Purchasing these types of things must be planned carefully in advance so that they can be obtained in the ports where they are available. In the modern world shipment by carriers would seem to be an easy solution, particularly since some indicate "guaranteed overnight delivery." Unfortunately, we found that—for a variety of reasons—this promise was never fulfilled. Often, of course, the marina or port where you are located is remote. But the major reason for delivery delays is Customs. In general, most items for a boat in transit should be duty free, as they will be "exported" when the boat leaves the country. But the local Customs people often refuse to accept that rationale. Then they frequently "hold up" parts and other items for inspection, and follow that delay with a demand for duty. In France, I had to pay an exorbitant duty in order to receive a part that—although sent from the US—was actually made in the EU, and would then be exported out of the EU on *ESCAPADE.* But it was either pay up or not get the part, which we (literally) had to have before we could sail again.

I strongly recommend that you have a full supply of propane or butane for cooking prior to departure. Since propane is not available in the EU, you must convert to butane. This may require changing the valves and nozzles on the burners of the stove. In other areas of the world, propane is available, but it comes with different connectors. Adapters are often available.

The chef needs to know the food preferences of the crew, which is not always the case, for example, when visiting crewmembers come aboard for a passage. It is necessary to communicate with crew before they arrive to determine their food likes, dislikes, and allergies well in advance.

Since we had six crew aboard for the Atlantic passage and five crew for the Pacific, the amount of food required—understandably—was considerable. Also, in order to cover a variety of contingencies, it is prudent to have enough food and liquids onboard for a voyage that could take 50% longer than expected. This meant that for the Pacific passage we needed a 40-day supply. Please note that this will challenge the storage capacity of most boats—especially that of the refrigerator and freezer, in particular.

Other considerations include the requirement for some food to be prepared and served during heavy weather conditions, such as stews that can be cooked in a deep pan, and then served in mugs. During passages, crewmembers are up for the full 24 hours. This meant that, in general, crew fended for themselves at breakfast because not everyone was awake at the same time. However, nearly everyone was up for lunch and dinner. This also meant that during the middle of the night it was useful to have energy bars or other snacks available for those on watch to eat. Everyone was responsible for getting his or her own coffee, tea or hot chocolate—at any time.

Special meals—such as Thanksgiving or birthday celebrations—were always welcome. We usually had a "Half-Way" celebration meal, which would lift everyone's spirits because it meant that we were then in the "downhill" (this is a joke) portion of the voyage. If you are crossing the equator, then special celebrations are in order for those who have not crossed it before. This is when "pollywogs" become "shellbacks" by order of King Neptune (see Wikipedia).

It is understood that the chef must be prepared to cook and serve meals when the boat is underway, often in the trade winds. The ride is usually comfortable and smooth, but there can be quite a bit of rolling. On other passages, you can expect to encounter all types of weather and sea conditions.

We found that food shopping in the major ports throughout the world ranged from good to excellent. It may be difficult to read the contents or the instructions on a particular can or box, but the pictures help. Also, while not all of your favorite brands may be available, what you will find can be surprising. And the foreign supermarkets were always helpful. For example, in Thailand we asked the supermarket to separate our meat into meal-size portions, and then freeze them overnight for pickup the next day. One cruising shopping challenge, however, was getting our provisions back to the boat. This would often require a taxi, or renting a car.

You have to be creative to provision for such a long spell with such a small amount of refrigeration. For example, outside the US most countries have UHT milk that does not need to be refrigerated **before** it is opened. Also, many vegetables are available in cans, as well as meats—such as canned hams. These items may not be what you would serve at home, but they are most welcome when you are sailing in the middle of the ocean. Convenient boxed mashed potato mixes can be used, as fresh potatoes do not store well over long periods of time.

The food onboard needs to be consumed in stages—with the fresh fruits and vegetables first. We used hanging net bags to store items like bananas and apples. Bread is a problem because it will not last the whole passage, and would take up too much room in the freezer. We actually tried (with some success) baking bread. In some countries, you can buy pre-mixed bread dough that just

needs water, mixing, warmth and kneading before baking (don't forget to have a small bread pan ready). If you buy eggs that have never been refrigerated, they will keep several weeks. We tried coating the eggshells with Vaseline (as one source recommended), but since it didn't seem to make a difference we discontinued that practice.

One way to stretch food is to make pasta meals, which reduces the amount of meat or chicken needed per meal. Also, pasta is compact as well as easy to store. There are several cruising cookbooks available that will provide a variety of tasty ideas for your consideration.

For shorter passages, some meals can be prepared in advance, frozen, thawed, and then cooked while cruising. We kept a supply of drinking water (along with soft drinks and other juices) just in case the water maker failed. The water maker makes extremely pure water, and in some cases—like in Mexico—we only filled the water tank with water from the water maker. We made sure to never use water from shore, since it was suspect.

Bottom line, we found it useful to prepare menus for the complete voyage in advance. That way, you can make a detailed list of provisions, and know that you will have adequate supplies (and the right quantity of everything) onboard before you set sail.

Escapade at anchor at Isla San Fancisquito, Mexico

PHOTO BY ERICK REICKERT

CHAPTER 19

Weather *and* It's Implications

The Importance of Forecasting Sources

We must free ourselves of the hope that the sea will ever rest.
We must learn to sail in high winds.

ARISTOTLE ONASSIS

If you live on and travel by sailboat, weather is ALL IMPORTANT. It is something a sailor needs to understand and master. It is not that you can change it, but you need to work with the weather in order to avoid as many of the bad consequences as possible, as well as take advantage of the favorable conditions when you can.

I strongly suggest that you try to gain as much knowledge as possible about weather systems, including how they develop, and how to predict them. Also, learn how to read a weather map, and understand the impact of both the system around you and whatever might be approaching you. Take the time to learn how to interpret the visual indications you see around you—both in the sky and on the water.

When circumnavigating, it is useful to understand the basic weather patterns around the globe. For example, the existence of the trade winds near the equator is caused by the hot air rising near the equator, which then descends to both the north and the south. The air then flows back towards the equator, but develops a NE component in the northern hemisphere as well as a SE component in the southern hemisphere due to the Coriolis effect of the world's rotation. The captains of sailing ships from centuries ago knew these trade winds well. The existence of the north Atlantic high and the north Pacific high are important factors when sailing across those oceans.

For example, if you want to go from Mexico to Seattle, it is recommended that sailing to Hawaii is the best way to avoid the prevailing south-flowing current and northerly winds along the west coast of the US. Many areas of the Mediterranean also have similar local weather patterns. If you thoroughly research weather factors, you will be prepared—and better able to anticipate weather conditions.

It's also a good idea to learn the basic currents around the globe. While the Gulf Stream may be the best known, there are also currents that flow south along the west coast of Africa, the west coast of North America, and the east coast of Australia. There are, of course, many others, and several currents converge on the Galapagos Islands. This is why the water around the islands is so rich in sea life, but it also means that—when approaching the islands—you will be set off course substantially. These currents affect weather conditions because they are often at a different temperature from the surrounding water. Consequently, they can become hazardous when the wind is blowing opposite to the direction of the current.

Also, it pays to develop an understanding of the typical local weather patterns in the area you are sailing. These vary dramatically around the globe. One example is the Gulf of Tehuantepec in Mexico. There, gale force winds can develop in a few hours with no apparent change in the weather. This is due to a differential in atmospheric pressures between the Gulf of Mexico and the Pacific Ocean and the relatively narrow piece of land that separates them. Sailing across the Gulf of Tehuantepec requires careful study and good weather information sources. Another example is the Tasman Sea between New Zealand and Australia. There, frontal systems sweep around the southern tip of Australia and progress to the east toward New Zealand. While sailing to Sydney (Australia) from Nelson on the South Island, four fronts passed over us. These had gale force winds that we had to beat into, but between the fronts there was no wind at all so we had to motor. But based on the normal conditions we had been expecting at least two fronts. Access to weather information and weather forecasting is improving every year. But be wary of projections, as forecasting is still not a science that can be totally trusted.

My only major weather-related event occurred between Fiji and New Zealand—in the same area as the "Queen's Birthday Storm" (which occurred several years earlier). I departed on the 1,077 NM trip with the encouragement of two weather routers, only to be caught in a Force 10 to 11 storm with waves of 30 feet, (some larger), and winds in excess of 55 knots. This experience is something I would recommend that you avoid. But the lesson I learned is that you have to be prepared for whatever weather develops.

There are many sources of weather information, and they are increasing over the years. Quality-wise, they vary from practically useless reports to really good information on which to make sailing decisions. Since sources vary around the world, remember to change them as you move locations. It is always good to have a local source, because they are most familiar with the local patterns. Weather information can be obtained from VHF, SSB, Navtext, local radio stations, and, of course, the Internet.

The Internet offers a wide range of weather services from which to choose. In fact, you will have to spend considerable time to select the specific sites that you prefer and trust. And GRIB files which give wind direction arrows plotted on your electronic charts, are also available. Additionally, there are subscription services available that can provide more tailored weather data for your specific area or route. One can give the projected wind and waves for specific points such as a simulated buoy for several days (buoyweather.com), which I found quite useful.

Weather Routers are another valuable resource, as they tailor their projections for your specific route. These firms charge for their services, but I found it worth the cost—especially when you are planning to sail across oceans by yourself. They can also provide guidance regarding when to depart for the most favorable weather conditions, as well as a "go/ no go" recommendation. But, even the Weather Routers are not infallible. Whether you use Weather Routers or do it yourself, one of the most important things to take into consideration when making

weather decisions for a passage is a good understanding of the capabilities of your boat—this includes the crew's (and your) experience and tolerance.

In many cases, perfectly good boats have been abandoned so the state of mind of the crew is (obviously) all-important. That is often related to the experience the crew has had as well as the conditions they have previously encountered. I found that my tolerance for heavy weather conditions increased as I gained experience, and better understood how my boat handled in heavy weather.

If you are out sailing for many miles (and many days) you will encounter various degrees of heavy weather. The following is a summary of the Beaufort Wind Scale. It is useful to recognize that the forces and pressures on a boat almost double for each increment of the Beaufort scale (for example from 6 to 7). There are pictures (on Wikipedia) available that correspond to the various Force levels. The wave heights are for Open Ocean with deep water and an unlimited fetch (i.e. the distance the wind acts on the water). Both wind and wave height can vary considerably from the average level to height of the peaks. Wave height also can be greater when it is shallow or when there is a current present.

Beaufort Wind Scale

Force	Wind in knots	Wave height in feet
5 - Fresh Breeze	17 to 21	6 to 9
6 - Strong Breeze	22 to 27	9 to 13
7 - Near Gale	28 to 33	13 to 19
8 - Gale	34 to 40	18 to 25
9 - Strong Gale	41 to 47	23 to 32
10 - Storm	48 to 55	29 to 41
11 - Violent Storm	56 to 63	37 to 52
12 - Hurricane	Above 64	Over 46

Another major aspect that directly impacts the sailor is the period of the waves, or the distance between peaks. In the open ocean the period is long, but in shallow depths the waves become steeper and have more pronounced peaks. This occurs in the Chesapeake Bay, for example, and the result is far more jolting and uncomfortable than what is generated by the long waves in the ocean for the same wind and wave height.

Finally, in the open ocean there are often swells that have no relation to the wind waves we have been discussing. Swells can come from many miles away, and often come from a different direction than wind waves. The swells have very long periods, and often have no effect on a small boat since it can simply rise and fall with the swell. And while swells can also be a precursor to winds that will follow later, they can also add to the wind waves.

A lot of research has recently been conducted on "rogue waves," which apparently occur with more frequency that previously thought. These are extremely high waves—often 60 to 90 feet high—that occur singularly. One theory is that they are a localized result of a wave that accumulates energy from the waves both in front and behind, which produces a huge wave. For this reason rogue waves appear to be preceded by a smaller wave and a "hole in the sea." The resultant giant wave is two to three times the height of the average waves, which have to be in excess of 30 feet. These are still very rare, but apparently occur more frequently in specific places—especially where currents exist such as off South Africa in the Agulhas current. Further research may define the required conditions, as well as the probability of a rogue wave occurring. I never encountered a rogue wave nor have I met anyone who saw one. There are, however, a number of documented cases of extremely large rogue waves.

In summary, when planning a passage—or just a day sail—it is important to evaluate all the weather data and information that you can assemble, and compare that to your capabilities and those of your crew. My experience has taught me that when sailing, you should expect to encounter gale level (Force 8) conditions at various times. You should have enough skill to feel comfortable sailing in gales. You may also encounter even stronger weather, with winds in the Force 9 to 10 levels—possibly even at Force 11. Be prepared for this possibility. Trade wind sailing is usually Force 6 or 7, and will generally be consistent for days on end. While this can be comfortable if you are going down-wind (from east to west), small storm cells (which can move faster than your boat), may pass over you, and disrupt the wind conditions for short periods of time. These storm cells can be dangerous.

There are many other weather conditions that are potentially dangerous, and require strong sailing skills. Fog is probably the worst, but a sailor can also encounter plenty of rain—and possibly snow and hail, as well. So be prepared to sail in all types of conditions.

As we stated, weather is ALL IMPORTANT for sailors. Learn to understand and predict it. Make climate conditions your friend, and avoid bad weather whenever possible.

I will discuss various heavy weather strategies and tactics in the next chapter.

Escapade at sea in the Pacific

PHOTO BY ERICK REICKERT

CHAPTER 20

Heavy Weather Sailing
and Tactics

Alternatives, Plus a Personal Example of What to Expect

Look into nature, and then you will understand everything better.

ALBERT EINSTEIN

As mentioned in the previous chapter on Weather, be prepared and expect to occasionally encounter Gales of Beaufort Force 8 level. Gales have winds of 34 to 40 knots and seas of 18 to 25 feet. You should also prepare for wind conditions that are even higher, up to at least Force 10 and 11.

Obviously, having a sound boat that is well prepared is most important. When going to sea it is desirable to have minimal items on the deck (like jerry cans), and to have everything lashed down well. The dinghy should also be well secured. Remember to prepare for huge amounts of water that will rush down the deck. Of course, everything down below also needs to be secured. It is dangerous for things to be flying about, with cabinets and drawers opening during a gale. All bunks should have the ability to be made into sea berths with lea cloths.

The boat should be well built and inspected regularly. *ESCAPADE* had a solid layup below the waterline, and all internal components—such as bulkheads, cabinets, seats, etc.—were fiber-glassed to the hull. This made the hull extremely stiff, and it did not flex or bend. If a boat flexes, all sorts of things can go wrong which puts additional loads on many components. Production boats with drop-in interiors are simply not as stiff as custom yacht like *ESCAPADE*.

Also, prepare for the encounter in the dark. It is pitch black in the middle of the ocean with cloud cover, and any major heavy weather will extend to—or begin in—the dark.

The configuration of your sails will determine which type of storm sails will be required. If your sails are of the hank-on type, then you will need special storm sails. If you have roller reefing, then be sure that under high wind conditions you can reef to a minimum sail area (like one square yard or meter). With a staysail, the staysail can act as a storm sail. In fact, that is a good configuration because the reefed staysail is relatively low and actually it is close to the mast, as compared to a reefed yankee or genoa. My boat had a staysail, which was heavy weight, and as a result I did not have separate storm sails. With reefed main and staysail, I was able to sail quite well in winds that were in excess of 55 knots, and with a balanced force on the rudder.

The other important consideration for heavy weather is that as many operations as possible should be able to be performed from the cockpit. All crew should be wearing life vests (PFDs—Personal Flotation Devices) at all times, and they should be secured to the boat with a tether, even in the cockpit. Jack lines should be rigged on both sides of the boat so it is possible to move to the bow and to the stern while always being tethered. Any departure from the cockpit is extremely dangerous in high seas. I could perform all the reefing required (rolling up the yankee, and reefing the main and staysail) from the cockpit in all wind conditions.

There are two types of approaches to heavy weather—active and passive. Active means that you will continue to sail, steer the boat, and maintain control. This is not as easy as it sounds. One major catastrophe is if the boat gets turned sideways to the waves. As very large waves "break" or curl at the top, a sideways boat can get rolled to disastrous effect. Therefore, it is best to sail close to the wind when going upwind and basically slightly off downwind when going in that direction. In large waves, the wind at the bottom of the trough is much less than the prevailing wind. So as the boat rises to the top of the wave, it will get hit with the full force of the wind, thus pushing the bow down wind and increasing heel. If hand steering, this requires great concentration as well as effort and in the dark it is nearly impossible to maintain one's bearing without visible stars. *ESCAPADE'S* autopilot worked even in the storm because two actuators worked on the rudderstock simultaneously and powered the rudder. Thus, it was powerful enough to handle the huge forces involved in keeping the boat headed properly.

One of the easiest tactics is to "run before the wind" if there is enough sea room. This may take you miles off course, but it will make life aboard considerably easier and more comfortable.

The other approach to heavy weather is passive. This requires either trimming the boat to achieve "heaving-to," or to set a sea anchor. Either approach will allow the crew to retreat inside the cabin for the duration of the storm. Heaving-to requires practice, and—frankly—not all boats do it well. I did carry a sea anchor, but I never used it. The sea anchor requires a lot of set up including the anchor to weigh the line to the "parachute" so it is under water so the boat doesn't pull the chute out of the water. A floating buoy with a line to maintain the proper depth, is also needed, as is a way to spill the chute to retrieve it, a bridle line to achieve an angle to the waves, and a very long line (300 feet or more) so that the sea anchor is in the wave ahead of the one the boat is riding over. All of this must be rigged so that there is no chaffing to any of the lines. It also has to be set off the bow of the boat, which is a very dangerous position. At various times in the storm I was in, the bow was under the water by more than six feet. Bottom line, the sea anchor would need to be rigged before you got into the storm, but even so it would have to be deployed before the waves became too large. If the sea anchor broke free of the water, the boat could be quickly turned sideways to the waves. Lying ahull is not recommended, as there is no control over which direction the boat is facing, and it might end up sideways to the waves.

In any approach taken, consideration has to be made of the sea room available before landfall, and the expected duration of the heavy weather. I also carried a drogue, which is deployed off the stern to slow down the boat. This might be necessary if—while heading downwind—the boat was going too fast, plunging off the top of the waves, and burying the bow into the trough of the wave. This could lead to the boat pitch polling and—subsequently—disaster. I never used the drogue.

Escapade at sea in the Indian Ocean

SPINNAKER POLED OUT AND ON AUTO PILOT
~ PHOTO BY ERICK REICKERT

Generally, weather situations worsen over a period of time. I had a rule that if you begin to think that it would be a good time to reef, then the time is NOW. You can always let out the reef if the conditions do not worsen.

To give you a feeling of what it is like to be in a storm, I will describe my own experience. I was sailing between Vuda Point, Fiji and Opua, New Zealand, a distance of 1077 NM. This was expected to take around a week. There was a crew of five, including myself. I had hired two weather routers (one in the US as well as one in New Zealand), and had proposed a departure date that both routers said was an acceptable time to go. One projection said that there would be winds from the north at 30 to 35 knots, which would be quite comfortable and make it a quick passage. There was a stationary front to the west, which did not appear to be an issue.

After a little over a day underway, I received e-mails from both weather routers expressing concern. The low had started to move east, into our path. The worst part was that the winds were now projected to move to the south, nearly directly on our nose. One of the routers strongly suggested that we make as much "easting" as possible. This advice turned out to be extremely valuable. Since we were aiming for an island, it was critical to maintain course as much as possible because missing New Zealand would mean that the next land would be Antarctica.

The situation continued to worsen, and the New Zealand router said that one of his scenarios indicated the front could become a "curved back wave front," similar to the one in the severe Queen's Birthday Storm, which had occurred a few years earlier in the exact same location. In that storm, many sailboats were lost with loss of life. This was not comforting to say the least, but he was telling us so we would prepare for the worst.

The first thing we had to address was the bimini. In the tropics, we sailed with it up all the time, but as the wind increased it became clear that we had to take the bimini down. That is because with the extreme heel of the boat the bimini was acting as a sail, and it could not take the wind load. So with considerable effort, the first mate and I were able to untie it, hold onto it, and finally stow it below.

The storm first hit at night. You could not see the seas, but you could hear the approaching waves. The wind climbed to a steady 50 knots with gusts over 55 knots, at least the ones I caught on the meter. We shortened sail to only a square yard in both the main and staysail. The wind sounded like a banshee in the rigging, with a very eerie high-pitched whine. The overall noise was intense, as the sound of the waves and the water rushing by the hull added to the wind noise. Daylight showed us the full extent of the storm. It is very hard to judge wave height, but they appeared to be 30 to 40 feet with occasional

ones that were even higher. The tops of the waves were breaking, and the sea was white with huge patches of foam. The waves were approaching like moving gigantic ski slopes.

There were other sailboats out in the same area of the ocean, and each one chose a different action. Some tried to run before the wind, but as Fiji is surrounded by reefs, I did not like the idea of returning to Fiji. Some boats were too far west so they fell off and tried to lessen the load on the boats. Maybe some tried heaving-to. Since we were making good progress—and I felt I could lay New Zealand—I decided to push on, in an active sailing mode. The autopilot was coping well and maintaining a good angle with the waves—but the problems kept mounting. When three of the crew became sea sick and incapacitated, it was down to the First Mate and me. We were taking so much water over the dodger that the First Mate's PFD inflated as though it were underwater while he was sitting in the cockpit. In fact, we had up to four inches of solid water come over the dodger, which was over nine feet above the water, and over 40 feet from the bow.

We were 500 NM away from land, and there was no hope for assistance. Plus, we were not in a shipping lane. In any event, the waves were so high; that I don't think any rescue would have been feasible. The bottom line is that we were on our own, which was a very sobering thought.

The conditions onboard became extreme, with *ESCAPADE* in VIOLENT motion at all sorts of angles. In fact, the boat was falling off the top of the waves for ten or 15 feet, and then crashing into the wave trough. The boat would shudder to a stop, then sail up the next wave. Then, when at the top, we would be hit with the full force of the wind, and heel far over. We went so far over that the water intake for the generator, which is on the bottom of the boat on the port side, would take in air. This meant that the generator would stop because of overheating. But we really needed the generator to keep the batteries charged because the autopilot was using a lot of power, and we really could not hand steer in such a powerful storm. The angle of heel was simply too great to run the engine. But with the redundancy that had been built in the boat, I was able to close the raw water intake on the port side, and open the raw water manifold crossover valve to draw water from the starboard side.

The motions were random and unpredictable. This required holding on with both hands or else you would either be slammed against something hard or be thrown across the boat. It seemed like we couldn't take any more of this beating, but it continued to get worse with more ferocious motions. Remember that while taking this prolonged battering, understandably, you still have to eat, sleep, and go to the bathroom. Every mundane task became challenging, difficult and hazardous—with a high likelihood of physical injury. We even put the washboards in place to seal out the waterfall that would otherwise enter the interior. And we kept a person in the cockpit at all times, just in case we had to take over the wheel. In addition, I had to navigate, and try to communicate with New Zealand by SSB (Russell Radio), which was giving us updates and encouragement.

The forward cabin became unusable due to the boat falling. With each wave, anyone in there would levitate. Since even the amidships cabin had violent motions, everybody tried to sleep in the salon. We used the cockpit cushions as mattresses, and people tried to wedge themselves into various corners. From a motion standpoint, the aft cabin was the best, and I was able to wedge myself into the lee side, mostly resting on the wall. I could at least relax from the fury by using earplugs to diminish the sound. In order to keep my hands free at the nav station, I had to force myself into a corner with my legs.

At first, the motions were so bad that we could not cook. So we resorted to relying on energy bars and cookies for food. Later, when things improved, we were able to cook canned stew in a deep pot and then eat it out of mugs.

What I learned from that storm is that the individual—and specifically yourself—is the weakest link. As Captain, I had to maintain a positive attitude, but I did not fear for our lives. Maybe I should have been afraid, but the conditions were just so terrible that you simply did not want to be there. You just wanted it to end. It was akin to being beaten continuously, but you have no control over the situation. Under those circumstances, it would be easy to despair, especially as the storm conditions deteriorate. You are powerless, and if there is any breakage on the boat it will only make matters worse—possibly much worse.

We were in the heaviest seas for nearly two days, which felt like an eternity. Then the wind declined slowly to gale force levels, the seas diminished, and it finally felt as if we were out for a Sunday sail. By the time we approached the North Island of New Zealand, we were able to put things back where they belonged, and tidy up the boat.

In retrospect, I am convinced that the strategy we took of active sailing was the best approach. Passive approaches would have been either dangerous or not have worked. By the time daylight had arrived, it was too late to deploy the sea anchor. It would have been dangerous to work at the bow in any event, and we probably could not have done the complicated set-up. I would not have trusted the boat to heave-to, and not become sideways to the waves.

I was not expecting the large difference in wind velocity between the trough of the wave and the top of the wave at the height of the sails. This would have made heaving-to difficult. Even trying to run before the wind would have been difficult—and practically impossible at night. It would have required falling off and then jibing on the forward face of the wave. This would have required

perfect timing and maneuvering under power to assure enough boat speed to maintain steering control. Then, we would have had to maintain a slow speed to avoid going fast down the face of the wave.

Fortunately, nothing on *ESCAPADE* broke, and the crew survived with no injuries, and just a little worse for wear. We achieved the passage at an average of 6.6 knots, sailed a true distance of 1100 NM, and completed it in 162.7 hours (6.8 days). All other boats survived, but they took many more days to reach New Zealand.

There are many lessons to be learned from our experience:

- Be prepared for the worst.
- Have enough crew to deal with the situation.
- Know how to handle heavy weather mentally and physically, even though it is not predicted.
- Have a strong, sound boat that is properly equipped.

Among other lessons, I do not ever want to go through another storm, but it really raised the bar regarding what conditions that I knew were survivable. From then on, gales seemed rather tame.

In the fall of 2013, there were two rallies that went from the US to the Caribbean. The Caribbean 1500 departed a day early to avoid a weather front, and all boats reached their destination. The Salty Dawg Rally departed around the same time, but each skipper was responsible for picking their departure time. The boats that left later were faced with heavy weather. Four boats were abandoned, and the Coast Guard had to rescue the crews. The weather was not as severe as what I have described above. So why did the boats leave late into heavy weather? Were they prepared for the weather they encountered? Were the boats sound and well maintained? Did the crews know what to expect or did they panic? Just some sailing issues to think about.

CHAPTER 21

Living *Onboard*

The Implications—and Impact—of Living on a Boat

When the new becomes commonplace, people become accustomed to it.
That is a tribute to our sense of adventure.

— JOHN GLENN —

Living onboard is an adventure. Since the boat is in the water, there is always a movement—even at a marina, the boat moves. In fact, if it becomes really still you somehow think something must be "wrong." Getting to and from the boat is generally a problem because even in a marina, the docks or pontoons have to be negotiated. And if you are anchored off, the trip to shore requires a dinghy as well as a place to land it.

Sailboats are inherently small inside, and it takes getting used to living in a confined—often cramped—space. I preferred to think of the space constraints as "cozy." With additional crew onboard, of course, there is very little private space. All the basic amenities are there, but it takes cooperation to make things go smoothly.

When living on a boat, you must be continually aware of the battery charge status, fuel levels, holding tank levels, power connections, water level in the tanks, etc. If any of these require attention—such as adding water, charging the batteries, or empting the holding tank—then actions have to be undertaken. Nothing can simply be left to operate by itself.

The dock lines or anchor chain always need to be monitored, and a sudden gale can put the boat in danger. When staying a long time, pump outs of the holding tank will be required. These may require moving the boat to a pump out station, or sometimes a pump out boat can come to you. In any event, it is an undesirable, but necessary, operation. In general, pump outs come at a cost. There are a few enlightened communities where there is no fee for the pump out because they trust that everybody will utilize the service if it is free.

TV reception is often difficult, and if you are in a foreign country—unless you speak their language—you cannot understand it anyway. We depended upon DVDs to provide onboard entertainment in English, and on our schedule. If Internet is available, streaming is another possibility.

Refrigerator and freezer capacities are limited, and stoves (as well as ovens) are small. But they are generally quite good, and excellent gourmet meals can be prepared.

Sleeping onboard will be different from doing so at home. Most nights will be spent in port—anchored or tied up to a dock or pontoon. This means that the beds will be level, but the boat may still have a rocking motion. The ports and hatches are not light tight, and temperatures can vary. Further, there are many unfamiliar sounds, both inside and outside the boat. These include possible noises from shore and other boats, pumps running, rigging banging, and water lapping, etc. If any of these conditions bother you, I recommend using earplugs and eye masks.

The weather affects you more than living on land because the direction and force of the wind impacts how the boat rides as well as the noises generated—especially when at anchor. Rain can be a real issue as many boats have poor ventilation when hatches and ports are closed. Also, getting to and from the boat in rain requires good rain gear—especially in the dinghy.

In many parts of the world—including the Mediterranean—the ports are in the center of town, which means you are in the hub of activity. In the US and other areas, the ports are often remote from a town—so it's more of a challenge to get to restaurants and stores.

A major issue when cruising is that you generally do not have an automobile at your disposal. We carried two folding bicycles onboard, which we found invaluable in many ports. These provided an extended range for our activities. Otherwise, you are limited to walking or local transportation—such as buses and taxis. We also rented cars if we needed to provision substantially and/or wanted to explore the surrounding countryside. Some rental agencies would even deliver the car to—and then pickup from—the marina.

In every new port, it was always a learning experience to understand the local situation, and identify where the stores and restaurants were. And, remember, you need to navigate around the town with your knowledge of the local language. It often seemed as if—just when we were getting acclimated comfortably—it was time for us to move on to another port. But that is part of the adventure. These days, staying in touch with the rest of the world has become much easier with the wide use of the Internet, mobile phones and the availability of Wi-Fi. This "connection" has improved dramatically since we started cruising.

When cruising, the boat is also your home. So, in addition to all the required sailing and maintenance equipment, you will also need the things that are normally involved when living in a house. This could include clothes, luggage, and gear necessary for travel off the boat when in a variety of weather conditions, or for a side trip of skiing or golf. The amount of "additional stuff" can quickly get out of hand, and where to store everything can become a major issue.

*Erick and
Lady Susan Reickert*

AT ROCHE HARBOR, WASHINGTON, USA ~ PHOTO BY RICHARD MALONE

Obviously, living onboard requires detailed organization and planning in order to maintain control of your financial matters as well as your shore-based activities or property. Income taxes still come once a year—no matter where you happen to be. Bank accounts and credit cards now can be controlled via the Internet, and I arranged for most of my land-oriented bills and accounts to be paid by direct debit. This handled 80 to 90% of the recurring bills, but there were other—often annual—bills that varied year-to-year, and could not be pre-paid. One example would be some insurance premiums. So I had my mail directed to a mailbox, and one of my relatives picked it up once a week to check for those types of bills and unusual communications. If there was anything important, she notified me by e-mail. She also had the ability to pay non-recurring bills from one of my bank accounts. In summary, handling your financial matters while cruising will require some ingenuity and planning, but it can—and must—be accomplished.

I went home four times a year, which gave me an opportunity to catch-up on a variety of matters. If you do not go home that frequently, then other ways will have to be developed to handle issues. These visits home also kept us connected with family and friends. And, at various times, land-based family and friends also came to *ESCAPADE*.

Additionally, the visits home provided a time for our regular health check-ups, let us renew medical prescriptions, get vaccinations, as well as things like malaria pills for when we would be entering specific countries. Also, the visits home provided us with the opportunity to buy needed spare parts. It was always easier to bring parts to the boat in luggage—rather than have them shipped. Shipping involved Customs in most cases, and that was generally a problem.

In summary, living onboard adds another layer of complexity to the operation of the boat. Every cruiser will have to develop his or her own method for handling these added requirements, and for interacting with the outside world.

CHAPTER 22

Cruising Risks *and* Ways to Evaluate Them

Methodology for Identifying, Categorizing, and Addressing Risks

It takes courage to know when you ought to be afraid.

———————— JAMES MICHENER ————————

Sailing and cruising—like almost every challenging activity—involves risks. But, is there a way to evaluate if the degree of risk is acceptable, and determine if it is possible to minimize the risks? This type of objective discussion is not helped by the many "disaster" stories—accompanied by comments on "lessons learned" published in many popular sailing magazines. Although dramatic and interesting, these isolated incidents may (or may not) be applicable to all cruisers. And, of course, they are not set in a framework of all possible risks or the likelihood of the event actually occurring.

To continue this logical discussion of cruising risks, I have given a lot of thought to the issue, and have asked cruising friends about their views. This chapter will attempt to present these thoughts in a structure that can help everyone be better able to discuss risks within a rational framework. This will definitely be helpful during your preparations for going to sea.

To do this, potential risks should be evaluated in terms of frequency, possible outcomes and the kind of responses.

Frequency, or possibility of occurrence. What is the likelihood an event will occur?

All risks are not random occurrences. They are influenced by where and when the sailing takes place, the condition of the boat, and—of course—by the skill and expertise practiced while sailing. For an obvious example, not going out in possible bad weather will minimize many associated potential risks. Thus, many risks can be avoided, or minimized, by a Captain's own action.

Some risks—like hitting a submerged container—are true random occurrences. In fact, there is a very low probability of ever hitting a container. That said, it's not practical to keep a lookout at night, in high seas and for days on end. There may be more risk in areas near busy ship-traffic lanes, as well as during the winter and spring—when storms make it more likely that containers are washed overboard from container ships. But remember, the consequences of hitting a container could be severe—with the possibility of losing a rudder, or even sinking—depending upon the type of collision (glancing, head on, scraping by, etc.), and the construction of the boat.

Possible Outcomes

The second way to categorize risks is by their potential severity. Outcomes can range from minor irritation at (one end) to the other extreme, which is death. The necessity for an action plan increases with increased severity, no matter the possible frequency. Obviously, risks that combine high severity with high likelihood are the most critical.

"Planning and response actions" should be selected to reduce the severity of an event, if it occurs. For example, keeping a fire blanket near the stove to smother oil or fat fires before they get out of control is a simple, good, and logical idea. This action reduces the potential severity without addressing the possible frequency.

Responses to Emergencies

Equipment and boat design options can be considered in advance. There is a lot of equipment sold to specifically handle different risks. These may, or may not, be good solutions to the risks. How much of such equipment needs to be purchased will depend upon the evaluation of that potential risk, the cost of the equipment, and how to store it onboard. Nevertheless, I had a lot of equipment that I hoped to never use (starting with the life raft).

One of the most valuable exercises—which is for the Captain to mentally review what he would do in response to all possible risks—costs nothing. That exercise might suggest the acquisition of possible equipment. If such a crisis occurs he will then be much better prepared. The Captain should share these concerns and solutions with other crewmembers so they know what to do, as well as what they expect the Captain will do in an emergency. In some cases (such as man overboard drills), responses can be practiced in advance. It is also desirable to prepare checklists for things such as departure procedures, "go bag" contents, necessary stores, passage plans, as well as lists of equipment, spares, and tools onboard and their location in advance. The more advanced planning that can be done, the better.

Spontaneous or "jury rig" Responses

Skilled sailors can devise creative and ingenious solutions to problems. Repairs can be made using other items found on the boat, but to do so requires "thinking out of the box." In that sort of situation, consider temporary solutions that work but may not be permanent or pretty. The objective is to overcome the impact of a specific problem or failure until it is possible to get to port and fix it properly. Don't give up until everything has been done to solve the issue—some incredible things have been done with "jury rig" approaches.

Other Impacts of Risks

Risks and responses should be evaluated on the basis that **no outside assistance will be available.** Also, many risks occur at the least desirable time—such as at night, in bad weather or near other dangers. Getting caught in a floating net is one thing when it is daylight and there is a calm sea, but it is a quite different matter when it is night, there is a heavy sea running, and a current is forcing the boat towards a rocky shore.

All actions onboard should be aimed at minimizing the possibility of risks occurring and/or to minimizing the impact if one does happen. For example, pay particular attention to watch keeping in high traffic areas to avoid a possible collision with a ship. Also, when dealing with flapping sails and lines it is important to act carefully so as not to be injured, which is would compound the impact of the first issue.

Unanticipated events often occur in a series with ever increasing risk. For example, bad weather causes inability to maintain course, and then engine failure occurs due to fuel problems as a result of boat movement, which then causes loss of electrical instruments and navigation due to inability to charge the batteries, which contributes to hitting a reef. It is therefore REALLY important to avoid getting into a **downward risk spiral.** This can be done by addressing the initial issue as quickly as possible, so no additional or further issues will occur.

The state of the crew is often critical when it comes to avoiding risks and minimizing the possible outcome. In particular, bad weather can frequently require shorthanded crew to be on deck or on watch at the same time, or (equally threatening) result in seasickness of some of the crew. This can then lead to sleep deprivation, and subsequent ill-advised or inadequate responses. Additional experienced crew is definitely a safety factor. Plus, one objective should be stress-free sailing, which places fewer burdens on the crew before an emergency occurs.

Redundancy of equipment is a way to minimize the impact of a single failure. Having hand-held or spare GPS units that can substitute in the event of a failure of the main GPS unit is a good back-up strategy. Redundancy can also take the form of alternative ways of achieving the same result. For example, my auto pilot steering rams acted directly on the rudderstock, which allowed me—if the manual steering cable broke—to still steer *ESCAPADE* using the autopilot.

Being able to repair items and equipment while underway is an important element of self-sufficiency. This requires having proper spares and tools onboard, as well as the knowledge to perform repairs on the whole boat and all systems. In my experience, I had to repair nearly every system on *ESCAPADE*—including the autopilot, engine, generator, sail handling, toilets, etc., while underway.

Exhibit 9 CHART OF CRUISING RISK PROBABILITY VERSUS SEVERITY

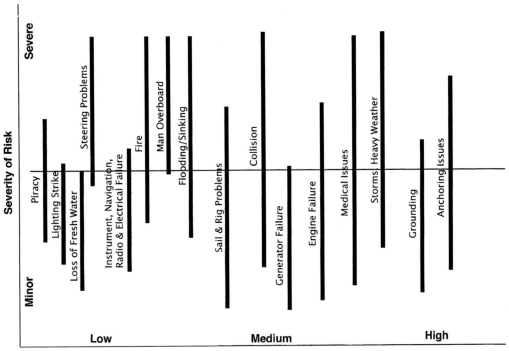

Probability of Risk

© Erick Reickert
December 2, 2008

The ability to do this is extremely important and the value of being able to fix systems while at sea is critical to safe cruising.

Obviously, cruisers have determined either through analysis or intuition that the potential risks of their passage are acceptable or can be managed. When considering going to sea, each individual will have to do his own analysis and assessment.

Potential Risks

To provide a starting point for a cruiser's own analysis, the following is a list of risks that might be considered. They are grouped into three probability categories, based on my experience and that of other cruisers with whom I have talked.

High Probability

- Anchoring issues   - Grounding

These are "high probability" because a cruiser is always entering new areas, generally without local knowledge. In other words, cruisers often place themselves at risk unknowingly, or have no other alternatives.

Medium Probability

- Engine failure   - Medical issues

- Generator failure   - Storms, Heavy weather

These are medium probability because engines and generators are mechanical devices that are prone to failure, even if all recommended preventive maintenance measures have been taken. Medical issues relate somewhat to the fitness of the crew, but boating is an inherently dangerous environment, and many crew still suffer seasickness. Weather predicting, even by experts, is still not an exact science, and—if you are sailing a lot of miles—it is simply not possible to avoid all bad weather.

Low Probability

- Collision   - Man Overboard

- Electrical failure   - Navigation failure

- Fire   - Piracy

- Flooding/Sinking   - Radio failure

- Instrument failure   - Sail and rig problems

- Lighting Strike   - Steering problems

- Loss of fresh water

These are low probability because they are usually rare occurrences, and most of them can be reduced in potential frequency and severity with good seamanship as well as appropriate preventive measures.

Chart of Risk Probability versus Severity

Exhibit 9, on the previous page, is a chart that portrays the relationship between various risks and their probability versus severity based upon my experience and data from various publications. Of course, this is a generalized concept, and the severity can vary over a wide range for each risk. The probability can be dramatically affected by the cruising area involved, the condition and type of boat, as well as the skill and practice exercised by the crew. It is the responsibility of each Captain to make his own assessment of every potential risk, and then develop plans accordingly.

Conclusion

What can this approach do for the cruiser? In our case, we traveled over 70,000 miles, including circumnavigating the world. Since we had no major crisis, I would view the voyage—and fifteen years of cruising—as relatively stress-free. Does that mean we did not have problems? Definitely not. We were in a Force 10 storm, endured many equipment failures, hit a submerged sleeping whale, and *ESCAPADE* was damaged while at a marina in a sudden gale. We were able to address most of these problems, often at sea, so that nothing major happened as a result, and they did not turn into crises.

I believe we minimized possible negative occurrences by prudent sailing, plus careful and detailed navigation. We carefully selected our boat and equipment to address most types of emergencies. We thought through all types of emergencies, and devised plans for responding. But even so, we have nearly as many stories as the days we were afloat, so things did "happen." But we were prepared. Were we lucky? Possibly so. But I don't think it was just luck. It is essential to plan well in advance, and to prepare for possible eventualities. Safe sailing.

In Suez Canal

A LONG SAND DITCH ~ PHOTO BY ERICK REICKERT

CHAPTER 23

World Cruising Grounds

Criteria for Evaluating and Rating Cruising Grounds

In still moments by the sea life seems large-drawn and simple.
It is there we can see into ourselves.

— ROLPH EDBERG —

After a circumnavigation, four years in the Mediterranean, several years in the Caribbean, the East Coast of the US many times, Alaska and the west coast of the US, as well as Central America, I am frequently asked what cruising area is my favorite. That is hard to answer because all areas have features that make them attractive to cruisers. Some, however, also have negative aspects that make the experience less than ideal. But I can honestly say that I enjoyed nearly every single port and cruising area.

My criteria for rating cruising grounds include the following:

- Good sailing conditions (including useful and dependable winds plus adequate water depths preferably in protected waters inside islands or barrier reefs)

- Pretty scenery that is lovely to look at

- Multiple choices of where to go by boat

- Secure anchorages that are protected and have easy shore access

- Availability of good marinas and boating support

- Some isolation, if "getting away" is on your wish list

- Interesting things to do on land, and worthwhile places to visit

- Local water activities—such as swimming, snorkeling, scuba diving, etc.

- Places to provision or get supplies that are close to the boat

- Access to airports for crew and friends to visit

To meet all these criteria, of course, a great cruising ground has to be a very special place. Everyone has their own opinions, and may not be in complete agreement with my evaluations. Also, local sailors often believe that their home area is the best, and—naturally—a cruiser will have a different viewpoint than a charterer. A charter skipper flies in, picks up a provisioned boat, and often wants to just "get away." The cruiser, on the other hand, may have just completed a long voyage, and—in addition to seeing the area—is seeking to connect and provision. But let's begin the discussion with my list, in which I have placed major cruising grounds into one of three categories—Best, Good and Fair. Please accept that I have used generalities, and have been very brief. Obviously, each cruising area deserves—and has its own cruising guide—as well as its supporters.

★ ★ ★ BEST

Croatia's Coast

Has everything, but may have become over crowded since 2003. This is one of my favorites, and I consider it a must-go experience. Avoid charter flotillas.

Australia's Whitsunday Islands, and Gold Coast.

Has everything, but is far away from the US and Europe. It is protected by the Great Barrier Reef, and the Australians are boat lovers. A great place to cruise.

Greece's Ionian Islands

Has everything, but does not have the classic Greek white buildings with blue doors. Easy area to sail and very interesting. Avoid charter flotillas.

Turkey's Coast

Has everything except protected waters in some areas. This is my third most favorite area in the Mediterranean.

Thailand's Phuket area

Very dramatic scenery, but few marinas, and sometimes little wind. A most exotic area to cruise. Good boat support is available.

USA's Long Island Sound

Not many anchorages and little isolation, but a great area to cruise. Generally more wind than the Chesapeake Bay with cleaner water.

Canada's BC Pacific Northwest and Seattle's Puget Sound

Requires a lot of motoring, otherwise has everything. Dramatic scenery. Interesting islands. A good cruising ground.

Panama's San Blas Islands

No marinas, little boating support, and difficult to get to—but a great area because of the pristine islands and the Kuna Indians. A real treat, and a wonderful experience. Be careful of the reefs.

Mexico's Sea of Cortez

Few marinas and little boating support, but it excels on the remote side. Abundant fish and dramatic, stark scenery. Memorable.

USA's Alaska, Southern portion

Absolutely breathtaking and remote. Incredible scenery and glaciers, but practically no wind for sailing. Cool temperatures even in mid-summer. Always cold water.

★ ★ GOOD

USA's Chesapeake Bay

Many shallow areas, muddy water, and light winds in the summer. But interesting with an abundance of boats and marinas.

USA's Maine Coast

Fog and lobster pot floats detract from pleasurable sailing, plus a lot of hard rocks to avoid. The scenery is very nice, but not dramatic.

USA's San Francisco Bay

Many shallow areas and limited in size. There are, however, dependable winds that enter the Bay through the Golden Gate. Many marinas.

Greece's Aegean Islands

Poor anchorages and unprotected waters detract from an otherwise interesting area with many classic Greek features and treasures.

France's Riviera

Very crowded, limited anchorages, and hard-to-get-into marinas. But the ambiance is genuinely outstanding. You must work hard to make it pleasurable.

Corsica

Interesting to circumnavigate, and Bonifacio is nifty.

Italian Coast, Sicily and Sardinia

Many interesting and nice ports, but you need to get into marinas.

Spain's Balearic Islands

A nice area to cruise with good boating support.

Spain's Canaries Islands

These are generally visited on the way across the Atlantic, but the islands are nice and quite unique like the black island of Lanzarote.

England's South Coast

Quaint and interesting area. The Solent has pleasurable sailing.

BVI's

Best of the Caribbean. There is protection in Sir Francis Drake Channel, but it is a high charter area.

Caribbean Islands

Good consistent winds. The boat boys are bad, and not that many marinas.

Fiji's Yasawa Islands

Reef area requires diligence—no marinas, but interesting natives.

Tonga's Vava'u Group of Islands

No marinas, limited boat support, hard to get to, but pleasant.

New Zealand's Bay of Islands

Limited area, interesting anchorages.

French Polynesia including Society, Marquesa and Tumotus Islands

Interesting, and a good respite from the Pacific crossing. Difficult to enter atolls. Live the Pacific life.

★ FAIR

Belize

Very shallow, few good anchorages, and mostly beside mangrove islands with bugs—only one small marina. Best feature is the barrier reef where there are no anchorages. Expensive by comparison.

Maldives

No protection until inside atolls, very deep anchorage at Malé, and remote.

Bahamas

Shallow depths, but close to the US. Good destination from Florida.

Atlantic Coast of France, Spain and Portugal

Interesting and challenging.

What do you think? Why not set a goal to visit them all so you can challenge my ratings?

Simi Greece

ESCAPADE IS THE BOAT SECOND FROM RIGHT ~ PHOTO BY ERICK REICKERT

WORLD CRUISING GROUNDS

CHAPTER 24

Our Circumnavigation

A Summary of What Went Right and What Went Wrong

If you can dream it, you can do it.

WALT DISNEY

As published in Blue Water Sailing, July & August 2003

We completed a circumnavigation on our yacht, *ESCAPADE*, and we are pleased and proud of the accomplishment. If you expect a disaster story, better find another article because for the most part it was a successful voyage and generally stress-free. We certainly enjoyed it. However, there are things that went wrong and things we would do differently.

It is still hard to believe that we actually did it. We had so many experiences and visited so many places that it is hard to recall them as a single event. But when we think of a specific country, or a specific passage, the memories flood us with the events that made up the accomplishment.

We started in England, where we received delivery of *ESCAPADE* on June 14, 1996. We sailed southern England and the Atlantic coast of Europe that year. During 1997 we explored the eastern Mediterranean, going as far east as Antalya, Turkey. In 1998 we cruised the western Med, and then crossed the Atlantic with the ARC (Atlantic Rally for Cruisers) in November. That was a good introduction to an ocean crossing, and highly recommended. From there on, we did it by ourselves around the world. In 1999, we cruised the Caribbean

North from St. Lucia and then day sailed up the East coast of the US from Key West to Boston. In 2000 we went through the Panama Canal and crossed the Pacific. That included stops in the Galapagos Islands, Marquesa Islands, Society Islands, Cook Islands, Niue, Tonga, and Fiji. We day sailed the coasts of New Zealand and Australia in 2001 before heading through Indonesia and Malaysia to Thailand and back to the Mediterranean via Sri Lanka, the Maldives, the Red Sea and the Suez Canal. We arrived back in Antalya, Turkey, on April 8, 2002, 4 1/2 years after departing there on October 6, 1997. We did not hurry, nor did we go as slow as many cruisers.

Overall, for the six years we have owned *ESCAPADE*, we have sailed 47,000 NM, visited 48 countries, entered 547 ports and anchorages, and lived onboard 1,173 days. We met countless people of many backgrounds and made many friends.

The Boat

Our first major decision was selecting and equipping the boat. We chose an Oyster 55 for many reasons. Primary among these was that it is a superior blue water cruiser, with raised deck saloon for light airy living, center cockpit, stern "sugar scoop" for easy boarding and swimming, great stability and capable of short handed sailing. We had it built to our specifications. After six years we are totally confident of *ESCAPADE's* ability to deliver us safely and comfortably through all the worlds' oceans and seas. Whatever boat you choose make sure you have confidence that it will handle what the oceans will throw at you, for it will be tested at some point. In discussions relative to the weight of the boat versus speed, I would recommend fast, but not at the expense of enough displacement and the proper hull shape to make the boat seakindly with motions that the crew can tolerate. Most modern boats can survive extreme weather conditions but a really good boat will permit the crew to not only survive, but to maintain acceptable living in all weather conditions. In *ESCAPADE* we often achieved 200 miles days, and with 50,000 pounds displacement we were able to beat into a Force 10 storm without altering our watch schedule while doing it on autopilot.

For another example, as we were sailing up the east coast of Australia we were in trade winds from the southeast nearly every day. The winds were generally 20 to 25 knots on the aft quarter so we were making extremely good times for our day sails. As we passed various harbors we could overhear other cruisers on the VHF discussing if the conditions were calm enough for them to leave the harbor after several days being "trapped". Those are conditions *ESCAPADE* loves and we enjoying the sailing. Very seldom were we confined to harbor unless there was a full gale or worse outside. (We may drive our boat harder than most cruisers and enjoy, or tolerate, higher winds and seas.) Yes, we are very satisfied with the Oyster as it met all of our requirements.

Rig

ESCAPADE is a cutter-rigged boat with an MPS (asymmetrical spinnaker) and spinnaker pole. It has in-mast power furling of the main, and both foresails are roller furling. We don't carry any storm sails as the staysail works well in heavy weather, and it can be reefed in storms. The boat can be balanced well with a reefed staysail and reefed main. Thus, in most instances all sail handling can be performed from the cockpit. Trade wind sailing is usually down wind sailing so it is imperative to have a good sail plan for wind near dead aft. We put the yankee on the pole so it is held out. (a yankee is a high cut genoa.) This wing-on-wing plan works well. In fact we often pull out the staysail to catch any stray wind. We can hold full sail up to 35 knots true. Then the yankee can be reefed without taking it off the pole. There is a preventer on the boom, which has prevented more than one accidental jibe. I call this our "bullet proof" arrangement as it will take high winds without constant attention and the autopilot handles it well. Thus it is good for night sailing. We can even sail with the wind slightly by-the-lee. The only negative is that the boat can roll a lot, but this is due to the quartering seas. In the Pacific we achieved 1,200 NM in

six days while feeling comfortable doing it. In fact, below deck there is very little sensation of speed.

In lighter winds we use the MPS, which can be set off the bow or off the pole. The problem with the spinnaker is that it needs constant attention, thus we very seldom used it at night. Overall, the sail plan is very flexible for all conditions.

Twice we made mistakes. On the Atlantic crossing, at night, while wing-on-wing, one crewmember hit the autopilot buttons by mistake and the autopilot was turned off. The boat rounded up and the yankee back winded with tremendous force. This pushed the pole into the mast and bent the pole track severely. From then on we took more precautions to prevent inadvertent touching of the autopilot, including putting the cover on. When the boat was new, we abused the in-mast furling by attempting to furl the main in a gale with rain without relieving the pressure of the sail on the mast enough. As a result we burned out the motor. This never happened again after we learned how to reef in a gale without having to point into the wind. It is trickier, but just a little bit of flapping will do the trick.

Equipment

ESCAPADE is fully equipped with items like lead bulb keel, dual ram autopilot, power winches on main and yankee, bow thruster, generator, solar panels, water maker, electronic charting, water computer, air conditioning, inverter, battery monitoring system, SSB radio, Inmarsat-C, Iridium satellite phone, GSM phone, weather fax with Navtex, forward facing sonar, radar, air conditioning, microwave, and laundry machine. Safety equipment includes a 6-man life raft, MOM-8, Lifesling, drogue, sea anchor, offshore medical kit, flare kit, 406 and 121.5 EPIRBS, and pre-packed "Go bag". Some important details make world cruising much more comfortable such as the dinghy mounted on stern davits, a good Passerelle, and the boat wired for 240 VAC. This equipment served us well and we would not change much. Although I was concerned about our inflated dinghy being carried on davits while at sea, it was perfectly safe in even the worst conditions. Only a few times did a wave even splash onto the dinghy, and it was not much water at that. The outboard was kept on the pushpit rail and a cover on the dinghy to keep water out of it. (I was prepared to cut the dinghy free if there was a threat of the davits breaking.)

We did alter some equipment during our cruising. For example, in the Pacific we increased the anchor chain from 60 meters to 90 meters. This became critical when the shallow spot in the anchorage at Male, Maldives was about 36 meters. If we dragged off the hill the depth increased to 42 meters. Although it was less than 3:1 scope, the anchor held. There were other instances where we needed nearly all the chain as well. I could have attached a rope rode to the chain if it was deeper or if the wind increased. An all chain rode is important when anchoring in reef areas. With that much chain and anchor out it is necessary to have a strong windlass. In fact, the original windlass, a Lewmar, was inadequate and it broke, as the design was similar to a winch. I switched to a Lofrans, which is a better design. (Lewmar has since changed their design.) In our experience, it is impossible to have too large an anchor and chain, too long a chain or too big a windlass.

For the Pacific we added Inmarsat-C E-mail. It has worked well everywhere, but is somewhat expensive. When near shore we use a GSM telephone connected to our computer and utilized a local AOL number for E-mails. For voice communication we added an Iridium telephone which, although it does not have perfect voice quality, is usable anywhere. We came to place high value on communication systems, which worked anywhere, anytime.

Our most trouble prone piece of equipment is the Onan generator. I would never again have a generator with brushes. Also, it is a 3,600 RPM unit as it generates 240 VAC at 60 hertz. Apparently 50-hertz units that run at 3,000 RPM are not only quieter but have better reliability. (I reduced the speed to 3,000 RPM later.)

The TV and video systems on board a cruising boat need to be world capable. We have totally changed our system. Originally the boat had a Grundig universal TV, but we had a series of problems with the unit. Also, we started with a VHS tape player. Now, DVD's are a better media for movies as they take less space and are not bothered by humid air. Our new solution is works very well. We are using a Samsung multi-function LCD flat screen monitor (171MP), which has a built-in TV receiver and two speakers. As we purchased it in the US, it is a NTSC unit. In addition we can connect one of our laptop computers to it and play DVD's. To make it universal, we also have a Samsung worldwide video VHS unit (SV5000W). This unit will receive any type of TV signal, either from an antenna or from a VHS tape, and convert it on the fly to any other type of TV signal. It will program the local TV stations automatically. Thus, you can receive in PAL or SECAM and play on the NTSC monitor. You can also rent VHS tapes locally and play them. The system works well and the image is sharp and clear.

In the discussions on simple versus well-equipped boats, I conclude that well equipped wins hands down. It certainly makes life more comfortable and enhances the overall cruising experience. In general, most of the equipment was trouble free. In many cases we had alternative means of achieving the same results, especially with the electrical systems. This provided backup if one part failed. For example, the generator, the high output alternator on the engine and the inverter all failed at one time or another, but not together. Thus we were able to devise

work-around strategies to keep the refrigeration, battery charging, etc. going. In every case the ultimate backup was to revert to non-equipment operation. There are more maintenance issues to consider, which I will discuss later, but why deprive yourself of something convenient just because it might fail? In fact, most of the cruising boats we encountered that were circumnavigating were very well equipped as well.

For handheld equipment, we depended upon our ITT night scope as it gave the best indication of objects around us at night (better than radar). We have two handheld VHF's so we can communicate with two shore parties and we have handheld GPS units for backup of the main unit. Finally, we have a handheld depth sounder, which was very valuable for scoping out the depths in various situations.

Overall, we are very pleased with our equipment selections, with the exceptions noted. The equipment matched our cruising plans and the conditions we encountered.

Planning

A circumnavigation may seem overwhelming when first considered, but when broken down into individual passages and cruising areas, it becomes manageable and the ease of doing it becomes apparent. Jimmy Corrnell's World Cruising Routes was our basic resource to plan the timing of all major passages. The cruising sections were then fit into the overall plan. We kept to our plan, often within a few days, for the whole trip. As a result we went on the long passages only at the best time of the year for favorable weather. ESCAPADE was put up on the hard each November/December so we could go home to be with family and friends, and we made at least two other trips home each year. Also, we included side trips by air to places near where ESCAPADE was located. These included Machu Picchu when ESCAPADE was in Ecuador and Cambodia when ESCAPADE was in Thailand. We attempted to maintain a good balance between the cruising lifestyle and home and family.

We had additional crew with us the whole way. One permanent crewmember was onboard for the whole circumnavigation. His presence made the trip much more pleasurable and provided flexibility for us when the boat could not be left on its own. For all major passages, we had either five or six experienced sailors onboard so we could handle a three-watch system with ease and assure that all were rested at all times. Passages this way are enjoyable with no strain on anyone. Further, it is far safer than only two crew, which are subject to sleep deprivation in difficult and strenuous situations or if one becomes ill. When coastal cruising we had friends and family join, but they did not have to be sailors. Day sailing this way permitted many more friends to participate, to our delight. One plan that worked well on the east coast of the United States was that we had another crewmember drive our car between marinas each day. Thus when we arrived at a marina, our car was waiting for us. She slept on *ESCAPADE* every night. Our crew strategy is discussed in more detail in the article entitled Crew– Help of Hindrance? in the December 2002 issue of Blue Water Sailing.

Cruising involves many more aspects than sailing. In fact, sailing is probably the easiest part of the whole adventure. Detailed planning in all other aspects made the whole experience pleasurable with minimum hassle. I did as much research as possible in advance: such as the legal requirements for all the countries to be visited including immigration, customs, quarantine, and cruising permits. We obtained all of the charts, electronic and paper, which we needed for the planned route plus any alternatives

in advance. There are pilot books or other sources of information for nearly every area of the world. Some are better than others, but we obtained every possible source of information we could lay our hands on. Of course, we always supplemented our data bank with local knowledge whenever we could. Sailors everywhere are very willing to share their experiences and knowledge. We also had courtesy flags for every country to be visited. Check www.noonsite.com, it is Cornell's latest effort and has lots of useful information on nearly every country in the world. We chose a marine insurance company in advance that would keep us insured all the way around the world. It is Pantaenius, and they were supportive of our sailing plan. And we made sure we were out of the hurricane areas as specified by them.

In the Panama Canal

SECURING TO LOCAL TOUR BOAT ~ PHOTO BY ERICK REICKERT

Our planning worked remarkably well. This made sure we were at the desired places at the desired times. With our crew strategy, we had to commit months ahead to where and when we would have crew join and leave us. None of the 88 crew who have been on *ESCAPADE* at one time or another ever missed a flight or did not find us in the appointed place. We also booked our flights home in advance and made reservations at marinas in advance as appropriate. To achieve this we researched our proposed itinerary thoroughly and identified all ports that we intended to enter to confirm that our length and draft could be accommodated, the facilities were as desired, and if it was a port of entry, if required. We booked the places where we put *ESCAPADE* on the hard at least 6 months in advance. As a result of the advance planning, we had less "flexibility" in our schedule than nearly all other cruisers we met. However, we provided enough cushion in the schedule to handle weather or maintenance delays, if necessary. Thus, we were sometimes ahead and sometimes behind schedule by a few days. If we were really delayed we could always do a short passage or overnight to catch-up to the schedule. Some may view this planning as not consistent with cruising "freedom". That may be, especially by those people who do not like to plan ahead. However, it worked for us and I would recommend it.

One part of our planning we would not do again. When we decided upon an Oyster, we elected to have it delivered to us in England, where it is built. Our original plan was to have our new boat delivered in Florida. However, we wanted to go to the Mediterranean so we thought it would avoid one ocean crossing. But, this placed us on a very steep learning curve. Not only did we have to learn the new boat, we had to get used to large tides (like 40 feet in the Channel Islands), contend with foreign languages, learn the skill of Med mooring, and handle foreign port entry plus other complexities all at the same time. We would definitely recommend to start out cruising in familiar territory, if at all possible. But we would still do a shake down passage and some day sails close to manufacturers support.

The legal and governmental requirements for all the countries that you will encounter are diverse and many. It takes a lot of effort to conform to all requirements. We tried to do everything "by the book" although we noted that many cruisers did not. Early on, when we were in Europe the law specified that a non-VAT paid boat could remain in the EC only 6 months out of a 12-month rolling period. As a consequence our whole cruising itinerary was based on this requirement. The law has been revised to 18 months, renewable by exiting the EC. This makes life much easier but is still a factor to be considered. The cruising permit for Indonesia took several months and a lot of paperwork to obtain. Other countries simply make things difficult. But I never had to pay a bribe. In many countries you are forced to utilize a yacht agent. For example in Sri Lanka, the Maldives, and the Suez Canal. We also used agents in Malta, Venice, Rhodes, and the Panama Canal. Although sometimes expensive, I would use agents more than we did. They can save a lot of hassle, ease the paperwork, and get you into places you might not be able to go by yourself. It is always helpful to have a local speaking on your behalf. If he is a good agent, he will be able to assist in obtaining the lowest cost fuel and boating services.

Maintenance

Before departing, I developed an extensive maintenance and spare part strategy. We followed a strict periodic maintenance schedule and made frequent checks of all equipment to keep *ESCAPADE* in top-notch condition. The schedule was derived from the recommendations of all the manufacturers of the systems aboard. We obtained spare parts for all items that might wear or break. In remote places it is very difficult to obtain spare parts, even if you have them sent to you, because of transportation issues and customs requirements. Thus, we carry many spares (some people say I could build another boat with the spares, but that is not quite true). If any part needed replacement, I always obtained two parts on the assumption that if it failed once, it may fail again.

It is necessary to learn and understand all the systems on the boat as often you will be the one that has to perform the service, either because you are at sea and no service facility is available, or because there are simply no adequate service people near the port. I would not let anyone touch my boat unless I was convinced they knew what they were doing. I "tested" them by asking questions on what went wrong, why, how they proposed to fix it, etc. I heard of several cases where local hack "mechanics" or "electricians" did more harm than good to other people's boats. There were very good mechanics in New Zealand and Australia. We had our transmission thrust washer replaced, the water maker rebuilt and the engine heat exchanger rebraised there. I was very satisfied with their work ethic and the promptness in attending to our issues. On the other hand, in Tahiti the fuel injection pump on the generator failed. Even though there was an authorized agent for our pump manufacturer, he did not have bench test equipment to test any repair. So I had a crewmember bring a whole new pump in his luggage and avoided the local mechanic.

Of course, this means you need adequate tools, including special ones for specific operations. Also, it is important to have manuals for all systems readily at hand. Manuals should include not only operator's booklets but also mechanics maintenance and repair manuals and parts catalogs. This is especially true of the engine and generator. It is always reassuring that you know how something is put together before you start disassembling systems that you know nothing about. After repairing many things

I learned more about some systems that I really wanted to know. The Oyster after sales department is a big plus to owning an Oyster. Without them I would have been desperate many times. They help in the diagnosis of the problem and identifying the necessary parts, can get parts to you anywhere in the world, and it is reassuring that you know they will do everything in their power to keep you underway. If you do not have a supportive boat manufacturer, then utilize a family member or friend at home to be the one to track down and ship parts to you. There are also companies that will perform this service.

Our maintenance strategy worked well. But we did have to do repairs while underway at sea, sometimes in heavy weather. We fixed the engine, generator, autopilot, toilets, electrical systems, GPS, fresh water system, and more while at sea. During long passages we would even do preventative maintenance, like winch greasing. A good sense for mechanical and electrical things is a required trait for a cruiser.

Shore Facilities and Fuel

Marinas and shore facilities are quite good around the world and after overcoming the language problems, things would generally go smoothly. The most common method of securing at a marina or dock is "Med moor," or stern-to. Besides having a boat that will back down well, you need the equipment to facilitate the operation. We have three large fenders for each side so we can force our way between other boats. The ability to lay the anchor chain from the helm and a bow thruster make the operation easy, even with some cross wind. A good Passerelle (gangplank) is necessary to get off the boat, and a long one makes sure your stern is well away from the dock. On *ESCAPADE* we have the ability to drop the dinghy, while still attached to the davits, deploy the Passerelle and then pull the dinghy up out of the water under the Passerelle. It is a very neat solution to storing the dinghy while at dock.

We like to go to marinas whenever they are available as we like the convenience of getting off the boat and because *ESCAPADE* is power hungry. Docking space was generally always available with very few exceptions. In most cases the local people would do their best to accommodate us, even if it meant tying to the fuel or ferry dock during off hours. We had difficult times in Lisbon, and some French ports. The highest prices were in the US, the lowest in the Pacific, and Europe was in between except for places like Capri, Porto Cervo and Venice, which were high.

Nearly all-overseas marinas have 240 Volt AC power that is 50 hertz, so world cruisers should be wired for 240 volts. We collected a large number of plugs to handle the variety we encountered. The most common, however, is the European small blue three-pin type. (There is also a larger

one.) I have a pigtail lead available for quick connection to any nonstandard variety. In addition I have a "reverser" adapter, which switches the polarity of the hot leads as not all power connections are wired with the same polarity.

Diesel fuel was available worldwide. In the more remote places it was obtainable only by jerry can, like in West Timor (delivered by dinghy). On the atoll of Ahe it was delivered to the dock by SUV in a drum. In Safafga, Egypt it was brought by pickup truck. In general, diesel availability has improved over the past several years. In terms of price, Europe is the most expensive area, with France leading in high prices. The lowest prices were in the US and duty-free ports like Gibraltar.

We have special equipment for fuel handling like a Baha filter for questionable fuel and an electric pump to transfer fuel from shore to boat or from dinghy to boat. In addition we have a spare Racor filter, which can be used in conjunction with the electric pump to "polish" the fuel in the tank. In the Caribbean we picked up fuel with fungi and have since treated the fuel with anti-fungal additive. The fuel has slowly improved since then. But because of this contamination, we cut our fuel filter replacement period to 125 hours from 250 hours. That has resolved the issue. (We later had to completely clean the fuel tanks and system.)

Navigation

For me an electronic charting system is necessary today, and it is our base system. I depended on our system many times, generally when visual and radar observations were not adequate. The key is to use charts that you believe are the most accurate. As a result, I now favor British Admiralty ARCS charts. You know you are seeing all the information that there is on the paper chart (like depths). I use the MaxSea program, but several programs will handle ARCS charts. I also have coverage with paper charts as backup, just in case. To minimize complete duplication I try to get the electronic charts in as much detail as possible, but depend upon chartlets in pilot books to provide the paper details, assuming good pilot books are available. Our charting strategy is explained in more detail in the article titled Electronic Charts- One System That Works in the January 2003 issue of Blue Water Sailing.

I created my own passage planning and daily log forms. These provided me with a wealth of information. For every day sail or passage I developed a passage plan in advance with all the waypoints identified from start to finish and then entered them into the GPS. These were adjusted while underway if the conditions required. It also assisted many times in entering ports in difficult conditions (at night, rough conditions and even sand storms). In England it is now a legal requirement to have a passage plan on paper before a yacht goes to sea. The plan should include tide and weather considerations as well.

These navigation systems work well, and were refined during our circumnavigation so I wouldn't change them. One misjudgment did cause some discomfort in the Cook Strait, however. In our previous experience *ESCAPADE* was not bothered by overfalls, so I became blasé about them. When crossing the Cook Strait in New Zealand, which is famous for having turbulent waters at times, we left Wellington on the backside of a gale. The conditions were reasonable, but I had plotted our course over some overfalls identified on the chart. This time we were suddenly in a "washing machine" with short peaked waves all over. The ride became uncomfortable to say the least. I then noticed that there were no white water waves only a short distance off our beam. After a quick change in our course we were out of the overfall area and back into normal conditions. That is one reason why all the information on a chart is important.

Provisioning

Cruisers must depend upon local stores and markets, but these vary widely in what is available. In Europe, nearly everything is available, and your menu has to be tailored only slightly. In the Pacific and Indian Ocean regions much less is available. In most cases, however, you must manage the local language. The pictures on the cans help, but it takes patience to find the item you are seeking.

Provisioning for one to three months is required and is an art into itself. My wife developed her skills well, and we always had plenty to eat and drink, even in the most remote areas of the world. So we provisioned when we could, and calculated usage requirements well including planning of all meals. Some hard to obtain items we brought from the States. All of our storage is in dry areas. We tried many of the storage tips provided at cruising seminars and they either didn't work or actually shortened the storage life of goods. For example, washing potatoes is worse than storage as purchased. We kept eggs in plastic egg containers and did not coat them with Vaseline. Our freezer was able to keep things frozen continuously so we were able to keep meat and fish for long periods. The only item, which required preparation, was bread. Bread will not last long and in some areas like Indonesia, it is not available locally. So we made bread onboard, and our favorite method was using bread mixes from England. These worked well and took minimum preparation.

We carry clothes and gear for all weather conditions and shore requirements. Plus, as *ESCAPADE* has been our house for years, we have all the things that make her a home. I had to raise the waterline, because of this and all the spares!

Weather

The weather was great most of the time (like 98%); we even had minimal rain. This is to be expected as the route was in the tropics and in the good seasons. However, weather information is not always readily available as might be expected. We found weatherfax transmissions hard to come by and not always with suitable coverage for the desired areas. Inmarsat-C provides weather messages, but generally only notification of gales and storms. This is very valuable information but does not cover normal sailing conditions. Navtex is sometimes the best source of weather information as it is often in English. This applies to European waters but not to the Pacific and Indian Oceans. Local forecasts on VHF are often in local languages and mostly not suitable. Not being able to surf the web, I felt that I did not have enough weather information. So I contracted with a weather service provider for the longer passages. As they knew *ESCAPADEs* normal speed and our tolerance for weather conditions, they were able to provide a five-day forecast for *ESCAPADE* in the positions where we were expected to be. They also provided routing advice and a go, no go recommendation prior to departure. We communicated by Inmarsat-C so we received updates while underway. This proved to be extremely valuable in the Red Sea as there the winds have a tendency to turn against you quickly. We were able to go from Djibouti to Suez with only three basic stops. In between, we waited in harbor for favorable winds. As a result, our experience was probably as good as the Red Sea gets. For more information on our trip see the article Notes on the Red Sea in the September 2002 issue of Blue Water Sailing.

After six years I have learned a lot about weather, but have concluded that weather forecasting is best done by experts. Even they have difficulties making forecasts when they have two or three computer weather prediction models at their disposal. Often it is hard to get consensus on a forecast. Those people that say a really fast boat is the way to go because they can get out of the way of bad weather assume that they will know what the weather will do. No one can do that with certainty at present. Remember the windjammer in the Caribbean a few years ago, which tried to avoid a hurricane only to have the hurricane change course several times and sink them.

Probably the worst thing we did wrong in our circumnavigation was to depart on a passage in front of a stalled low. We were traveling from Fiji to New Zealand and because of the area I had enlisted the aid of two weather services. One was my usual one based in the US, and the other was a noted New Zealand local. Both of these recommended leaving when we did. Actually there were many other boats out there as well. At the time there was a low stalled to the west of our route for several days. The forecast was for northerly winds up to 30 knots, which was suitable. (Remember this is the southern hemisphere.) After we departed the low started to move east. In fact, I believe we ended up going through the center. We were advised to make as much easting as possible, which was good advice. However, we were beating into 55+ knot southerly headwinds for 12 hours, then into 40+ knot headwinds for five long days. At one point one of the weather models predicted that the storm might turn into a "curved back wave front", similar to the Queens Birthday storm a few years earlier in the same area. Luckily that did not happen. We never stopped sailing, we maintained life aboard, and we did the 1,077 NM passage in 1,100 NM at an average of 6.8 knots. However, I never want to go through a Force 10 storm again. It is nearly impossible to convey how VIOLENT the motion was. I was never concerned for our safety, and always felt *ESCAPADE* could handle the situation. The key is the mental attitude of the crew, and making sure they have had enough sleep, even in the extreme conditions.

After that, lesser weather seems tame by comparison. We experienced a lot of gales, but if they are from behind they are hardly a worry. The Tasman and Red Seas lived up to their wicked reputations. So plan on lots of good weather, but expect a few challenging times. The major crossings of the Atlantic, Pacific and Indian Oceans were all very pleasant, and we did them quickly compared with other cruisers crossing at the same time.

Special Cruising Situations

One specific is the transit of the Panama Canal. This is a unique and awesome experience, and one that is adrenaline filled for a boat owner, as it is fraught with danger. We were able to transit it without damage, but the boat we were paired with experienced transmission failure just as we were docking against a tug. It took quick action to avoid damage to our boat. We were able to tow the other boat out, lashed to our side, so he avoided expensive charges related to delaying the canal. Mostly we went center lock. But what I would do differently would be to negotiate with the other boat to swap line handlers. This is because if line handlers fail to secure the lines, the other boat is the one that is swept into the wall.

We did a lot of anchoring, 181 times in total. So it is imperative that you get to be proficient at it. Early on, in Turkey, we dragged anchor at night in a very small harbor. That incident, which we could only resolve by leaving the anchorage, put us on warning. From then on we always made sure the anchor was well dug in, no matter how many times it took. We tested the set by a significant pull on the chain and by a crewmember with his foot on the chain during the pull to confirm no slippage or bouncing of the anchor. In Great Harbour, Yost Van Dyke (home of Foxy's) it took us six tries to get the anchor to dig into the hard sand. Our dinghy, with a see-thru bottom, is also used to check the set of the anchor. Our main anchor is a CQR, which I trust. It sometimes takes a bit of dragging before it digs, but it holds well. Our secondary anchor is a Bruce, which digs quickly. It has proved useful many

times as a secondary anchor, as a stern anchor, and to pull us off a dock. We also have a third anchor, a Fortress, for emergencies.

Sailing among reefs takes extreme caution. Too many boats come to grief. We know of six that were sunk, but many more suffered damage. It takes complete concentration, continuous monitoring of your position, sailing only in good light and a sense of where reefs might be. We also installed a forward facing sonar. It only works at slow speeds, but for creeping among reefs it works well. Even with all our caution, we still got caught. At one island in Malaysia, there were permanent mooring buoys installed, as anchoring was not permitted. These were along a beach. On arrival, we carefully approached the second one on the inside and tied up. No problems all night. In the morning we left and proceeded past the first buoy, but on the outside. We were only 20 feet away from the buoy when we hit coral and bounced over into a pool. If we had tied to that buoy we would have hit the coral while attached to the buoy during the night! A crewmember dived and saw that we could get *ESCAPADE* out of the pool with no more damage. He directed us from the water. We let our guard down (the sonar was off), and assumed the buoys would not be near any coral. Mistake!!

Safety and Security

Other than a few minor bumps and bruises, we had no major medical problems. I attribute that to a very safety oriented attitude aboard. All new crew were given a talk about safety and were instructed on emergency procedures. These are also listed on a plastic laminated exhibit for reference. One rule was that crew on watch had to wear shoes so they could moves quickly around the deck without stubbing toes. Everyone always wore inflatable PFD's with built-in harness at night and in rough weather, and in rough weather all crew were tethered to the boat. There are tether points in the cockpit and jack lines running bow to stern. For additional security all crew at night wear personal EPIRBS, which are water activated. If any person fell overboard a loud alarm would sound.

A concern of many cruisers, especially after the events of September 11, is potential piracy. We went through the Strait of Malacca, the Gulf of Aden and the Red Sea, all noted for piracy. We followed all recommended procedures such as staying far off shore, proceeding quickly, maintaining VHF silence, etc. In the event, we had absolutely no problems, and I heard of none from other cruisers in 2002. We do not carry a gun onboard as most reports on pirates say they are well armed and a gunfight is not an option. There are no guarantees, but I believe that the risk of piracy is a lot less than many other risks, which must be considered and dealt with if caution is exercised while sailing.

Summary

There is a lot that I would not want to change, or ever forget. The experiences are a treasure to remember forever. The passages were great, with a relationship with the sea that is not possible when close to land. The conditions are ever changing, ever fascinating. There is the challenge of being totally responsible for your own actions, with no "help" readily available. You are truly alone in a vast sea world. Sea life is always near, always interesting. The weather impacts your life far more than on land, so it is of greater significance. Even small changes in the wind or seas are of importance. The nights have their own special memories. Clear, moonlit nights are wonderful. Dark nights sometimes permit seeing displays of phosphorescence, which are incredible. But dark nights also give you a sense of excitement as the boat rushes headlong into a black void. The sounds of the wind and the seas are always in the background as well as the motion of the boat. Subtle changes in the sounds or motion can wake you if you are asleep. They are at once a comforting reassurance that all is right, or a warning that conditions are changing.

The places we visited and the people we met are too numerous to recount. But some stand out such as the lovely and remote anchorages inside the Great Barrier Reef, the atolls of the Pacific, and the islands with the Kuna Indians in Panama, the dramatic islands in Thailand, the French Riveria, and anchorages in Croatia. We also spent time in marinas in the heart of many large cities such as New York, Boston, Miami, Baltimore, London, Lisbon, Auckland, Sydney, and Wellington, as well as innumerable smaller cities and towns.

One question we are asked is if we had a favorite place. We enjoyed it all! (Some places more than others.) Each place and passage was unique and had its own special charm or character. Of course, we wanted a good sail, a safe and secure anchorage or marina, and interesting and accessible shore based activities and sights to visit. We didn't have everything every time, but we had plenty of good and great days. It was all memorable.

Once underway things fall into place and a routine develops. In short, although it takes a lot of forethought and planning, it is easy to sail around the world. And it is great fun. The rewards for a circumnavigation are many, besides the accomplishment.

CHAPTER 25

Cruising Australia
and New Zealand

Planning for—and a first-hand description of—this trip

To reach a port we must sail—sail, not tie at anchor—sail, not drift.

FRANKLIN D. ROOSEVELT

As published in Oyster News, Winter 2001

Is New Zealand out of the way when you are going around the world? The owners of *ESCAPADE* don't think so. After traversing the Pacific in 2000, having taken the traditional route from the Panama Canal to Ecuador, the Galapagos, Marquesas, Tuomotus, Tahiti and the Society group, Rarotonga, Niue, Tonga and Fiji, a decision was needed as to where to go next. It was getting close to the cyclone season, requiring leaving the tropics for the summer. New Zealand, although south, is a perfect solution. Not only is it cyclone free, but it is also a fabulous place to cruise. The Kiwi's are warm and friendly, the cruising grounds excellent, the support services and workmanship first class, the food good, and the country is beautiful with a dramatic coastline. That, combined with the opportunity to cruise Australia afterwards, made our decision to go easy. Besides, cruising with us is a Kiwi crewmember who wanted to show off his country.

Overall Plan

The time to leave the tropics is usually around October. It is spring in New Zealand, making the timing is ideal. Going to New Zealand then gives you the whole summer to enjoy. We left Fiji on 21 October, 2000, and arrived Opua, New Zealand, on 28 October.

We chose to put *ESCAPADE* up on the hard at Gulf Harbour Marina (40 minutes by car north of Auckland) for November, December, and January, as we like to be home with the family over the holidays and visit the London Boat Show in January. Gulf Harbour is a full-service and self-contained community. However, others might want to utilize that time in New Zealand, as it is summer. We returned in late January and started cruising in February. After nearly two months there, we crossed the Tasman Sea to Sydney in late March. We then utilized their fall to go north along the east coast of Australia to arrive in the Whitsundays around mid-June, in their winter. We kept going to Darwin, from where we will leave for Indonesia, Singapore and Thailand. So, time wise, it fits the seasons perfectly.

Places worth visiting

All told, we visited 19 ports/anchorages in New Zealand and 53 in Australia, so we had a great exposure to both countries. New Zealand has several major cruising grounds; but by going home for 3 months, we didn't do it justice. Our first experience was the Bay of Islands, where the usual first port of call, Opua, is located. The area is only about 12 by 24 miles but there are many islands, bays, and coves for anchoring places. Being an easy, pleasant area to relax on a boat, one could spend weeks.

Besides Opua, there is Russell, and Whaitangi where the treaty with the Maori's was signed. As a result, there is historical significance to the area as well as being a popular holiday destination for Kiwi's. The town of Russell has importance to sailors, as Russell Radio is located there. Des, the radio operator, has helped many boats on passages to and from New Zealand, including *ESCAPADE*. A steady, calm person on the other end of the SSB is very comforting during times of stress. One anchorage was Opito Bay where we encountered our first experience with the friendliness of the Kiwis. A couple dinghied over to our boat; they had been sailing the S. Pacific for ten years, just returned, and were missing meeting the cruisers so they came over to say hi. We invited them aboard and obtained a lot of local info.

Between the Bay of Islands and Auckland there are several good stops, including Tutukaka, which has a nice marina, well protected behind a narrow, rock-edged entrance,

which is a little daunting going through the first time. One very picturesque anchorage was Kawau Island on which the restored residence of a former NZ governor is located. Great Barrier Island is remote and fjord-like, a nice place to stop with good shelter, and mostly uninhabited except for the mussel farms.

To get to Auckland, you pass through the Harakari Gulf, where the America's Cup races were held. For our arrival, we were rewarded by getting to sail among eight Americas Cup boats that were out practicing (in four pairs). So we set our colorful MPS and sailed between them (sorry, we could not keep up with them). In Auckland, we stayed in the Eastern Viaduct, which is across from America's Cup Village, next to the Maritime Museum, and near many upscale restaurants. All services you will ever need for a boat are available. Being there was very convenient for walking into town for a morning Starbucks coffee, a favorite of one of our guests who was "picked up" in a

Escapade in Sydney, Australia Harbour

PHOTO BY HEATHER REICKERT

bookstore by a woman. After they talked for a while, she invited the four of us over to her home, on Waiheke Island, for coffee and muffins. It wasn't on our itinerary but we did go. She met us at the dock and took us on a tour of the island then to dinner back at their home, which has a fantastic view of Auckland and the surrounding islands. She wanted us foreigners to have a memorable experience with real Kiwis, and this is one we will never forget!

In the Bay of Plenty, we stopped in Tauranga to take a side trip to Rotorua but then had to wait out the easterlies so we could cross the Bay. Tauranga is a good-size town and has a beachy arm with lots of resorts and bistros. The hot spring baths and the luge ride down the mountain were highlights in Rotorua. Finally, the wind subsided enough for us to leave. The exciting part of this trip was going within a mile of an active volcano, which continues to spew smoke (being blown the opposite way; no soot on our deck!). There are only a couple of ports between Tauranga and Wellington so we chose to do a 3-day passage to get there.

We found Wellington to be a neat city and fully accessible by walking! Our marina was right next to the new TePapa Museum, the country's museum for the people which houses a first-class restaurant and virtual rides so one could spend all day there. We went to two plays to take advantage of the cultural aspect of a large city, visited the botanical gardens via tram, the maritime museum, and thoroughly enjoyed the whole city very much. We left Wellington on the tail end of a gale (as we had an appointment to keep) and saw why the Cook Strait has the reputation it does. Going into (then out as quickly as possible) the washing machine-like overfalls proved again what tough, sea-worthy yachts the Oysters are.

On the northern end of South Island is another great cruising area, the Marlborough Sounds. We called in only at Picton and Port Ligar before going to Nelson, but there are many more possible anchorages and various fjord type arms to explore. A lot of the bays are deep requiring us to do our deepest anchorage at 20 meters. We laid out 80 meters of chain and stayed put! With time, you could spend weeks just gunk holing around in sheltered waters.

Nelson was our base from which the west coast was explored by car down to the Franz Josef Glacier. Taking a helicopter ride around Mt. Cook and landing on the glacier was a thrilling highlight.

From Nelson, we sailed directly to Sydney where we tied up ESCAPADE in Pyrmont Bay, right next to Darling Harbour, near the heart of the city, the Maritime Museum, Harborside shops, restaurants, and lots of activity. Sydney is a very alive city and welcomes visitors.

Sydney's harbour is one of the best in the world next to a large city. With the bridge, Opera House, and the Rocks area, it is a pleasure to sail. (You just have to look out

for all the ferries, jet boats, jet skis, and other sailboats.) There are many places to explore by boat and it could take weeks. There are yacht clubs and marinas spread around the various arms of the harbour to make it interesting.

Just north of Sydney is Pitt Water, another great sailing area that includes some remote anchorages in a national park. It is wonderful to have such an area so close to a large city. There are a large number of boats kept there and there are yacht clubs and friendly places to stop. It reminded us of a lake more than anything else.

Sand bars at the entrance of many southern ports have to be crossed requiring accurate timing relative to tides. After getting in, they were worth the effort. Some memorable ones were Port Stevens, with a new waterfront complex with some of the best marina facilities we have seen (i.e., marble showers), and Yamba, where after crossing the bar you have to wind your way around sand islands to get to the marina. The town was small, but was a nice flat town for us to get our bicycles out to ride around. It was a fun place.

Southport is the port for the Gold Coast and Surfers Paradise, which is very similar to Miami in many respects. We chose Marina Mirage, associated with a shopping mall and hotel, for enjoying all the "big city" type activities. The area is "pumped up" with tourist activities, but there is an excitement in the air. We drove to Brisbane, as it would be out of the way to get there with ESCAPADE. We considered going up the Broadwater passage to Moreton Bay but realized it was not passable due to overhead power lines too close to our mast height for comfort, as well as the depth. But we had a fast sail around Moreton Island to Mooloolaba, which is on the Sunshine Coast, and a yachting center.

After crossing the Wide Bay Bar we made a stop at Tin Can Bay, which is a laid back small town south of the entrance. Going there and through the Great Sandy Strait took a lot of motoring because it is shallow and the channels have to be followed precisely. Even so, we "kissed" the bottom twice as the sand bottom shifts continuously. It lead to Fraser Island, a unique all-sand island with a rain forest, fresh water lakes, and miles of beaches on which SUVs roar up and down and planes land. We anchored off Kingfisher Resort, which offers tours of this lovely, unique place. We hoped to see whales in their migration north as the timing was right, but except for a glimpse from the beach at Fraser Island, they didn't appear near our boat.

One of the most incredible cruising grounds, and our personal favorite, is the Whitsunday Islands. Some people go for a week and end up staying for years! The islands are peaked and lush, bordered by beautiful fine white sand beaches, have well protected anchorages and they are close together. Plus, they are behind the Great Barrier Reef so it is generally smooth sailing. Snorkeling is also good. The islands have it all: a marina on Hamilton Island, luxury resorts, casual resorts, camping, and remote anchorages. To double our exposure we stopped at one anchorage for lunch then went to another for the night. However, with the high-peaked hills, you have to contend with "bullets"; wind gusts blowing down the mountain. In fact, there are many interesting islands south and north of the Whitsundays, which we visited as well.

Returning to the mainland on our way north, Bowen gave us our first experience of tying up to pile berths, which turned out to be easier than expected. The yacht club was friendly and the town gave us a taste of the informality in the north of Queensland. Townsville was an exception, and the facilities were good.

We chose to go through the Hinchinbrook Channel, which is composed of many offshoot river ways, all lined with mangroves giving protected anchorages. Again, it is quite unique and interesting. All along the coast the scenery is dramatic but some of the bays are quite shallow and shoal gradually. One night, we had to anchor more than a mile from shore to stay in deep enough water.

Cairns and Port Douglas are in tropical north Queensland. In Cairns, taking a side trip to the rain forest is fun either by train or the new Skyrail, a 7 km gondola ride that gives you a bird's eye view of the forest. Two stops along the way allow you to view Barron Gorge with its spectacular (in the wet season) waterfall and to walk over a boardwalk through the forest. Cairns offers the visitor something for everyone. Port Douglas, just north of Cairns, is a nice resort town with a good marina. After that, the area is very remote with no civilization until Thursday Island. The coast is low and contains a lot of sand dunes. It feels strange being close to land, which is not populated.

We day sailed up the entire east coast of Australia to Torres Strait. Great southerly winds favored us the whole way, even before reaching the SE trades, giving us fast, record-setting sails. There was a two-night passage from Thursday Island to Gove, which has a yachtie-friendly yacht club on aboriginal land. We chose to do another passage from Gove to Darwin, but one could make stops along the way recognizing that you cannot go ashore on aboriginal land without prior permission. One potentially exciting experience is going through Hole-in-the-Wall (or Gugari Rip), which is part of the Wessel Islands north of Gove. There is a 12-knot current at mid tide, so one wants to pass through it at slack or near slack water.

Getting there and back

The hardest part of this plan is getting to and from New Zealand. Although we were using a weather routing service to provide advice on when to leave (and they predicted 40 kts from the N), a Force 10 storm hit us, with SE winds above 55 kts on our passage between Fiji and New Zealand. The waves were 12 meters or higher. It was not pleasant, but with *ESCAPADE.* under staysail and reefed main, we endured the storm very well. We are continually amazed at how well Oysters handle rough weather. We have become extremely confident of *ESCAPADE.* and her ability to bring us through the toughest circumstances. In fact, during this passage, we kept to our watch schedule, getting proper sleep, and sailed continuously. We were always moving at 6 or more knots. Other boats around us were heaving to, reversing course, or running before the wind. We kept on our course, which was beating into the wind. However, we did become tired of living life heeled far over for five days! When we arrived, the Customs officer did not believe we just come in as the boat looked so neat; the other boats he saw were in disarray. People who left a week before or after we did had to motor most of the way. It's all in the timing.

While crossing the Tasman Sea from Nelson, New Zealand, to Sydney, four fronts passed us. Two were simply wind shifts. The other two were a gale and near gale. The gale was not bad and actually speeded our crossing. The near gale was not much wind wise, but we had 8 meter plus waves coming from down south on our beam. That meant a lot of rolling, but it didn't slow us down. We crossed in seven days, better than the Challenge boats did a few weeks earlier.

Summary

New Zealand and Australia are great places to cruise, and they can fit in well with a circumnavigation plan and timetable. They offer a wide variety of experiences, and we highly recommend a visit. Our Oyster was always an eye-catcher wherever we went. We were also out sailing while others waited in harbour for lighter weather—another true test of the benefit of an Oyster.

CHAPTER 26

Pirates, The Red Sea *and* The Suez Canal

Experiences from the Midde East

*I could not tread these perilous paths in safety
if I did not keep a saving sense of humor.*

ADMIRAL LORD HORATIO NELSON

As published as Notes on the Red Sea in Blue Water Sailing, September 2002, with major added detail

The Red Sea has the reputation of being a very difficult body of water. Some have described it as their most difficult passage of all those around the world. We were among the class of those going through the Red Sea in March/April of 2002, and it upheld its wicked reputation.

Before getting to the Red Sea, we had to contend with the threat of pirates in the Gulf of Aden. Pirate attacks had occurred recently, and I plotted where they had happened. They were generally located near the center of the Gulf of Aden (both east/west and north/south). The threat was real, but they seemed to be targeting ships—as opposed to sailing boats. To compare the risks, I did an analysis of what it would take to go around Africa. We wanted to return to the Mediterranean, so going around Africa would have entailed another year, and many more miles of sailing. It meant crossing the South Atlantic to Brazil, and then sailing back across the North Atlantic. It was something I did not want to do if I could possibly avoid it. The political atmosphere in the Middle East was tense—as the Taliban captured Kabul in 1996, and The Gulf War had been in 1990/91. The general feeling was quite anti-American, and I was concerned about political

protest actions against civilians. In the end, we however, decided to take the risk of pirates.

In fact, 2002 turned out to be a relatively good time from the pirate standpoint—certainly better than the years from 2008 to 2010. There were many foreign warships patrolling the Gulf of Aden. We saw French and German fleets as well as an aircraft carrier and support vessels of undetermined flags. Other cruisers saw British fleets, and were overflown by patrol aircraft. Plus, we heard American and Italian warships on the VHF. So there was a lot of military activity, and I did not hear reports of any piracy against a yacht. We took the "middle" route by keeping more than 100 NM off Somalia and more than 30 NM off Yemen. We also went as fast as we could, maintained VHF radio silence, ran without navigation lights, removed our American flag, maneuvered away from any approaching boats, went through the most risky area at night, and went directly to the city of Djibouti from Male in the Maldives.

Other boats that we were in SSB contact with stayed closer to Yemen, but traveled in a group within sight of each other. We used a prearranged code to describe our positions on SSB. We could have joined them, but a group can only go as fast as the slowest boat, and it is difficult to keep close enough to be of assistance during the night. In their case, they were traveling at 5 kts or less.

So I decided to go it alone. For most of the way down the Gulf of Aden we had favorable winds, so the passage was fairly fast and not at all difficult. In addition, the seas were sufficiently high that it would make boarding our boat difficult. Once, when a local boat seemed to be targeting us, I turned on the engine and went maximum speed while sailing until they broke off and changed course.

Djibouti was an exotic, but safe, port. We anchored off the yacht club, which provided a haven from the town. Getting diesel was a challenge, as we had to take a taxi to the oil company, and pay for a quantity of diesel in advance. After that, we had to move ESCAPADE to the commercial dock at an appointed time, and that's when a tank truck appeared. But as their hoses were too large for our boat, the fuel had to be dispensed into barrels, hauled to the boat, and then poured into the tanks. Local men—who knew what would happen—fought their way to be the ones to handle the barrels. There were near fights, and I had to pay more men than the ones who really worked. It was a wild scene, but we did get the diesel.

The challenge began in the Red Sea. About three days before we entered, a large catamaran with a German couple aboard was demasted in the Bab el Mandeb Strait. They were unable to cut the mast free, so they issued a Mayday. They abandoned ship, were picked up by helicopter and taken to Djibouti. It was reported that the boat was recovered later, but it had been stripped. Three other boats were reported lost, but there was no loss of life. A French boat, Chamoise (with two crew aboard), went on the reef at Marsa Mubarak at night when they were attempting to seek shelter. The boat was holed and sunk, but they were able to save personal possessions. A large Chilean boat, Hussar 3, went on the reef near Sharm el Sheikh. The boat was reported to be lost. Finally, a New Zealand boat, Cariad (with a couple aboard), went on a reef. The boat was pulled off, but sunk before it reached shelter. This information is as it was reported on SSB transmissions in the region. I had no first-hand contact with any of these boats or crew after the reported incidents, although I had previously seen several of the boats.

To go through the southern entrance to the Red Sea in daylight (known as Bab-el-Mandeb), we chose to anchor offshore at Obock in Djibouti. That worked well. The entrance to the Red Sea was challenging because the seas were large and confused. The winds were 40 knots with gusts at 50 kts, but in a favorable direction. ESCAPADE took these conditions in stride. Later, the wind dropped, changed direction, and was generally fickle.

In our case, we did sail the Red Sea about as easily as it gets—especially based on all of the experiences that we'd heard about. We were in daily contact with a group of boats also going up the Red Sea, and we followed their progress. Our plan—as our insurance company had requested—was to sail from Djibouti nonstop up the Red

Sea. We hired a weather router, and for the first part—since the winds were favorable—we were making good progress. But our hopes of a quick passage were doused when the weather router contacted us to say that the wind would turn to the NW, almost on our nose. He recommended that we seek shelter immediately. The only port that was somewhat near was Port Sudan. So we turned toward it just in time as the wind did, in fact, go to the NW. The seas became very choppy with sharp waves, much more so than in the open ocean. In my planning, I had always considered alternative ports, and was prepared with charts and data for Port Sudan.

What we were not prepared for was a sand storm that reduced visibility to about 0.1 NM. It was really eerie to be sailing while in the middle of a sand storm. In fact, on the boat the sand built up to a depth of a half-inch on the forward side of the mast and rigging. Thanks to accurate electronic charting, we were able to enter through the narrow gap in the reef—the radar was of no use. We tried calling Port Sudan Port Control, but did not get a response, so we went in anyway.

Port Sudan is an exotic port. We anchored, and tied the stern to a huge block of concrete in the harbor. In the morning, after the storm had passed, there were camels walking along the bank near us. The city was filled with people from both parts of Sudan, all black. Given the war issues in the rest of the country, Port Sudan was quite peaceful. One family wanted their picture taken with me, as I was the only white person to be seen in that part of the world at that time.

Since Port Sudan is only about half way up the Red Sea, we set sail again as soon as the winds changed. This time, we were able to reach Safaga, Egypt, before the wind turned against us again and rose to 30 knots with gusts to 35 knots. We had to pound into a bad chop of peaky and fierce waves for six hours before we reached the harbor. This was our entry to Egypt, so there were a lot of formalities to take care of. We tied up alongside a commercial dock, but had to move in order to provide room for a ship that was expected later. In the middle of the night, we were awakened by the ship that was tying up near us, and then the noise of hundreds of people milling about on the dock waiting to board the ship. They were men going on the "hajj" to Mecca in Saudi Arabia, which is on the east coast of the Red Sea. In the morning, the ship had departed and all was quiet again, but the litter on the dock gave proof to the events. We were able to fill up with diesel from a truck that brought large barrels to the dock.

To stay out of the northerly winds, we decided to motor north inside of a reef. But we promptly ran aground so we had to kedge off using our anchor. Crew in the dinghy used the hand-held depth sounder to find a deep enough channel for us to follow in ESCAPADE. We arrived at Hurghada, but had to anchor off because the customs people were giving us a major hassle. Early in the morning we departed and went to an island called Endeavour Reef, in the mouth of the Gulf of Suez, to wait out the winds.

We waited nearly two days and (with a forecast of the wind shifting to the SE) we departed before it happened as all crew were becoming restless—borderline mutiny. Since the island is only six feet high we were protected from the waves, but not the winds. But it was bare sand, and there was nothing to do.

The wind did change to the SE as predicted. Then it increased and increased to 30 knots, gusting to 35 or 40 knots, all with sand. As a result, we made the passage quickly, while dodging the oil platforms. Upon arriving at Suez city, which is the south entrance to the Suez Canal, we found that the port was closed because of the winds. So we hid behind a huge, long breakwater. The waves were so large they were actually breaking over the breakwater. Our anchor was well dug in and we were very safe, but two large ships in the bay dragged anchor and drifted toward the beach. It was very exciting to watch.

We were permitted into the Yacht Club the next day, where *ESCAPADE* was measured and we had crew changes. Had to pay the Agent for the fees for the transit of the Canal, but received clearance for leaving Egypt—so we would not have to stop when were departed the Canal. A Pilot arrived the next morning and we motored north, keeping clear of the southbound ships. There are no locks

Escapade's Red Sea Crew

L to R back row– Paul Fenn, Erick Reickert, Jack Pryde
L to R front row– John Hancox, Dick Hinsley, Charlie Scott

PHOTO BY HEATHER REICKERT

PIRATES, THE RED SEA AND THE SUEZ CANAL

in the Suez Canal. We stayed overnight at Ismailia, and another Pilot joined the next morning. We gave each Pilot a carton of cigarettes and some cash. Concerned they might take something, we did not let them go below unless they were escorted. When we arrived in Port Said, a boat came alongside to take the Pilot off. I never let the Pilot steer, as his job was to keep the Canal Control informed of our progress. The actual trip up the Suez Canal was uneventful, and even boring. But it was strange to be in a boat surrounded by a sand desert. There were a few rusting tanks left over from the war on the banks. After that, it was just a few minutes before we entered the Mediterranean. It was a tremendous emotional relief to have the pirate areas—and the Red Sea—safely behind us.

We sailed directly to Larnaca, Cyprus. We had planned to leave *ESCAPADE* there for a couple of months, but they said they did not have room—even though I had "booked" six months before. In total, it took us 19 days (March 16 to April 4, 2002) to sail from Djibouti to Cyprus, a distance of 1,682 nautical miles. We were happy and relieved that it was over, and we were finally back in friendly and first-world waters again. One reason we were able to sail successfully in such trying conditions was that we had a full complement of six crew aboard which let us handle watches with ease. Even when three of the six crew became ill in the bad seas, we carried on without concerns. We also used a weather routing service (Commanders Weather) that proved to be very accurate in predicting wind changes in our specific location.

Ultimately, we were able to arrange to leave *ESCAPADE* at Antalya, Turkey so we sailed there. This, actually turned out to be a better plan because when we arrived in Antalya, we completed our circumnavigation. It gave us an even better reason to cheer and break out the champagne. And did we ever savor the accomplishment! We had departed Antalya on October 6, 1997, and returned on April 8, 2002—four years six months later.

Escapade under Sail in Oyster Regatta off Palma, Mallorca, Spain

PHOTO BY OYSTER MARINE

CHAPTER 27

Cruising *from* Alaska to Maine

Cruising around North and through Central America

If one advances confidently in the direction of his dreams,
and endeavors to live the life which he imagined,
he will meet with a success unexpected in common hours.

HENRY DAVID THOREAU

As published in Oyster News, Winter 2007 and expanded

It was a wonderful, exciting and delightful voyage, filled with a few challenges and many rewards. In total, my wife Susan and I sailed 12,700 miles but were never more than 100 miles offshore. It took nearly 18 months but we went around North and Central America and cruised most of the coast of the United States. It included the Pacific and the Atlantic Oceans as well as the Caribbean, and went from icebergs and bergy bits to tropical waters. We visited six foreign countries, but skipped several others. All told, it was a fabulous experience filled with many pleasurable adventures.

ESCAPADE, our Oyster 55, has been the boat that opened the world to us for the past ten years. We had previously circumnavigated the world, and spent four years cruising the Mediterranean. *ESCAPADE* had been positioned in 2004 to be in Vancouver, BC, Canada, so it was the perfect opportunity to go to Alaska in 2006, and then continue to Maine.

Our overall plan was determined by the following basic weather considerations:

*   Be in Alaska during June and July for the best weather.
*   Leave Seattle southbound before early September, before the fall storms begin.
*   Don't leave San Diego southbound before November, so the hurricanes are over.
*   Be in the Caribbean between January and April for the best weather.
*   Be as far north as the Chesapeake Bay by mid June, before hurricane season starts.
*   Be in Maine in August and early September for the best weather.

This plan worked well and we were blessed with good weather for the whole trip. The importance of this type of planning was underscored by the fact that a hurricane had damaged some of the towns in the Sea of Cortez a few months before we arrived. Plus, hurricanes hit Cabo San Lucas and Belize after we were there. So timing is everything.

In general, this was an easy voyage with many opportunities to make stops along the way. The longest passages were about five days, and they were between Seattle and San

Francisco at 826 miles, and then between San Diego and Cabo San Lucas, Mexico at 750 miles. I concluded that we had to go directly to San Francisco because the ports along the west coast all had sand bars in the entrances, and in case of bad weather these bars become nearly impassible. So, if bad weather developed, we would not be able to enter any port, which meant that—whatever the weather—we had to go non-stop. A situation like that focuses one's thinking. For the San Diego to Cabo leg, there are places to stop, but we wanted to stay ahead of the Baha Ha Ha (a cruisers' rally) that makes two stops. There were two passages that were slightly over 500 miles, and one was 453 miles. All other legs were less than 355 miles.

There are many very good cruising grounds along the way. The hard part was to keep moving so as to stay on our time line. We could write articles—or even a book—on each of these cruising grounds because each one has its own special appeal and character. But I will summarize our feelings.

Alaska, Glacier Bay and Tracy Arm in particular

This is a different type of cruising. The grandeur, the wilderness, the vastness, the desolation, and the areas devoid of human impact are simply overwhelming. It is a majestic wilderness that cannot be conquered by man. We saw dozens of humpback whales, orca whales, porpoises, seals, sea lions, sea otters, bald eagles, bears, and other wildlife. Most of the time, we stayed in anchorages with no other boats. So if you want a sense of remoteness and isolation, Alaska is the place. Suffice it to say, we truly enjoyed Alaska and the unique experience it provides.

The first part of our adventure was to go to Alaska and back. It took us six weeks to travel the 1,500 miles each way from Vancouver, BC. Our primary objective was to visit Glacier Bay and Tracy Arm, in order to view as well as get close and personal with the glaciers. We accomplished that and—in a remarkable bit of good luck—we had magnificent weather for both visits, with complete sunshine and clear blue skies.

Overall, it was a very interesting and exciting experience. We did not sail at all in Alaska, and there were only about five days (in three months) that we sailed at all. Those were during small craft and gale warnings in the Dixon Entrance and the Queen Charlotte Sound. But, as usual, that is the kind of conditions that *ESCAPADE* loves and we enjoy. So do not go to Alaska for sailing! Winds, when they occur, travel up or down the arms so they are either on your nose or on your tail and the arms are generally too narrow to tack.

The distances are quite large, and often there are very few facilities for cruising boats. So it is a different cruising experience with many challenges. These include navigating among rocks and reefs in very close quarters (down to 20 feet), negotiating rapids with currents of up to 7 knots, and—if you get it wrong—competing for space with fishing boats, deep, rocky anchorages (up to 92 feet deep) with little swinging room, and sometimes practically no communications (the high mountains often cut off the GPS, the satellite phone, and Inmarsat-C). Points of interest include waterfalls (some of which are at sea level), hot springs where you can bathe, and trails in the woods (some on boardwalks). Although you are surrounded by land, much of it is impenetrable. The locals are very friendly, and they speak English! It is a very different area to cruise, but—added to our prior experiences—helped make a more complete picture of the world. You need to develop the skill of winding around icebergs and pushing aside ice-bergy bits to be able to reach the face of the glaciers. In terms of towns, we stopped in Prince Rupert, Ketchikan, Wrangell, Petersburg, Sitka and Craig, in addition to Juneau. Basic supplies are available, and most towns cater to cruise ship tourists. But it is life on the rustic side.

Taking cruise ships to Alaska is quite popular now, but the experience pales when compared to being there on your own boat. For example, only two cruise ships per day are allowed into Glacier Bay National Park, and they must be out by sunset. In contrast, we spent four days in Glacier Bay—including three overnight anchorages, one in front of a glacier. We were able to go up arms and see glaciers where cruise ships are not permitted. We spent hours drifting in front of the Johns Hopkins Glacier on the Fourth of July, where our "fireworks" were the glaciers themselves. There would be a sharp crack, a deep rumble, and then a splash followed by a wave. It is a real challenge to try to feel the isolation and solitude of Alaska on a ship with hundreds of people.

Since there is rain—often with dull overcast, low-level clouds and sometimes fog—the weather is not always cooperative. Of course, that totally destroys the view of the snow-capped mountains. Still, we were able to move and keep on schedule on all days except for one. You need to have electronic charting and radar for safe boat movements. The temperatures are cool to cold and can run in the 50's (F) but that becomes downright cold with no sun, a bit of rain, and some wind. During the day, however, it can reach 70 degrees in the sun. We kept the cockpit enclosed with clear plastic side curtains that kept the wind and rain out, which considerably improved the comfort level. I had previously added a diesel heater to *ESCAPADE* and it made all the difference when it came to enjoying comfortable life aboard.

We went north in the Inside Passage, but returned south sometimes on the outside so we could visit Sitka and other ports, which was well worth it. We also visited the Queen Charlotte Islands, including the Gwaii Haanas National Reserve Park in the south. That is a protected area, and only a limited number of people are permitted in at one time to protect the heritage sites of First Nation peoples. These are truly impressive, and best seen by private boat. Permits are required in advance to visit both this area and Glacier Bay National Park.

Puget Sound, Vancouver Island, the Bay Islands, and the San Juan Islands

This is a wonderful area to cruise, with many options in terms of anchorages, marinas, as well as towns and cities to visit—plus the distances are short. Mostly protected waters, but not a lot of wind. For sailing, the Strait of Georgia was the best. There is something for everyone, and one could explore the area for years. Roche Harbor and Friday Harbor are great, and are good ports of entry to the USA. Roche Harbor has an outdoor sculpture park, performances of Shakespeare under the stars, and fine dining—all in one stop. I liked the Canadian Bay Islands better than the San Juan Islands, and there are more of them—with a greater variety of things to do. A circumnavigation of Vancouver Island is a quite nice little exploration, and the northwest coast (on the Pacific side), is especially rugged and remote. In the inside passage there many interesting places like Desolation Sound, with several anchorages. The farther north you go, the more remote it becomes. The weather is nice during the summer, and inside of Vancouver Island the microclimate is quite moderate.

Escapade in front of John Hopkins Glacier

IN GLACIER BAY NATIONAL PARK, ALASKA, USA ~ PHOTO BY ERICK REICKERT

The city of Vancouver is a wonderful, modern city with many activities, and the city of Victoria is a unique and special place to visit. The harbor is full of activity—with floatplanes landing and taking off, small and large ferries, water taxis, as well as pleasure boats of all descriptions, all moving about at the same time. Docking in front of the Empress Hotel is nice, and high tea at the hotel is not to be missed. Butchart Gardens on Vancouver Island is world-renowned, the flowers change for every season, and they even have a special boat entrance. We spent two summers in the Pacific Northwest and still did not get to see everything.

San Francisco Bay

This overall area is relatively small, and there are shallows in some corners. But when the temperature in the valley rises, there are consistent winds in the afternoons that pull air into the Bay through the Golden Gate. There often is a layer of marine fog close to the ocean in the morning, which generally burns off by noon. Angel Island has several bays, one of which has mooring buoys. It is an easy island to explore by foot. We especially enjoyed Sausalito, Oakland and San Francisco itself. From Benicia we took a limousine tour of the vineyards in Napa Valley. We happened to be there during Fleet Week, and that made it possible for us to anchor in the Bay near Alcatraz Island along with hundreds of other boats. We were able to watch airplane races—and the Blue Angels—fly overhead. We enjoyed the Bay area, with relaxed and pleasant cruising and nice sails. There were more sailboats out sailing there than anywhere else in the US.

Sea of Cortez

This is a unique area that is generally desolate and arid. The scenery often consists of dry rock formations in a multitude of colors. These colors appear to change during the day—from sunrise to sunset—so it is a never-ending kaleidoscope. The sea life is overwhelming, and the fish seethe beneath the surface—especially at night. In fact, they just about jump onto the boat. We did not see any whales, as I don't think they had migrated from Alaska yet. There were very few cruisers around at the time we were there in November, but I believe that it is busier in the winter. Except for La Paz, it is anchoring out sometimes just behind a point of land like at Los Muertos. We liked Puerto Escondido, Bahia Santispac in Bahia Conception, Aqua Verde, and Isla Partida. There was good swimming and snorkeling. La Paz is a more typical Mexican town, unlike Cabo San Lucas, which is touristy to the extreme. It was interesting to contrast and compare the Sea of Cortez to Alaska bcause they were so different in physical appearance, but quite similar in the remoteness and isolation from civilization.

West Coast of Mexico and Central America

This is a long coast that changes from arid to tropical as you head south. We made stops at Mazatlan, Nuevo Vallarta, Laguna Navidad, Ixtapa, Zihuatanejo, Acapulco and Huatulco in Mexico. Visiting a Montessori school in Ixtapa allowed us to see some of the needs of local children. Susan was able to invite the school to be part of her global initiative "The Art of Peace". We also stopped in Bahia Jiquilisco in El Salvador and Golfito in Costa Rica. We choose to skip the countries of Guatemala, Honduras and Nicaragua primarily because of security concerns, and the fact my insurance company would not cover us in those countries. The legs were between 95 and 521 nautical miles, so they were one- to three-night passages. In several of the stops we stayed at marinas associated with luxury hotels so we had the ability to use the hotels facilities including the beaches, restaurants, swimming pools, etc. We left *ESCAPADE* in Nuevo Vallarta for Christmas when we went home for a few weeks. In Acapulco, we stayed at the Yacht Club, which has fine facilities that are located in a quiet part of the bay.

In other stops we anchored off or stayed in marinas. The atmosphere was very much like a multi-stop holiday; and we enjoyed the variety of towns, and took inland excursions as well. In general, provisioning was good. One interesting stop was Isla Isabela, which is a bird sanctuary that had the feeling of a Galapagos island, but with the ability to approach nesting birds closely. The entrance to the river at Bahia Jiquilisco was very threatening because you must enter between a reef and a sand bar in a curved path between breaking waves. But the marina sent a boat out into the Pacific to guide us in which removed much of the worry. All told, an interesting coast.

Panama Canal

This was our second time through with *ESCAPADE,* but this time we were going northbound. Although the transit is fraught with a high possibility of damage to the boat, we got through with no damage. By selecting an aggressive agent, we were able to transit on the date we specified, and made it through in one day. *ESCAPADE* was alone, with no other sailboats. We up-locked tied alongside a local small cruise ship, and down-locked tied alongside a tug. That avoided the issues associated with center-locking, but we were glad that we had rented covered tires to supplement our fenders. Even so, it is intimidating to be in such a tight space with the bow of a huge ship towering above you. It was dark by the time we reached the Panama Canal Yacht Club, where we returned the lines and tires to the agent. Overall, we were very pleased with the entire experience. There is nothing quite like transiting the Panama Canal in your own boat, but if it is your first time be sure to learn and understand all the issues associated with the transit before you attempt it.

San Blas Islands in Panama

It is 75 miles up wind in the Caribbean to get to the San Blas islands, which are east of the Panama Canal. Since we did not want to get beat up too badly, it took us three days. But it was worth it because the San Blas is a unique and special cruising area that is filled with gorgeous, tiny, sandy and palm tree-covered islands. They are the classic image of tropical islands surrounded with clear, calm water. Actually, many are at the edge of the archipelago, so while you are anchored in a serene and calm anchorage, you can hear the Caribbean waves crashing on the outer edges of the reef. It can be a bit unnerving, but you get used to it. The swimming is great, and there is some good snorkeling. Essentially, the whole area is picture perfect and wonderful. But what we found to be especially delightful are the Kuna Indians, who still live in traditional fashion and get around in dugout canoes with sails. The women dress in their classic costumes of molas and beads, and while you're at anchor, they come in their dugouts and offer molas, fish, and other goods for sale. We also went ashore and visited Kuna villages on the islands of Carti Sugtupu and Isla Tigre. They live in grass huts with no furniture, and only small hammocks in which to sit and sleep. Since the Kunas are not allowed to marry outsiders, the race is pure and they look like they just stepped out of a history book. This was my second trip to the San Blas, and I would put it on a "must visit" list for all cruisers. But do not expect to find any provisions there.

Western Caribbean

For us, this comprised Panama's Bocas del Toro region, the Colombian Island of Isla Providencia, Belize, and Mexico's Yucatan. We skipped the Rio Dulce in Guatamala for two reasons. First, I was concerned about security, and secondly, the sand bar at the entrance seemed to be just too shallow for ESCAPADE—even at high tide. This is a less-traveled area than the eastern Caribbean, but is interesting in its own right. Bocas del Toro seemed like a modern-day version of the Wild West. There was a lot of growth and potential but it was still very rough and basic, which makes an interesting blend. We visited a butterfly farm that had a huge netted enclosure with thousands of butterflies. Isla Providencia is off the beaten track, and it was easy to tour the whole island in a few hours by taxi. When we rounded the corner of Honduras, we stayed well off shore as because the local rumor was that the government impounded cruising boats if they got too close to shore. Belize, from my viewpoint, was not as good as I'd expected for cruising. Many areas are very shallow. For example, if you wanted to anchor off Belize City you would be over a mile from shore, and other towns were not accessible without a lot of risk. So we skipped San Pedro on Ambergris Cay, but we did travel north through the country inside the barrier reef. We started with Punta Gorda, which is an open roadstead, to Belize City, and stopped at many Cays and Placencia, which does have a good anchorage. Most of the small islands, or Cays, are covered with mangroves. These often have bugs at dusk, no protected anchorage, and you cannot land on them due to the mangroves. There was good snorkeling on the barrier reef, but we took a local dive boat out to the reef, as there are no anchorages at the reef. The reef is the second longest barrier reef in the world.

We stopped at Puerto Aventuras in Mexico, which was a good decision. It is a good place from which to explore the region, and we drove to Tulum, a Mayan ruin, and swam with dolphins, which was a treat. We also took a ferry to Cozumel, as there are no good anchorages along the west coast of the island. The whole area close to the town is covered with tourists, huge cruise ships, and many local snorkel tour boats. In short, it is bedlam. We toured the island by taxi, and got a feel of the tourist hype. It was a quick sail to Isla Mujeres off the coast from Cancun, which is where cruisers stop, because there is no good place in Cancun itself or on the coast north. We rented a car on the mainland, which is a short ferry ride away, and explored Cancun as well as the Yucatan, including Chichén Itzá—a very large Mayan ruin. Our tour of Isla Mujeres was by golf cart, and the sculpture park at the south tip was interesting.

Florida Keys, and the Eastern Florida Coast

It is 350 miles to Key West from Isla Mujeres, going west of Cuba. It wasn't wise for an American boat to go to Cuba at that time, so we skipped Cuba again. It was nice to get back to the States, but make sure that every non-American has a B1/B2 visa. Otherwise, the Immigration people get very uptight, and a person without one will be deported. We were in Key West at the time of the reenactment of the Conch Republic war. It was all great fun, with the Coast Guard participating in boat-to-boat water fights and bread throwing, plus airplanes dropping toilet roll "bombs." This event commemorates the time when Customs officials blocked the only road to Key West. To retaliate, the local business community decided to create the Conch Republic, secede from the USA, declare war on USA, immediately surrender, and then ask for reparations. They did not get any money, but Customs did remove the roadblock.

It is pleasant to sail in the inside passage up to Miami because it is protected, but you must stay inside the channel or it gets shallow. This time, I decided to skip a lot of the ports I'd stopped at before, and selected only the ones I really liked. So we stopped at Fort Lauderdale, West Palm Beach, St. Augustine, Hilton Head, Charleston, and Beaufort, NC before getting to the Chesapeake Bay. I enjoy Fort Lauderdale because it is one of the three major boating centers on the East Coast. It is also a good place to get anything repaired or replaced, as everything for boats is available. Any mast height above 65 feet requires sailing in the Atlantic Ocean as that is the controlling clearance on fixed bridges over the ICW (Inter Costal Waterway). There is one area (since all the bridges open), that is passable on the ICW, which is the stretch between Fort Lauderdale and West Palm Beach. For a change of pace, we motored that stretch—plus, it is impressive to see the homes lining the ICW. We spent one night at the Boca Raton Resort marina, which was delightful. West Palm Beach and Palm Beach are interesting, and offer a lot activities. St. Augustine is a great little place that has a lot of history. As we came into the harbor, we learned that there was a temporary lift bridge over the route to the marina, which was not on the chart. After several quick radio calls to the bridge operator, we found out that we could get under it with a little bit of clearance. It was nice to be back in the USA, and we really enjoyed all the ports along this coast.

Chesapeake Bay and Long Island Sound

These are the two biggest and best protected cruising grounds on the East Coast. You could spend a whole season, or a lifetime, in each. The distances are small, the marina and anchorages are numerous, and both Annapolis and Newport are major yachting centers. Each has its own advantages, but I like Long Island Sound because it has cleaner, deeper water, and you don't have to motor up tributaries in order to find anchorages or marinas. Connecting these is New York Harbor—with the Statue of Liberty—and the East River. Motoring around Manhattan is breathtaking, and not to be missed because it is so dramatic and so very different from the norm. One especially enjoyable stop was in Mystic, CT at the Mystic Seaport Museum. You can tie up at the Museum, and be immediately immersed into the recreated whaling seaport of the 19th century. And you are there at night when all the other visitors leave.

The Maine Coast

This was new territory for me, and it was an interesting and pleasant area to cruise. We visited eight ports and spent two weeks in Maine with only one day of fog, which was good. The main detraction is the numerous lobster trap floats. Often they are no more than ten feet apart, which requires constant steering to avoid them. Frequently, there are several routes to choose from, including going outside, but constant attention to navigation is required due to the many rocks and shallows. And of course, when the fog descends, accurate electronic charts are required. But the reward is pretty scenery and protected waters. Our northern most point was Mt. Desert Island, and we liked the ports there—including Bar Harbor, Northeast Harbor, and Southwest Harbor—all of which had a rustic feeling, as Acadia National Park is on the island. We arrived at Bar Harbor on August 27, 2007. Camden is the quintessential Maine port, and both Portland and Rockland are interesting towns to visit.

Challenges

During the cruise around North America there were sailing challenges like rapids, reefs, the Panama Canal, fog, tides, and fiords to keep us on our toes. To get through each of these safely requires advance preparation and planning. The most important things required were accurate electronic charts, tide and current tables, along with local weather information. The rough spots were the Gulf of Tehuantepec (at the southern end of Mexico), the Gulf of Papagayo (off Costa Rica), the Gulf of Panama and crossing the Gulf Stream between Mexico and Key West.

The Gulfs are challenging because of the northerly winds, which funnel between the Gulf of Mexico to the north and the Pacific over the relatively narrow necks of land. Due to air pressure differentials in the two oceans, the winds can come up suddenly and reach over 55 knots. We tried to time our passage of the Gulf of Tehuantepec, but were off by about four hours. We used the "one foot on land" strategy by sailing close to the shore to minimize the wave heights, but, of course, it does not reduce the wind. The plan was to go north to the head of the Gulf and then turn to southeast following the shore. But the wind, which was predicted to be 25 knots, rose to over 45 knots. So we struggled into it for four hours before getting relief when we turned to the east and then southeast. In the Gulf of Papagayo, we had to stay off shore due to the configuration of the land, and again the wind exceeded 45 knots on our aft port quarter. It was a rollicking ride for 24 hours, but *ESCAPADE* handled it well. I was concerned about the Gulf of Panama because you have to go north to the Panama Canal, but this time the weather God was on our side, and we were able to motor into relatively light winds.

We kept to our timetable the whole trip, and achieved all of our goals. The main goal was to have an experience of a lifetime, which was fulfilled in wonderful measure. So you don't have to cross oceans to have a memorable adventure filled with a wide range of sailing conditions and experiences.

CHAPTER 28

Shipping *Escapade* by Ship

Transporting a Boat on a Ship

I will find comfort in the rhythm of the sea.

CHARLOTTE ERIKSON

We have sailed *ESCAPADE*, an Oyster 55, for eight years, have circumnavigated the globe, and know she is capable of delivering us safely to anywhere by sea. So why would we put *ESCAPADE* on a ship, and have her moved that way? Because it is fast. So that is what we did.

Moving a boat by ship has several advantages over sailing. Primarily in the speed in which it can be accomplished, plus the time of year is not as weather dependent, and it results in reduced wear and tear—compared to long ocean voyages. For motorboats, it can also save a lot of fuel, but remember that the shipment is quite expensive.

After spending four years in the Mediterranean, we wanted new sailing challenges. We decided on the Pacific Northwest of America and Canada. To get there by sea from the Med would have taken two years because we would have had to time our crossing of the Atlantic for the next November, and then we would have had to go north along the west coast of America—not a desirable cruise because of the prevailing northerly winds and currents. Instead, we shipped *ESCAPADE* from the Med to Vancouver, BC, Canada, in time for the summer sailing season in 2004.

We chose Dockwise Yacht Transport for the job. They have ships that regularly go to various ports around the

world, and they have scheduled ones that connect the Med to Vancouver. The ships are constructed like floating dry-docks, so they partly submerge to allow the boats to motor into the open hold of the ship. A diver places tripods under the boat that act as a cradle. The ship is then refloated and the boats settle onto the supports. Sailboats are also snuggled up against the side of the ship so that they cannot fall in that direction. Straps are placed around the mast, and are also tied to the deck cleats to prevent falling the other way. In addition, after the ship's deck is dry, large supports are welded to the deck of the ship to support the sailboats. It seems quite sturdy, as long as the transport ship is not in very large seas. In preparation for loading, Dockwise asks for detailed drawings of all boats in advance so they can plan the arrangement of boats on the ship and the necessary supports.

Dockwise requires full payment prior to the ship departure. That is the only way to guarantee a position on the ship. Since most yacht insurance policies will not cover the actual shipment, it is also necessary to arrange for special insurance of the boat while it is cargo on the ship.

Although we first contracted for a ship leaving Toulon, France, that ship was canceled—so we ended up shipping from Savona, Italy. As *ESCAPADE* was on the hard in Croatia for the 2003-2004 winter, we had to sail her around Italy in April, which was not nice due to bad weather. But that is another story. By choosing the ship from Savona, we had to go to Fort Lauderdale, Florida to take *ESCAPADE* off one Dockwise ship and put her on another Dockwise ship bound for Vancouver. We utilized the 10 days between the ships to equip *ESCAPADE* for Canada and the US, as contrasted to Europe. Had we chosen the ship departing from Majorca, it would have been the same ship that went to Vancouver so unloading and loading would not have been necessary. Interestingly, there were only two boats (*ESCAPADE* and a large power boat) on the ship from Savona as that was "against the flow." But the ship to Vancouver was totally full of small as well as large motorboats and sailboats. They were packed in just inches apart.

How did it work? Overall, the shipping achieved what we wanted. *ESCAPADE* was delivered halfway around the world in two months (from May 9 to July 5), and suffered only very minor damage. The starboard navigation light was knocked off, and the mast had some scratches on it from the strap used by Dockwise to hold the boat upright.

On the first voyage, we avoided scratching it by placing a soft towel around the mast. On the second voyage, the towel fell out—probably because the Dockwise ship had unloaded some boats in Mexico, and the strap became loose during the process.

When loading in Savona, there was a surge that worked its way into the ship. This caused *ESCAPADE* to slam against the side of the ship, but she was not damaged because of her rub rail. Dockwise stated that Savona is one of their worst ports for swell. There were no problems in either Port Everglades (Fort Lauderdale) or Vancouver.

The ship's exhaust emits a lot of dirt, so Dockwise washes the boats prior to their arrival. However, small particles of iron were still on the fiberglass and teak surfaces. *ESCAPADE* had just been waxed and polished before the trip, but she needed a complete re-wax and polish to get the particles off. Some of the other boats were shrink-wrapped or had canvas covers, which was probably a good idea.

Savona, Italy

ESCAPADE IS THE BOAT IN THE FOREGROUND ~ PHOTO BY ERICK REICKERT

Escapade on Shipwise Ship just after arrival

PRIOR TO SHIP LIFTING ~ PHOTO BY PAUL FENN

To minimize problems caused by the exhaust, of which we were aware, we removed all sails, as well as the dodger, bimini and running rigging so they would not become dirty. We would take the same extra effort if we did it again. This action also reduces the weight aloft thus minimizing the forces on the boat if the ship encountered seas. In addition, there were minimum levels of fuel and water in the tanks to reduce weight and any sloshing action.

The issue that caused us the greatest concern—and the most problems—were the timing estimates versus the actual timing. It is absolutely essential that someone representing the boat be at the departure and arrival ports at the time the Dockwise ship is loading and unloading. Dockwise provides estimated "windows" for arrivals or departures that narrow as the actual day approaches. The problem was that the actual dates fell outside the original windows. However, we had made airline flight reservations well in advance. In Italy, we ended up changing our flight three times. Plus, we needed hotel and car availability during the periods we had to wait. In Vancouver, I had scheduled my son and his family, including three grandsons, to join us for a week's sail on *ESCAPADE*. This was scheduled four days after the end of the window. In the event, *ESCAPADE* did not arrive until three days into the planned sailing holiday. So we missed some sailing, and we all had to stay at a hotel while waiting for Dockwise.

In our experience, Dockwise was never early. If we did it again, we would allow plenty of time even beyond the windows they predict. Flexible flight arrangements are far better than unchangeable flights so make the reservations as late as possible, and have hotel arrangements organized for possible delays.

In summary, it did work and it is a way to quickly move a boat over long distances. We would do it again if the circumstances demanded it, but it was a strange feeling to know that the shower we were taking onboard in Florida was using Italian water!

CHAPTER 29

These are the
Good Old Days

Why this is the Best Time for Cruising

*We live in a wonderful world that is full of beauty, charm and adventure.
There is no end to the adventures that we can have if only
we seek them with our eyes open.*

JAWAHARLA NEHRU

As published in Cruising World, July, 1999

Cruising means many things to many people, but most agree that it is among those human activities that are the least limited or controlled. In turn, this requires a high degree of responsibility for ones own actions and decisions. Cruising has meant to some the act of "cutting free", of being independent and without limitations. Cruising does give a sense of freedom, though there are those in governments around the world who want to limit that freedom.

What is freedom? Freedom is choice, the opportunity to choose what, when and how you want to do things. It is not withdrawal from society, though there are those who suggest that is what cruising is about. Cruising can mean freeing oneself from many land based systems and requirements, but there are still many restrictions and formalities that must be considered. These include natural phenomenon such as weather, tides, and currents, as well as COLREGS, governmental regulations, harbor rules, etc. We can never be totally free, but cruising comes very close, especially when compared to most land based lives.

Cruising can be successfully accomplished on many levels, with a wide variety of boats and equipment. But cruising does not need to be self-denial or self imposed

austerity. Why not cruise in luxury and comfort, if it can be afforded? Technology is providing more freedom, and more choices. It is enabling the handling of larger boats by small crews, and adds to the enjoyment of the whole experience. The best possible scenario is living the cruising experience while minimizing drudgery and inefficient effort.

I first sailed on a wooden boat with no engine, no outboard, no galley, no radio, no instruments except for a magnetic compass, no lifelines, and no life raft (among other things). I look back on those times fondly, but would I exchange that boat for my modern blue water cruiser with all modern equipment? No way. My range of enjoyment is expanded now.

Take winches. My first ones were the small single speed type with the slide-in handle. My present ones are larger in diameter, two speed, self tailing, and powered. I do not miss those old ones at all, especially their tendency to clip the ends of your fingers when you removed the handle. I expend less effort to trim the sails now, and my enjoyment is greater.

Technology has added new dimensions to sailing. It requires a larger skill and knowledge base on a wider variety of systems. It provides additional challenges and learning opportunities for these more diverse systems. Notwithstanding new technologies, the basic skills required have remained the same, such as sail trim, anchoring, navigation, etc.

Technology is continuously changing, and the change may be occurring at a faster rate. But only those who do not take the time to study and learn about new technologies will be blinded by them or by ads and hype. Life is change. Just look at your own body. Life is enhanced by continuous learning and new challenges. Those who handle change well have learned how to live well. Change is exciting.

Additional equipment and systems brings more complexity on board, and the possibility of malfunction or breakdown. That said, why give up the opportunity to have an easier existence simply because something could go wrong? Reliability is increasing for all types of gear. Roller furling, refrigeration and radios have all been problem sources in the past. Now they can be reliable, and quite useful. Even if they fail, the backup is the old system. In the future, cruisers will not even consider denying themselves the advantages of such systems because they might fail.

However, there is logic to say that new sailors should learn to sail on a boat with a minimum of equipment, so they may become familiar with the basics of sailing. This knowledge of the basic principles, and the fact that sailing does not require all modern equipment, should be deeply ingrained. It also will provide a confidence that will stand the sailor well in the future, no matter what new technologies are adopted and what situations in which he finds himself.

Communications is a unique technology. It has, and will increasingly provide the ability for the cruiser to stay in touch, if he wants. Cruising in the past has required withdrawal from society, and from easy and quick contact with family and friends. To some that may have been a plus, as they wanted to escape from the modern world. But to others it represented a major negative. Now, modern communications will permit staying in touch at all times. This may expand the number of people who are willing to go cruising and it will improve the experience for many others. It is not about the fear of cutting the umbilical cord with society; it is about a way to experience cruising while remaining a participant in life and the world around us.

Freedom is about choice, and the ability to choose. Technology has increased those choices. However, cruisers must never let technology overwhelm them or make them overconfident. The sea is still an alien place and a major challenge to all who sail. Backup alternatives and plans must be considered for all possible scenarios, be it a failure of a radio or GPS, of a dragging anchor, or of severe weather. Technology does not substitute for good sense and thorough planning, or for experience. Responsibility for the safe conduct of the boat and crew still rests with the individual skipper. It is his decisions on how to manage and deploy all systems of the boat, which are important, no matter what technologies are involved.

Now is the best time for cruising. There are affordable as well as luxury boats. There are wide varieties of equipment to choose from for each cruiser's particular needs. There are a vast number of very desirable cruising grounds. Don't look back—the "good old days" were never as good as some make them out to be. The changes in yachting have been expanding, exciting, and good. The future can only get better (if we keep the bureaucrats at bay).

Erick Reickert at Escapade's Bow

SAILING IN THE STRAIT
OF GEORGIA, BC, CANADA

PHOTO BY SUSAN REICKERT

CHAPTER 30

ESCAPADE Journal 2002

What Types of Day-to-Day Things Happen Onboard

*We are like islands on the sea, separate on the surface
but connected in the deep.*

WILLIAM JAMES

This is a complete, and unaltered, record of what happened in 2002. It gives a day-by-day and sometimes hourly account of what happened. The problems, issues, and accomplishments are all described. It was written each day so it is a fresh and a real account. The problems with customs, the arrival and departure of crew, maintenance issues, changes in the weather, worries about going through the pirate zones, contacts with other cruisers, provisioning challenges, commissioning the boat after winter storage, etc. This is the real picture of cruising in some of the toughest areas of the world. It also records our completion of the circumnavigation.

The objective for the year was to start in Thailand, sail across the Indian Ocean, go down the Gulf of Aden through the pirate area, up the Red Sea, cruise the Mediterranean, and finish the year at an Oyster Regatta in Palma Mallorca.

I think you will find it interesting. If you find there is too much detail, then these are some of the key dates so you can skip to the subjects of interest to you:

January 19	Start the year on the hard in Phuket, Thailand
January 31	Start crossing the Indian Ocean
February 28	Depart Maldives for the passage to Djibouti (the pirate passage)
March 16	Passage up the Red Sea
March 31	Suez Canal
April 8	Completion of the Circumnavigation & Cruise Turkey
June 11	Cruise Greek Islands
July 2	Cruise Croatia
July 17	Arrive in Venice Italy & Cruise Italy
Aug 6	Malta
October 18	Menorca & Balearic Islands
October 21	Engine problem at sea
October 24	Oyster Rally in Mallorca
October 29	Put *ESCAPADE* up on the hard in Alcudia, Mallorca

Friday, January 18 - Siem Reap to Bangkok

We arrived in Bangkok from Siem Reap, Cambodia. Although we had a brand new Bangkok Airways 727 on the way there, we had an old turbo prop on the way back. Spent four days visiting Angkor Wat and 18 other temples. It was great, but it is sad to see a country so ravaged by war. Checked into the Amari Airport Hotel; were upgraded to executive floor again. Paul is due to arrive late so left message for him. Did E-mail. Had dinner at the bar-type restaurant at the hotel.

Saturday, January 19 - Bangkok to Phuket

Checked out at 0710 and Paul was there. Caught a 0900 Thai Airways flight to Phuket. It was a big Airbus that was totally full. Took taxi directly to the Boat Lagoon and *ESCAPADE*. She was exactly where we left her, but the bottom had been painted and the topside waxed and polished. The anchors had also been re-galvanized. She looked great! The bottom had been repaired well; there was no trace of the coral incident. We had a fork lift truck lift the bags up. Everything was in place down below. Went to the new hotel, now the Boat Lagoon Resort. Checked in and had lunch there. I checked with the marina and asked if they could put us in the water on Monday, January 21 instead of Tuesday. That seemed to be OK, but they still said they were full so we would have to leave immediately. I said that was not acceptable. Will have to talk to the headman on Monday morning. Started to work on the items needed to put the boat in the water. Got the outside items completed. Replaced all zincs except the bow thruster, which were nearly new. The prop is in great shape. When moving the rudder there was a scraping noise, which we discovered were the two cables on the quadrant were on the same slot. Moved one and the steering is fine. The house batteries appear to be fine, and fully charged because of the solar panels. One engine start battery had only 4.5 volts on it so it does appear that they will need replacing. It was really HOT so we knocked off early and went swimming. It then promptly rained. Had dinner at the hotel.

Sunday, January 20 - Phuket Boat Lagoon

Got going at 0700 to beat the heat. Continued to do all items necessary to splash the boat. Completed all except buying new engine start batteries. The battery on the PC computer was dead flat and wouldn't accept a charge. The knob on the port window is stripped. Other than that, all is in good shape. It took some doing to get the nav computer to run MaxSea after loading the new ARCS chart license. Had to start it in demo mode first! Ate at the sandwich shop at the marina. Got our E-mail at the Internet place. Found out that Max Grody decided not to go through the Red Sea this year. Sea Glass arrived today. Did more work on the boat. Went for a swim. Jack and Margaret arrived at 1800, just after Heather went down to the boat to wait for them. Had dinner at the hotel. Went to bed tired.

Monday, January 21 - Phuket Boat Lagoon

Started again at 0700. The sun is bright and blazing all day long and it becomes oppressive in the heat. Went in to the Marina at 0800 and they said we could have a berth for 3 days. Great! Saw Andy when he arrived, and he will have the bottom of the keel painted after the boat is lifted at 1300. Checked the raw water impellors for the engine and generator. The engine one had a torn vane and the generator vanes were worn so I replaced both of them. Went over to the battery shop across the road and ordered two engine start batteries. They agreed to deliver them by 1100; in fact they were early. They took the old ones and we were able to squeeze the new ones into the same location as before. Started the engine and it started right away. Had lunch at the hotel. Promptly at 1300 the travel lift arrived and it all began. We were in the water by 1400. They told us to go to G1, in front of Sea Glass and near the marina office. Just as we were sorting out the A/C units (had to bleed the saloon and the forward one) they came and asked us to move and tie along side a boat they were just launching. After some discussion they said we could stay where we were. The water arrived at 1600- 600 liters in 20 liter bottles. Filled the forward (small) tank and put the rest in the aft tank. Paul scrubbed the deck that was filthy. *ESCAPADE* started to look just fine. Started the water pressure pump and one of the inlet ports broke, so I had to replace it with a new one. Went to dinner at Scampi's. Food was very good. Retired by 2115 as all were tired. But we accomplished at lot.

Tuesday, January 22 - Phuket Boat Lagoon

Checked out of the hotel by 0730 and put everything aboard *ESCAPADE*. We had arranged for a van for 4 hours and we departed at 0800. It was a long morning. Dropped H & M at Tesco's and proceeded to Immigration, but they weren't there. We were told to return at 0900. Found some plastic bottles for fuel for our long Aden and Red Sea passages. Returned to Immigration and were told to return at 1100. Tried to find a battery for the Toshiba laptop PC. Couldn't find the stores. Went to Rolly Taskers and picked up the sails. Asked for a Sudan flag but they were out- "have them tomorrow". Went to Dive Supply, and got the regulators. He was also willing to refill the tank without a hydro test. Went back to Immigration and they were there and got the letter for my Bond. Went to the bank and got the 20,170 Baht (with interest) back. Returned to Tesco and the girls had only just finished 15 minutes earlier. Had 5 trollies and the meat was being frozen for pickup tomorrow. Got back to *ESCAPADE* at 1300. Worked more on the boat and went to dinner at Scampi's again. Erick started diarrhea again (joining Heather). Went to bed tired and sick.

Wednesday, January 23 - Phuket Boat Lagoon

Put up the sails even with a bit of wind on the beam. H got the laundry. E paid Marine Services the remaining 30,950 Baht in cash. Got on the Internet for a short period. Continued the checks. The generator worked fine the first time. The fresh water pump pressure switch failed so I replaced the micro switch in the assembly. The port dinghy davit spring broke, which allows the dinghy to free-fall. Replaced it with a new spring. The icemaker wouldn't run. Later found out that TV would not respond to the remote control. Had lunch of egg sandwiches on board, even though E and H didn't feel well. Got a van for 1300 and departed for Canal Village at Laguna to go to a Jim Thompson's shop. Then went to Rolly Taskers to pick up a Sudan flag. On the way dropped J & M at Chalong Wat and picked them up later. Dropped H & M at Tesco's and we went to find another computer store. Found this one but they would have to order the battery and it would take a month! So skip that. Returned to Tesco and went inside to help with checkout. Returned to *ESCAPADE* at 1600. H & E took a nap and then E installed the connection for the second Macintosh G4 computer. E & H stayed on *ESCAPADE* and had tomato soup. Turned on the TV to watch a movie and discovered that the remote does not activate the set. And the remote is essential as it controls all functions. Changed batteries and nothing worked. Went to bed early.

Thursday, January 24 - Phuket Boat Lagoon to Ko Rang Yai 5.0 NM

Had a good sleep. E feels much better but still has the runs (H too). A bright sunny day. Got to work doing remaining items. Went to the Internet place for two hours to get all the last minute messages out via AOL. Had lunch at the sandwich shop. Decided to leave at around 1600. Tested the bilge pumps. Paul washed the deck one last time. M & H washed up and cleaned up. *ESCAPADE* was shipshape Bristol fashion for our departure. We changed our destination to a closer island as E wanted to leave as late as possible (high tide was at 1800) but the harbormaster said 1530 was OK. We waited anyway. E paid off the marina and we left at 1633. Unfortunately it wasn't long before we got stuck. Just after leaving the marina by the first bend. Took us 20 minutes to get off, between water getting higher and us going back and forth. Lots of boats passed us, creating wakes that helped. Finally got unstuck and headed out again. It was very shallow; *ESCAPADE* bounced along the channel all the way out going aground several times. There was much more water when we came in. However, at last the depth read 3 m, which gave us peace of mind, and then we were out! The water suddenly changed color from brown to blue indicating deeper water. Decided to go to Ko Rang Yai based on Danny's (Sea Glass) recommendation. It was a lot closer than Koh Phanak meaning no dark entry. Plus he said there was a restaurant ashore. Took us an hour to get from the marina to the beginning of the channel and another hour to get to the anchorage. Were anchored at 1808. The island is very pretty. A lovely white sand beach is on the west side. After anchoring, J,M,P,& H went ashore. E not feeling well so he stayed on boat. Turned out there was some shindig at the restaurant. One couple told us there was a convention so we walked around. Hundreds of people. The Oriflame Diamond Directors were having a party and the restaurant was closed because of it. However, the bartender was kind enough to say we could have take-away, which we did. Had drinks while waiting. Called E via VHF but battery went dead so he didn't hear the entire message. Brought food back to boat and ate. It was excellent. E didn't eat much; still not feeling well. E&H went to bed early. Nice breeze but wave slap. Wind was from S when first anchored but switched to N by the time shore patrol returned.

Friday, January 25 - Ko Rang Yai to Koh Phanak 14.4 NM

Had good sleep even w/o a/c. Slept till 0700. Lovely, sunny day. E feeling better; H still has runs. Started up water maker, purged the system and made 18 gallons. Left at 0930. Motored north into the light wind and anchored at 1202. The tour boats were just pulling out so we had lunch in the bay by ourselves. Later, J,M,P went to see the caves and were gone a long time. H & E went by themselves later. The first Hong was interesting in that you had to paddle under a low hanging rock arch which was covered with shells into a small round pond with sheer rock walls going up nearly 200 feet. It was very dramatic and had great echoes. After paddling out, and the tide was

rising, so you could get trapped in there. We motored north. The outside wall of the island has overhangs with jagged pieces hanging down from the ceiling. Impressive! Such erosion. Then we took some pictures of *ESCAPADE* against the sheer rock wall background. Entered the cave by paddling and it soon became very dark. Even our good flashlight did not seem to light anything. Went in a ways, but something was jumping in the water and the tide flow inward was quite strong. H got concerned so we decided to leave. Took all our effort to go against the inbound flow. Had dinner onboard of steak. E even had some and began to feel better. Went to bed at 2200. Set the intruder alarm for the first time. Had horrible wave slap keeping H awake. She thought she heard someone on boat several times and got up, setting off the alarm herself. Once she thought we were aground and turned on the instruments but there was plenty of water. It was so still to have such loud wave slap.

Escapade anchored at Koh Phanak. Thailand

PHOTO BY ERICK REICKERT

Saturday, January 26 - Koh Phanak to Koh Daeng Yai to Koh Pan Yai 5.9 + 7.7 NM

Got up at 0630 and read some before starting the jenny at 0730. Another pretty day but with wind from the N. Left at 0830 near high tide to have plenty of water to go over shallow bit. Got down to 4.7 m, but there was no problem. H had first solid BM--yea, the ordeal is over! As we were anchoring at 0905 near Koh Hong, a couple came alongside with their long boat. We bought some shrimp for 400 Baht, cheaper than at the supermarket. H was skeptical but they were OK. E,H,M,& J went in the dinghy to see the Hong. It was very open and pretty, but not so unique, possibly because it was high tide. Returned to *ESCAPADE* and departed once more at 0940. There are so many dramatic islands around it is hard to tell them apart. Had to negotiate around a submerged rock. Never saw it or hit it so we were OK. Anchored in a fairly protected area just to the west of James Bond Island. But it turned out that there are many longtail boats passing by. So it is not too quiet. J,M& P went to JBI to check it out. Turned out to be very touristy and busy. Had lunch on board. All rested in the heat of the day. At 1500 E & H went to JBI. H stayed in the dinghy. E walked to the bay (used J's ticket; was 200 Baht). Still some tourists but much quieter. Returned to *ESCAPADE* and decided that we should go on to the stilt village as there was not much more to do here and probably not at the village. Calculated that there should be enough water by 1700 and we should be able to get there before dark. So we departed at 1657 and slowly went through the shallow bits (getting down to 3.6 meters). After crossing them, the run north to the village was quite easy. Anchored at 1817. All but M (her feet bothering her) immediately went to the village. All the major restaurants are set up only for lunch for the tourists. So it was deserted in that part of the village. Walked around the store and home section and most locals were surprised to see foreigners there at that time. The call to prayer began just as we passed the Mosque (it is a Muslim village). It was dark and not very nice. There was even a school with cement volleyball court. If they need more space, they just build out over more water. Returned to *ESCAPADE* to have dinner of the shrimp that we purchased that morning. They were very tender and delicious.

Sunday, January 27 - Koh Pan Yai to Koh Pak Bia to Ao Nang Bay 32.4 NM

Woke to a bright sunny day. The village looked much better in the sunlight; took some pictures but didn't go ashore (wish we could have seen it during the day with all the hubbub). The water is very muddy so didn't make any water. Left at 0832 so we could catch the high tide at the place we had to cross the low spot. Made it fine. The wind seemed enough to sail so we pulled out the yankee and then the main. Looked good. But, of course, then the wind died and we had to motor again. Arrived at Koh Pak Bia and anchored at 1150, perfect for lunch. We were directly behind the "mushroom" rock. Had tuna sandwiches. Rested a bit then went to the little beach and crossed over and had to walk a great distance out over a very rough water area (it was low tide) before we could start swimming. There were a lot of sea urchins around. The snorkeling was fair to good. The water was slightly murky, the coral had some variation and there were some fishes. Overall, a 7 out of 10. We left at 1503 and motored to Ao Nang Bay. The wind really increased from the east, sometimes reaching 16 kts. We were towing the dinghy, but it was OK. Anchored at 1720. M,J& P went on a scouting party and found a restaurant. Went in for 1900 and J&M bought. Walked after dinner along the tourist strip. People were from all over, but not many from the US. Had a drink at a bar and returned to *ESCAPADE*. The evening cooled off nicely.

Monday, January 28 - Ao Nang Bay to Koh Dam Khwan to Phi Phi Don 20.6 NM

Woke and started the water maker. H did a load of laundry. P & J went into town. Left at 1008 and motored to the near-by Koh Dam Khwan. The winds were gusting to 24 kts on the beam. Did not anchor where the book said, but behind the north island to get some shelter from the wind at 1047. Also, we were very near a snorkel spot that turned out to be OK. After snorkeling and then lunch of BLT's, we departed at 1300. The wind was still from the east so we were able to sail all the way to Phi Phi Don. It started at 18 kts but diminished to 11 kts. Good sail though. Anchored very closed to the spot we used last October. This time we got off the boat! Went in soon after arrival and had to use a beach landing spot at nearly low tide. Pulled the dinghy quite far up the beach. Strolled all the way through town and then decided to have dinner (about 1730) rather than go back to the boat. Chose a nice looking beachfront restaurant. The food was so-so and the drinks expensive. At about 1845 E was getting worried about the dinghy and the rising tide as he expected to be going back by then. Also, it was getting dark and he expected to be back before dark (had no flashlight and did not turn on the anchor light). E left the table after P & J decided they wanted desert. When E got to the dinghy it was OK, but the surges were increasing by the minute. Tried to turn the dinghy into the waves, but couldn't, especially after water started coming into the dinghy. So the dinghy was swamped with water up to the seat level, submerging the fuel tank. E felt so helpless, he could not do anything to prevent it and he did not have a curly cue so he couldn't start the engine to pull the dinghy off the shore. Sill no one in sight so he ran back to the restaurant to get aid. They had just left and were walking slowly back to the dinghy. With P & J helping, finally was able to push the sunken dinghy into the water with the bung removed and Paul was able to motor around a bit to drain some of the water. We all then got in and made it back to ESCAPADE quite wet. Paul bailed most of the remaining water and we were able to haul it up on the davits to drain the rest of the water. Now worried about water entering the fuel tank thru the vent relief tube. Will drain it tomorrow. Turned on the water maker and took a shower. Decided we should proceed to Ao Chalong tomorrow.

Tuesday, January 29 - Phi Phi Don to Ao Chalong, Phuket 29.8 NM

The wind died and the seas calmed down over the night. Did not drag anchor at all and were in the exact same position in the morning. Turned water maker on again and nearly got it topped up. Left at 0907. Motored to Phi Phi Le to go into Maya Bay. Several boats anchored there which we went around. Then it was directly back to Phuket, in Ao Chalong Bay. Anchored at 1345 in 4.2 meters of water, at about half tide. The tide is nearing springs and the range today is 2.1 m. The low will be 1.0 m at 1700, but will be 0.7 m tomorrow morning. Figured we had enough water for tonight, but might be touching the bottom tomorrow. So we re-anchored at 1420 from 3.7 m to 4.2 m. Hope that the additional 0.5 m will be sufficient. The crew seems to be very lazy because we have extra time here. M is writing post cards. The bay is very large, but it is quite shallow with a light turquoise color. They have built a new concrete pier and seem to have a fuel dock on one side. The pier is VERY long. We took the shuttle bus to the land. Went in around 1500 to look around. First had a drink at Jimmy's Lighthouse Bar and then went by another bar that now seems to be the cruiser's hangout. They also do laundry and have Internet. Met Americans from the east coast who are still planning on going up the Red Sea. They are late because they had to rebuild their engine in Port Dickson. Went on to the main street and found an ATM. Then bought some more Frosties in bigger boxes. Got a new snorkel tube and then got on the Internet- all within a few blocks of the pier! Returned to Jimmy's and had dinner. The people at the next table were off the Sunsail boat next to us. They were from Austria and recognized Erick as they had read the article in the Oyster News. The wind had kicked up to 15 to 20 kts so the seas in the bay were quite large with short wave peaks. We all got in the dinghy and proceeded to get quite wet on the way back to the boat. Just as we arrived, a man from the Halberg Rassy came by to inquire about two boats to our port side that seemed to be close to touching. In fact the people for the front boat arrived at that very moment and they proceeded to move their boat away. The man knew of us and that we were going to meet up with Hygeia. He is also going up the Red Sea. Small cruising world when everyone knows everyone. Stowed the dinghy on the side. Played Uno before going to bed. E was given a series of bad cards and got in a bad mood--very un-sportsman-like.

Wednesday, January 30 - Ao Chalong, Phuket

Quite windy overnight with lots of wave splash. H slept in the saloon. It was a clear sunny day, but still windy. Got on Rowdy's net at 0700 and they said there was a disturbance over the south China Sea and it was windy along the whole west coast, well down into Malaysia. P took H, J, & M in to take the laundry in and do the last minute provisioning. He returned to ESCAPADE and we emptied the gasoline from the outboard tank, which had been underwater, into the new jerry cans and swished them out. We then went in to the fuel dock and got 110 L of diesel in the 6 jerry cans plus filled up our gasoline tanks. Returned to the boat and poured all the diesel into the tank. It is now completely full. Opened all the ports and cleaned, then Vaselined them. J called from shore and we went in to the steps and picked up the groceries and returned them to ESCAPADE. We then went to shore and all of us ate at the cruisers hangout, the Chalong Sunrise. E & I then bought some engine oil and disposed of the bad gasoline. Found a pair of thongs for E on the way back to the pier. Met M and we returned to *ESCAPADE*, leaving P & J at two Internet places. We should be able to leave tomorrow, one day ahead of schedule. Went in for drinks at Jimmy's Lighthouse and met Richard and Martha from Transit there. They are staying for one more year and their boat is at Boat Lagoon. Had dinner at Chalong Sunrise. Returned to *ESCAPADE* with all getting doused as the wind and waves have not diminished.

Thursday, January 31 - Ao Chalong, Phuket, Thailand to Sri Lanka 1095.0 NM

A bright, sunny, but very windy day. Weather forecast from Rowdy is 16 to 21 from the east to the Nicobars. Sounds good. Had a lazy time waiting for 1000 to start to do our last minute chores. H stayed on the boat. The bay was very choppy but the ride in is fairly dry. I went to the closest Internet place but it was closed so went up to the main road and the place there. The report from Commanders Weather was waiting. In short it said: Favorable conditions over to Sri Lanka!!! Plenty of breeze the next several days!!! So we are off. Went back to the port office. It took nearly an hour and half, but it was painless and easy. Immigrations, Customs, and Harbour Master were all in the one building, within 20 feet of each other. Cost 500 Baht but by 1150 we were cleared out. Called Jack, and they had just received the laundry and were re-packing it. They came to the root of the pier and we walked out. The dinghy ride back to *ESCAPADE* was very wet. Had lunch and got ready to depart. Pulled up the anchor at 1304 and motored south out of the bay on high tide. Started heading west again. The wind was from the SE to East so we went wing-on-wing. After 1600 the wind moved south and dropped to 10 kts so we were in a beam reach. Before we left VHF range a boat, Lasqueti, called. Tavi said they were departing tomorrow as he had a problem with his engine header tank. They are going in company with Jenny. We agreed to keep in contact on 4024.0 at 0730 each morning. They are going to Cochin, India, but we should be in touch all the way across. Saw some dolphins. During Paul's watch, the autopilot went crazy and twice jibed *ESCAPADE* and only the preventer prevented disaster. Found that the flux gate compass was 30 degrees off. P hand steered while I turned off the system and then back on. Seemed to correct the issue, but we switched to steering a course (not track).

Friday, February 1 - At Sea in the Andaman Sea (1095.0 NM)

A bright, sunny day with winds of about 15 kts from the east. Been making quite good time, but the wind has generally been directly astern. Started yesterday on a port tack, with the wind even on the beam, but it moved aft and then north until we had to jibe last night. Now on starboard tack but have to go about 6 degrees north of track so by noon we were at 6 miles cross track error. During the night E had to dismantle the generator, as it would not start but it was probably the DC control circuit shutting down because of heat in the generator compartment. Will run the fan next time. A later start went OK. At dawn three fishing trawlers approached from the port bow, crossing our path. Obviously, we had limited ability to change course. We went in front of the nearest boat, and behind the farthest. The issue was with the middle one, which had to alter course. Quickly they were gone. This all occurred during the morning chat on Rowdy's Net. I got our position in and heard a little of the weather but did not hear it all. At 0730 I called Lasqueti but got Perdika in response. They will be leaving today as well. Jibed around 1900 to head for the waypoint as the wind never went to the NE. Heard from Kiko and they will be in Galle until 7 February. Maybe we will see him there. There are strange areas of water turbulence which you can hear before you see them. Not a problem, but the water is very deep so don't know what is causing it. The bilge pump did not pump water so I replaced the impeller. Tested it and discovered it was leaking from behind. Took it apart and replaced the shaft seal. All seems to work now. The autopilot steering rams were making louder than normal noise along with some clicking sounds. Emptied the lazarette and checked them. The port side one, which is original, shows some signs of stiffness. As it is under the dive tank we will replace it in Galle. The starboard one is the loud one with the clicks. Both seem to be working OK, even on their own. Don't really want to disconnect either one in case it fails. So we put everything back and hope that it continues to work. Had lunch of those crazy Thai pastries with a sausage in it. At 24 hours we had covered 162.7 NM for an average of 6.78 kts. Dinner was steak. The seas were somewhat confused and the sails were flapping badly. Had trouble starting the generator until I left the side open and took off the two top access openings. I think it was too hot for the over-temperature switch. Filled the water tank. The wind continued to die so finally at 2350 we turned on the engine and pulled in the yankee.

Saturday, February 2 - At Sea in the Andaman Sea and the Bay of Bengal (1095.0 NM)

E had the 2400 to 0300 watch. Nothing happened. The day dawned with lots of clouds, nearly overcast. We were back to track and the wind improved so we shut the engine off at 0750. At first there was a favorable current and we were nearly sailing at 8 kts SOG. But that slowed down. In the middle of the Sombrero Channel we could not see any of the Nicobar Islands. Oh well, they must be there. Nothing new on Rowdy's net, but reported our position. Talked to Tavi on Lasqueti and he said the three boats are proceeding in company. They are 96° 44 East so they are 3 ° behind us- 180 NM. E's watch starts at 0900. The ram sounded worse, maybe we should change it. Had lunch of ham sandwiches. Jack tried a sun shot. At 1400 and we still seem to be in the grips of the channel current. We have had more than 2 kts against us. Speed is slowly increasing as we get to the 1,000 meter line. Going through the channel was interesting as there was a series of wave areas, all well defined where there were standing waves. Had to pass each one in turn, and in between there was relatively smooth water. The sail turned into a very pleasant one with gentle movement. After we broke free our speed increased to sometimes over 8 kts, SOG. Had dinner of pasta and salmon. Went to start the generator at 1930 and it wouldn't turn over. The DC control was not cutting it out so the problem was something else. Tried jumper cables but that didn't help. Started tearing the generator all apart. Kept tracing the circuit and noted that when the starter switch was pressed the voltage dropped to near zero. Finally, after much work and postulating we traced the problem to the positive terminal on the battery, which wasn't making good contact. After cleaning, it worked. That was at 2230. So it took three hours of hard work in hot conditions to sort it out. But the good news is that for once the problem was not the generator. Finally got to bed around midnight and that is before my watch at 0300 tomorrow. Jack forgot to put on lotion and is very red. He must be suffering.

Sunday, February 3 - At Sea in the Bay of Bengal (1095.0 NM)

E had the 0300 to 0600 watch and the generator started right away. At the 0700 Net, it was just turning light so we do need to set the clocks back today. The weather report is still more of the same, and to not drop below 7° north until as late as possible. Talked to Perdika and they were at 94° 53 East, or about 3° 45 behind us (about 225 NM). The winds have been light, down to around 12 kts, and our speed has not been too great- in the 5 to 6 kts range, but the SOG has been around 7 so there is a good favorable current. The day is bright and sunny and still hot. Saw a group of about 30 dolphins. H&M sat on bow and watched them play in the bow wave. Watched the DVD America's Sweethearts. Set our clocks back one hour. At 1204 (72 hours underway) we hit 478.5 NM, or 167.5 NM in the last 24 hours. That is a 6.64 kt average for the whole time or 6.98 for the last 24. Had lunch of hamburgers and leftover pasta salmon. E showered early and H cut his hair on the bow. The wind increased slightly to 16 kts and we hit 9.4 kts SOG! It is confusing on what time Sri Lanka is. The computers and the guidebook say +6 hours to GMT. The pilot book and the world atlas say +5.5 hours. Watched Driven on DVD. E had the 2100 to 2400 watch. H not feeling well.

Monday, February 4 - At Sea in the Bay of Bengal (1095.0 NM)

Tried sail change just before dawn but so did the wind so had to put the yankee back on the starboard pole. E had 0600-0900 watch and ran jenny; started right away. Pretty day with some cloud. E talked with Lasqueti and they are still at 94° 53 E, or about 6° 40 behind us. E spoke to Hygeia on the SSB. Sri Lanka is at +6 hours. Can go stern-to to a pontoon, but no power. H made banana muffins. Another hot day. The autopilot steering rams don't sound so good so we will look at them today. Talked to Kiko by Iridium phone. He gave us some hints about the harbour. Like be careful of the Customs people who come aboard as they steal things. He will be standing by on VHF 72 as we approach. At 1204 (96 hours) we hit 653.4 NM, or 174.9 NM in the last 24 hours. That is a 6.81 kts average overall, and 7.29 kts for the last 24. Lunch was egg salad sandwiches. Went to change the ram but upon listening again, it was clear that both rams were clunking when the direction changes, and the movement was a series of jerks in one direction. Further, the area above the autopilot computer was what Heather commented on as being very hot. So we changed the autopilot computer for a new one and it seems to have eliminated the clunks. The motor sound is, if anything, louder, but the action seems to be better. We will run this way for a while and see if it is better. Dinner was beef stroganoff. E had the 2400 to 0300 watch.

Tuesday, February 5 - At Sea in the Bay of Bengal (1095.0 NM)

Another bright, sunny day which promises to be hot. The autopilot is running well, but it is very NOISY. Don't know why changing the autopilot computer has so much effect on the sound level. H made bread. The only issue now is our time of arrival. At 0830, we were about 270 NM from the waypoint, and another 30 to Galle. The 300 NM will take 40.5 hours at the current rate of 7.4 kts. That would put us in at 0100 on February 7. Thus we may have to putter around until 0800 until we can get in. We will just keep sailing till we get closer before we attempt to reduce speed. At 1005 we had to jibe as the wind had moved to the east. By noon it was swinging back to the ENE. At 1204 (120 hours) we hit 828.3 NM, or 174.9 NM in the last 24 hours, the same as yesterday. That is a 6.90 kts average overall, and 7.29 kts for the last 24. H baked some bread rolls for use with leftovers. Talked to Dick Hinsley by Iridium phone and found out he will not arrive till noon on the 28th. By late afternoon we concluded that we could not make landfall before dark on Wednesday, as we had 220 NM to go. The only alternative is to slow down so that we arrive at daybreak on Thursday. So we rolled up the main at 1615 and then at 2400 furled some of the yankee so as to keep our SOG down to around 6 kts. Had dinner of tacos. The winds increased in the night to 24 kts and the ride was quite rolly.

Wednesday, February 6 - At Sea in the Bay of Bengal (1095.0 NM)

It was a clear starry night, somewhat chilly with the wind in your face. The day dawned bright with a few clouds forming. Talked on the SSB and it seems that all the boats behind us are complaining of no wind. A recent departure had hardly any wind prior to the Sombrero channel. Lasqueti and Perdika also have little wind and she said if they saw 6 kts they were happy. They are 6 to 7 degrees behind us (360 to 420 NM). Talked with Hygeia, but Kiko was very hard to understand. He knows of our arrival tomorrow. Probably can't get in the inner harbour before 0800, but the Navy will at least see us approach. Rolling was severe last night and today. H didn't sleep well. Finally E took pole down and put sails on same side. Helped a lot. Cut rolling dramatically. All were getting fed up with the constant roll so this was much better. Had sandwiches of peanut butter and c/o egg salad. The day was much cooler than the prior several, partly due to a bit more wind across the deck. Shifted the sails to a normal configuration but both reefed to keep the speed down. Tried to call Windsor, the yacht agent, on Iridium but the mobile and office numbers did not ring. Another number did ring and I left a message, presumably at home. Also tried sending an E-mail via the Inmarsat-C. Dinner was salmon special (from the cover of the cookbook). Margaret was first to see land. Three large ships came charging at us, one going astern and the others across our bows. They were all heading NE. Still trying to get to the waypoint at 0200, so that the 30 NM beyond will take 5 hours and get us there at 0700. Still adjusting sails to achieve that objective. We were warned to hide all things from sight when the Navy and Customs come aboard. Also got out cash to pay Windsor. Everybody seems happy with Sri Lanka except for the detonations in the harbour all night long.

Thursday, February 7 - approaching Galle, Sri Lanka (1095.0 NM)

The night was really pleasant, calm seas and good wind. Sailed beautifully until about 8 NM from the waypoint into Galle harbor when the wind died. P had been running the generator but then the engine went on. H decided to get up and do the laundry. Running the engine also gave a good charge to the batteries before getting tied up. Lots of fishing boats out near the shore. One row along the shore and another further out. Seems we are going right down the middle. All very well lit. Can see the glow from Galle lights in the distance. Even after going very slow we arrived at the harbour entrance at 0730. Puttered for a bit, then anchored, as there is a floating barrier across the harbour mouth. Ran the water maker to top off the tank. The total passage took 163.43 hours, covered a distance of 1095 NM (1099.3 on the GPS). That is an average of 6.70 kts, but we were trying to go slow for 36 hours. Could have done it 8 to 10 hours quicker. Waited until nearly 0845 until the Navy guys came out to do an inspection. We were then permitted into the harbour where we tied up along side Hygia. Yang Shou and Mazy were also here. Went stern-to to a floating plastic pontoon by 0910. It is not connected to the shore so we still have to use the dinghy. Probably better as we then go to the corner of the harbour with the dinghy, which is closer to the gate, and it is probably more secure. Waited for Customs to visit. Got through both inspections OK with only a pack of cigarettes for each of the four guys. But they wanted whole bottles of booze, or wine, or other substantial gifts, which we politely refused. In the middle of all this the pressure relief valve on the water system let go. Erick went in to finish the clearing in process, which started at Don Windsor& Co. The total cost was $170, but they were not very pleasant or value added. We had a little get together on Hygia. As they were leaving at 1500, this was the only time. H was fully briefed by Myles and Kiko also briefed us on their trips, which were good experiences. Decided we would use Marlin for the sightseeing and trip. He organized an A/C van and we first went to the bank to change money and then to the Ramparts Hotel for lunch. Quite good, and a absolutely beautiful view. Marlin then took us on a tour of the town, pointing out all the places we might want and some places where not to go. Also stopped at a "factory" for lace, batik, jewels, etc. H bought some gifts. We were all very tired from the previous night, so we returned to *ESCAPADE*. E & J worked on the water system and after taking apart the pressure relief valve, determined that the problem is probably the pressure switch on the pump as the pressures seems to be too great. Decided to work on it tomorrow. Had dinner on board of shrimp added to the rice from lunch. Went to bed by 2100 and the explosions were not as bad as we thought. They are sharp cracks, like a hammer blow rather than a boom. But they are very random and vary in intensity and character. A few mosquitos around, but the electronic mosquito repeller seemed to work.

Friday, February 8 - Galle, Sri Lanka

Had a good sleep, in spite of the explosions. Everyone feels much better. Had a lazy morning. J & M headed into town. E & P worked on the water system. Turned out to be the micro switch in the water pump pressure switch. It is the one I installed only two weeks ago! Replaced it with the other spare I bought in Boat Lagoon and all is back to normal. The pressure relief valve is holding fine, and we removed the clamp from the overflow hose. Need to get some more micro switches. But also found that the main water filter and two shower filters were clogged so I cleaned those. We went over to the fisherman's dock with our jerry cans and the dinghy and bought 130 L of diesel. Came back and filled our tank. Up to the brim. About then J&M returned and we had lunch of sandwiches on board. Went to the Internet cafe at Unawatuna and stayed and had dinner at the resort hotel.

Saturday, February 9 - Galle to Ella, Sri Lanka

Started our tour with Wijaya Sevena and his van. Left the port at 0720 after retrieving Margaret's purse that she left on board. Jack took a bicycle back to the boat but Paul noticed the bag and brought it to us. It took a while for Jack to return. Set off east and came upon the stick fisherman at Koggala. They perch on sticks stuck in the ground where the water is shallow and hook fish. Looks uncomfortable. Popular surfing beach there as well. A house stands on a small island owned by an Englishman. Passed a lace center. Matara is a large city w/ busy traffic. The Star Fort built by the Dutch is part of the old town. Visited the Buddhist temple of Weherahena where a guide explained about it, and why it was underground. Passed through the small town of Dickwella that had a large, yellow modern building. Stopped in Tangalle at The Chalet Restaurant for a break, which looked out over a beautiful bay. Outside of Hambantota, we passed salt flats that are covered with pink chemicals to protect the salt. Near Bundala fresh buffalo curd is made. Started heading north into jungle territory and had lunch at Flamingo Bundala Sanctuary Safari Hotel near Werawala. Proceeded to climb up into the mountains until we reached Ella. Stopped first at Rawana Falls, which is quite spectacular and attracted a lot of people. Chose the Ravana Heights home, which is run by a man and his wife. Was OK, but probably paid too much and they do not look after the drivers so well. Tried to reserve seats on the train for tomorrow morning but could not do so. They said to get there at 0930 for the 1007 train. Had candlelit curry dinner at the home, in the dark due to the power outage. The chocolate ice cream w/ bananas for dessert was the best part (we all were in heaven, especially E). Went to bed early as not much to do in the dark.

Sunday, February 10 - Ella to Kandy, Sri Lanka

Had breakfast of fruit and eggs w/toast then a leisurely morning. It was raining at first. Got to train station at 0930 but they still did not know if there were seats on the first class observation car. In the event, we had to wait until the train arrived and then found they had space so E paid for the tickets and jumped on the train, which then pulled out. The seats faced backwards. We sat in the back, without a good view and the conductor came and said, sorry the seats we were in were taken; we would have to move. He then kicked some people out of one of the front row of seats and sent us there! Great, couldn't be better. The train ride was very good. Saw a different view than from the roads. Gorgeous scenery, with tea plantations. Many villagers use the tracks as a path so as the train passed they came back on the tracks. The speed was very slow, often no more than 15 mph. Started raining and that gave another view. Arrived at a station and Wiji was waiting for us. Went to Nuwara Eliya that looked like a displaced England. It was where the English came to get away from the heat of the coasts. It is about a mile high. Had lunch at the Grand Hotel pastry shop and then toured the hotel. Truly grand. Drove towards Kandy. As we declined we were in the tea growing area. Stopped at Labooklie and had a factory tour and tea tasting. Continued down through more tea plantations to Kandy. Selected a hotel that thru Wiji we would only pay 2100 Rupees (about $23), including breakfast. Left quickly and tried to catch the cultural show, but arrived with only two dances to go (but didn't cost anything). Saw the fire eating and fire walking, however. Then went to Senani Restaurant, which overlooks the city. Returned to the Riverdale Hotel expecting a good shower, but there was no hot water; a man came up and said they would turn on the switch. After 45 minutes it was warm enough for E to take a shower. H had a hot one in the morning.

Monday, February 11 - Kandy to Sigiriya, Sri Lanka

Left the hotel at 0800 and went to look over the city and then walked along side the lake. Went to the Temple of the Tooth and watched the ceremony blessing the food. Then we visited the National Museum after buying our Cultural Triangle tickets (for a discount) at an out of the way place in the back of a garage. Had lunch in the van after picking up stuff from a roadside bakery. Went to a "spice farm", which had a display of various spice plants and then a sales pitch for us to purchase various mixtures for various ailments. They wanted to give us a massage, but, after an hour and a half, we had had enough. H succumbed and purchased a bunch. Stopped at the rock temple at Dambulla, which required a climb up a hill. The caves, which have outside walls added, are over 2,000 years old. They contained many Buddha images and painted walls and ceilings. The night's accommodation was a remote lodge, Phlefrhara, near Sigiriya. No hot water, and the mosquitos were fierce. Had dinner there.

Tuesday, February 12 - Sigiriya to Anuradhapura, Sri Lanka

Got up early and tried to have breakfast at 0630 but they were not ready yet. Left by 0730 and went directly to the Sigiriya site. This turned out to be the highlight of our visit to Sri Lanka. First you walk through a vast area of pools and fountains (some still work in a fashion), then you begin climbing up stone and brick steps at the west face of the huge massive rock, some 1,000 feet high. After quite a distance you come to a horizontal gallery with the "mirror" wall, constructed about 1,500 years ago. So called because it had a polished inner surface. From there you climb a spiral staircase to the ledge which had half nude damsels painted on the walls and ceiling. Back down the spiral staircase, and out further over a platform projecting out from the stonewall. Then up some more stairs to a terrace. Thru the legs of a lion, then up a vertical steel staircase and then up a sloping staircase affixed to the stonewall before reaching the top area. It was actually quite large, with a reservoir and swimming pool. The royal palace was at the very top. Radioed down to M who saw us waving. Returned most of the way back down but then deviated to the car park. It was the right time to climb as the sun was not too hot and we avoided the crowds that slow things at the congestion points. There were only two couples before us! The site rivals Matchu Pichu and other ancient sites for being spectacular. Proceeded on to the Polonnaruwa area. Visited the museum first, which was great as it put everything into perspective. It also showed what the buildings would have looked like when new, with their roofs etc. Had lunch at the Suru Hotel, which overlooks one of the "tanks" or large reservoirs. Visited around five different buildings in the area.

Quite good, and it reminded us of Cambodia. Proceeded to Anuradhapura where we visited four guesthouses before selecting the Shalini Rest Home at 1,850 Rupees. Had hot water, but no generator. Very basic. Went to the Grand Rest house for dinner, where we had a set menu of local food. Good, however, but we would have preferred to order from menu and know what the price was. Went back to the Shalini, which was still in the dark, but the place next door had a noisy generator running. Luckily the power came back on and the generator stopped and we went to sleep in quiet.

Wednesday, February 13 - Anurahapura to Galle, Sri Lanka

Had breakfast at 0630 so we could get an early start to the day. Picked up a guide and proceeded to the site area, which is not as well defined as the prior areas we visited. First went to two Buddha temples, which are functioning. Probably significant for Buddhists, but they were not what we expected for an ancient site. Then we looked at a couple of building ruins. For having been the capital for 1,000 years, there is not much left. We were disappointed compared to the other sites. Dropped off the guide and headed south. Arrived at the Elephant Orphanage just after 1300, in time for the feeding at 1315. It was not much, just three baby elephants tied up inside a shed and being feed milk in large bottles. One had 3 bottles in succession then cried when one of the other babies got his. Looked at the herd on the hilltop and then proceeded to a restaurant that overlooks the river in which the elephants bathe and cool off. We ordered our lunch and waited for the elephants. They walk down the street where there are stalls leaving "deposits" in their wake. They put on a good show. One bull was getting frisky with a female, but she was being coy. Then we left for the long drive back to Galle. Took an inland route of lessor roads before reaching the coast road south of Colombo. Stopped for dinner at a place only a few km north of Galle. Then we reached the harbour by around 2100. P was in bed and had turned off the VHF so Jack walked around and hailed him. P came to get us. It was a great trip and we saw a lot of Sri Lanka, but it was tiring.

Thursday, February 14 - Galle, Sri Lanka

Valentines day! Clear sky, that promises to be hot. Organized the laundry. Decided to buy a new generator start battery as it was using a lot of water; so I measured the box. Everybody went into town. J & M set off by themselves. We went to Mikes and ordered a bunch of groceries. Then bought a battery that will just fit. Had it charged. Got more cash at the bank. Saw the museum. Posted cards. Looked at another grocery store. Went to an Internet place and then to lunch at Lady Hill, which turned out to be quite good. It overlooked the coast and seemed so far from the city. Returned to the boat. J&M had arrived earlier and Jack rowed out to *ESCAPADE* and then rowed back to meet Paul. When we got to the boat, Ocean Jaywalker, an Oyster 435, and Windsong had arrived at our pontoon. They were awaiting customs. We installed the battery and lazed around in the heat. P,J&M went in to go to the beach and then to The Villa. E picked up the passports so we are now cleared out of Sri Lanka, with the exception of an inspection by the Navy before departure (to confirm the people on board). We waited around before going to dinner. When we were ready to shower, we tried starting the generator. It wouldn't start, even with jumper cables to the house battery. Just wouldn't turn over fast enough. Discovered that it was low on oil (Paul had just checked) and maybe the friction was too great. Added oil, which seemed to help, but did not fix the problem. Finally had to give up on it and we headed to shore. Decided to go to the Lighthouse Hotel for our Valentines dinner. It is the best hotel in town. Took a tuk-tuk across town and found a great restaurant on the second floor. No one was there, but they were open and air-conditioned. Had a great meal, and it was a lovely setting. Near 2100 it started lightening outside. Then by 2120 it started to rain, and it was torrential rain. We had left some of the side ports open on *ESCAPADE* so we feared the worst. Tried calling J, but no response. H had a great pavlova desert, but we asked for the bill as soon as she got it. Left the hotel at 2130 and it was still raining very hard. The tuk-tuk had to lower the side curtains to protect us. Started back east. When we got to the city center it was raining less, but the ground was very wet. By the time we got to the turn for the port, it was not raining. When we got out, there was no rain and the ground was dry! We couldn't believe it. Called *ESCAPADE* several times, but no answer. Finally Jack answered as they had just arrived, and *ESCAPADE* was not wet. What a relief. After getting on board we talked about the generator problem and then decided to tackle it in the morning. We ran the engine and inverter to run the refrigeration. Also gave the new generator battery a little charge with the separate charger.

Friday, February 15 - Galle, Sri Lanka to Male, Maldives 419.0 NM

Erick got up early to work on the generator. Paul, who is usually a late sleeper, also got up. The basic problem seemed to be that the new battery was not fully charged, and possibly the connection Paul had worked on a few days ago was suspect. I first cleaned the terminals to the new battery so we had good metal-to-metal contact. Also took completely apart the connection Paul had worked on and made bare metal. Then tried to start, far better than before, but the new battery was too low in charge (had 12.28 volts). Then jumped from the engine battery directly to the starter motor on the generator and it started immediately. Great joy! The battery was charging at over 13 volts immediately and then soon reached 14.2 volts. So maybe it will hold the charge better than the old battery. P,J& M went in to Mikes for internet and fruit and veg shopping. We went in about an hour later to Mikes. The stuff was already loaded on a tuk-tuk. Got on-line and received the weather forecast, which said we would have NE winds all the way. Possibly some thunder showers around. Looks good to go! Paid in a combination of rupees and credit card. Took stuff to the boat including the frozen food. J & M had returned as well. After putting things away, we all went in for lunch at Closenberg Hotel, as it was close. Turned out to be the worst meal we had in Sri Lanka, and it took over and hour to get it. We went back to get Marlin but he was in town so we went to his house and picked up the laundry and left his wife with payment for the laundry, our remaining rupees and some dollars. Returned to the boat and the Navy were there. They completed the inspection quickly and then we were able to leave. Pulled out smartly and departed at 1510. The winds were from the SSE, Force 3, and quite good so we could sail after we cleared the outer harbour entrance. However, by 1815 we had to turn on the engine as the wind turned against us from the SSW. This lasted until 0330 in the morning. Had some large swells coming at us from at least two directions so the motion was sort of corkscrew. Not too comfortable. No moon, very dark. Lots of ships heading both directions.Relatively few fishing boats. But we were underway, and away from those nightly depth charges.

Saturday, February 16 - Galle, Sri Lanka to Male, Maldives (419.0 NM)

A good day, with some hazy sky. Cleared up a bit after noon. Tried the SSB and could barely talk to African Queen, who was still in Phuket. He talked to Hygeia, but I couldn't hear Hygeia. The winds had shifted to the north at 16 to 21 kts and we were rocketing along always above 8 kts and frequently in the 9 kts range. At this rate we could make Male before dark on Sunday. At 1510, or 24 hours, we did 179.2 NM, or an average of 7.47 kts. The generator started straight away and we made 54 gallons of water. Later the winds dropped, as well as the swells. It was a comfortable night, but speeds had dropped to the 6.5 to 7 kts range. This means we will arrive in the middle of the night. Lunch was toasted cheese sandwiches. Had dinner of fish that M had bought for the second night.

Sunday, February 17 - Galle, Sri Lanka to Male, Maldives (419.0 NM)

E had the 0300 to 0600 watch. Haven't seen any other ships in 18 hours. Finally filled the water tank. Made 120 gallons all told. Going well, in the 7 kts range. A clear sky day so it will probably be hot. Not as much splashing so we will be able to keep some windows open. Heard Hygeia but could not communicate. He sent e-mail to use Iridium on the hour. Trouble was, the signal is not sufficient to stay locked in so we did not talk. Talked later when I plugged the antenna in better. He is leaving the Maldives on 20 February for Oman. He will E-mail me the code for use on positions. I think we can find the anchorage at night so we will not try to adjust speed. Set the clocks back one hour at noon, to +5 hours to GMT. Now on Maldives time, so sunrise and sunset are at about 0600 and 1800. Lunch was of tuna sandwiches. At 1410, or 48 hours after departure we had done 345.4 NM, or an average of 7.20 kts. For the last 24 hours we did 166.2 NM for an average of 6.93 kts, down from the first 24. Called the agent, AMSCO, and he said arriving after dark was OK; just call the Coast Guard upon approach. We will get cleared-in in the morning. Don't know about the security check. Had dinner of oriental stir-fried beef. At 1845 turned on the engine as our speed was declining and I needed to either start the engine or the generator. We are back to arriving at the waypoint between 0000 and 0030.

Monday, February 18 - Galle, Sri Lanka to Male, Maldives (419.0 NM)

Had Male in sight at 2150, at least there was a glow and a rotating beacon visible after the moon disappeared. The GPS positions turned out to very accurate despite warnings on the chart. E had the 2100 to 2400 watch, which was the approach. The lights at the airport were the first ones really visible. It took awhile for the town of Male to become visible behind the airport. Came in right on track. Contacted the Coast Guard and reported our arrival; no problems. Had to go north on the west side of Male to find an anchorage. Turned out there were a lot of boats- fishing, local tourist, and some cruising yachts. Approached slowly as all were lit or unlit strangely. The strangest one was a floating dry-dock with a yellow submarine inside. Turns out they were anchored over the shallow spot so we ended up circling them. Finally found a spot at 32 meters, less than most of the surrounding area of 42 meters. Were anchored by 0122. All went to bed. In the morning, we were in the same spot (we saw two local boats dragging later). The agent called on VHF at 0710 and said he was arranging things. Everyone had a nice lazy morning waiting. The Security people (3 of them) were out by 0945. They conducted no inspection but I had to fill out several forms. Now waiting again. Finally, Customs, Immigration, and Health officials came out along with a person from our agent. After filling out several more forms, and using our stamp, we were cleared in. They left at 1315 and we took down the yellow Q flag. Had lunch of nibbles. Then went into town in two shifts to keep drier. The channel is quite rough due to the wind and all the powerboats roaring by. Made it OK. Went to AMSCO, our agent, to discuss details. The most troublesome problem is that the anchorage at the airport has been closed due to construction. This means we will not be able to dinghy to the airport as it is too far away from the anchorage we are in on the west side of Male. We will have to use a water taxi or take the boat from downtown Male. Received our cruising permit. Converted $50 as the banks were closed by that time and they will be closed for nearly a week due to holidays. We took a walk around town, which is small but interesting. They have a big building boom, as contrasted to Sri Lanka. Looked over the supermarket to know what they carry. Had dinner at Twin Peaks, an Italian restaurant. Great pizza. Returned to the boat in the dark. We forgot to turn on the anchor light and to bring a flashlight. Made it OK in one go and didn't get wet or run over. The exciting bit was as we approached *ESCAPADE*, the water suddenly turned light green. It was the submarine doing a night dive. Just about went over it but its surface boat waved us to go around. After we got on *ESCAPADE* they blew their tanks and rose to the surface. Everybody relaxed on board.

Tuesday, February 19 - Male to Laguna Beach Resort, Maldives 7.5 NM

The ferryboats started at 0600; sometimes two were racing and they would go on both sides of *ESCAPADE*. Lots of noise and bouncy swells. Went into town a little after 0900, each to do his thing. We confirmed H & M's flights on Emirates Air. Went to AMSCO and found a "pilot book" which are pages from an old Sunsail book when they operated here. At least it is more than we had. Went to the Internet place and sent some last minutes E-mails. All of us were there (and no one else). Returned to the boat and departed. Took a long time to haul the anchor up from 32 meters! Left at 1207 and had lunch of BATs on the way (bacon, avocado, tomato). As we were approaching the Laguna Beach Resort we were hailed on the radio from Flash. We tried to enter the channel, but it looked too shallow so we backed up and decided to go the long way around the reef and up from the south. This was easier and we were able to spot the break in the reef. Anchored at 1335 in 11 meters of water. Such a difference.Shallower, no wind waves and no wakes from the powerboats. Went over to Flash as they were going to leave in an hour. We had met Robert McKown and Ingemar first in Tonga (they were in the race) then in Darwin where Paul helped pull their rudder off, and now here. They have been cruising Maldives for 3 weeks. Got all the low down of the places they visited. Their experience at Ari Atoll was not good, and some other places were not good because of difficult entrances, and/or unfriendly staff toward cruising boats. They had a difficult time at Male as they don't have a windlass. It took them four hours to raise their anchor by using a winch. They also had a slow time from Thailand to the Maldives with little or contrary wind. Paul gave *ESCAPADE* a good wash down and cleaned the hull so she looks good again. H, E & P went in to the resort and reported in. They welcomed us and we made a reservation for dinner. Walked completely around the island on the shaded path. J & M went in later. The resort is a bit of heaven. It is well constructed of cement bungalows in a circle around the whole island. So each has access to the beach in front. There are also over-water units, which don't look as smart. The water is gorgeous, and the white sand beaches are lovely. Went in for dinner and had a BBQ buffet at the Palm Grill restaurant. It was great, with a lot of goodies, but it was the most expensive dinner we have had at $30 US per person. Returned to *ESCAPADE*, and all had an early night, and a good sleep.

Wednesday, February 20 - Laguna Beach Resort, Maldives

A bright sunny day. Lounged around; made water. J, M &P went in to do E-mail. E took a nap. It was late before we realized it was lunchtime. Had lunch of salami sandwiches. H went on the island to relax and swim and J & M went snorkeling on the reef. They were VERY impressed with the number and variety of fishes, but the coral was dead. They returned and M went on the island to join H. E took a second nap for the day, after getting up late! Nearly shook the cold, the first in the tropics. Stopped coughing and the nose has stopped running. We all went in for Chinese dinner. What promised to be a good meal, turned out to be a big frustration. It took nearly two hours to get the main courses, and then they were lukewarm when delivered piecemeal, and Jacks order never came. Returned to *ESCAPADE* disappointed. But had a good nights sleep.

Thursday, February 21 - Laguna Beach Resort to Embudu Village, Maldives 6.6 NM

Another bright sunny day. Did laundry, made water, charged battery, and refrigerated all at once. All went snorkeling (H looked thru the bottom of the dinghy), but the sea was up and quite rough so there we weren't as many fishes as yesterday. Returned to *ESCAPADE* and departed at 1040. Had called Taj Lagoon but they are closed for renovation. Called Embudu Village and made a reservation and confirmed the use of their south buoy. Left by the way we entered. Motored all the way and came in from the south. Good we did so as the buoy is tucked up in-between coral fingers. Picked up the buoy's line at 1200. Had lunch of leftovers from last night. We went in to explore. It is much the same layout as Laguna with rooms around the perimeter, all with sand beaches. The rooms are clustered in groups of four. Most floors are sand; in reception, dining room etc. It is not as upscale but very nice. Seems to have European clientele, somewhat younger. On the other side there is a jetty and at the end there were many fish. So we decided to snorkel from the pier around the island counterclockwise. That way we would drift with the current. Returned with our snorkel gear and E, P, J & M swam to the end of the jetty from the beach. What followed was the most amazing display of tropical reef fish we have ever seen. The reef is dead, although there were some new coral growing. But we encountered a "wall" of fish of all descriptions. They were everywhere, some by themselves and most in small groups of like fish. All sizes and all colors. Stripes, spots, translucent, snouts, big lips, you name it. Drifted west without having to move. The scene was incredible. Absolutely great. The sun was slanting through the water and you could see the reef drop into deep blue. It rose to just under the surface. In some places it was hard to swim over it. The light made it dramatic. I then crossed a shallow area of reef to the sand bar, which was very wide. The reef resumed and fell off into 40 meters of water as I approached *ESCAPADE*. The buoy has a very heavy chain and heavy concrete block at the bottom. No worry about *ESCAPADE* moving! What an experience. It was like being in an aquarium. After showering we had cheese, crackers, & salami. Dark rain clouds in distance giving us a sprinkle. When in for dinner at 1900. Had drinks first on the deck-overlooking *ESCAPADE*. It turned dark and you could only see the anchor light and it's path. It was BBQ night and we ate in the one large dinning area. They were three local singers dressed in cowboy hats and shirts singing calypso songs. There was plenty of food, and Paul really liked it. Not much ambience, however. Cost only $65 for 5. Quite a bargain after expensive Laguna Beach.

Friday, February 22 - Embudu Village to Taj Lagoon, Maldives 1.8 NM

Heavy rain at 0215 woke us to close hatches. Quickly got hot; turned on the fan. Rain didn't last long. E woke early & read. H got up to make bread. At 0930, a local boat came out and wanted to tie up on the buoy so we quickly got ready and left. Had only a mile and a half to go. The Taj resort is being renovated so all ashore is a mess. Have great anchorage. Still can't believe the color of the water, pale aqua to deep blue. H made banana muffins, which were great, hot out of the oven. H & M worked on menu organizing for guys' trip. Bread not quite ready by 1200; first loaf was made into open-faced sandwiches of cheese and ham. P went windsurfing. E played on computer. After lunch, P went windsurfing while M&H continued working on the menus. J tried the windsurfer but got frustrated by it. More power to him for trying. Erick talked to Dick, who had received the Oyster parts and also got his passport details. Then we dinghied to the island to check it out. There was debris everywhere; a frantic beehive of activity even on a Friday. While we were walking down the beach, two men hailed us. We thought they were going to ask us to leave but they wanted to have their picture taken with us -- just like the Japanese! They were very nice; told us the resort would be finished in two months. Some of the newer bungalows were very nice. The lobby had marble floors, as did one of the units we peeked into. They appear to have doubled their capacity by building out more bungalows over the water. It will be very nice when done. H made oriental beef with eggplant and garlic for dinner. Seriously dark clouds in the sky over the island; let out another 10 meters of chain for a good nights sleep.

Saturday, February 23 - Taj Lagoon to Kuda Bados Reserve to Giravaru Resort 12.9 + 7.6 NM

Bright sunny day, and there was no rain overnight! The other two boats were still there when we first got up. The wind is a constant 13-14 kts from the ENE. Could hear African Queen on SSB, but she could not hear us. Evening Star, anchored in Male, acted as relay. Don't know why we didn't reach. But Hygeia still had over 600 NM to go to Oman. Lazed around until 0930. Left at 0945. The wind is up to nearly 20 kts from the NNE but we went out of the South Male Atoll toward the east. The original course took us east of the north Male Atoll until we got to Full Moon resort. But because of the swells, we decided to head into the North Male Atoll just east of Male Island. That reduced the swells considerably. Called Full Moon resort and they said they were full and we could not even anchor there. Then we switched our destination to Kuda Bados Reserve, and uninhabited island used for day outings. The anchorage is close to the reef. Had lunch of sweet potato croquettes and coleslaw. Very good. After lunch, we decided to head to another anchorage because this one left us unconfident. Good decision because we had actually dragged anchor. Looked at Giravaru, which appeared to have a very sheltered lagoon. We called to see if we could come in and they said yes. So we were off. The "pilot book" said there was a new channel to the lagoon but we could not find it. P&J went in dinghy to check out depth. Turned out there was only 5 feet so no go. The island said they would send out a boat. Five guys came out and one came aboard. They led us to the harbor which they said was 3 meters but it got down to 2. Didn't hit bottom, however. J got back on board and worked the anchor. Stern got a little too close to the breakwater and was churning up sand. E very nervous about backing in with the cross wind. Finally got the boat heading right and backed down into the slot nicely. Secured the stern and tightened the chain. All OK! We can stay two nights after all that effort. We can also run a tab. Made reservations for dinner at 2000. The dockage charge is $15 per night but it is worth it. Also we can buy diesel at $0.37 per liter, versus the $0.50 from AMSCO. Took a walk around and although it is a little old, it has all the amenities, including Internet. Pool, tennis, volleyball, ping-pong etc. The lagoon is in back and it looks great. This was the Sunsail base, and my guess is that since they left, they did not put the channel thru to the lagoon. We are sitting nicely. Now to work on our toilet, as the motor stopped working. H & P got their TV fix--there is a TV in the lobby with HBO. While H was watching TV, E fixed the Vacuflush toilet. It required a new pump, but it was a messy, dirty operation. But now it is fixed and working great. Wind seems stronger (30 kts) and is howling into the mast furling opening. Really glad we are in the harbour. Bet the boats at Male are bouncing and dragging anchor. Had drinks at the bar. Found out that the main dining room is closed and there is an outdoor BBQ, but we were shown to a table in the coffee shop, next to the disco. Had a good dinner, ala Carte, and then watched the disco a bit before returning to *ESCAPADE*. H watched the Wedding Planner.

Sunday, February 24 - Giravaru Resort, Maldives

Another bright, sunny day, but still very windy. Winds were up to 35 kts during the day. The seas are quite lumpy and we are glad we are safe and quiet in this harbour. And everyone can step on and off the boat when they want, without getting wet. Organized getting diesel and after a while they took our jerry cans and then brought some of theirs so the first load had 11 cans and the second had 7. All told we got 420 liters and put about 85 in the flexible bladder forward of the mast and 132 in the 6 jerry cans which are set at the rail just forward of the stern seats. The other 203 went in the tank, which was last filled in Sri Lanka. They helped by bringing it on the boat and filling the tank. Took some time and spilled some on the deck but by lunch it was all done. That means we have a total of 1,277 liters on board, for a motoring distance of 1,200 NM. And we did it without the boat bouncing about, like at Chalong in Thailand. Had lunch at the coffee shop of cheeseburgers. E took a short nap. Then he changed the water maker pre-filters, which had become dirty. H cleaned the head. J & M spent some time on the island. H cut Erick's, Paul's and Jack's hair. Great barber! H watched Chicken Run on the TV. We went to the BBQ on the beach for dinner. It was great; the table was only 10 feet from the water, the moon was bright (nearly full), and the water lapped quietly. Took a romantic walk on the beach. Watched a little of the band, but there were not many people there so we went back to *ESCAPADE*.

Monday, February 25 - Giravaru Resort, Maldives

Another bright, clear day. The wind seems to be somewhat diminished. Talked to African Queen and tried talking to Hygia, but Kiko was having a hard time hearing. Having trouble sending E-mail to Commanders Weather via Inmarsat-C. Keep getting "failed" message. Called them on Iridium and confirmed their address is the same. But they also said they had not received one from me. Tried sending Craig a message and it went thru. Sent another one to CW with them also addressed in the body of the message. Still don't know if that worked. Went into reception and asked if we could stay another day and they said yes. Tried to get on to AOL to send the message to CW but after 24 minutes did not even get our password recognized. Bummer! Will have to try from Male tomorrow morning. Everybody lazing around. Had lunch at the coffee shop. J, M, & P did some snorkeling. H packed for her trip to London and we shifted the provisions from the lower bunk in Paul's cabin so John will have a place to sleep while H is still onboard. Also made it up. H then made chocolate chip cookies. Yummy. I received a response from CW on Inmarsat so they did get the message. Don't know what failed. Also got one from Craig; they had a great time at Michaywe. It is going to be sad to see Heather go. Had dinner at the coffee shop and then paid the bill- $715, including $155 for the diesel. Had a walk on the moonlit beach. Went back to *ESCAPADE* and H watched a little video.

Tuesday, February 26 - Giravaru Resort to Male, Maldives 5.5 NM

Another clear, sunshine day. Confirmed the checkout. Left at 0755 and motored toward Male. Called AMSCO to ask if we could get into the NW commercial harbour and he said that it was possible. Just give him a 1.5 hours. So we dropped anchor just to the west of the island at 0917 in 36 m of water. H & E went in to AMSCO to take in the laundry and H & M's passports to clear them off the boat. He thought we had a good chance to get in so H picked up the hard groceries and we returned to *ESCAPADE*. Waited quite awhile, but finally AMSCO called and said it was all arranged, and we could go in, but to call Harbour Control on VHF 10 before entering. We pulled up the anchor at 1142 and then called Harbour Control as we approached. They said wait. After more than 15 minutes we called them again and they said it was OK to enter and to tie up along side the German Swan, Ra. We proceeded in and dropped the Bruce anchor off the stern as I made a big turn and then Paul took the dinghy and took the bowlines ashore. Did it as pretty as could be done. H stayed onboard and E went to AMSCO and picked up H & M's passports. They have been signed off and they have departure cards. E had a quick sandwich at Food Bank and then went to the Internet place. Returned to *ESCAPADE* and the wind seems to be dying. E replaced the starboard davit spring as it broke. J & M returned with bread and they found out how to get a boat to the airport. E & H walked around town, and met everyone at Twin Peaks for dinner at 1930. E, J, & M went to the airport by dhoni and met John, who's plane arrived on time at 2200. Took a dhoni back to Male and walked to *ESCAPADE*.

Wednesday, February 27 - Male, Maldives

Woke to a partially cloudy sky. John was up early. H hung up the laundry and then it rained a little. A French boat, Skopea, came in beside us on the west. They don't seem to be competent, so I hope we do not get any damage from them. Went into town and cashed money at the bank, Gave the passports to AMSCO. Got the weather forecast at the Internet place. The forecast is fairly good, with the only problem being the first couple of days when we will have scattered showers with variable winds. Went to the National Museum where we met J & M. It was a rather shabby display of items from the Maldives past. But they do not have much in terms of physical history. Had lunch at Seagull Cafe House, which had the best ice cream in Male. Went to the smaller supermarket and did some more shopping, including cheeses. Returned to ESCAPADE and it began to rain again. J & M did the vegetable shopping. Paul and I changed the generator oil, oil filter, and Racor filter. Also checked the engine zinc, which is worn, but still usable. Cleaned the raw water filter of the engine side.

Thursday, February 28 - Male, Maldives and depart for Djibouti 1976.0 NM

Got up early and the water taxi came at 0610 and took us to the airport. H & M left on Emirates. J & I could not go past the first checkpoint so we did not get to the check-in counter. So said goodbye to H and kissed at 0630. Returned to Male by dhoni and went directly to the boat. Jack picked up the bread on the way back. After we were on board it rained very heavily. Saw the Emirates plane take off at 0850. Waited until 1000 to go to the Internet place and then was able to pick up the laundry at 1040. All items were there. Stowed all items in plastic bags etc. J & I went to the airport and caught the 1215 dhoni. Had lunch at the airport and then met Dick who was late coming thru immigration as they questioned him well, and even called AMSCO to confirm his story (and what was on the letter I sent him). Returned to Male and I went directly to AMSCO with Dick's passport and they went to ESCAPADE. He sent off our documents and then I paid the bill, which cost $433. The charge for the two nights in the harbour was $60 because they count it as three days at $20. They finally delivered the passports and the Clearance paper at 1620. We got underway immediately and pulled up the anchor at 1625 and pulled the dinghy up the davits inside the harbour. Departed the harbour at 1633 just before the French boat and before a tug pulled the barge at the west end free. Did between 9 and 10 kts heading west with 3 knots of current. John prepared crab cakes for dinner, which we had with the gazpacho that Heather had prepared. A good start to the passage! Turned NW, basically on our long course, and the wind was on our beam at 10 to 12 kts, and we were sailing at around 6.5 kts SOG in a very calm sea. It was very pleasant. The galley sink pump ceased pumping water. After inspecting the pump, which was OK, we blew the pipe clear of some blockage. It then worked fine. We have one atoll (Rasdhoo) and one island (Thoddoo) to clear before we are free of the Maldives. I took the 2100 to 2400 watch so that I would be on watch when we passed. Saw it on radar and then by lights visible on the island. Were able to change course to 301° true for our long leg of 1144 NM. All free and clear! No boats or ships in sight. But this will be the pirate passage. Been thinking about it for two years but now the die is cast.

Friday, March 1 - In the Indian Ocean (1976.0 NM)

A bright sunny day. The dark clouds seem to have moved westward and we then had a clear blue sky. Talked to African Queen but neither of us heard Kiko. I sent Kiko and Reunion E-mails asking where they were. Received a message from Laura saying that Heather called and said she was in London but the computer would not work. The wind was staying at 14 to 17 kts from the ENE to NE and we were really moving quickly, between 8 and 9 kts SOG. Really great sailing. Couldn't be better as the sea is still slight and it is a comfortable ride. All crew are happy and the new arrivals are working thru their jet lag. John made lunch of grilled cheese and ham sandwiches. Talked to Heather, who had a Mercedes drive her and Margaret into London. She could not get the computer to start, and had a blank white screen. Still making good time. The clouds stayed away; we may be north of most of the disturbance. Got an E-mail from Kiko. He arrived in Oman this morning at 0830. Cleared-in in 10 minutes. Jack, helped by Dick, made dinner of mince and pasta shells with carrots. At 24 hours, we did 191.3 NM, or 7.97 kts. We had a sudden "wind shift" and the seas turned flatter. Turned out that the current basically reversed itself and the autopilot had to steer more north to compensate. That brought the wind more on the nose. Although our SOG is now 7.5 to 8 kts, it is still pleasant and a great sail. Jack became ill.

Saturday, March 2 - In the Indian Ocean (1976.0 NM)

John and I had the 0000 to 0300 watch. The wind kept decreasing and finally at 0040 we turned on the engine. Mostly the wind was at 6 to 7 kts true. The problem was that there were a series of dark rain clouds with lots of lightening that were disrupting the trade wind. The engine went off at 0500 and we began to sail- slowly. By 0830 the winds were at around 10 kts and we were doing 6.7 kts SOG, in the right direction although we got 0.28 NM off course to build up speed. The current is still subtracting. Talked to African Queen, but no Kiko. By 1000 we were up to 8.0 kts SOG, but hard on the wind. Had lunch of salad and sandwiches of luncheon meat. Talked to Heather and she took the computer in for service. Margaret was at home by now. The wind held at the 13 to 15 kts range and we continued to bound along, although the current was subtracting some speed. Healed over to port, but not too far. By 1400 we were north of 7° and the weather appeared to be somewhat better with only high clouds. (Commanders Weather said we would have to get north of 8° to get clear trade winds.) Sent Charlie a message via his father. The refrigerator would not run. It had an air lock due to the seas and angle of heel. De-powered the main to straighten up and then bled the system and it worked. At 48 hours, we did 358.9 NM, or 7.48 kts overall. The last 24 hours were slower, at 167.6 NM and an average of 6.98 kts. Paul made lemon chicken for dinner. Nice sail.

Sunday, March 3 - In the Indian Ocean (1976.0 NM)

Had the 0300 to 0600 watch. Having trouble with responding to Helmuth & Veronica. They sent a message from markhb@, not hellbick@ as they expected after February 28. Responded to both, but received a failed notice. The night sky had brilliant stars all over. Some dolphins made phosphoresce trails. In the morning we set the MPS at 0750 as the wind had dropped to 10-12 kts. The sailing is nice, but the halyard groans. Could not reach AQ or Kiko as some ham was doing a contest of contacts. But he was from Mexico and we heard many from the US. Nothing heard on 4417, the frequency Reunion is on. Tried calling Flash at 1000 on Iridium but there was no answer. At night, on the VHF, an American warship called a cargo ship and questioned him. They were at least 800 NM away. Never heard if they boarded. Had trouble with the refrigerator again. This time I bled it at the breather tube. Worked, but there must have been air trapped in the breather tube for it not to work. Hope it is OK now. Turned into a bright sunny day, and hotter than previous days. Turned the clocks back one hour to +4 GMT. Had lunch of fried egg and bacon sandwiches made by John. Talked to Heather again. She still did not go to the Internet place yet. Asked her to order the light bulbs and get a Spanish/English dictionary for Paul. Took the MPS down at 1310 as the wind increased to around 14 kts, and it looked like it would increase further. At 72 hours, we did 528.3 NM, or 7.34 kts overall. For the last 24 hours we did 170.3 NM for an average of 7.10 kts. Of the 72 hours we have motored only 6 hours. Great; and per plan. Erick, with the great help of John, cooked dinner of salmon pasta. Good! Got long E-mail from Kiko about how or if we want to meet. It may be difficult so I said maybe they should leave early so we can catch up and sail thru the fleet. I have the 2100 to 2400 watch. The wind has increased to a Force 5 from the NE. Generally ranging from 16 to 20 kts. So we are going great guns at 8.0 to 8.5 kts SOG. Quite comfortable as it is a beam reach and we are not healed much at all. Got an update from Commanders Weather and they predict lighter winds, and very light in the middle of the Gulf of Aden. But the strategy is working so far and as long as we sail at least 200 NM to the major waypoint, we will be able to motor all the way to Djibouti.

Monday, March 4 - In Indian Ocean (1976.0 NM)

Got a little lumpy overnight as the sea built a little. But on our 0600 to 0900 watch, the wind dropped to the 12 kts range so we pulled out the main at 0750. Later, the wind increased somewhat to the 15 to 18 kts range at 1130. Talked to AQ easily. Also heard Reunion and we changed frequencies twice, but could not get clear connection. Believe that he is 3 days away from Djibouti. Still going fast as the current is now somewhat favorable. Maintaining 8.5 to 9.0 kts SOG. The day is bright and sunny with no clouds in the sky. We have broken free of the weather disturbances to the south. Had lunch of ham & cheese sandwiches with chips. At 96 hours, we did 730.7 NM, or 7.61 kts overall. For the last 24 hours we did 202.4 NM for an average of 8.43 kts. Wow! Even had to reef the main to reduce heel for dinner. Paul made steaks, with potatoes and beans. Got H's E-mail. Sent another note to Kiko to update him, but noticed that the one I sent yesterday is not on the composed mail list. Strange. Wonder if it was sent. Heard another US warship on the VHF, but they are much farther north.

Tuesday, March 5 - In Indian Ocean (1976.0 NM)

Had the 0000 to 0300 watch. Got E-mail from Kiko and he apparently got both messages. He and the group (Hygia, Mazy, Yang Show, Fyn, R Phirst, Wanabe, Flash & Perdika) plan on leaving Salalah mid-day on the 6th. They expect to be near my waypoint #8 at 1700 on the 9th. My projection is that we will arrive #8 between 0600 on the 9th and 0100 on the 10th. Probably toward the later time if the wind dies. Plan to use 4146.0 on SSB for communications. Still going well, but slower at 7.7 to 8.1 kts SOG. Saw about four ships last night, none really close. All were going SE. The day dawned bright and clear with no clouds. It is slightly colder. At night I wore long pants for the first time. At 0800 it was still a nice temperature, and cooler than previous days. AQ was not on the radio, but I was going to tell him that I would not be on in the future. A rather pleasant day. The swells were down and with the wind on the beam the ride was nice. Slower with winds of 12 to 14 kts. Had lunch of ham and cheese sandwiches. Tried to call Heather but she had already left the flat for Wyn's. At 120 hours, we did 924.5 NM, or 7.70 kts overall. For the last 24 hours we did 193.8 NM for an average of 8.07 kts. Dinner was sausages and mashed potatoes prepared by Dick. Put a new Trimble Inmarsat-C antenna on the to do list. If they only last 2 years, then we will need a new one shortly. John left the bath sink tap on and the floor of the bath was filled with water before we noticed that water was flowing continuously. Called Heather on her mobile phone when she was at Wyn's. We hit a floating net, or it's buoy and support wire. Some heard it scrape along the hull and then a bang (probably hitting the skeg), then nothing. No buoys followed us so it must have broken free. Saw the line of buoys; we crossed over near the end. Basically the line was parallel to our course, but the end hooked around. Later, just near dusk, we passed over another floating net, but did not hear anything. They are hard to spot and harder yet to avoid. In both cases there was a fishing boat nearby, but not that close. The winds are holding in a reduced state and we are still moving nicely through the water. After dark I had to put on both long pants and a fleece jacket. Believe that is the first time since we were near Sydney in the beginning of 2001.

Wednesday, March 6 - In Indian Ocean (1976.0 NM)

Woke up early for my 0300 to 0600 watch. At 0130 we just passed half way for the complete passage-- we passed 1000 NM. That means we will be able to skip Oman as we should have enough fuel to motor the total rest of the way to Djibouti, if necessary. In fact, we have only motored for 6 hours. We have run the generator for 24.5 hours so I think we have used about 100 liters of diesel (30 before we left Male). But with the 200 liters on deck, we should be able to motor 1000 NM. Also, it is all-downhill from here! The steering rams are making a lot of noise, making sleeping difficult. It bothers me, but they seem to be performing properly. We are slower than before but still going well. The sky is clear with a brilliant star display. Wrote Kiko about our current position. Could not reach Kiko by SSB, but talked to Reunion. They are only one day away from Djibouti. Apparently the bulk of the boats are already in the Red Sea. He knew of no pirate attacks this year. He also said that the Gulf of Aden is being patrolled by 25 to 30 ships from several nations. Another boat, Okiva, called on VHF 16 as they were approaching from Galle, Sri Lanka. Saw them and they are a large ketch, which seemed to have the sails reefed and was rolling heavily. Really did not want to talk as he was asking all the wrong questions for VHF. He was also going only 50 NM north of Socotra. That is too close for me. He tried to use SSB but he couldn't get his radio working. It was a pretty day, but the wind kept diminishing. We set the MPS at 0945 and continued to sail. Had lunch of steak sandwiches. Kiko wrote back and changed times/frequencies of the SSB schedule. Finally at 1445, with the wind at 8 kts, we took the MPS down and started the engine. With the main and yankee we were going 7.5 kts SOG at only 1500 RPM. The issue is that we really don't want to get to

Djibouti before March 13 as we can have 72 hours there without a visa, and Charlie arrives at 0810 on March 16. But, we also want to keep up with Hygia and others so we will have to maintain at least 7.5 kts until we met up. Got an update from Commanders Weather and they say the winds will be less than 10 kts in the entrance to the Gulf of Aden, but that the wind should pick up on Saturday and Sunday, when we get farther west. At 6 days (144 hours), we did 1103.6 NM, or 7.66 kts overall. For the last 24 hours, we did 179.1 NM for an average of 7.46 kts. By 1645 we were able to turn the engine off and pull out the yankee. We were able to do 7.1 kts SOG on the modified course. Talked to Kiko at 1700 on 4146.0 and he said the group of boats left at 1300 and were motor sailing at 5 kts as they did not have enough wind. They sill intended to make their waypoint on time and would remain at 5 kts for 3 days. They might even stop! The waypoint is only 25 NM off Yemen, but that is where they want to be. He confirmed that the Germans are patrolling the Somalia coast; the French the Yemen coast and the British were in-between. I thanked him for the offer of diesel, but said we did not need any. He said that he had to motor the last 3 days to Salalah. Had dinner of salmon patties, per Heather's recipe, made by John. Pleasant sailing that is very smooth. Our watch is 2100 to 2400. Not much happened. The phosphoresce was quite good. The wind kept declining.

Thursday, March 7 - In Indian Ocean (1976.0 NM)

The engine was started at 0005. The day was bright and sunny with no clouds in the sky. Getting warm again. With motoring everybody is reading. Talked to Kiko on SSB and he still wants to go only 25 NM off the coast. He also wants to go between 48° 50 and 47° 50 at night as that is the largest risk area. The risk area is consistent with White Rabbits conclusion. I still want to keep to my course as I think that is safest. So I said not to wait for us and we agreed to go our separate ways. Received an E-mail from Heather. She enjoyed Lord of the Rings. Will return to London on Sunday. The day is peaceful, lazy and boring. Motoring along with a very flat sea, nothing in sight- not even any ships. May have another 48 hours of this. Had lunch of peanut butter and jelly sandwiches (Paul had honey). The battery charge is improving. By 1430 it was up to 476 amp hours. Will get it back up to full later today. At 7 days (168 hours), we did 1268 NM, or 7.55 kts overall. For the last 24 hours, we did 164.4 NM for an average of 6.85 kts. Dinner was chicken with garlic and balsamic vinegar on pasta and mushrooms with pears for desert, by John. Got a little wind (10 kts) but then it dropped again. Got second E-mail from Heather. We went into the full anti-pirate mode, and are running without nav lights now. Everyone seems compatible and happy. Absolutely nothing happening on the watch, which is the best thing. We are all worried.

Friday, March 8 - In Indian Ocean and entering Gulf of Aden (1976.0 NM)

Had the 0000 to 0300 watch. It is a very, very dark night. Rather eerie as it is impossible to find the horizon. The ink black sea just blends with the ink black sky, even with the night scope. The stars are visible right down to where the horizon should be. There are star beams on the glassy ocean. Have 1 kt of current against us so we are doing only 5.9 kts SOG. No wind to help. Nothing to see. No ships, nothing. The day dawned brightly with no clouds. The day continued hot and airless. The only wind is that which we make. Talked to the fleet and told them we were behind as we have had an adverse current. They are ahead. So I said to proceed without us and make their own speed decisions. Apparently their formation worked at night with four abreast in front and three abreast behind. Jack made Chiapatta bread buns and we had sandwiches of ham and cheese. The wind is not projected to increase until afternoon tomorrow, Saturday. No e-mail. Just a lazy day. Talked to Hygia at 1300 and they are still going at only around 5 kts, but they have had a favorable current of up to 0.5 kts. Also talked to Belleau, who left Salalah on March 8. They are behind us and very near the coast. Saw a large sea turtle; oh what excitement. Got another E-mail from H about travel Scrabble. At 8 days (192 hours), we did 1417 NM, for 7.38 kts overall. For the last 24 hours, we did 149 NM for an average of 6.21 kts. At 1645 we had the excitement of seeing a warship, unknown, pass us heading east. It was followed by a tanker, Front x from Oslo. Both were going rather slow. Talked to the group again and Yang Shu is 84 NM ahead of us. Tomorrow night will be the pirate high-risk area. Had dinner of hamburgers with Chiapatta buns and coleslaw made by John. Had pineapple for desert. Motoring without lights again but keeping sharp lookout for ships. Will turn lights on if we see a ship, but not for fishing craft. I had the 1800 to 2100 watch. Pitch black again, but not quite as misty. Made 44 gallons of water but had to run the generator at the same time as the engine. Not quite a full tank yet. At about 2000 we entered the Gulf of Aden.

Saturday, March 9 - In Gulf of Aden (1976.0 NM)

Had the 0300 to 0600 watch. Just as I came on watch a ship approached crossing our bow. Switched on the tri-color and they then saw us and aimed a light at us. We deviated 10° to let them pass slowly. Switched off again. Nothing more happened but we did get to 3/4 of the way to Djibouti. The wind slowly increased from the SW, but even by 0800 we were not able to sail, especially with 1 kt against us. The forecast by CW says that the wind will increase all day today, possibly moving to the NE. Although toward the Yemen coast it could be SE. The day started late, nearly by 0700, but it was a clear sky. So we shall turn the clocks back today. Everyone was up by 0815 and puttering around. Got a message from Charlie, he is home from Geneva and will depart for Paris on the 12th. The flight that arrives Djibouti is only once a week so we will have to live with it. H will return to London today. At 0930 we poled out the yankee wing-on-wing and made sufficient speed so we can sail. By 1145 the wind dropped so we had to turn on the engine again. Saw several ships. Turned the clock back one hour to GMT +3. Had lunch of sandwiches with bread we made. Talked to the net twice. They had a British warship go through their formation twice! All were taking pictures. It is good to know that there are friendly forces about. A fishing boat came from the Yemen shore towards us. We sped up and pulled ahead; he broke off aiming at us and continued on course and passed behind us. At 9 days (216 hours), we did 1568 NM, for 7.26 kts overall. For the last 24 hours, we did 151 NM for an average of 6.29 kts. At 1700 the autopilot gave a warning that it was not steering. We took the lazarette apart and determined that the starboard ram was not working (the newer one). Also, the ball joint fitting on the port ram was destroyed. Apparently the rams were fighting each other. We swapped the ball joint fittings and disconnected the starboard ram. The system seems to be now working fine, including on track. The sound level seems to be quieter. Whew! I thought for a while that we might have to hand steer for the rest of the way. Working on the steering rams while sailing as a person is hand steering is tricky as everything is moving about. We had dinner of macaroni and cheese, plus frankfurters (the dry packaged ones from Thailand) made by John. We will be entering the most risky pirate area tonight. The wind has been just about exactly as predicted by CW, but in that case the wind should increase by tomorrow for good sailing. The seas are somewhat confused as there are large 2-meter swells coming from the SE but the wind is from the east or NE. The result is not too comfortable and it keeps shaking what wind we have out of the sails. But the seas also make boarding by pirates difficult so we were pleased. At 1800 a fleet of warships passed us- a small aircraft carrier on our starboard (only half a mile), and a destroyer and other vessel on our port. It was just at dusk so we could not get any pictures, although we saw a flash from the carrier as someone took a picture of us. We could not tell the nationality of them, and they did not call us on the radio. The destroyer had red numbers and none seemed to be American or British. We heard an Italian warship farther northeast previously, but we don't think he was one of these. At least we got our protection, and didn't leave all the warships to Kiko. We turned on the tri-color and will probably leave it on for a while. Turned it off later. Kept the engine on to ensure maintaining over 7 kts SOG. It is best to keep going fast.

Sunday, March 10 - In Gulf of Aden (1976.0 NM)

Paul turned the engine off at 0050 when the wind increased to around 16 kts. We were moving at 8.1 kts SOG at 0200. The day dawned with lots of cloud cover, but it soon burned off leaving a cloudless, bright day. We are still moving quickly, up to 9.1 kts SOG. Talked to the group and although they are nearly 20 NM towards shore, we have nearly caught up with them. We will probably beat them to Djibouti. They were thinking about slowing down as the slowest boat (Wanabe) was falling behind. I still want to go as fast as possible in the high-risk area. If the weather forecast is correct, and it has been quite accurate, then we should be able to sail all the way to Djibouti. At 1000, we could reach Djibouti in 29 hours, or at 1500 tomorrow. Wow, only one more night! We still have around 500 liters of diesel in the tank, as best as I can tell. So fuel is not a problem with another 200 liters on the deck. We will not have to touch the deck reserve and will simply fill the tank, thus avoiding double handling. Lunch was of Thai "noodles in a cup". Were they hot! Had peaches to help cool off our mouths. Talked to Yang Shou and they were only making around 6 kts SOG. Mazy was having a hard time going slow enough. They had 240 NM to go to Djibouti and we had 238 to go. Seems that we have pulled ahead slightly. Hygia did not answer. The wind is up slightly, now a force 5. But the sailing is very smooth with no rolling. Am going slightly off track at 2.7 NM to the north as the wind is exactly on our stern. Jibed to the port tack as the wind had moved to the east. Going very fast- up to 9.6 kts SOG; wind peaked at a force 7. Did not see anything all day long. At 10 days (240 hours), we did 1752 NM, for 7.30 kts overall. For the last 24 hours, we did 184 NM for an average of 7.67 kts. In the afternoon chat I said we were going to go directly to Djibouti and will not rendezvous with the group. Heard a yacht calling Djibouti Harbour Control. Had dinner of bloody Mary chicken with peas and pears for desert. Jack & Dick made dinner. Had popcorn later. Ran with no tri-color light. The wind declined dramatically and we turned on the engine at 1915 to maintain at least 6 kts SOG. Concluded that we would not arrive before nightfall, so the exact time of arrival is not critical, but we did not want to get there too late. By 2000 we were out of the high-risk pirate area. At 2245 we turned off the engine as the winds had increased and there was a lot of vibration as we surfed down waves. We were going well, and very relieved.

Monday, March 11 - In Gulf of Aden to Djibouti (1976.0 NM)

Had the 0000 to 0300 watch. Had quite a lot of ship activity. Only once, when what we believe was a military ship crossed our bows did we turn on the tri-color. Most times they were well north of us going east or west. One, however, came within one mile and it had two giant poles with a lot of what appeared to be net piled on the aft deck. Not like any fishing boat we have seen, as it was quite large. One ship turned to go into the port of Aden. The day started somewhat overcast, with winds in the 25 to 30 kts range. The seas are 2 to 3 meters, but it is still comfortable on *ESCAPADE*. Not good for pirates, however. Anyway, we are past all the risk areas in Gulf of Aden, with the possible exception of the final approach to Djibouti. But we are approaching from the NE so we are closing on Somalia on a steep angle, which should be safe. When we leave Djibouti we can go further north and stick to the Djibouti and then Eritrea coasts, keeping to the west of the Bab-el-Mandeb channel, thus keeping away from Yemen. This avoids the pirate areas there. A day north we should be totally out of pirate territory. Saw a yacht heading towards Aden in the morning but he was too far away to wave to. At 0800 we had only 77 NM to go to our waypoint just outside Djibouti. There is another 8 NM from there to the anchorage at the Yacht Club. Talked to Yang Shu and Hygia. They are still going slow and they now have 130 NM to go, compared to our 76, so we are 54 NM ahead. They expect to arrive in daylight tomorrow morning. By noon we were 59 NM ahead. The day turned very hot and sticky, after the wind dropped. Started the engine at 1220 so that we had some chance of arriving in daylight. Had lunch of tuna sandwiches by John. Talked to Heather. She will pick up the computer this morning. She did not go to the Internet place yesterday. Everybody is anxious to see land after 11 days, and very relieved that we did not encounter any pirates. At 11 days (264 hours), we did 1942 NM, for 7.36 kts overall. For the last 24 hours, we did 190 NM for an average of 7.92 kts. At 1515 I tried calling the Yacht Club but got no response, at 25 NM. The light was falling as we approached. However, it held long enough for us to see the whole situation. It was dark, however, for our final approach into the harbor. Had dinner of beef stew, sauerkraut, and poppadum. Called Port Control and received no answer. Entered and found the anchorage really easy. We were anchored by 1922 in 5.6 meters of water. It was very still and calm and we all enjoyed the relief of the finish of the passage without pirates. Overall, it went very well with lots of good sailing. We still had at least 450 liters of diesel in the tank plus the 200 on the deck. We had beers and V&Ts in the cockpit. The harbor was busy with activity, especially at the container ship, which was very close. The passage was a total of 1,975.7 NM and took 268.82 hours, just over 11 days. We averaged 7.35 kts. Used the engine 94.17 hours for 35% of the time. We made 310 gallons of water.

Tuesday, March 12 – Djibouti

Woke up early and got busy as the offices are open from 0630. Called the Capitainerie and received a response. He said to come in to his office. Put the dinghy down and installed the outboard and went in. Found the Capitainerie and checked-in. Said we arrived at 0100 in the morning of March 12. Went to Immigration and turned in the passports to get 5 day visas for all except John, who already had a visa. Cost $80. I will be able to get them back by 0900 tomorrow. That completes formalities. While I was ashore, Hygia contacted us. They said they were within one hour of arriving. Went to the Yacht Club and paid a $100 deposit so we can charge food and drink. Talked to Christina, who is in the Club's office, and she gave us a map of the town with the locations of all the important places. All crew were busy cleaning ESCAPADE so she soon looked spick and span. All the other boats arrived by 1000 and anchored near us. Told them what we had found out. Had lunch at the YC. Spent most of the afternoon sitting in the YC as everything is closed until 1600. Did go to the fuel station and no one was there. Will have to sort out the diesel bit tomorrow morning. The guys went into town at 1630 and I returned to ESCAPADE to do the route planning up the Red Sea. Decided that we would stop the first night at Obock, Djibouti so that we will go through the straight in daylight. Had dinner at the YC. We were told that boys/men swim from the shore at night and board sailboats to steal things. So we have removed everything from the deck, put the dinghy on the halyard, will lock-up and will set the motion detector. Looks like another very calm night at anchor.

Wednesday, March 13 - Djibouti 0.4 NM

Woke up early to work on the fuel. The day was bright and sunny and hot. At 0640 I went to the fuel dock, or more appropriately the dock with the fuel pumps. Turned out that was not the place. We had to go to the Shell facility behind. After much discussion, some in French, we learned that a tanker would deliver the fuel to a dock if you pay for it first (in local Djibouti francs). They suggested 1200 at building #8, but I needed to confirm it with the harbormaster. However, the tank truck had no meter or nozzle. The driver controlled the flow. He said that he would attach a smaller hose than the standard 4" one. There was no refund on fuel not used. I was trying to arrange this also for all the other cruising boats as well. Returned to visit other boats to confirm such arrangements. Then went to the harbour master (which took 20 minutes or so before he returned). He said 1200 and #8 was OK. Returned to Shell and paid for 600 liters, which was only $0.23 per liter duty free. Returned to the boats and told them to get their duty free forms from the Harbour Master and to order the fuel from Shell before 1100. But they were not that quick and the last order was not placed until 1115, partially because the harbour master could not be found. The location was at the end of the mole and we could squeeze on to a 45° end. It also turned out that the tanker truck was normally empty and they filled it with only the amount of fuel you purchased. We motored over there and tied up at 1100. But 1200, then 1300 went by. We did not have lunch but had crackers and cheese to tide us over. The ship beside us left, but they were pulled clear by the tugs. Another one came in while we were waiting.   Finally, at 1400 the truck finally came. The truck had three compartments. One was for ESCAPADE at 600 L, the second was 520 L for Ynag Sho (140), Hygia (270), and Mazy (110), the third was 465 L for R Phirst (165), Flash (100), and Fyn (200). All other boats wanted it in jerry cans. We had already poured our jerry cans into the tank. We asked the driver to fill a jerry can. He had very little control over the flow, especially at the beginning. So we concluded we had to have him fill the jerry cans and we would pour the cans into our tank. So we began the operation. Two local guys, who said they were security people, helped out without being asked. It was a slow process, as we wanted all fuel to go thru the Bahia filter. We filled the tank and a lot squirted on the deck thru the breather. We then filled all the jerry cans. All told we used about 593 liters as there was about 4 L left over from our compartment, but we also spilled some. Told the other boats to bring their cans. The scene turned into a circus with more and more locals trying to get paid and all the boats scrambling to fill their containers. I paid the helper and the truck driver with dollars and cigarettes. They were making noises that they would report us for polluting. We re-anchored at 1510 and by the time we got the boat back together, it was 1630. Went to the YC for drinks and stayed for dinner. Jack & Dick in the meantime went to the Egyptian embassy to get visas. They returned for local currency and passport photos. Had dinner at the YC with Flash, as there were only 2 of us. It was a buffet, but for starters and desert only. Ordered steak kabob. Anyway, the passports will be available for pickup tomorrow. Missions were accomplished but we were beat after all this. All the other boats were satisfied.

Thursday, March 14 – Djibouti

Another bright day. Went in early to the supermarket. Walked so that I would see some of the city. Most everything is available, but cokes are in glass bottles only. Took taxi back. The forward head blocked up so Jack spent a long time, all very messy, working on it. It finally required cleaning the entire hose from the toilet to the holding tank of calcium deposits. We did that by using the hose and pumping salt water thru it. But that resulted in a lot of water in the shower drain so the drain pump was being used a lot, and it developed a noise. Turned out we had to replace the drain pump with a new one. Then the filtered fresh water flow in the galley diminished. So I changed the Seagull filter, which brought the flow up to normal. Completed the route plan to Egypt. Decided to go to Hurghada Marriott Marina based on White Rabbits comments. So that reduces the mileage to around 1100 NM to when we can get fuel. As long as we sail some in the southern portion, we will have enough fuel to motor the whole distance. Sent E-mail to Commanders Weather asking for a weather forecast on the 16th. Bought some beer and cigarettes duty free. Tried to check out but wasn't successful. Went over in the morning and found the harbour master but he said he wasn't on duty until the afternoon and said to return then. When I returned, there was no one in sight. We put the new steering ram into position, but did not connect it up, as the boat will steer with only one ram. Went to dinner in town at the Figero restaurant. When walking back, there were many people sleeping along 6side the road. Had a drink at the YC.

Friday, March 15 – Djibouti

A partially cloudy day, but still bright with sunshine. Worked on the boat- changed the Racor and fuel filters on the engine, added oil to the engine and generator, filled the batteries, and put a new zinc in the engine. P, J, and J went into town for the Internet. Dick & I stayed aboard. Talked to H. Did a second load of laundry. Had lunch on board but had ice cream at the club. Paul went windsurfing. Took a nap. Went to a party on Flash. Had dinner at the restaurant above the Hotel Historil.

Saturday, March 16 - Djibouti to Obock 26.2 NM

Slightly overcast day, more so than in the past. Got up early and went to the harbormaster at 0645, but he did not arrive until 0730 (should have been there from 0630). He wrote out a form to take to the port office, but their computer was down so we went back to the boat, as I had to go to the airport to pick up Charlie. Paul returned to carry on the checkout wars. Went in a taxi with Miles (from Yong Shu), as he was picking up crew as well. The airplane was early and Charlie came out quickly. We were back at the Yacht Club at 0855. The other guys had gone into town to do the last minute provisioning. I took Charlie back to the YC so he could go into town to look around and to get a passport photo for Egypt. Just as we were entering the boat area, we ran out of petrol. There is a petrol station right outside so I filled up and then the guys arrived with the groceries. Took them to the boat and went to Immigration, but he wouldn't process the passports without the Port Clearance so I had to return to the boat to get it. After I presented the document, he stamped all 6 passports quickly and we had completed the formalities, for no extra cost. When in to pick Charlie up and pay off the Yacht Club. All told, we spent $300 there ($200 additional). So, finally, we were ready to prepare the boat for departure. Pulled the dinghy up, put the jerry cans back on deck, and re-strung the sheets. Pulled up the anchor at 1141, slightly ahead of the target of 1200. Lunch was ham and cheese sandwiches on French bread. Had to motor all the way to Obock as the winds were from the NE. Went in behind the reef, and anchored quite away from shore, but it appears to be protected and should result in peaceful sleep. It will permit us to go through the straight of Bab-el-Mandeb during daylight. John made dinner of shrimp and rice. As usual, it became more rolly after dark.

Sunday, March 17 - Obock into the Red Sea 612.0 NM

Got up early to an overcast sky. The most clouds we have seen this year. Later in the day it became clear sky. Pulled up the anchor at 0632 and motored into the wind and waves to get around the Ras Bir Point. Took quite awhile as we were only making 4 to 5 kts SOG. Finally got there and were able to pull out the staysail. Things started to improve immediately and when we reached the next waypoint we could sail. It was great going with about 16 to 18 kts of wind from the SE. The problem was that the seas were large and confused. They had a long fetch down the Gulf of Aden and then the bottom shoals as it gets to Djibouti. The ride was not bad, however. Talked to Yang Shu, and they, plus Hygia, Fyn, and Mazy were leaving in the next hour for Obock. When we got to the beginning of the strait Bab-el-Mandeb, we went wing-on-wing. The winds were in the 20 kts range and with the current with us we were doing 9 to 11 kts SOG. Charlie got sick and retreated below. He recovered enough later to have a little bit of dinner. Received the weather forecast from Commanders Weather and it was right on for the bit out of Djibouti, and it predicted we would have favorable winds through Wednesday. But Thursday it could turn against us. Lunch was sandwiches of luncheon meat on rye bread. Talked about the catamaran that was abandoned with a broken mast near here. The winds suddenly increased to the 40 kts range, with peaks at 50 kts. We reefed both main and yankee but still kept speed in the 9 to 10 kts range. The seas diminished as we got farther north in the strait and then later they increased again as a result of the winds. The port autopilot ram failed, possibly due to all the stress on it. I disconnected it and replaced it with a new one. It was a good thing that I had two spare rams. There were a lot of ships and we had to dodge a few in the evening. By the time we got to waypoint 10, which is south of the Hanish islands, we had passed the major pirate areas so we were free of those dangers. Thank God, it is such a relief. Now we only have to worry about weather and other things like ships and reefs. The next waypoint is 700 NM ahead at a course of 331°. To the west is Eritrea, where several of our friends are going. Heard some cruisers on the VHF, but saw none. Had dinner of spaghetti Bolognese. There is a new moon, with a sliver on the bottom.

Monday, March 18 - In the Red Sea (612.0 NM)

Had the 0000 to 0300 watch. Lots of ships around. Pulled out the yankee to maintain speed. At 0100, all changed. The wind suddenly changed to the W, and dropped to 15 kts. Had to reach on port tack. The wind kept changing until it was directly on our nose so we began to motor. It was only 9 kts so we are still making 6.4 kts SOG. A report from R Phrstn said the boats ahead have no wind or light wind. So it looks like the Red Sea is maintaining it fickle reputation. It is overcast today, and not very pretty. It cleared up later, with a sort of hazy look. Even so, at 24 hours we had done 201.5 NM, for an average of 8.40 kts. Shows how fast we were sailing when we had the high winds. Started to tack while motor sailing with the main and staysail. John made BLT's for lunch. Heard some American warships on the VHF, but could not tell where they were. Continued to make steady, but slow progress motor sailing. A dohu came sailing, sort of aiming at us. We sped up, and he suddenly changed course, seeing that he would not intercept us. Had dinner of hamburger patties, potatoes and corn, made by Paul. John had started steaks, but the meat had gone off so we switched to the hamburger. John felt a little queasy after being in the galley for a while and Paul completed the dinner. Received an update from CW. The adverse headwinds are due to a small high passing over the middle of the Red Sea. They are now predicting the winds to return to the SE for Tuesday and part of Wednesday, before a low comes through on Thursday and Friday. The low could bring 30 kts headwinds and sharp seas so we are considering going into Port Sudan to wait it out. We should be able to make Port Sudan just before the high winds hit. At the end of our watch at 2100 the winds had already begun to drop, down to 6 kts, from 11 most of the day.

Tuesday, March 19 - In the Red Sea (612.0 NM)

Had the 0300 to 0600 watch. Not much to see or do. The day dawned bright and clear. Heard from Kiko and the four boats that are heading for Massawa in Eritrea. At 48 hours we had gone 359.5 NM, for an overall average of 7.49 kts. The last 24 hours was 158.0 NM, for an average of 6.58 kts, all motoring. Worked out a new course to Port Sudan, and it is about 240 NM from us at 0900. So it may be possible to get there before dark on Wednesday. That would be just as the headwinds would be developing. The pilot books make it out to be a big hassle to go there, but we can fuel up and ride out the winds. A lazy day, but the winds did shift to the south, as predicted, but still light at 8 kts. Shifted to the new course and was able to go on track by 1015. Had lunch of ham and cheese sandwiches. VERY hot day with little wind to cool things off. But making 7.9 kts SOG. Should arrive at the waypoint to turn toward Port Sudan by 0100 tomorrow morning. Sent E-mail to CW asking them if the winds will still happen, how long will they last, and if it is a good idea to go into port. John made curry chicken with rice for dinner. Received report from CW. They strongly suggest going into Port Sudan, and think we can resume on Saturday. The front may come thru between 1100 and 1300 tomorrow. That is a little before we are projected to get there, but the higher winds will lag the front by a few hours, and then will back from the east. As our final course is 281°, we should be OK. At the moment, there is no indication of possible strong winds from the NW in 20 hours. The sky is clear, and full of stars. The wind is gentle, and from the south. We are heading NW at 321°. I have the 2100 to 2400 watch, and a full night sleep after. Now running the generator and water maker along with the engine, as I want a full tank of water before we go into the port.

Wednesday, March 20 - In the Red Sea to Port Sudan (612.0 NM)

Woke for my 0600 to 0900 watch. The sky was clear and the sunrise looked like a sunset with a bright orange disk rising from the sea. Paul had turned the engine off at 0350, and we polled out the yankee at 0610. But it was to no avail, and the wind continued to drop. So we started the engine again at 0630. At 0632, or 72 hours, we had done 544.4 NM, for an overall average of 7.56 kts. For the last 24 hours we did 184.9 NM, for an average of 7.70 kts. The wind began to back as predicted and the sky was beginning to fill with clouds from the north. By 0920 the wind was from the NNE, but at only 7 kts. We will be able to head directly to Port Sudan after we pass waypoint #13, as the course will be 281° true. Due to the current flowing toward the NE, we will have to steer around 268° to maintain course. That should not be a problem if the wind increases from the north. Before dawn a ship passed on a reciprocal course to our south, then at 0900 one going into Port Sudan passed to the south. We passed the reef where the Finnish boat was lost last year. Talked to Hygia, and the four boats are 60 NM from Massawa, but they don't expect to arrive until tomorrow. Apparently Flash got hit by the same type of winds we got in the strait, but it was very uncomfortable for them. They lost the use of the foresail because the head broke free. We set the clocks back one hour at noon to +2 from GMT. We are now in the same time zone as Turkey! The wind slowly increased and backed as predicted. By the time we were 50 miles off, it had increased to 20-22 kts from the north. The seas were increasing, with very sharp waves, as it was wind over current. We were all glad that we were going into a harbour. The sky darkened, and it looked like rain. But it turned out to be a sand storm. It was very fine sand, but there was grit everywhere. The visibility was less than a half-mile and we were approaching reefs! Received no answer from Sudan Port Control on VHF 16. So went in anyway. Saw a few boats anchored and some larger ones anchored and tied to a bollard at the stern. Although the wind was abeam we anchored and pulled our stern to a huge bollard so we were out of the turning area for the ships. Anchor was down at 1510, and the stern was tied up by 1550. All told we had come 612 NM, in 81.63 hours for an average of 7.50 kts. Before we had the anchor set an agent, Chico, came out to the boat by dinghy. Hired him to do the clear-in process ($50); gave him the passports, two crew lists, and one photo each for the shore passes (at $27 each). Hope they return! He should be back tomorrow morning by 0900. We are confined to the boat until then. Called Heather on the Iridium phone; she was back at the flat from Tony and Irene's. While talking a couple of camels walked by on the street behind *ESCAPADE*! Had dinner of smoked salmon and salad by Charlie. All had drinks and we all were very pleased with the passage. We are just off the Hilton hotel. An Italian, Roberto, on the boat next to us came over and he said this was a secure place. Hope to get diesel tomorrow. Watched a large ship from the north of the port depart. The tugs had to turn it completely around. The boat is very still even though the wind is singing in the rigging. Hope to have a good night sleep.

Thursday, March 21 - Port Sudan

It was very peaceful overnight. There was a chilly wind in the morning. The sky is overcast, but the visibility is better as the sand in the air has diminished. Not much activity in the port at 0600. Charlie made French toast for breakfast. The agent came with the Health Officer and we were cleared for pratic. He gave us our shore passes and then I went to Customs across the harbour to clear in. Paul emptied the jerry cans into the tank and we gave them to the agent. He said he would return in an hour with fuel, including some of his jerry cans so we can get 400 liters in one go. But his sister was getting married today so he never returned. Probably won't see him until Saturday. John, Charlie and Jack went into town to get some groceries (bread, veg's, etc.). We set the Bruce anchor off the windward side of *ESCAPADE* to reduce the strain on the anchor and to reduce movement. Worked well. Also set the trip line buoy so the anchor location is marked. Replaced the generator water pump with a new one, as there was a lot of salt build-up on the side of the generator engine. This is probably the source of the water in the bilge as there are no other indications of leaks. Rebuilt the water pump with new seals, but I will also buy a new one. Had lunch onboard of sandwiches. The guys returned with some veg's and baguettes. They changed money at the Hilton hotel. All relaxed during the afternoon. Found out that Sudan is at +3 hours, not +2 as we have our clocks set. Oh well, we will keep to our time as it is the time for Egypt. The wind is blowing at 25 kts in the harbour, but gusts are probably higher. But we feel snug and calm even though the wind is whistling in the rigging. There is still sand flying about but it is not the sand storm as it was when we entered. Charlie made gazpacho for tomorrow. Heard from Kiko and they had a "horrid" sail into Massawa today with 30 kts headwinds for 25 NM. Everyone else went to an Internet cafe. Had drinks onboard and then went to the Hilton for a good dinner. It has been open only 3 months and it is very nice inside. Everyone relaxed before going to bed. The wind seems to have diminished a bit.

Friday, March 22 - Port Sudan

A bright sunny day with clear sky. There was no wind at first, with the water glassy, but later it resumed from the north abet lightly. All lazed around. Paul re-did the leather on the yankee sheets. Heard from Yang Sho and they are in Massawa, after the rough sail yesterday. All are waiting to go north. The diesel arrived. They brought our six jerry cans and a large plastic drum of fuel. We used the electric pump to pump from the jerry cans into the tank. We shuttled back and forth with the jerry cans until we had received 12 and then we brought the blue drum to the boat from which we pumped the remainder into the jerry cans. We put the original 6, plus the 12 into the tank, which filled it. There remained 4 jerry cans to put on deck. Thus we bought 360 liters. We now have about 1000 liters in the tank, and 178 liters on deck as the bladder is still full. That should be sufficient for a 700 NM trip, even if we have to motor hard into the wind. We will get all the deck fuel off in Suez. Paul then hosed down the boat with salt water. Had lunch of gazpacho soup and ham and cheese sandwiches on baguettes. Took the bad ram apart but did not see what was wrong. Charlie, Jack, Dick and I went into town and walked around. It is a dry, dusty, dirty place with very wide streets and very poor people. Returned to *ESCAPADE*, a wonderful retreat among the squalor of Port Sudan. The capital is Khartoum. Received the weather forecast from CW and it appears that leaving tomorrow is just as good and may be better than any other time to head north. Roberto, from the boat next to us came over and he had a weather forecast from the Internet that said much the same. Had dinner of ratatouille chicken with bow tie pasta. Paul, John, Charlie and Jack went into town and tried the hookah (water pipe) at the Hilton. They said it was very sweet tasting with a hint of apple flavor.

Saturday, March 23 - Port Sudan and heading north in the Red Sea 498.0 NM

Woke to a bright, clear morning, but cold. I had to use the blanket during the night and a fleece after I got up. Others said I had been in the tropics too long. John and Charlie went in to get bread. It is a still morning, with a glassy surface on the water. Chico is due at the boat at 0730 our time. Chico came at 0740, but he took until past 0900 to return. In the meantime we let the lines to the bollard go and hauled up the Bruce with the windlass, as Paul couldn't get it up by hand. We swung at anchor until we departed. After Chico returned, we both went to Customs and received our Port Clearance. Our passports were not stamped, and Chico left the crew list and ship declaration onboard. The total cost was $420 ($162 for diesel, $162 for shore passes, $33 port charges and $63 for the agent and fuel helper). We were able to haul up the anchor at 0940. Motored out the harbour, which we could now see the full extent. There were 18 ships anchored out, just north of the port entrance, which we did not see in the sand storm. Will start watches at 1200 with mine so that we are sure that we are well at sea. At 1600 we are motoring slowly into 9-10 kts headwinds. At 1700 RPM we are making 5.4 to 5.6 kts SOG. This is the "worst" time of day for headwinds so the rest of the day should be better. We may get a better wind angle, or reduced wind and thus reduced seas. At 5.5 kts we will reach Suez late Thursday 28th.

At 6.5 kts we will get there late on Wednesday 27th. Wrote Heather an E-mail stating this and suggesting that she fly to Cairo on the 27th. If we arrive later, she can stay at the hotel an extra day. After we reach the next waypoint (#6), we will be heading more NW. Now we are heading 006°. Had dinner of hamburgers, prepared by John. Very good. The SOG dropped to 5.0-5.1 kts for much of the evening as we had adverse current.

Sunday, March 24 - In Red Sea (498.0 NM)

Had a good nights sleep until 0530. During the night we passed WP #6 and then picked up a favorable current and by 0400 were doing 6.6 kts SOG. Later at 0800 we were up to 7.5 kts SOG. At least we are making good time. At 0940 we did 143.6 NM, for an average of 5.98 kts SOG. Called Heather and she had not checked with Egypt Air yesterday, as it was too late. Said we probably will arrive on March 28. May go into an anchorage overnight the 27th to time our arrival for daylight if we get there early. Had lunch of soup and bread rolls. The day is beautiful and the seas are calm. Most of the day we were doing 7.2 to 7.5 kts SOG. Can see the mountains off in the distance to the west. Mid-day we passed into Egyptian waters (north of 22°). The wind started to clock to the east so we had a better wind angle. Then we reached WP #7 and we fell off 10°. We were then doing 8.0 kts SOG. Trying to get in as much mileage as possible while in calm conditions. If the weather forecast holds true, then we will have at least 36 hours of favorable winds. Decided that we will anchor at a bay just south of where you enter the canal entrance to Suez. That way we don't have to worry about the exact time of arrival. But it should be during daylight on the 27th. We will go to Suez between the north and southbound convoys on the 28th. That should be between 1000 and 1400. Assuming we can get the formalities completed on the 29th and then transit the canal on 30/31 March. I was on watch for the sunset. It was perfectly clear, with no clouds on the horizon. The sun was absolute perfection. Then we saw the green flash!!! At least what we believe it is. There was no flash, but just as the sun dipped below the horizon, there was a green dot of light where the sun had been. Dick made dinner of vegetable corned beef hash. It was an original creation. The ride is very comfortable as it is smooth and consistent. Wrote Heather another E-mail telling her of the latest plan. She doesn't seem very interested in organizing the flight after we have been working so hard to get there. She is too busy enjoying doing things in London. The moon is getting larger each night. Now it is about 70% full so there is plenty of moonlight at night. It was as though you could get "moon burn". It is absolutely gorgeous.

Monday, March 25 - In Red Sea (498.0 NM)

The day is bright with scattered clouds. At first there was virtually no wind and then we got some from the NE. Paul pulled out the yankee at 0710. Still motoring and there seems to be a slight counter current. Talked to Yang Sho and they will be leaving Massawa tomorrow, but Hygia and Mazy are leaving today. It is a very light wind day. Sometimes it read 0.0 kts. Passed our first oil platform. It appeared to be a floating exploratory one. There was a support ship hovering around it but there did not seem to be any activity on the platform. Charlie made omelets for lunch. Making 7.5 kts SOG at 1300. Heard some cruisers on the VHF, but did not know them. Wrote Heather another E-mail, but she has not answered the last three. Had chicken Cherbourg for dinner, courtesy Charlie. A cruise ship approached from the rear, but they were weaving back and forth across our stern. So I called them on VHF and asked their intentions and they said they would pass to our port. They did, but they were going very slowly. The wind came from the SSE and finally, at 2320 we were able to turn off the engine. I received a new forecast from CW and they now predict high winds starting tomorrow.

Tuesday, March 26 - In Red Sea (498.0 NM)

At 0150 the wind dramatically changed direction- it was now from the WNW and we had to put the engine back on. The winds increased to 30 kts, with gusts to 35 kts and the seas dramatically increased very quickly. I was on the 0300 to 0600 watch and it was totally black, as the moon had disappeared earlier. The wind was on our nose, and we had to make sure we avoided a reef. We had fallen off earlier as it increased our speed, got us closer to the coast to reduce wave size, and were heading toward Safaga, Egypt. We continued, but the waves got very peaky and fierce. The motion was harsh and Charlie, John and Dick got sick. John especially went many times over the rail. The Red Sea would not let us go without giving us a lick of some punishment.

We motor sailed as tight as we could but the wind was always from the direction we wished to go. Decided to go into Safaga as we did not want to take 48 hours of this punishment. Headed in that direction but we had to take a tack to the NNE as we were heading directly for a reef. As we went away from shore the waves got larger and more vicious. Everybody was wearing foul weather gear. The sky was clear and it was a sunny day through all of this. We finally limped into the harbour at 1230 and we tied up at the dock by 1345. We were met by a group of Egyptians who welcomed us to Egypt. Had to go to the Harbour Master first, which was quick and then I went to Immigration, but they said I had to go to the bank to get Charlie's visa. Returned to the boat and sent Charlie, then he and I went to Immigration. By the time we were done Customs was closed. We made a deal to get diesel at $.30 per liter, as it would be easy at dockside. They arrived within an hour in a pickup with three 200-liter barrels on it. They pumped it to *ESCAPADE* and we essentially took it all. We were told that another ship would come in at midnight and go stern-to where we were tied up so we moved *ESCAPADE* forward to just behind a pilot boat and the cruise boat that passed us yesterday. Had dinner of spaghetti Bolognese made by Charlie. Paul, Jack and Charlie went to a pub in a building near the dock, but it turned out to be nothing. Talked to Heather and asked her to delay the flight. It is getting cooler the farther north we go. This evening is chilly.

Wednesday, March 27 - Safaga to Hurghada 35.2 NM

Overnight there were hundreds of people on the shore near our boat. They had come off a ferry and were waiting for transport, but they were loud, noisy and there were loudspeaker announcements as well. The ship that came in did not tie up where we were. In fact, we were all by ourselves in the morning. Decided to clear in and out so that I would not have to return to the port from the anchorage. Thought we would go to Abu Tig Marina as we can get there hugging the coast and not getting into large seas. But Customs did not arrive until 0930 and by the time we cleared (and paid) them, and the harbormaster, we were finally able to leave at 1037. We promptly ran aground in the narrow gap leading to the anchorage to the north. We used the Bruce anchor to kedge ourselves off and the dinghy to locate the deepest channel with the handheld depth finder. We got thru OK, and then recovered the dinghy. At that point the autopilot stopped working. We had lunch of the packaged meals, which people found to be OK. Discovered that the large pin that went thru the steering shaft arm fell off. It was simple to replace it, even though the threads were somewhat buggered. The autopilot was working again! Given the late start, and the going aground, we could not make it to Abu Tig so we will look for an anchorage near Hurghada. The land here is desolate, with nothing green. It is brown, dusty, dry and dull looking. The hotel strip didn't look very good and it is rather depressing. Sure don't know why someone would want to holiday here. At the point we passed a hotel development with a golf course. There was some green there. You just don't realize the need for vegetation in your environment. The wind is 13 kts from the NE today, and the seas are quite calm. Not too bad to motor, and we were able to sail some distance as well. It was nice to have the engine off for a while. The wind dropped and moved to the north so we had to start the engine again. We decided to anchor off the Marriott marina south of town. It took us a long time to get the anchor set and then a dinghy came out with the marina manager and a "coast guard" man. They said that we would have to take the boat to the town dock and check in and get a stamp before we could anchor or go to the marina. It was 1630 and it was getting close to dark. But they said the coast guard was there 24 hours. There were no anchorages close by that did not require spotting reefs. So we had no choice than to anchor off the town dock. We dropped the hook, while people on the shore were whistling (probably didn't like where we were anchoring). We dropped the dinghy and went in. The passports were inspected and they confirmed that we had cleared into Egypt. Two of them came out to inspect the boat. Don't know what they were looking for, but we passed. They asked a lot of questions, and wrote the answers on a blank piece of paper that I provided. They said we were OK to stay until tomorrow- first they said to 1500, and then they said to 0900. They asked if we had an agent here or in Safaga. They were perplexed that we didn't. Turns out that the piece of paper described to me as a Port Clearance from Safaga they took as a permit. As it was for only one day, they said we had to arrive in Suez by tomorrow. I asked if we could go to Abu Tig marina, but they said we needed a permit that lasted longer. He suggested an agent, and I said that maybe we should talk to one. They said that they would have one come to the boat tomorrow morning. Sure confusing! The issue is whether we need to have a cruising permit as well. So whereas we thought we would have dinner at a hotel, we had to have it onboard. After they left we had cocktails, and we were glad that we had completed the Red Sea. So we had cooked cabbage, baked beans, corn, and mashed potatoes from a mix. The wind came up as we were motoring to the town dock from the NW at 15 kts. After dinner the wind was whistling and it made us glad that we were not trying to go up the Gulf of Suez. It is quite chilly tonight and I wore a fleece during the day.

Thursday, March 28 - Hurghada to Endeavour Harbor 22.9 NM

Woke to another clear, sunny day. The night was cold, and I needed to have the blanket folded so I had four layers over me. Even so, I was cold. Talked to Kiko and they were close to Port Sudan. R Phurst said he had heard that if you stayed in Egypt more than 10 days you would be fined $1200. The pilot book said that Hurghada often charges $300 for a cruising permit and the agent fee is $100. Abu Tig marina is within the Hurghada area so they would be covered. It also notes that there are representatives of the coast guard at the marina to ensure things are enforced. So we decided to leave before the agent arrived. Pulled up the anchor at 0748 and headed north. Talked to Heather and she is still coming on the 1st. Hope to meet up on the 2nd. We selected Endeavour Reef on Tawila Island as the place to hang out without being disturbed. The wind was generally about 12 kts and the seas were not bad at all as most of the area is within reefs and islands. Arrived and dropped anchor at 1143. The island is low, sandy, and barren. There are some building ruins and crumbling docks. Obviously been abandoned for a long time. It is only about 6 meters high so there is no protection from the wind, but the shelter from the waves is good. Came in directly on a bearing due west and skirted the reefs on each side of the opening and around the old dock. The anchorage is over sand in 7.5 meters. There is continuous wind noise, but it is peaceful otherwise. John had made bread on the way and we had lunch of toasted cheese sandwiches with tomato soup and some reheated mashed potatoes. After lunch most everybody crashed out. A little later a local fishing boat came in and asked for water. I gave them one of our large bottles. Near sunset, after Charlie, Jack and Dick went in to photograph *ESCAPADE* at sunset, a dive boat came in towing a local fishing boat. They anchored ahead of us, and then decided that it was not a good location and moved to the north, over a shallow area. Then followed a circus of dropping a poor anchor on a rope rode, and then tying to one of the old jetty's posts, by a man who jumped overboard from a RIB. Then they turned on colored lights above the upper deck. Another fishing boat came in and towed the other fishing boat out. Dinner was salmon with angel hair pasta by Charlie. Desert of peaches. The wind has been between 18 and 24 kts all day long. Received another forecast from CW. The adverse winds will continue into Saturday morning, when they will switch to the SSE. As the winds decline at night, we will leave at dusk tomorrow so we can get out of the anchorage in some daylight. The winds should be light until they switch direction. Some played Uno, with Jack the champion.

Friday, March 29 - Endeavour Harbor

Woke to 16 to 18 kts winds from NW, but bright clear and sunny. On the net, everybody is in harbor waiting for favorable winds. Hygia is in Port Sudan, leaving tomorrow for Safaga, R Phirst is south of Port Sudan, waiting. Yang Sho is north of Massawa, waiting. A boat in Djibouti is leaving tomorrow for Obock and to wait there. Many boats have had difficulty in the Bab-el-Mandeb strait due to the high winds, even though they are generally aft. All crew aboard *ESCAPADE* are bored and just setting around and reading. Had lunch of ham and cheese sandwiches with made bread. All relaxed during the afternoon. John tried fishing. He caught four small fish that he threw back. Had a cocktail hour. Had dinner of sweet and sour pork chops made by Charlie. The wind at dinnertime was still 16 kts.

Saturday, March 30 - Endeavour to Gulf of Suez 165.0 NM

Woke early, about 0530. Everybody was up by 0600. The winds are still from the NW, but about 10-12 kts. According to the forecast the wind should have dropped to 5-10 at 0200 and by 0800 it should switch to 150-170°. So we decided to leave anyway on the basis that the change will happen, but a little delayed. The crew is definitely getting restless. Had to wait until we could read the water, as the sun was gleaming off the surface in the direction we had to go. Pulled up the anchor at 0618 and headed off. There is a general decline in the wind so maybe it will all come true. At 0900 the wind was 11 kts from the NNW. Dodged a few ships crossing the traffic lanes and then headed NW up the east side of the northbound lane. The seas increased, probably due to wind over tide as we were getting quite a current boost- maintaining 6.8 kts SOG motoring into the wind. Talked on the net. Hygia left Port Sudan at 0630 this morning. R Phurst, who is at anchor about 20 NM north of Port Sudan is staying put. Yang Sho, who is at anchor north of Massawa, may leave tomorrow if the winds decline (they have 24 kts from the NW). So all are hoping for a weather window. Talked to Heather and discussed her changing her flight from Monday to Sunday. Miracles do happen! (Or forecasts come true.) The winds had been declining all morning. By 1100 they reached 3 kts and the sea flattened out so we were motoring well. The current was with us as well so we were doing 7.2 kts SOG. Then the winds changed and came from the ESE and by 1400 were at 11 kts. We were able to shut the engine off at 1405 and by 1420 we were wing-on-wing. The sailing is beautiful, smooth and about 6.1 kts SOG. It couldn't be better. Really glad we spent the additional night at anchor. We can see both side of the Sea of Suez- Sinai on the east and Egypt on the west. The ships are going north and south and there are many oilrigs scattered around both sides of the traffic lanes, as well as in the separation zone. Wrote Prince of the Red Sea that we will be arriving tomorrow. Got an E-mail from Heather saying that she was able to change her flight to Sunday. Great! Later, around 1800 we were doing 8.5 kts SOG. Later still, the sped had dropped into the 7's. Had dinner of bloody Mary chicken with pasta, made by Charlie, and peaches for desert. Still have one more chicken and some mince left in the freezer. Heather did a good job of provisioning. Did run out of tea bags this evening and Jack is devastated. I had the 2100 to 2400 watch. Went quite well, with winds in the 20-22 kts range. Made good time. The wind seemed to drop so I pulled out the reef in the main for Jack and Charlie.

Sunday, March 31 - Gulf of Suez to Suez (165.0 NM) + 2.5 NM

I woke to Paul reefing the main and then the yankee. The wind had increased to the 30 kts range, with gusts to 35 and even 40 kts. At 0300 I got up, and so everyone was awake after John got up. Were approaching Suez rapidly so first we put away the main, then the yankee and were sailing on the staysail alone. Even with that we were making over 6 kts. Large ships were maneuvering and anchoring. But we counted on the channel to be free of traffic, and it was. I called our agent, the Prince of the Red Sea, on the Iridium phone and woke him up. He was not helpful and said to go to the anchorage at Green Island. There is no shelter there so that was not an alternative. Called Suez Harbour Control on VHF, and gave him some facts on ESCAPADE. He had me talk to another agent, Felix. He said it was difficult to go to the Yacht Club at night, so said to anchor behind the breakwater near the floating dry-dock in Ibrahim Basin. So we kept going. Sailed down the channel and then I took over as we peeled off to go beside the floating dry-dock. With winds at 30 kts, and gusts higher, it was exciting to say the least in the dark. As we passed by the floating dry-dock, which had waves breaking into it, I spotted a huge dark bollard and worried that there was a line from it to the dry-dock. But, luckily there was not, and we went past safely. Saw the breakwater, with waves breaking over it, and tucked in behind it. Dropped the anchor at 0510. Everybody was excited and pumped up and extremely glad we were safely here and at anchor. It was the most dramatic entry into a harbour ever, and it was at night in high winds! It was fairly peaceful at anchor but the wind howled around us. The passage was 165 NM and it took us 22.87 hours for an average of 7.21 kts. All went to bed. I awoke at 0845 and the wind had not abated. In fact, as the tide was up, the waves were crashing over the breakwater with more regularity. What a sight to behold. Heard on the radio that a ship at the Green Island anchorage was dragging anchor, so others are having difficulty in coping. Tried calling our agent, but got Felix again. He said it was not safe to move to the Yacht Club in these high winds. Later, our agent called us and said the harbour is closed to all ship movements so we should not move and that no boat could come to us. Talked to Heather and she will leave the flat in two hours. I will try calling her at 2200 tonight at the hotel in Cairo. Near noon the wind was still 35 kts with gusts to 41. It was a true gale. A small older ship was dragging anchor and drifted into the shallow end of the bay. A huge container ship came out of the canal and was caught broadside and had to power strongly forward to avoid drifting into the breakwater in front of us. The tide has risen and the water has been pushed into our end of the bay so the water is up 2.1

meters from when we anchored. The sea is breaking over the breakwater with regularity. An Australian boat came in, Foxtrot, with two people aboard. They anchored next to us. There seems to be no letup in the wind. Our anchor was well set and we were secure. Took a nap and when I got up the wind had dropped to 20 kts. Called Prince of the Red Sea and he said we could proceed to the YC (although the south bound convoy had not passed completely). Picked up the anchor and went in, going beside a huge tanker and tied to two buoys, bow and stern. The agent came aboard, and we arranged for measurement tomorrow. John will leave here, as we will clear out here and continue to go when we reach Port Said. Had cocktails to celebrate our accomplishment. Had dinner at the Red Sea Hotel in the restaurant on the sixth floor that overlooked the *ESCAPADE*. Walked around the town, which was built for the canal ex-pats. When we got back to the boat the wind was back to the north, at about 10 kts. Tried calling Heather at the Cairo hotel but the phone would not connect.

Monday, April 1, 2002 – Suez

Awoke to a bright, clear, calm day with hardly any wind. It has been such a long, hard push to get here it does not seem that in only two more days we will be in the Med. Got out the laundry we will send in today. The agent should be here at 0900, but he didn't come to the boat. The guys left for town to shop. Paul and I cleaned up the boat. At 1030 we moved *ESCAPADE* to the Yacht Club pontoon. Paul then washed down the boat thoroughly as it was covered with sand and salt. Noticed that the outhaul pulley in the deck organizer had a crack in it. We will have to live with it as it requires a whole new part. Heather arrived around 1100. Boy was it good to hold her! Paid the YC for the mooring and water- $28. Finally about noon the guys returned from shopping with their haul. The guy came for measuring the boat for the canal. He took the data and seemed quite efficient. I offered him 5 packs of cigarettes, but he refused. He has to review the data with his boss before we find out what the charge will be. The agent was here to make sure it happened. Heather cooked lunch of hot dogs and baked beans. Christened John's travel scrabble game. Moved back to the buoys and Paul changed the engine oil and oil and fuel filters. Heather put stuff away. We arranged with the agent to go to dinner and give him the passports at 2100 tonight. He will then clear us out so that we can depart Egypt as soon as we drop the pilot at Port Said. Went into town and ate at the Senator restaurant. Had whole broiled fish stuffed w/onions, baby shrimp and other goodies. Took the mini vans out and back. The agent came at 2100 to collect the passports and he brought our propane tank back. Heather, John and Jack played a game of Scrabble; she won.

Tuesday, April 2, 2002 - Suez into the Suez Canal and Ishmailia 45.0 NM

Woke to a bright and sunny day. Everyone was up and relaxed. The agent is due at 0830 with the laundry, our passports and bill. John will leave then. That didn't happen until after 0900. Finally got our passports and port clearance. Paid the agent $520 for all the formalities. A pilot boat came alongside, but it turned out to be another inspector who checked the safety equipment. Finally, a young pilot came aboard and said go! So off we went, leading 5 sailboats. He wanted the sail up in the first channel and we pulled out the staysail. Half way the first of the southbound convoys came and we kept to the left until we came to two lanes and we cut right. Got to the Great Bitter Lake, which is quite large, and at that point the last of the southbound ships passed. Heather and Jack played Scrabble; she got a scrabble and won. The pilot is very quiet, as he doesn't speak much English. He went below only once and that was to use the toilet. He did accept a carton of cigarettes and $15 but had to hide it from the police who were at the dock. Tomorrow's pilot came by and said to be ready at 0600. We were able to tie up to the yacht club dock and even had electricity!! Joy of joy!! Heather made Margarita Chicken and garlic cabbage that were eaten with relish. It is getting cold -- all are getting out fleeces. After dinner, we played Uno. We all went to bed fairly early, as we had to get up early.

Wednesday, April 3, 2002 - Ismailia thru Suez Canal to Port Said and Med 43.8 NM + 231.0 NM

Very cold morning but sunny and clear. Later turned overcast, probably the most cloud cover we have had recently. Erick walked around the Yacht Club, which is a good facility. The pilot came aboard and we left at 0618. He was an older man, who has been a pilot for 22 years. Not talkative, and smoked, but not too bad overall. The canal was more of a straight ditch today, but at the northern end there was some green shrubbery. Near Port Said, we pulled over to the Customs area and gave them a crew list and they waved us on. Prior to that I gave the pilot a carton of cigarettes and $15. As we got into Port Said proper a police boat came close, but after seeing the pilot they moved away. A small pilot boat came out near the Canal Authority building and the pilot got off and we said goodbye. We then proceeded another 2 miles to get out of the harbour. In the outer basin Erick closed out one leg and started another at 1155. It was a quick trip through the canal at 7.79 kts SOG average as we had a current with us nearly all the way. The two legs will separate the canal from the passage to Cyprus. The seas built as we moved away from land and into the Med. The wind was from the WNW so we could sail the 17° course to Larnaca. Turned off the engine at 1240. The winds were in the 20 kts range and the seas were large enough to give Jack and Heather problems. One peculiar wave broke over Jack and Dick and soaked them. The water was muddy for 25 NM off shore. Started the watch system with Erick taking the 1200 to 1500. As we arrived earlier than predicted, it will be longer before the wind backs to the south. The wind diminished a bit around 1800. Had dinner of chunky soup, as it seemed appropriate with everyone's tummy. Talked to the Larnaca marina and they said they didn't have room for us for a month, but we could stay a few days. So we will go there and try to talk our way in, or else we will have to go somewhere else (Limassol or Antalya). Sent E-mails to our family and Pantaenius Insurance letting them know we are back in the Med again. We are doing really well sailing with speed of 8.5 to 8.8 kts SOG. That means we may arrive Larnaca in the afternoon tomorrow. Hopefully in daylight.

Thursday, April 4, 2002 - Med to Larnaca, Cyprus (231.0 NM)

Our progress was still good when my watch started at 0600. It was overcast, and then began to rain. Had to suit up with full fowl weather gear including boots. The wind dropped, switched and generally was generally confused. Turned the engine on for 20 minutes, but then the wind returned to W or WSW and we were off again. Could hear Cyprus radio on VHF 16. We are well north of Israel. At the 0730 net, we had only 60 NM to go. Talked with Achates (Are-cades) and they had 130 to go. (They were with is in Ishmailia.) Yang Sho was still at the same anchorage, north of Massawa and Hygia was still at 22° north. All are staying put waiting for favorable weather in the Red Sea. At 1100 we had 32 NM to go to the waypoint, or about 4 hours at the current rate of 8 kts. There is another 6 miles to go after that, or about an hour. All seems favorable. The wind held from the SW and we kept going at over 8 kts. The rains came and went, but after we saw land, the sun came out. At 1155, or 24 hours, we did 201.3 NM, for an average of 8.39 kts. Saw the airport, then the city of Larnaca, then the marina. Heard another boat call the marina and they were very curt and said he could only stay to make repairs and then he had to leave. Called the marina and he was more courteous with us. But we still had to go against the north quay wall in the outer basin. Arrived at 1525 our time, which is an average of 8.40 kts. There was a surge even though the wind was not from the east. Mike, the harbour master, showed me three alternatives to squeeze *ESCAPADE* into the marina. I then went to the office building and completed Immigration, Customs, Police and Medical in short order. Went upstairs to the Marina office and they were aware that I had asked for a space last November. So we were discussing leaving the boat for two months. Thank goodness! They will give me a quote tomorrow. Went back to *ESCAPADE* and we moved her to between two motorboats, which were separated for us. It was a tight fit, as we had to shove them aside a bit, and roll the fenders, but we got in. Went about making *ESCAPADE* secure and deploying the passerelle and connecting power. Oh, all the luxuries! By that time the marina staff had left. Had cocktails and dinner of tacos on board. The men went out later to explore. Took showers after two days. This essentially completes our circumnavigation. What a sense of accomplishment. So we have traversed the major oceans- Atlantic, Pacific, and Indian; and the major seas- Mediterranean, Caribbean, Tasman, and Red. We felt relieved that were through the pirate areas, the Red Sea and the Middle East Arab countries. With all the war talk it is good to have that behind us. It confirms our decision to proceed. In fact, if anything, it was safer to do it when we did it than a year before. In any event, it is done and we don't have any more of those worries.

Friday, April 5, 2002 - Larnaca Marina

Woke to a bright, pretty, warmer day. But then a man appeared on the dock and said we would have to leave in 3 days. Bummer! Tried to get Yang Sho and Hygia, but could not hear them. Did talk to Notra Dom, who is 60 miles south of Suez and they had 10 kts from the south. Went to the marina office and they explained that we could not stay for two months. A few days, maybe, but definitely not two months. Heather made pancakes for breakfast, which were enjoyed by all. I couldn't get the telephone number from the old pilot book to work so I went to the marina office to get a number. They didn't have any information on Turkey, period. But a woman who came to get a laundry token said she might know someone who had a book on Turkey. So I met Ruth who took me to their boat on the hard and she lent me a book on Turkish marinas. Then I found out that you couldn't make a direct call to Turkey from Cyprus. But I was able to use Iridium to phone the Setur Marina in Antalya and they said they had room. So we will leave Sunday or Monday. Just need to change our British Air tickets. Went to Payless Rental Cars and rented a 5 passenger car. But they needed 45 minutes to get it ready so we went to lunch at McDonalds. Then returned at 1245 to get the car (the office is closed between 1300 and 1430). Drove to the airport and found the BA office. We were able to turn in our Cyprus/London/Cyprus tickets for Antalya/London/Antalya tickets with no penalty. We have to go through Istanbul and wait a couple of hours, but it will work out fine.Changed the date to the 10th, rather than the 11th to give us one day in London before our flight to Detroit on the 12th. So it has worked out well. Returned to the marina and picked up Jack and Dick and we drove east along the coast road. Saw Ayia Napa and Protaras, both tourist areas. Returned to the boat and then had dinner at the Crown restaurant. Went to the Internet cafe and was on-line for one hour. Caught up with most things. Went to bed tired.

Saturday, April 6, 2002 - Larnaca Marina

Woke up to an overcast and rain threatened day. Drove west with Jack, Dick & Charlie. Charlie decided to go to Lebanon after he leaves us. Stopped at Khirokitia, which is a Neolithic site about 9,000 years old. It consists of round dwellings made of stone and mud. We proceeded on and looked at the Limassol marina, which was also full, and not well protected. Went to the medieval castle in Limassol and had lunch at a Greek style restaurant next to it. Went to Kolosai, which is a medieval castle, and then to Kourion, a Roman theatre overlooking the sea. Looked at the "birth place" of Aphrodite, which are large rocks along the coast. Finished the day at Pafos, looking at mosaics from Roman houses. Had tea at a harbour side place and then drove back to Larnaca. Had dinner at Pizza Hut, and the pizzas were great. Everyone pigged out. Returned to the boat to read the weather forecast, which says to leave as early as possible.

Sunday, April 7, 2002 - Larnaca to Antalya 231 NM

Woke to a pretty, sun filled day. The sky was clear, and the wind was slight. Much better than yesterday. Took the car over to the rental place and parked it and gave the keys to the taxi office. Charlie will go there on Monday to make sure they got it. Picked up our passports from the police (there were 5 officers there). Charlie got off and we departed the dock. Picked up the dinghy and left the marina at 0703. The wind was about 8 kts from the SW as we headed south but when we turned to go SW it picked up to 14 kts and it was so close to our bow we could not even have the staysail out. But it was a pretty day to start the last leg of our circumnavigation. We kept going and the wind increased to 22 kts on the nose, the seas increased, and we still had to motor into it. Luckily the waves were from slightly to port. Our SOG dropped to the 4's but we were still making headway. Tacking would not seem to be productive as we would have to go a lot longer distance and the starboard tack would be directly into the waves. So we kept going. On my watch we passed Cape Gata. It was very lumpy, probably because of the cape and the shallow depth (32 meters). A passenger ship approached us but deviated around, giving us room. Finally we got past, and we were able to head more north. Still had to motor sail as the wind kept following us around (actually following the shore). But when we got to the SW tip, we could head for Antalya at 326° and we finally were able to shut off the engine and sail at 2230.

Monday, April 8, 2002 - Larnaca to Antalya (231 NM)

Had a good sail on my 0000 to 0300 watch. The lights of Cyprus finally disappeared. But by 0605 we had to turn on the engine as the wind had dropped and turned against us again. But with only 8 to 10 kts of wind the seas dropped and we were making good time- 6.5 kts SOG. The sun came up and it was lovely on my 0900 to 1200 watch. But at around 1130 the wind picked up to 18 kts on the nose and the seas rose quickly. Soon we were pounding into it again. The wind finally tended to go north a bit so we fell off to the south 10° so we could motor sail. But even so our speed dropped to 5 kts SOG. I am hoping that the wind will continue to clock, as predicted, and we can gain some speed and head in the right direction. Suddenly, at 1510, the wind shifted to the SW and we could shut off the engine and sail. The wind continued to back and we could point Antalya while making speeds of 8+ kts. It turned out to be a great sail as the seas dropped and we were making great speed with hardly any motion. Just before dusk we could see the mountains to the west of Antalya. Then, as we got closer, we could see the lights all around the end of the bay. It was nice and pretty and very pleasant. As we approached we had three checkpoints. First, we crossed the longitude of the Antalya old harbour at 2019. That means we have circumnavigated 360° around the globe. Hurray!! Then we crossed our outbound track when we left Antalya on October 6, 1997, at 2054. That officially completes the circumnavigation. Finally, when we arrived, we had returned to the city from which our circumnavigation had begun. It was very dark as we approached, but it was clear. We had to turn on the engine at 2023 as the wind died. There was a large ship anchored just north of our track, but we saw him as we approached. The red/green lights of the harbour entrance were visible when close and we turned in. Just then a fishing boat was coming out. At first he did not see us, but finally he turned away. Called the marina and they said they would have a dinghy to help us. Turned toward the marina entrance, and there was the dinghy signaling us. We followed him, and he was going to put us at the far end of the large boat dock. So we stopped, dropped the dinghy, turned around, and backed down the row and then into the slot. He passed Paul the "laid line" that turned out to be a chain. The man stayed to help us put the passerelle to shore and to connect the power. We were very pleased for the assistance. We were tied up by 2147. Tidied up then had a champagne toast to the finish of the circumnavigation. We went to bed tired, but extremely satisfied and proud.

Tuesday, April 9, 2002 - Antalya Marina

The day dawned bright and clear, but cold. The wind is up compared to when we entered last night. Heather made corned beef hash for breakfast. It warmed up nicely during the day. Spent the day clearing-in and organizing for repairs to the dinghy, TV and dodger. Had lunch onboard. Gave Zafer, the Marina Manager who we met at the Cruising Association house Med section meeting in January, a summary of our circumnavigation for submission to the Cruising Association. Finally got the passports back at 1700. Took the free marina shuttle into town for dinner. Walked to the old port and choose the Marina Restaurant for dinner; it turned out to be good. Walked around the old town and then to where we thought the shuttle made a pickup at 2300. Well, we were close, and they waited until we got on.

Wednesday, April 10, 2002 - Antalya Marina

Another sunny day. Ayhan, the tech services manager, came by and took the TV, dodger, and dinghy, all for repair. Also bought a new plastic gas tank for the outboard to replace the original steel one. I replaced the fuel tank inspection ports with new ones, installed a larger split pin on the top of the autopilot ram, and glued the cockpit speaker bars. While we were away Paul re-varnished the cockpit table and mug rack and replaced the forward head outlet house with a new one. Talked to the marina about having parts shipped in and concluded that it is much too difficult to do. Guess I'll bring spares in my luggage. Paul will stay onboard while we are away. Arranged for a taxi at 1200 and departed for the airport. We had a Turkish Airlines flight to Istanbul and then a BA flight to Heathrow. All went well.

Monday, May 13, 2002 - At Home

Received an E-mail from Kiko, who is back in London. Hygeia is in Gocek, but they arrived only around May 4. He said that now four boats have been lost in the Red Sea this year. These include the big German catamaran that was demasted in the Bab-el-Mandeb before we went through. They were in Galle with us. Then there was a French couple on Chamoise, who were in Darwin with us. They had heavy weather south of Safaga and tried to enter Marsa Mubarak at night. They hit the reef, couldn't get off, and were holed in a couple of hours. A large Chilean yacht, Hussar, which took our place in Galle also went onto a reef. He had no details. Finally, a New Zealand boat, Cariad, who was in Djibouti with us, also went on a reef. They were pulled off but the boat sank before they reached shelter. No loss of life. Very sobering. The Red Sea is a dangerous place.

Wednesday, May 29, 2002 - Antalya Marina

Flights from London went well. Craig Marks surprised us at the international arrivals in Istanbul. Walked to domestic terminal together where Anne was waiting. She looked terrific in spite of the three long flights they had from Florida-Detroit-Amsterdam-Istanbul. We all flew together to Antalya. The driver E arranged w/marina never showed so, after waiting half and hour, we took a taxi, which was basically, the same cost. The boat was in great shape thanks to Paul's efforts while we were away. The beds were made and looked so comfy after our long day. Did simple unpacking while visiting then went to the welcoming bed. P went to the symphony w/ friends. Heard him come in, also heard Craig come back from toilet as fwd head had a problem.

Thursday, May 30, 2002 - Antalya Marina

Finished unpacking our three huge duffels. The table was piled high w/parts to be put under the fwd bed. E installed a new autopilot ram and carefully adjusted the two rams so they were in sync. They are now really quiet. Possibly some of our problems were because the rams were fighting each other. E hired a car so we could drive to a Migros supermarket and provision the heavy items. First had lunch upstairs at the food court. There were so many familiar chain stores. Spent hour and half in the store and had two full shopping carts. Good thing we had car. Afterwards, dropped C&A off at a museum and returned to stow food. There was lots of room. Worked on getting H's clothes out from storage then got ready to go into town. Visited old harbor and walked around old town. Anne wanted to stop at every shop and enjoyed the atmosphere. I thought we would go to dinner at the restaurant where we were supposed to stay 4 years ago but once there, we didn't care for menu and accordion player. Too bad because we passed lots of lovely places. Then E wanted to go to the first place we came to but I wanted something w/atmosphere. Shortly found the Blue Paradise w/terrace overlooking harbor. Very nice. H had great sea bass, C&A also had fish, E&P had mushroom chicken. Drove back to marina. As E sat at the computer before retiring, his tummy began to gurgle. That meant upset tummy. During the night, he had the runs, getting up several times.

Friday, May 31, 2002 - Antalya Marina

E didn't sleep well and was very weak this morning. Lovely sunny morning. We planned to go sightseeing but he elected to stay onboard near the head. Smart. We got ready to leave. Anne was going to shower on shore but was stopped by arrival of Craig and Miles who took a pump and the kettle. She didn't want to pass them in her robe. Delayed us some. Now we were on Anne's time, not Reickert time. First had to go to Avis office to add Craig to contract. Next went to Perge. Best part of site is roman arch. The theater is not open to public. Rest of area was in ruins. Showed long main street w/trench for water. Headed toward Aspendos but took a wrong turn and passed a great store w/jewelry, leather, and rugs. Anne was very interested in jewelry and I wanted to check out the rugs for the powder room. When Anne didn't see anything she absolutely had to have, we went to the carpet area. I honed in on the silk rugs; they brought out dozens and finally brought one that had the right colors and pattern; the dimension is short but it will work and be lovely. Don't really want silk under the toilet anyway. H did not bargain for the price! C&A could not find one they really liked so we left then went to lunch at a nearby restaurant that wasn't bad. Nice and cool. Finally we were on our way to tour. Checked out Aspendos to see where to park then proceeded to Side (pronounced seedy). Drove through the ancient site and went to go through town but were directed by police to park in the car park. The town was made up of tourist traps: jewelry, leather, carpets, clothes, purses, candy, restaurants and narrow streets. No wonder cars aren't allowed; there is no place to park! We wandered around and found the old harbor that has a nice breakwater for local boats. Then saw the temple of Apollo in the distance and walked over to it. It was an incredible sight with the sunlight reflecting upon it. We continued up the east side of the peninsula and found a restaurant for dinner, walked back to the roman site, went into the theater. Anne wanted to shop before dinner so C&I perused further the site. Nothing else was open or open to the public. So we talked with the police to see if we could take the car to the restaurant. After our feeble attempts to state our case, he let us go through. With the narrow streets filled with pedestrians, we began to doubt our decision. There was no parking near the restaurant, Karides, so we kept going to the temples where there were a few spaces. A joined us after a while excited about her purse purchases. After a quick dinner, we headed to Aspendos where we were meeting E. Because we were late, he was already there and saving seats. Parked at the back, hoping no one would park in front of us. E had already radioed to get our ETA as the crowds were trying to infringe upon his territory. Went to toilet, then joined the throng of people entering the arena. E was in the first row center of the upper level. Even by the time he arrived the lower half was full. We wended our way through the seated people and finally got to E. Great seats. He brought cushions. The symphony and tenor were fantastic. Hearing the music in such a beautiful setting was pure magic. The acoustics were incredible. The finale was the full-length Ravel's Bolero, played as never heard before. The crowd roared appreciation. After that, with a heavy German audience, the symphony played some favorite German songs to which they sang along. We were able to get out easily and walked quickly to the car that was not hemmed in. We were probably the first car out of the car park. On the way home, we stopped to fill the gas tank. What a marvelous day! E had a nap to 1330, then another hour later. Had half a peanut butter sandwich for lunch, and whole one for dinner. With Paul they replaced the line organizer on the cabin top. Got our cruising permit. Checked out of marina. Got on-line with AOL via the GSM telephone. Oh joy! Had to move the AOL Global Net Plus cell to AOL 4.0 as 4.0 didn't have it and 5.0 would not communicate with the GSM modem; changed to the other phone number, and called during the right time of day. Was able to get all mail downloaded/uploaded and signed off in one go. Hope it will now work reliably.

Saturday, June 1, 2002 - Antalya Marina to Cineviz Limani 29.8 NM

E feeling much better, and was able to sleep through the night. Bought some oil for the engine. Turned the car in to the Avis guy. Did all the things to get ready to sail. At 0930 we pulled out and were dispatched with much horn blowing by boats that Paul had become friendly with. The day started out somewhat sunny but soon turned overcast as we headed south. We were headed into a rainstorm but it parted so we got to the harbor with only minor rain. Anchored at 1405 among eight boats, but some of the local gulets left quickly as they were day-tripper gulets. There are sure more boats and people than last time we were here. There was even a dock and a makeshift shelter serving food. After lunch of sandwiches it started to rain harder. Lazy afternoon of reading and napping. Rain stopped and calm set in. Had bloody Mary chicken w/cauliflower, creamed corn, and rice, along with Greek salad. Decided that we would go to Finike, Kale Koy, Kalkan, Fethiye, Wall Bay, Ekincik and Marmaris. Watched the Mexican. The TV kept shutting off, even though we were running it on AC and we just had it fixed.

Sunday, June 2, 2002 - Cineviz Limani to Finike 27.1 NM

The day dawned bright with a clear blue sky- just like we remembered the Med. The bay looked much better with the sun on the rock sides. Also, after the gulets left there were only about four small sailboats there so it was far prettier. More like we remembered. Took our time to get going so it was relaxed. Pulled up the anchor at 0930. Motored in very still waters. Went close to shore so we saw the land really well. After we rounded the point, we were able to sail. It was only about 6 knots of wind to begin, but it was a pleasant sail with smooth water. Lunch was sandwiches made with bread that H had just baked. As we approached Finike the winds increased so we were doing over 7 kts SOG. Everybody loved the sail. At the marina, they put us along side a fixed pontoon near the end. Friendly staff. Had to wire our plug with a French type 2 prong one, which we had in our stockpile. Checked in and paid the marina- $32. H,A,&C walked into town, found the grocery, had a look around for restaurants but didn't find much. Took some photos. It has more boats than last time and is quite nice. The bathrooms are great and there is laundry (service type). Anne & Craig went shopping and bought a wool carpet for $600. Ate dinner at Petek Restaurant near the marina; food OK. Believe that we ate there last time. Went to bed by 2300.

Monday, June 3, 2002 - Finike to Kale Koy 18.3 NM

Woke to an absolutely gorgeous day. Bright sunshine hitting the town and deep blue sky above the green trees on the hills. The temperature is still somewhat cool. Wearing shorts during the day, but need a fleece or jacket at night. Nice for sleeping as we are under the bedspread with all but the head window closed. But it is cool enough that it does not make me want to swim although there were two people swimming in the bay at Cineviz Limani yesterday. Got under way at 0900; water perfectly flat so H did load of laundry while motoring. The area is more developed, including some docking beneath the castle that offers power and water (if you eat at the restaurant), but it is still beautiful. Went behind the island into the bay and anchored next to another cruiser at 1200. Had lunch onboard. H stayed on the boat while the rest of us dinghied around to the base of the castle. Walked up, but it seemed easier this time. It was definitely less hot. Had drinks at the restaurant where we docked. Cruisers can dock for free, with free electricity. Met an American boat, Cinabar, who had just come up the Red Sea. H hung out at the laundry and read her book. It was very relaxing. Had nibbles of cheese & crackers onboard and then went to Ibrahim's for dinner. Walked around town and had drinks (Hot apple tea) at a very moody, unique bar. Ran the generator and water maker and went to bed.

Tuesday, June 4, 2002 - Kale Koy to Kalkan 29.5 NM

The day started bright, but there was a thin dusting of light clouds. The wind dropped last night. Ran the generator and water maker and filled the tank. Got the two loaves of bread promised by Ibrahim last night. They were delivered to the boat before breakfast. Picked up the anchor at 0850. Motored all the way as the wind kept following us around. Could have sailed the last two miles. Arrived and med moored stern to the dock at 1332. The harbormaster stayed and helped with the passerelle. Had power, but not enough to run the AC plus other items. The breakwater was badly damaged by last winter's storm. We heard that there were 20 to 25 meter waves last winter that did the damage. The town seems prettier than before. It is definitely larger with lots of new buildings: restaurants, shops, and grocery. A boat at right angles had their anchor under our chain and the boat next to us, as we both arrived after the other boat. We slacked off our chains and they were able to lift their anchor and drop our chains. We lost some scope, but it should be OK. Welcome to the Med! Later, more than 8 charter boats came in, most in a flotilla. So the harbor became very full, especially after the local boats returned as well. We had dinner at the Ibo Restaurant, on the rooftop. It was more expensive than others, but wonderful, with different food. Returned to the boat. The boat was discharging, even though the charger was on. However, the shore voltage was down to 180 VAC. When it increased to 190, then we started to charge. The girls stopped to shop on the way back.

Wednesday, June 5, 2002 - Kalkan to Fethiye 40.3 NM

Another gorgeous day in paradise. Music played quite late; kept me awake. Craig as well, turned out. Wind from W so we are motoring, again. Slight swell. Cool air. Left at 0830; no problem raising anchor. Flotilla left much earlier as did the large motorboat. A&C went to store to buy bread and fruit. Loved Kalkan. Didn't get to walk around last time here as we took an excursion to Xanthos. After lunch, Anne presented all of us with a t-shirt from Kalkan that says "Sailing Paradise". All are on deck reading. Hope to sail as we head more northwest. E called an agent in Rhodes to reserve spot; also called Marmaris to make sure they had room; all okay. Were not able to sail; wind followed us around the coast. Saw lots of sailboats as we came around corner. Fethiye is a large sailing harbor. There was plenty of room at the quay so we backed in at 1504. As we approached, one yacht was leaving and someone on the dock was yelling, "did you pay"; after they raised anchor they went back. E took care of our docking fees upon arrival. A&C headed off in to town. Found a place for dinner, but didn't buy anything. I prepared the watermelon and made gazpacho for tomorrow's dinner. Left at 1930 for dinner. Wandered through the pedestrian streets lined with rug, leather, jewelry, spice, knickknack shops and restaurants before getting to the restaurant, called Cuisine Restaurant. Food not bad but nothing great. Roamed streets after dinner; Erick found an ATM after sixth try to accept our card. Came back to boat and went to bed early. A&C stayed out late buying stuff.

Thursday, June 6, 2002 - Fethiye to Wall Bay 14.7 NM

Slept in. Peaceful night at dock. A&C bought jewelry last night; good buy. She really likes to shop. Also got some placemats, napkin rings, and glass mats. Very nice stuff. They went off to have breakfast and look at the tombs. I cleaned up our cabin and went to store. Ran into Paul there. E & I had lunch on boat. Decided to leave before 2 and left at 1325. At first, wind was on the nose but then we were able to sail as we changed course. Had a nice couple of hours sailing. Lovely day; A&C are very happy they decided to come. Going behind the island shifted the wind so the sails disappeared and motor was turned on. There is a lot more vegetation on the hills. And many boats are sailing in this lovely bay. We come down to Wall Bay and picked our spot between two boats. This bay is fabulous; very deep; took stern line to shore that has bollards on which to tie lines. (An improvement by the Turkish Marine Environmental Agency.) Were secured at 1605. People were swimming; the water was very clear. The day became really hot; had cold watermelon after arrival. A guy came along side selling Walls ice cream (Magnums) in which we indulged. We all went to shore and took a walk around the bay; and took some great photos of *ESCAPADE*. The guys went to the restaurant and looked at the 20 or so charter boats tied to a rickety pier. Had dinner onboard of Persian chicken and gazpacho soup. It was great. Watched the movie Memphis Belle, about the WWII B-17. Very realistic I thought, but all that probably did not happen to one plane on one mission. Ran the water maker. Have been having trouble with the basic G-4 computer freezing or locking up. Sometimes with no app running, other times with various operations being performed, sometimes when it is in sleep mode. Reduced the extensions to the basic set and the problem went away. Will increase the number of extensions slowly to see if I can identify the problem. It did not start until I played around with AOL 5.0. Possibly the problem lies there.

Friday, June 7, 2002 - Wall Bay to Ekincik 29.5 NM

The day dawned clear with the sun rising over the hills, and it was very still in Wall Bay. The water was like glass and so peaceful. Anne swam before leaving; said it was so refreshing; showered on stern. Picked up the anchor at 0905 and headed out into no wind. Calm seas. The mountains in the distance were hazy. It was very beautiful. Went through a small channel between an island and a peninsula of the mainland. Depth got to 15m. No problem. Very lazy day. Nothing to do but motor along, read, and watch the coastline. Computer is having no problem after E got rid of extensions. Got to Ekincik and found that there is now a dock which you can tie stern-to. And there is power! Tied up at 1330. It is free as long as you eat at the restaurant. A big Red go-fast motorboat (Magnum) was here but they left later. Turned out a former president of Turkey was aboard--all men. Made arrangements for tomorrow. Spent a lazy afternoon; H,C&A played Scrabble. Had dinner at the My Marina restaurant located up the hill. Didn't think much of the meal; and it was expensive. Had an early evening.

Saturday, June 8, 2002 - Ekincik

Took a large tourist boat at 0900, and we had it all to ourselves. It was stable but the water was calm and it had a bimini. The sky was light gray as was the sea, could not tell the horizon. Showed us a cave from one side then the other. At first, we thought we were going through it. Passed Turtle Beach, and entered the river over a sand bar. There were some huts and hundreds of beach chairs lining the shore. Went first to Ancient Caunos, which we toured for 45 minutes. H stayed on the boat. It left to pick the group up further up the river. She thought frightening thoughts for a few minutes but then realized we were following the channel. There was some overcast so it was not too hot. The main buildings are the theatre, Roman baths, church, and a round foundation. Saw many turtles on the ground. Proceeded on into Dalyan, where we had lunch and bought some floating "noodles". It was market day; fun seeing the stalls of fruits and veg. From there you can see the Lycian rock tombs carved into a cliff high above ground. Returned directly to Ekincik and arrived back at 1400. C&A went swimming and tried P's windsurfer. She finally got it to stay up. Sun had come out; hot afternoon; turned on A/C in salon. H worked on cross-stitch. Made Turkish meatballs for dinner then went up to the restaurant for drinks. E&H took the funicular; quick start and stop but slow and pleasant going up. Bar area was lovely with grape vines being silhouetted by the mountains in the setting sun. No one else there. Returned to the boat for dinner of the meatballs, fettuccini and garlic cabbage. All sat visiting in the cockpit afterwards.

Sunday, June 9, 2002 - Ekincik to Marmaris 19.9 NM

The morning dawned clear and bright. The surface of the bay was like glass so we could see the bottom very clearly. So still and peaceful.Another day of motoring.Left at 0853. There were trees on the surrounding hills and not as barren and rocky even though some mountainsides go straight up. Anne gave me a book called The Pull of the Moon to read about a 50-year old woman going on a journey to find herself. Good reading, but I don't really understand that type of woman. Think Wendi would enjoy. Practically no wind and the sea was glassy. Arrived at 1158 at C-dock. Had lunch at Pineapple. They had ESCAPADE in their computer at the marina! We tried to find the small restaurant we liked five years ago, but it must have closed. Made reservations at La Campana right near the boat. E went to Ocean Jaywalker and talked a while. They will be returning to England (Gosport) by October so will not attend the Oyster event in Mallorca. But both of us might receive the Oyster circumnavigation award in January. Anne was shopping all afternoon. Had pictures taken on the stern. A large junky boat came in and just about hit us. Had to fend off and the marina dinghy acted as bow thruster. The marina people put them two spots over. Had dinner at La Campana restaurant, an Italian one overlooking the Marina. Quite nice. We went to bed early and C,A& P had a walk.

Monday, June 10, 2002 – Marmaris

Another hot and sunny day. Anne and Craig left at 0920 in a minivan with a driver for Ismir. Collected all the laundry and took it over to be done. We did all of the preventative maintenance items to bring us up to date. Both the engine and generator are less than half way to oil changes. H got her clothes organized and cleaned the aft cabin. Bought some large bolts to make substitute pedals for the bikes. Checked out of the marina. Can't get duty free fuel under 2,500 tons, which comes from Ismir in a tank truck. Bought a few grocery items including four bottles of wine. Veronica and Hellmuth called on the GSM phone and they are in Crete. Paul started the movie Vertical Limit, and Heather then had to watch it all the way through. So we had soup for dinner. We then went walking in town and through the bazaar at night. The sky was cloudy and we spots of rain. The wind was up from the west, a rare occurrence at night. The weather forecast at the marina office showed no gales, but westerly winds. Should be OK as we are heading south (193°).

Tuesday, June 11, 2002 - Marmaris to Rhodes 25.4 NM

The morning was much brighter with sunshine. There are more clouds about, but they are light and fluffy. It was cool as P&H left to get the laundry; H stopped at a store to buy pop w rest of P's money. E went to harbormaster to check out then had to go to Customs & Immigration. After he returned, we left the mooring and went to the fuel dock. Even though the hose would have reached where we were docked, the marina's policy was to not dispense fuel in the marina -- we could understand. Took 575 L. Got away at 1050. Clouds disappeared. Harbor calm and two naval vessels were anchored. Were able to sail out of harbor w/engine then turned off engine w/reefed main, staysail, and yankee flying. Doing 8.1 SOG. Saw three submarines just off the coast, as they were on the surface.   The wind was generally at 20 kts, but did get up to 24 kts near the end of the trip. Was still blowing 15 to 20 in the harbor which made docking tricky. I called A-1 Yachting, our agent at 2 hours to go, then again at 30 minutes to go. Still, after we got into the harbor we were asked to wait 10 minutes. Just as entered, two French boats came in and were circling as we were, causing confusion and they squeezed into some tight places. Finally, our agent appeared next to the Kon Tiki floating restaurant, at a private berth next to the Coast Guard boats. We dropped the anchor and while backing down the wind kept catching us and tossing us to and fro. Finally pulled up on the chain, which straightened us up so we were able to get the stern lines ashore. "Lightly kissed" the small motorboat next to us with the outboard propeller, but there was no damage. The transmission would not engage in forward and the wind forced us back on it. Finally at 1500 we were secure enough to stop the engine. Whew! The check-in office is about 50 feet behind us. The man for the power came right away. Later, more boats were circling trying to find places. Glad we hired the agent compared to last time. For dinner we walked the new town and finally found an Italian modern restaurant, Angeli Di Roma. It was good, and we thought we would have enough Greek in the next few weeks.

Wednesday, June 12, 2002 – Rhodes

It was another bright, clear day with the wind still blowing strongly, but slightly less than yesterday. E went searching the old town, and then reserved a car for tomorrow. Went to take the bus to the airport, but it just left at 1040 and the next one was 1130. So he took a taxi to the airport and arrived just before Helmut and Veronica's flight from Athens arrived. But he did not see them and although the baggage just started arriving they left quickly in a taxi. Veronica called as they were in route in the taxi but they didn't have E with them. After calling Heather, E got a taxi back to the port. Bummer to have missed them and had that expense. After they unpacked, we had lunch of BLT's on *ESCAPADE* and then walked the Old Town and visited the Grand Masters Palace. Returned to *ESCAPADE*. Had dinner at the same restaurant we ate at in 1997 on a roof overlooking the old square, but it was windy and cold and the food was not as good as it was before (Elazzo). Walked back to the boat.

Thursday, June 13, 2002 – Rhodes

A bright and clear day. The wind has diminished somewhat. Tried to get money via ATM, but none of them, including the one I used before would give any money. Borrowed E200 from Hellmuth. Picked up a car-Fiat Punto. Everybody piled in and we headed south. Stopped at A-1 Yachting but they did not have the bill prepared. Bought a yellow Q flag at the chandlery on the first floor. Arrived at Lindos late morning and had to park up at the top of the hill. Walked up to the acropolis. H very out of shape, got winded, and affected by heat. They were in the process of reconstructing the Temple of Athena. Had lunch at a creperie in Lindos and then drove back to Rodos town. Stopped at a good Spar supermarket and stocked up with provisions. Stowed everything on the boat and then went to the beach on the west tip of the island. H&V went in the water while H&E sat on the recliners. Water was a bit cold. Returned to the boat and H&V played scrabble. Went to look for a restaurant mentioned in our old travel book and found that it was closed. Walked a bit and then ate at Nireas restaurant. It was quite good, inexpensive and very Greek. The plates were brought individually. Returned to *ESCAPADE*. Called Comerica bank and they said the daily maximum was $500, which is what I thought. But the reason the ATM card was not working was they showed a charge of $383 (for 400 Euros) charged today at 8:30am. But I made the withdrawal at 1812 local time on the 11th. That should have been around 1000 Detroit time on the 11th. Don't know if one of my other attempts was charged to me or the 11th debit was not booked until the 13th.

Friday, June 14, 2002 – Rhodes

It became windy overnight and in the morning there were clouds around. But it cleared up later. The wind is still out of the west. We left the boat late, and first stopped at A-1 Yachting. They still had not prepared the bill yet, but they did so as I waited. Then the credit card machine would not work. We drove to the Valley of the Butterflies. It was a pretty, shaded valley with a creek running down it. But it was a long walk up, with steps and bridges, then we continued to the Monastery where we rested in the shade of a tree with the wind cooling us and had donut holes and fresh orange juice. It was easier to walk down although the stones were very uneven. Ate at the cafe at the bottom; lunch of ham & cheese sandwiches. Drove to Ancient Kamiros and visited the site. H stayed in the car. It is a mediocre site. Returned to Rhodes and stopped at a supermarket which was supposed to have more US items, but it was not really much different from Spar. H tried to buy tickets for the Greek dance show tonight in the Old Town, but the ticket office was closed. Went again to A-1 and the Visa card machine still was not working. They claimed that the banks had changed their number in the last few days. The bill is reasonable. E45 for the transit log, E100 for the Greek cruising tax, E75 for 4 days dockage, and E100 for the agency fee. Returned to the boat. H&V played a game of Scrabble (H got 91 points for one word). Yang Shou has not been seen. Finally paid A-1 Yachting with a dollar check (except for water and electricity). Dropped the car at Butterfly Car Rentals before going back to the Angeli Di Roma Restaurant. Was able to get 310 Euros at an ATM machine. After dinner we walked quickly to the place in the old town where the Greek dancing show is performed. Although listed as 2120, they did not start until 2135 and the 10-minute break became 20. The dancing was so-so, and the dancers were older and not really fit. Erick & Hellmuth did not like it but H&V did. Returned to *ESCAPADE* late.

Saturday, June 15, 2002 - Rhodes to Simi 23.6 NM

The day dawned partially cloudy. The wind is still from the west, but moderate. People came to read water and electric fairly early. Agent came to bring transit log & receive payment. Then we had to wait until the 0900 departing ferries left. Harbormaster advises when they can leave so it was an orderly exit. Our departure was orderly and without panic as well as P rigged a line to another boat to keep us from being blown on to the small powerboat to our starboard. All went smoothly; nothing hooked on the anchor (like the last time in Rhodes) and we departed at 0924. Motored into the westerly wind so that we could get an angle to sail. Turned off the engine at 1130 and had a fine sail. But as we went behind Simi, the wind dropped so we had to turn the engine on at 1240. Had lunch of sandwiches. Came into view of the harbor and it was just as pretty as before. Lovely. Went well down into the harbor to find a space to dock. There was a cross wind which turned out to be greater that Erick thought. Thus we had to abort the first approach and drop the anchor a little more upwind. This time it was a very smooth approach between a sailboat and a powerboat. We were attached at 1355. The local official came to the boat to collect a 2 Euro fee. What a bargain! Turned out it was only for catching lines. Most went exploring. The day was now bright sunshine and it was hot walking around. A one-day tripper boat left after we arrived. So most of the day people will be gone for the evening. I checked the records and found that we first moved on to *ESCAPADE* was exactly 6 years ago today. We started sailing on June 19, 1996. A man asked for the captain and said I should go to the harbormaster. E was nervous about having all 5 crew on deck as only 3 are on transit log. I went and had to show the Transit Log and pay another 7.60 Euros. A powerboat squeezed its way in between the larger powerboat and us. We didn't think it would fit but it did. The kids aboard it were yelling and screaming. So much for our peace and quiet. We went to dinner at the Hellenikon Restaurant, on the side of the street at the end of the harbor. It was good, with different Greek food. Returned to run the generator. We started a movie, but then the Germans in the boat next to us came back and complained about the generator fumes. So we shut it off without a full charge or refrigeration hit. That stopped the movie and computer playing. We all went to bed.

Sunday, June 16, 2002 - Simi to Tilos 34.0 NM

The day started bright and clear with very little wind. The church bells tolled as the sun glistened off the cream and yellow colored buildings. Veronica went to get pan au chocolat for us for breakfast. It was fresh and delicious. Smooth exit after two boats hemmed us in; left at 0845. H went to turn on the inverter after leaving to run the refrigeration but there was a failure with the inverter. E concluded that the inverter failed and needed major work, so we will have to live without it for a while. Had to turn on generator as fridge was at 5 and needed a hit, so water maker is being run as well. Had to motor the whole way as the wind, light at first, was on the nose until just before Tilos. Came around the south point and into the bay, which was very wide. It is on the south side of the island named O. Eristou. A swell rounds into the bay so we went into the far northwest corner and anchored at 1420. Hellmuth and Paul went into shore, found a taverna, watched football, and walked around a bit. A basically deserted island. Later, the swell seems to roll *ESCAPADE* side to side too much so we re-anchored the main anchor to make sure it was dug in and then set a stern anchor to hold the bow into the swell. It improved the situation dramatically. Had dinner of curry chicken with rice. Watched the movie A Knights Tail, with the generator on and the washing machine running, then with the water maker on.

Monday, June 17, 2002 - Tilos to Astipalaia 46.9 NM

It is another clear sky, sunshine day. Before I got out of bed Hellmuth was putting away the washboards. Paul got up early and had the stern anchor aboard and stowed by 0720. The water was so very clear. We could see the whole bottom through 8 meters. It was still and serene. ESCAPADE started to roll as soon as the stern anchor was released. Paul started to pull in a little chain so we left as soon as Heather started her log. It was 0738 as we pulled away. The wind is on our nose again, especially as our long (43.5 NM) leg is at 283°. But we could pull out the staysail and a little of the main to speed us up about a knot and smooth the ride. I got on-line before we left, although it appears we have quite complete GSM coverage even between islands. Talked to Yang Shou and they arrived in Rhodes yesterday (June 16) because of further delays in Antalya. The Navtext indicates that a medical helicopter went missing last night, and in two separate incidents, there were 10 red flares seen, and in the other a single red flare. No indication if anyone was found. We hope the anchorage tonight will be nice and snug. H took a nap in afternoon and woke as the anchor was laid at 1600. Were able to motor sail most of the way. The anchorage was basically deserted; a couple buildings on the NE side and a boat in another small bay on the S side. Very windy. Paul went windsurfing and had a super time. V&H played scrabble. Made penne bolognaise for dinner. Watched Ocean's Eleven and had popcorn. E ran generator & made water. All went to bed early, but H was nervous about wind strength & how close it was putting us to this little rocky outcrop. She got E up but he felt it was okay and not worth putting out a second anchor. He went back to bed; she stayed up on deck until 2:30, but nothing changed in those 4 hours. Figured it would stay the same. Down below, the wind seemed much less but it was not really.

Tuesday, June 18, 2002 - Astipalaia to Santorini (Thira) 63.8 NM

Day dawned sunny and clear but very windy from N. Left at 0658 in Force 6. The motion was good. As we were heading 260° we could sail. It was a fast nice sail. Heather thought we were heeling too much but it was good to get in some sailing after so much motoring. The seas remained relatively calm for winds of at least 25 kts, and gusts higher. Near islands the wind would reach 34 kts. Had lunch of mac and cheese. Arrived at Santorini at 1615 and there are no good anchoring alternatives. As we were circling another sailboat came in and went close to the dock and a motorboat with men on it came out to attach their lines to the buoy. We deployed the dinghy and Paul was in it but they ignored us. Then a ferryboat came in near the buoy so we had to wait for them. Finally we came in and the men (Union Boatmen of Santorini) attached our lines. The winds were in the 20-knot range and there is a small chop that kept things stirred up. After several maneuvers we were attached to the buoy, and at rest. The time was 1630. The sailboat beside us will leave at 0900 tomorrow morning. There is also a motorboat here and they don't want the sailboat anywhere near them. Went up into the Chora by cable car. Walked the town and had dinner at a very nice, but expensive restaurant that had a roof top view of the sunset (Ampolo). Quite romantic. Walked down the hill in the dark among donkey dung. Not a good idea. The motorboat had left and the sailboat had repositioned so we were relatively fine. Had a somewhat OK night.

Wednesday, June 19, 2002 - Santorini to Thirasia 3.8 NM

It was another bright clear day. The sailboat left at 0900 and we then positioned ourselves into the wind so ESCAPADE was riding better. One of the fenders was missing so Paul & I went looking for it in the dinghy. We just about gave up hope when we spotted it way down the shore. The surf was breaking on a rocky shore so we put the anchor out to hold the dinghy into the swells. Paul dived in and walked down the beach to retrieve the fender. I tried to let the dinghy drift closer to the shore but I took three large waves over the bow. Had to pull forward to avoid being swamped. But at least we recovered the fender. Heather agreed that it was better to go directly to the Peloponnesus rather than to Milos as that would require motoring directly into the wind. Later a light home-built motorboat came in along side us and caused all sorts of havoc. He did not know what he was doing and did not have proper dock lines etc. First he got close to our bow and came up under our anchor and cut a slash in his deck. Everyone went ashore except Erick and he had lunch of a peanut butter sandwich. E replaced the Gebo pelican hook on the portside lower lifeline as the old one broke. Then the motorboat caused damage to *ESCAPADE*- a ding in the aft starboard side Gebo port and a nick in the rub rail. Even though I had placed 4 fenders near the stern, the boat came bow first at us and then ducked under the fenders and I could not reach it with my feet before it had risen and caused the damage. I then positioned the dinghy there to act as a buffer. Paul returned at 1315 and he prevented further damage in much the same fashion later. Just then the owner of the powerboat returned and took it away. Whew! The seas are getting larger and maybe it is time to leave. But Heather must have turned off the VHF because I have been trying to reach her for an hour and there is no response. Finally she called. They will return directly to the boat. Heather suggested that we go to the north end of Santorini for the night. When she returned, we looked at other alternatives and concluded that the anchorage at Thirasia would give us protection from the winds and swells better than the north end of Santorini. So we concluded we will do that and if it wasn't good we would proceed to the next place. The winds increased to over 20 kts and the waves were getting larger at the anchorage. Paul went in to use the Internet and then tell the boatmen we would leave. He returned quickly as the Internet place was occupied and he noticed that two boats were coming to the buoy, one a sailboat and the other a powerboat. In fact the powerboat looked at the situation and took off at over 20 kts. The boatmen arrived and untied us and we motored nicely away at 1515. They then got busy attaching the sailboat. We later discovered one of our dock lines had nearly chafed through. The chop was large as we motored into it. Spray was flying. The winds were up to 30 kts. As we approached the Thirasia everything became still and the seas turned flat and the wind dropped to less than 4 kts. The problem was that there was no place to go. There were buoys, but they all appeared to be privately owned. The depths were severe with over 40 meters very close to shore. We were attempting to scope out anchoring at the north end under the cliff when a local boat came out. We asked him if there was a buoy we could attach to and he said we could use his, and pointed to a buoy in front of Captain John's restaurant. As we were circling and lowering the dinghy, a rowboat came out and said we could tie alongside the fishing boat on the buoy at Captain John's. They even had a man on board the fishing boat to catch our lines! I approached very nicely and just kissed the boat as we came along side at 1615. It is still, not rolly, and seemingly perfect. We also took a stern line ashore. The man said the buoy was very large and strong. H&V played Scrabble and P&H went on shore to scope things out. They also have donkeys to go up the hill to the Chora above. Everyone was pleased with the decision and the selection of port. We will leave tomorrow for the mainland. Ate at Captain John's. It was simple food and there was no menu. We ordered by looking at the availability in the display case. It was quite OK. H & I took a short walk around the waterfront, which consists mainly of abandoned fisherman's buildings.

Thursday, June 20, 2002 – Thirasia

Another bright, clear day. Not as hot due to the strong winds. Near gale force 7, locally gale force 8 through most of the Aegean. Went to take a donkey up the hill, but as we were there at 1000, there were none as they start work at 1300. So we walked up. Then walked south on the top of the island. H,P,&V continued on the dirt road, saw another couple who said there was a monastery further along. We walked until we were close enough for good pictures then turned around. H was going to wait for us at the restaurant but turned out that he & E waited for us at the windmill. Found an old windmill, then returned to town and had lunch. Saw another sailboat heading toward the bay so Paul went down the hill quickly. We followed after visiting the rest of the town. Paul told the other boat, which wanted to raft to us, to go to the other side of the fishing boat. That would equalize the force on the buoy, as the fishing boat would be in the middle. Had ice cream at Captain John's. Paul sealed the thru hull port which was damaged yesterday. He worked on the fwd head pressure relief, which was blocked before the vent filter. The head seems to work much better now, with less back pressure. H&V played Scrabble again. Then a charter sailboat used our bow as a target for backing exercises. Made us very nervous. Had dinner at Captain John's again. Good, but not special, food at very reasonable prices. The latest weather forecast says that decreasing winds in many areas will occur. Also, the winds in the southwest Aegean will be north northeast. Hope it will be good for tomorrow. Went to bed early and had a good sleep.

Friday, June 21, 2002 - Thirasia to Porto Kayio, but at sea 141.0 NM

Another bright, clear day. Everyone got up late and just relaxed. Reading, and H&V played Scrabble. H made gazpacho for later. The sailboat on the other side of the fishing boat left early. We went in to Captain John's for lunch at 1230. Had a good one, and H bought some groceries. Also got some tomatoes from the restaurant. Had some ice cream there and brought some back to the boat for later. Watched the first day-tripper boat leave then a couple on shore started waving their arms. The boat came back for them after the ferry departed. We left smoothly at 1330 knowing it would be blowing more outside our sheltered bay. We said goodbye to Yannis. They were really very good to us, and we really appreciated all they did for us. We reciprocated by giving them business and tips. Headed out from behind Thirasia and into the chop. Were able to set sails as soon as we headed west (our course was 268°). The sea was somewhat confused which resulted in a bouncy ride. The wind varied from 25 to 30 knots. As we headed west the seas smoothed out somewhat and the ride became better. Heather even said if it stays like this she would be happy. Had dinner of margarita chicken, corn and rice. It was quick since most was prepared ahead of time. The night was beautiful with nearly a full moon and lots of light. We were going so well we would get to the bay before daylight so we decided to carry on to Porto Kayio. E wanted to go all the way to Pilos but he & H compromised to PK.

Saturday, June 22, 2002 - At Sea to Porto Kayio (141.0 NM)

The Straits of Elafounsia was very busy with large ship traffic as we passed through. Hellmuth was on watch, but E&P were also up keeping an eye out with the busy traffic. H turned on radar. Another bright sunny day. Daylight came at around 0515. Once through Straits, the bay was very calm. Wind diminished, then had to motor. Entered the PK bay and looked at the western part and decided to go to the south part near the "town". Anchored at 0911. Everyone took showers & naps. P&H went into town for a look. H&V played Scrabble. E rested. Had lunch of sandwiches and gazpacho. Did laundry, and then ran the water maker. Chilled out. H&V played Scrabble again (H lost both times). It was a mistake to come in at 0900 in the morning as it resulted in a lost day. Went in to Akrotiri Taverna for dinner. Ran the water maker.

Sunday, June 23, 2002 - Porto Kayio to Pilos 60.5 NM

Sunny, cloudless morning. Was nice, cool night. Woke to smoke smells from shore, reminding us of Indonesia. Left at 0648.Calm seas; probably no wind. It was very hazy, in fact, at one point we turned on the radar as visibility was down to about a mile or less. Continued to motor. Later the wind increased to about 5 kts from the west so we pulled out the staysail and mainsail to give us about a one-knot boost. At one point we even tried to sail but with only 9-10 knots of wind we weren't going fast enough for our 60.5 NM day. The wind kept following us around and when we headed north we put the sails away. Saw Methoni, the place where we had originally thought we would go in. Looks quite small, but interesting with the castle. H&V played two games of Scrabble; V won both. Arrived Pilos and called Port Control on VHF 12, but got no response even though a sign at the entrance to the marina states that every yacht should call in. Tied along side the outer wall at 1646. The marina is not finished as the electrical cables are sticking out of the concrete. However, we should get a good nights sleep. H&V went into town to find a store and locate a restaurant. No store was open as it is Sunday. E went to the Port authorities and had to pay 15 Euros. Had a drink at a cafe in the town square waiting for the others to get into town. Then had dinner at Gregoris, a restaurant up the hill and in their back garden. Nice, but standard Greek food, and lots of olive oil. Returned to the square to have ice cream. Getting hot at night so we ran the A/C to cool off the cabins before sleeping--what a huge difference. It was very quiet on the boat and we had a great nights sleep.

Monday, June 24, 2002 - Pilos to Zakinthos 67.2 NM

Another clear morning. Pulled away at 0636. Water like glass. Decided we would go through the gap between the island of Pilos and the mainland. The detailed chart showed a minimum depth of 10 meters, which turned out to be true. But it was very dramatic and exciting as we went into the gap. As there was no sea running it was fine, but one can only imagine what it would be like in choppy seas. The wind was less than 2 knots so it will be a long motoring day. We are primarily heading 330° today to get to the island. H made bread, which turned out to be the best ever. H&V played two games of Scrabble; each won one. Tuna sandwiches for lunch. At 1400 staysail was put out. At 1510, the main and yankee were put out, engine off at 1515. Had a nice sail for about an hour then we came alongside the island and there was no wind. A more lush and populated island than we have previously seen. It was very hot with no wind. There was wind in the harbor which made going between two sailboats difficult. So we went along side a catamaran. This place was next to a sign that said DO NOT TIE UP HERE. Nevertheless a man on shore from another boat directed us there. They moved over so that we weren't so close to the sign. Later, another small charter boat came in beside us at the sign. We will see what happens. There is power and water on the dock, but you need a man to turn them on, and his office is way on the other side of the harbor, so we went without power for the short time we were there. Found out that there was one hose that worked and Paul went spray happy. A man came by and collected 5 Euros for the docking. Turned on the refrigeration and there was no water flow. Went to bleed it and discovered that the nipple fitting, to which the hose is attached, was broken off and water was leaking into the bilge. This explains why there was an air lock and why we were getting water into the bilge. E replaced the nipple with a new one. Turned on the A/C units and everyone had showers. Walked into town and found a restaurant with a garden. Had a great menu and the food was not bad. Named Village Inn; they had a pet peacock which liked bread V found out. Toilets were filthy. On the way back, we found a store open and bought tea then found a market where we bought some bananas and apples. Ran A/C a short time to cool off the cabins.

Tuesday, June 25, 2002 - Zakinthos to Ithaca, Vathi 42.3 NM

Sunny, clear, muggy. Left in glass water at 0740. Clean getaway; no tangled anchors. Everybody on boats either side of us were still sleeping. Motored north past Kefallinia Island. Not enough wind all day long. Had lunch of hot dogs in home made bread. Came beside Ithaca and curved anti-clockwise into the bay at Vathi. The town turned out to be prettier and more Mediterranean in style than we thought. Debated whether to go stern to in town or to go to the new "marina" across the bay. As there were electrical boxes at the marina, we decided to go there. Also, as we approached the town dock a noisy motor scooter went by on the road just behind the boats. In the event, we went along side a dock at the marina, arriving at 1400. Although there were power boxes, they were not yet connected to power. Oh well. The water was very clear at the boat so H,V and H went swimming at the boat. E thought it was cold on entry, but it was OK after you were in for a while. P&H went into town via the dinghy and checked out the tavernas. H&V played Scrabble for the second time today. Had dinner at the local taverna just beside the marina. The table was right at the waters edge. Watched the DVD Something about Mary. Wind came up so there was some wave slap. Got good sleep after the wind died.

Wednesday, June 26, 2002 - Ithaca, Vathi to Levkas 29.0 NM

Everyone was up relatively early so we departed at 0750. Other sailors were sleeping in their cockpits as we pulled away. Motored all day due to lack of wind. It was a very hazy day with poor visibility. But it was an interesting day as we went close to several islands, including the Onassis islands, Skorpios and Skorpidhi. They were quite lovely. In fact, all the islands here have many more trees than previous Greek Islands. Entered the Levkas Canal and motored easily through it. Many of the markers are missing but it easy to see the proper direction. The depth got down to 5.6 meters although the reported minimum depth is 6.0 meters. There is a power line but it is 40 meters high. Got to the marina and were directed into spot G06; secured at 1222. It has laid lines and power! But when we asked the attendant, he said there was no power. We were next to an Oyster 53, Liberté of Waterford Ireland. The owner was not there, only some workmen cleaning the inside. They need to clean the waterline, as the bottom is weedy! Had lunch of egg salad sandwiches after we were tied up. Paid the marina- 45 Euros. Found out they were working on the power today so there were signs saying that power would be back on in the evening. However, where we were we had power all day long. The marina complex will be great when they are done (by the end of 2002). In fact it is already the best facility we have seen in Greece. Today is a big day back home as Laura closes on her new house and Lynn flies to China. We all took a walk into town to scout out a restaurant. Watched 28 Days on VCR. Went to dinner at a taverna in town along the walking street. Not good, but cheap.

Thursday, June 27, 2002 - Levkas to Paxoi, Gaios 34.5 NM

Decided to go through the 0900 bridge opening so we timed leaving the dock no later than 0845. There is no charge for the bridge. It was a still, pleasant morning. Clear sky and sunny later. H&V went to the marina supermarket at 0830, when it opened. Warm bread was delivered at 0830 so they were back onboard by 0837. We had already disconnected power and filled the water tank (the water was good). After bringing in the passerelle, we dropped the stern lines and departed at 0840. Motored slowly but were the second boat in line of nine sailboats plus a day-tripper boat. The bridge is a floating one, which both ends lift toward the center. After lifting the ends to 45° the bridge rotates around one side. It actually goes quite quickly. They opened slightly late at 0905 but we were through easily, and there were no southbound boats. Had to wend around a point that silts up. Motored at 312° to Paxoi. Pulled out the staysail and main, but didn't do any good. Had lunch of sandwiches. Put sails away later. As we approached the harbor, the wind increased to 14 knots from the NNE. That would make tying up difficult but it dropped as we entered. Gaios is a very small harbor, essentially a gap between the main island and a smaller island. We went in the north end as the depth in the south entrance is reported to be 1.8 meters. Saw a boat tying up in the entrance area, near the big ferries. We continued and low and behold, there was an Oyster 56, Piperita, tied up in the center of town. Further, there was space beside him for us! Did a good stern moor in only 2.9 meters at 1440 (the rudder was very close to touching). We are right in the center of things. Great town. Later, a boat came in on our port. We encouraged them to get close to us so that no one would try to come in between. That opened room to his port side for another boat. There was an ice cream place just behind us, 6 feet away. Had drinks at one taverna then dinner at Genesis taverna. The food was good, but they were very slow due to a large group that came in just after us. Then they had some Greek dancing by two men. Everybody thought Paxoi was a winner. Paul went out with the group of men from the boat next to us.

Friday, June 28, 2002 - Paxoi, Gaios to Corfu, Gouvia Marina 34.1 NM

Paul woke us at 0500 by walking around the deck. The morning was nice, still and clear. Departed at 0834 cleanly. Motored north. Tried some sails but none worked as the wind went to the south and there was no relative velocity. There is a gale warning in the Aegean. Went close to southern Corfu. Some areas are very touristy and some are deserted. Did some work trying to figure out how to spend our time in Corfu and wondering if we can leave early (0600) Monday. That would probably mean checking out Sunday night. All will be revealed when we get there today. Motored all the way. Passed Corfu Town and it was busy. There were two cruise ships letting off passengers, a ferry leaving and people all over. Continued directly to Gouvia Marina and went first to the fuel dock, arriving at 1340. Took 486 liters of diesel. Left at 1400 and were docked at E21 by 1410. The transmission would sometimes not engage immediately in forward, mainly when hot. So we will keep a watch on it and accept delayed engagements. It is nice here but we are a long way from the land facilities. All things open at 1700 so we can do business then. Took the laundry in, and it will be ready by 1000 tomorrow. The port police were not there (even though it was their posted office hours). Reserved a car for 0830 tomorrow morning. Had dinner at the Argos taverna in the Marina. Fast service and OK food. There was a vintage car event in front of the marina. An odd assortment of older vehicles, but interesting. Went to bed early.

Saturday, June 29, 2002 - Corfu, Gouvia Marina

Woke to cloud cover! It later burned off and became sunny and hot, as usual. Paul stayed on the boat. Picked the car up at 0835. Drove into Corfu Town, then south and finally found Mon Repos, just recently opened as a museum. It was built in 1824 by Sir Frederic Adam and is where Prince Philip the Duke of Edinburgh was born. The restoration is good, but not faithful to the original. The grounds consist of a large wooded park. There are several ancient sights in the area, now uncovered. Saw picturesque Mouse Island, a small islet with a white convent on it. Farther south and up a winding road was Achilleion, built in the late 1800's by Empress Elizabeth of Australia. Kaiser Wilhelm II bought it and used it until World War I. Quite impressive, but we did not see the good rooms. (It was a casino for a while.) Had lunch at a small sandwich shop. Then we crossed the island and went to the Kaiser's Throne, a lookout with views of water both east and west. Then north to Paleokastritsa, which had many lovely beaches covered with tourists and a 17th century monastery. Some of the cars from vintage car event were there. Drove back to the marina by a different route and stopped at a bulk supermarket. Relaxed on the boat. Drove to the park near the Old Fort and parked and walked in the old town till we found The Venetian Well restaurant. It occupied a small square with an old well in the center. Fairly exotic food, but very good. They had a christening party that night as well. Returned to *ESCAPADE*. Still warm and muggy.

Sunday, June 30, 2002 - Corfu, Gouvia Marina

Rose to another good day. But it got hotter quicker. Loaded the car with all of Hellmuth and Veronica's luggage and took them to their hotel, the Corfu Palace. They left the bags there and we then parked in the Esplanade. Visited the Old Fort, which is very large, and then the Museum of Asian Art, which is housed in the original British Governors mansion. Then walked the streets of the Old Town and went to McDonalds for lunch. Went back for some more walking and finally went to the Archaeological Museum. H&V checked in to their hotel and we then cleared out of Greece at the new port, which had Port Police, Immigration and Customs all in one building. Some of the cars from the vintage car event were leaving on a ferry. Went to *ESCAPADE* and took naps. Returned to the Corfu Palace Hotel for drinks and dinner, which was very good. Said goodbye to H&V and returned to the marina, leaving the car in the parking lot.

Monday, July 1, 2002 - Corfu, Gouvia Marina to Dubrovnik 209.0 NM

Got up early, and it was very still. Called marina on VHF 69 and told them we were departing. Left at 0630.A rather hazy day. Motored close to Albania but then turned NW. A large ferry cut inside of us, traveling fast to the north. Set Heather up with her own E-mail address. She is happy and she sent out a notification before we got out of range of Corfu. Had lunch of pasta. The coast of Albania is very rugged and there are no buildings visible. The high peaks of 2045 meters come straight down to the water. Wind started building after 1300, but right on our nose. The seas built as well and we were pounding into it. Good thing lunch was out of the way. Wind reached 24 kts and our SOG dropped to below 4 kts at one point. As we came around the point the wind dropped to below 20 kts and the seas diminished. We were paralleling the coast, but we could not pull out any sails as the wind was following the coast. Later in the day the winds began dropping and we picked up speed. Much later the seas became far better. Had dinner of pasta with smoked salmon. Paul had the 6-9 watch, Heather took the 9-12. Kept solid progress on our course.

Tuesday, July 2, 2002 - At Sea to Gruz & Dubrovnik, Croatia (209.0 NM) + 2.8 NM

Erick had the 12-3 watch. It was a clear sky with lots of stars, even though the Italian VHF was predicting gales, primarily west of Italy, and an approaching front. The moon rose at 0140 but because it was about half it was not too bright. Heather got up for the 6-9 watch. Paul had pulled out the yankee and staysail as the wind, though still light at 10 knots, was from the ESE. At 0630 we had done 153.7 NM for the first 24 hours for an average of 6.40 knots. Better than expected. The day dawned bright and clear. The decks had a lot of dew on them overnight. The wind switched to the SE, but never got above 10 knots so we still had to motor. Had lunch of a cheese omelet and left over pasta. Saw Dubrovnik from the distance. Entered the harbor area and proceeded to Gruz so we could clear in and anchored at 1423. Actually at 1323 local time as Croatia is one hour behind Greece (the same as Europe, +2 for daylight savings time). Dropped the dinghy and a man on the quay waved at us so we dinghied in. He said we could go stern to if we wanted to stay the night there or we could go along side the quay behind the ferry if we didn't. He said Customs and Immigration wanted the boat alongside land or they would be suspicious. So we picked up the anchor and tied up at the quay. I first had to go to the harbormaster and he took the ships papers and stamped the crew list. Then I returned to the boat and Customs and Immigration came to the boat, but did not board. They stamped the passports right there. I then returned to the Harbormaster and had to pay about $280 for a cruising permit. Used an exchange place to convert money to pay for the permit. The ATM didn't work. Left the quay and proceeded to the marina, where we tied stern to (G68) with laid lines at 1520 LT. Paul was able to get the LPG tank filled right away, not more than 500 meters from the marina. The restaurant in the old summer palace that we wanted to eat at is not operating as it was damaged during the war. Heather watched a video. Had dinner at the marina cafe Bazen, which was not that great. Went to bed early, as we were all tired.

Wednesday, July 3, 2002 – Dubrovnik

Bright and sunny day but at times it was cloudy or hazy. All but Erick got up late. Can't get on AOL as the network is not responding. But called Greece and downloaded 19 messages for Heather on her own address. Paul washed the boat. Took a bus into the Old Town. Only waited about 5 minutes and it took about 20 minutes to get to right outside the Old Town west gate. Walked the wall first. Came to the Maritime Museum, which showed how much Dubrovnik was a maritime power for many years. Then we took a break and had lunch of pizza. Returned to the wall and Paul came by. He had biked into town. Finished the wall and walked around town, after having some ice cream. It is a really great place and all the damage from the 1991 war had been repaired. Took the bus back to the marina. Heather went swimming. Erick developed the plan for the period until July 27, in Pescara. It all fits if the weather cooperates. Tried calling John & Judy again but their phone is not on. All three of us took the 1915 bus back into town. Ate dinner at Dundo Maroje restaurant, which is on a small side street near the far end of the main street. Looked in at the church in the main square as the door was open and there was going to be a concert by a youth string orchestra. They did a great job playing several selections. One girl had a fantastic voice and one 5-year-old oriental girl played a violin solo. Her mother sang a couple of impromptu songs. It really added a nice touch to our experience in Dubrovnik. Took the bus back. At the bus stop a couple of crew from the powerboat that had been in Santorini and Corfu with us, were there so we had a nice chat and it used up the time. Heather went right to bed.

Thursday, July 4, 2002 - Dubrovnik to Ston 21.8 NM

HAPPY FOURTH OF JULY -- *ESCAPADE* ORDERED SEVEN YEARS AGO

Woke to pouring, at times torrential, rain! It is dark and rain clouds are sweeping the inlet. Wonder what we should do today? It has been 7 years since we signed the agreement to have *ESCAPADE* built, in 1995. Some more rain, then it slowed. Decided we should go anyway. The forecast is for improving conditions over the next several days. Checked out of the marina. H&E went to the supermarket and picked up a few things. Tanked up with water. Called John & Judy, and Judy answered! They just returned from Sweden. Thought we could get together at Vrboska in a couple of days time. Left at 0955. Motored out the inlet in rainy conditions. Turned and headed northwest inside the channel. The wind was from the SW so we pulled out the yankee and turned off the engine. Sailed quite a bit, but not too fast (5 to 6 knots). Had a few rolly spots as we passed between islands, but for the most part it was a smooth and easy sail. Had lunch of ham and cheese sandwiches. Clouds disappeared and sun came out. Very humid. Heather was worried about the channel to Ston so she called the harbormaster at Ston and he said there was space at the dock and that the channel was fine for 2 meters. So we proceeded into the channel. Just before the dock, there was a boat anchored off. As we passed, he shouted to be careful of rocks and depths (as though he had personal experience). John called back and also told us to be careful of rocks. Great advice, but the water was so murky we couldn't see a thing! There were two spaces at the dock, one too small forward of another sailboat and one behind. The trouble with the one behind was that is was close to the end of the bay. So I didn't want to swing around and approach up wind. Had to back down and hope there were no rocks or low spots. A man arrived at the dock and offered to help with the lines, thank goodness. Took Erick two tries to get the boat set up with the wind so we could back down to the dock. Came in smoothly with no problems. Tied up at 1335. A little later a small sailboat came in and they took the space ahead. Called John back and he gave a recommendation for dinner tonight, and we agreed to meet in Korcula tomorrow. Ston is a very sleepy hamlet, but you can see the old defensive wall that reminds us of the Great Wall of China. First Paul took a bike ride then Erick rode in to town and found the restaurant in Mali Ston. We left early so we could walk around both towns before dinner. Had a puppy follow us the whole way to Mali Ston. Had a good dinner at the Captains House (Kapetanova). Walked back and watched a DVD, Behind Enemy Lines.

Friday, July 5, 2002 - Ston to Korcula 36.4 NM

Did not have a great sleep. Heather neither as she coughed a lot. Woke when guys from a boat next to us crossed our deck. Plus they kept their spreader lights on the whole night. Another bright, clear day. Left at 0653 after waking the people in the boat tied to us. They got up and moved, but returned to the dock. We motored out fine, even though the water was down more than a foot. We could see many more things (sharp, pointy rocks, one engine) sticking up in the water. The wind had moved to the NE during the night and it was quite fresh. Later we heard it described as a Bora. Went out the narrow entrance, which did get to 15 meters, but it was fine even though Heather was worried. After rounding the corner we were able to sail. In fact it was the best sail we have had since Antalya. We were in the lea of the long peninsula so the sea was calm. The wind was 20 to 28 knots. The only issue was that there were gusts or bullets as we passed various mountain peaks. We had reefed yankee and main plus the staysail. Were doing 9 to 10 knots. Great! As we approached Korcula, the wind died so we were able to enter the marina with no problems. There was plenty of space, even though we were concerned as it is a small marina. Tied up to space #132 on the inside of the outer wall at 1155. Went into town for lunch. Had a hard time finding a place to eat as few had simple lunches. There was a fast food place with no food because they were out of gas, there were drinks only places, pizza places, and full restaurants. Finally picked one where we could see ESCAPADE from, and Heather had a salad and Erick had spaghetti Bolognese. Went to the supermarket and bought some cold beer and Frosties, and paid the marina. At 1415 we got a call from Lindisfarne on VHF 16. They said they were a half hour away. Paul washed boat. Lots of boats entering marina now. It was 1530 before Lindisfarne arrived. It was good to see John and Judy after such a long time. They had their friends, Galen and Mary Louise with them. They came over for drinks and we talked and talked. Then we all went for dinner at Adio Mare, which though they had been there before, was not that good. After, we walked the small town, which was quite active. It seems that nearly all places to eat are pizza places. The center of town is the high ground; so all streets go up to the center. Went to bed early.

Saturday, July 6, 2002 - Korcula to Vrboska, Havar 43.7 NM

Woke early to a bright and clear day. Heather went into town to buy bread. I showed John and Galen the computer plotting system. We said our goodbyes and departed at 0836. Motored all the way as there was very little wind and it kept moving around (W, NE, NW, etc.) Had to go east around the end of Havar Island, then west to Vrboska. Had lunch of chicken salad sandwiches. It was a very smooth ride all the way as we were inside the islands. Arrived outside of Vrboska and there were people all over swimming and sunning on the rocks (great way to spend one's day off). Docked stern to at 1536 between #44-45. Had some excitement because when we were nearly to the dock the bow thruster handle came off in my hand and it stuck on and forced our stern over to the boat on our starboard side. Our outboard propeller hit the stanchions of the powerboat but we did not do any damage. Paul and I fixed the control head by replacing the clip that held the joystick in place with a wire. But then the bow thruster wouldn't work. Found that switch was bad. Paul had turned off the switch when the bow thruster was on so the high current must have fried the switch. The switch should not go before the fuse. I bypassed the switch and connected the fuse directly to the power bus. So it now works. Need to get new parts, however. Tried to pay the marina, but the office staff had gone home. Walked into town and checked out the restaurants. It is a quiet, sleepy village that is quite nice (laid back). There is a little island in the center of the river just before the bridge. Had dinner at Trica-Gardelin. Food not bad, and was a busy place. Returned to the boat and did E-mails.

Sunday, July 7, 2002 - Vrboska to Split 28.9 NM

This morning there were some clouds over the mainland, but the day soon turned fine, but with thin cloud cover. Paid the marina and departed at 0815. Motored, as there was no wind. Ran the water maker. Turned corners and the wind stayed on our nose. Came to the Splitska Vrata, the gap between two islands, and there was traffic all over; two large ferry boats, over 20 sailing boats within one mile, a ship, and several powerboats. Continued north and it got cold and rainy. We put on coats and had lunch of pasta. Just as we entered the harbour, a large ferry was approaching from astern and a cat came out. We called the marina on VHF 17 and they said they would put us outside. The man came and directed us to an outside position. We actually got tied up but the bowline was too short and there was a large swell. So he said we could go to a place inside although we were really too big. Anyway we went in and it was tricky getting into the spot, but we did. Tied up at 1300 at spot #A19 on the outside key. The bowlines are just sufficient but we stick out. Hope no one hits us. Took our showers so we wouldn't have to return to the boat before dinner. Left the boat in bright sunshine and blue sky, but there was a black cloud over the mountains. Walked into town and we decided to stop to get a cold drink as we were warm. Just as we sat down, the rain started. It was heavy for nearly an hour. Paul was walking by and he sat down as well. Then it stopped and it became clear again. We walked into the Diocletian Palace (built in 300 AD), first into the basement, then above. It was great. People have lived in it since it was built. Went to McDonalds for a toilet and ice cream. Walked some more and then sat at a bench facing the harbor and watched all. Went to the only restaurant along the front, Adrana, at 1905 and first had drinks, then dinner. Walked into the old section again before walking back to ESCAPADE. Heather watched the video Diamonds.

Monday, July 8, 2002 - Split to Trogir 14.4 NM

Heather and Paul got up during the night as a Bora came through. They took down the sunshades, but the boat was riding OK. Lots of other people up at night as well. Erick got up at 0535 so he could take the laundry (5 towels) in at 0600. They did not open the shop until 0620, but they said they would have it done by 1300. E returned and got some more sleep. The day is bright and clear. Around 1000 the wind increased again from the north. E & P went to the local chandleries and bought some items. Replaced the broken outlet nipple on the refrigeration pump. Also bought a single pole, double throw, center off switch for the bow thruster. Now we need a plastic plate, as the switch hole is too small. Paul went into town on the bike to do Internet and brought back McDonalds lunch; yum yum! E went to see if the towels were done at 1230. No, had to wait until 1300. Heather was really worried about the winds and our leaving the marina. In the event, it was easy. We let go the lines at 1319. I just went to the left and then turned around and departed. Had to motor all the way, as usual. At first the winds were from behind, but too light to sail, then they went to the nose at 19 knots. When we entered the bay leading to Trogir, we were greeted with holiday hotels and beaches filled with people, a shipbuilding yard, a pretty full marina, and another pretty medieval city with a castle on the tip of an island. We tried calling the marina several times but got no response. Saw that there were yachts tied along side the town dock on the island where we wanted to be. So we went down there and a man signaled where we could go. He wanted us really tight with the boat behind us. In fact, our dinghy was over his passerelle that was extended into mid air. I backed down so we were facing the wind. We tied up at 1555. They have power and water as well. The only problems will be that we might have to let someone tie along side us, and the bars on the shore may be loud in the evening. Walked the old town, which is 100 feet from ESCAPADE. It is very nice, sort of between Dubrovnik and Korcula. No other boat tied to us. Had dinner at a restaurant in there, and then walked around the whole island. Had some ice cream, and everybody was eating ice cream! The area next to ESCAPADE is a real scene. While I was sitting in the cockpit watching the people, a man came up and asked if I was a former Chrysler Vice President. Wow! He said he had had dinner on ESCAPADE in Santander Spain in 1996. Both Heather and I didn't remember it at all. Later, we found his name, Klaus Völdner, in our guest book on August 28, 1996, along with Linsisfarne. The music and noise went to 0300.

Tuesday, July 9, 2002 - Trogir to Primosten 20.2 NM

Another bright, clear and calm morning. Left at 0908 after loaning the water hose to three other boats. Their fittings would not fit but our universal one with a hose clamp worked. Motored all the way in calm conditions. Arrived at Primosten and we thought the outer quay was too small to get in. We anchored at 1220 and had lunch. Paul went in into town and discovered there was plenty of depth to go stern to the town dock. So he returned and we motored in at 1310 and were tied up at 1320. Since then a whole slew of boats have come in to the dock, which became full. Have electricity. Everybody rested. Must have been that sleep last night was not good, and it was hot. H got fruit and veg's. E walked around town and found an ATM. Went to dinner at Amfora restaurant. It was the best we have had in Croatia. Had Greek salads, good chicken, pork and shrimp and a great local wine. All were happy. Walked around the island and up the new area. The concert quit around midnight and it was quiet. Good sleep.

Wednesday, July 10, 2002 - Primosten to Zlatna Luka Marina 40.5 NM

Another bright, clear day. Am still amazed at the clarity of the water near the dock. Paid the dockage fee at 0800 and departed at 0810. Heather made a bread run. Light wind from the NW at 7 knots so we are motoring. Went through the narrows of one Canal, in which the depth dropped to 5 meters, but it was not a problem. Had lunch of ham and cheese sandwiches. Went into the transit section of this HUGE marina. Docked stern to at 1450 in a space near the snack bar on the transit dock (no numbers). H&E took a tour of the marina by dinghy and then stopped at the market for H to get some things. E filled the dinghy with gas. This could be a place to leave ESCAPADE for the winter. It is close to Zadar, which is a large city and has an international airport. Had dinner on the boat of hamburgers. Went to bed early, as there is nothing to do. [It is about 5 miles into town and the bus runs infrequently.]

Thursday, July 11, 2002 - Zlatna Luka Marina to Simuni on Pag Island 30.7 NM

Another bright, clear, windless day. The high remains over Croatia. Left at 0831 and motored the whole way. Just as we left the marina, a sailboat (charter) without a mast, motored by, heading north. Passed the city of Zadar but the marina and port area did not look inviting. Had lunch of BLT's. On the approach we could see many campers and tents by the sea and lots of people in the water. Entered the harbor, which is a small hamlet and very laid back. Tied stern to at the marina, space #181 at 1331. Just then Veronica called and Heather talked to her. Lazed on the boat as it was very hot to move around, and hotter near the reception and restaurant. Paul went snorkeling. Had dinner at the restaurant at the marina as there is nothing else around. Not bad, but basic. They said that it got really hot in August. Watched the DVD All The Pretty Horses.

Friday, July 12, 2002 - Simuni on Pag Island to Losinj on Losinj Island 29.6 NM

Overnight the wind increased from the east to around 20 knots. Great! We have been asking for wind and this is about perfect, as we have to go west, then north today. Should be good. The day is sunny and clear. Left in about 20 knots of wind from the east. Pulled out easily as the wind was on the nose. Started sailing with the wind on our stern, it moved slightly by the lee but then dropped so we had to motor one again. Later, when we turned NW, the wind increased to over 12 knots but it was on our nose. Decided to go to the marina rather than the town docks as the wind was blowing down the length of the bay. We arrived in front of the marina at 1350 and were secured at 1400 in space #46, which is on the other side of a bridge from the marina office. Walked into town, about 30 minutes, and looked around. Had dinner at a Mexican restaurant, Jadran. Walked back to ESCAPADE. It was a quiet night at our dock.

Saturday, July 13, 2002 - Losinj on Losinj Island to Pula 41.1 NM

A bright, clear day again. Calm at the marina. Left at 0805 with no problems. As we were motoring out, the wind was at 13 knots from the NE so things looked promising. However, when we got outside the wind dropped and then ceased. For a while we had a boost from the wind, and at the end we had 13 knots from behind, and then on the nose as we turned into the harbor. It seems that the wind never stays in any one direction very long. Around noon we had a most strange occurrence with the GPS. It went out and could not acquire enough satellites, thus not giving us a position. We dug out the spare antenna and it did no better. The backup handheld GPS was also struggling to get a position. Finally, after about an hour, the GPS got a fix with the spare antenna. In fact, we had 6 of 8 satellites. At the same time the handheld GPS got its fix. When we got in the marina, I re-attached the standard antenna and it worked fine. We concluded that there was a problem with the satellites. (The last time we had a problem with the GPS was in 1998 in northern Italy, in the Bay of Genoa.) Erick developed a Movie file program so we could keep track of our VHS tapes and DVD's. Heather immediately proceeded to enter all the tapes we have on *ESCAPADE*, some 60. It will help us when we buy more DVD's, and we can keep track of where they all are. The sea was covered with white/light brown slime. It is gooey and even the water sounds different as it splashes. Later we learned it was a marine organism that lasts about a month. The harbor at Pula is huge with a large shipbuilding facility. The first thing you see is all the large strange looking cranes. A barge was taking ship modules that had already been built to an island for storage until they needed them. A large ship was under construction in the dry dock. We passed all that and went directly to the fuel dock, arriving at 1411, and took on 484 liters of diesel. As we were there, three powerboats came in to the marina, which made us worry about space. We left the fuel dock at 1428 and went to the front of the marina. One of the large powerboats was having trouble tying up at the pontoon so we stood by. Finally, the powerboat left that space. We were directed to take that space, #4, which we gladly did. Then they were having trouble with their windlass. Finally they dropped their anchor and went stern to the marina central area tying to the columns. It is very hot. Paul wanted to wash the decks, but we had a time getting the A/C going. First, the only circuit available was 10 amps and it blew thrice. Then, the A/C unit did not pump water. After the marina staff gave us a 16-amp circuit, we finally got the A/C in the salon working. Received an E-mail from the marina in Trieste and there will be a spot there for us. We went to dinner at Scaletta Restaurant, which had promise, but was hot. The food was good. Passed the coliseum, which was going to have a concert tonight. It is very complete and well persevered. Walked the town, which has a lot of Roman and Venetian stuff and buildings around. Returned to *ESCAPADE* and watched TV. Heather ironed the clothes that were washed earlier. Just before we headed off to bed, a thunderstorm hit us. At first there was lightening a ways off, with light winds. Then the winds increased as the storm closed in and ultimately hit 44 knots on our wind instrument. The rain was torrential. The high winds didn't last very long and soon it was just the patter of light rain, so we all went to bed. *ESCAPADE* rode fine, as did the powerboats either side of us. But across the pontoon two small sailboats were pushed sideways and were being tilted in the gusts.

Sunday, July 14, 2002 - Pula to Umag 40.0 NM

The morning dawned still and hot after last night's fury. There were a few clouds in the sky. Being Sunday morning, the church bells pealed their call. Erick went to the marina office to pay, and we left the dock smoothly at 0838. The GPS started up right away; in fact it worked well all day getting 6 of 7 satellites. Motored as the water was like glass. The islands we went around were very nice picnic and hotel ones. One even had a small marina on it. Talked to the agent in Venice. The E-mail address did not work, and I had to leave a message at the phone number in the book. He said there are no real marinas in Venice, and no ports with power. It seems that the 20th is some holiday there so it may be tough to get a spot. He asked how early we would be leaving on the 21st, as there was one spot that had a cruise ship coming in at 0800. I said we could leave before that. He will call back on Monday afternoon. The Umag harbor entrance is shallow, but we entered OK, and directly into the marina. Tied up inside on the outer wall at space #L3, 497 at 1444. We did our usual arrival procedures and were all secure when a thunderstorm hit. Winds hit 54 knots and the rain came pouring down. We sat quite well, while other boats entering and leaving were trying to take shelter as best they could behind the marina.

The refrigeration required bleeding. By 1630 the sun came out again. There were a lot of boats trying to get into the marina. It was a madhouse as the sky was threatening. A small boat must have lost his engine because he threw out a stern anchor then tied his bow to another sailboat. He weathered the storm that way. After it was over, a diver went down to dislodge his anchor as he apparently caught the mooring chain. They moved him to our side of the quay. By 1800 another thunderstorm hit. This time it was very black, and then it poured. Not as much wind, but more rain. For a long time after the storms, a surge came into the marina causing all the boats to rock side to side. We didn't have to worry about our mast hitting anyone else as we stuck out farther but it was uncomfortable. The surging stopped before we went to bed. We decided to have dinner onboard. It was Parma ham and melon plus pasta. Later, around 2000, it cleared up and people started to emerge from the boats. All boats, including us, were rocking back and forth. Paul left for a long walk into town and we did a walk around the marina and bought some items at the mini supermarket. It started to rain a bit so we returned to *ESCAPADE*. Heather watched TV, and the video of Slow Burn.

Monday, July 15, 2002 - Umag, Croatia to Trieste, Italy 19.3 NM

Awoke to a hazy, but calm day. It seemed so unreal after yesterday afternoon. There is a much larger tide here, nearly 2 feet. It seems to be getting larger the farther north we go. We also discovered why we were rolling so much yesterday. The quay was not solid underneath so the surge could get through. Paid the marina in cash and then used up our Kuna to buy some more groceries. Cleared out at the end of our quay. It was as about as simple as any country we have been to. They just stamped our cruising permit, kept our crew list, and entered *ESCAPADE* in their logbook. (No stamp in the passports.) We departed at 0826. Motored out in calm water, then when we turned NE, the 15 knot wind was on our nose. The forecast is for a day similar to yesterday, with the possibility of thunderstorms in the late afternoon. We hope to be in and tied up before there are any. Also, a low system is moving east and should reach the west coast of Italy today. We planned on staying in Trieste Tuesday, and going to Venice on Wednesday. Don't know when the low system will pass over us. The wind increased to 20 to 22 knots from the NE. Had to let a tanker with a tug go into the harbor before we continued. As we approached we hoped the wind would diminish, as we got closer to land. It didn't. Found the marina but there was no one about. Went south a bit but had a hard time turning around in the wind. There were no seas but the wind kept up. Were aiming at the outside pontoon of the marina to tie up until we could talk to someone when they saw us. In the event they sent out the dinghy and there were 5 men to assist. We had to come into the marina, in a narrow slot then proceeded north and then down a lane and reversed into the berth while attaching a bowline to a buoy. We did it very easy and made it look like there was no wind at all. We were secure by 1210 at #224. Whew! Boy, were we glad we were tied up. Got all docking procedures completed and had lunch of salami sandwiches with watermelon. Then Erick went to clear in. Came back for the bike. Finally found the Capitaneria in the Coast Guard building, but they were out to lunch until 1430. After waiting, they prepared a Cruising Permit (Costituto in Arrivo per il Naviglio da Diporto) for free. It seems they don't get many non-EC boats clearing in here. The process was helped with the translation by other customers such as from the cruise ship. I then had to go to the Immigration office (Polizia di Stato), which was in a totally different location. Without a map drawn by the cruise ship guy I would have never found it. It was behind a building on a pier, behind a locked door, and upstairs a dreary staircase. They also took a long time and had language problems, but again it was free. For some reason they want me to come back before I leave Trieste. For the cruising log, I have to turn it in when we leave Italy. Went back to the San Giusto Marina office and discovered that they are closed between 1300 and 1530. Anyway, I checked in and then she asked if we wanted power (which we had). It seems that they have a complicated system using "keys" which you "charge" the pedestal you are plugged into. You pay for the charge in advance. It took the staff two times to zero it out and recharge it. At least we still have power. I called the agent, Eddie, in Venice and he still had not worked out our berthing but he seemed positive even if it will take a move after two days. It could even start between piles. Hope to hear more tomorrow as I sent him an E-mail with all our data. A rainstorm moved across with winds up to 35 knots, which is a Bora. It cleared up for awhile then it looks like another thunderstorm may come. If I read the weather chart correctly at the marina, it predicts the low, now over Italy, will pass Trieste by midday tomorrow,

July 16. That would leave the 17th all right to sail to Venice. Just as we were ready to go out, it rained again. So we waited 15 minutes and it passed. Took umbrellas, as there were still sprinkles. Went to dinner at a Chinese restaurant. The food was OK, not good, and it was hot inside. Returned to *ESCAPADE* and H watched a video, Hit man's Run.

Tuesday, July 16, 2002 – Trieste

Woke to a dull, overcast day. It was cooler as well. There are some black clouds around so it may rain. There is no wind and everything is still. Erick went to clear Customs (Guardia di Finanzia) and found the office, but no one was there. A mooring service guy, Andy, who spoke English took pity on me and said he would call me on VHF 12 when the officials arrived so I could do other things. I did go back to immigration and got the stamp on the piece of paper, so we are cleared with them. Then I paid the marina so we could leave tomorrow if it is possible. It was 164 Euros, or about $80 per night. The weather forecast is not due until around 1130. I then got a call from Andy who said Customs would be there in 20 minutes or around 0950. We will see. It is raining a bit, but not hard. Went there and there was no one so I returned once again. The power then went off so I had to go to the marina office (by bike) to recharge the key with 10 Euros. While there, they had the weather forecast and it is better for today and tomorrow. At least there are no high winds predicted, although there might be some rain. So I guess it is a go for tomorrow. We then headed for the Modern Art Museum and discovered it was closed on Tuesdays. Could not find another museum so we met Paul at the Tea Room for lunch. We then walked up the hill to see the Cathedral and then to Castle San Giusto. Not much of a castle, but it had good views of the city. Returned via the city. The sun had come out and it became rather hot. We used the umbrellas as sunshades, and tied our red jackets around our waists. The Plaza Italy is especially impressive. Went by the Customs office and there was still no one there, so we left a sticky note on the door. We got two calls from Ed in Venice. He has arranged some berths alongside in the main channel. He warned us of rocking and rolling due to passing boats and he described the Fiesta on the 20th, which will include fireworks. It should be a rollicking time! Then I got a call from Andy to come and when I got there, there were three Customs agents. After Andy translated they said they were the wrong Customs, and that I had to go to another Customs in the old port. So with Andy's directions I biked there and after much discussion they said I did not have to notify Customs of my arrival. They understood that this was our first port of entry, and that we had an American flagged boat. Still, they said as long as we had nothing to declare, then Customs was not involved. Well, I tried. Heather went back to the supermarket for some small items. Went to dinner at a German restaurant, which was very good. Walked to the main square, which was lit impressively. Heather watched The Straight Story on video. There are dark clouds around, but it hasn't rained. Will have to see what tomorrow brings.

Wednesday, July 17, 2002 - Trieste to Venice 62.2 NM

It was overcast when we woke up. No wind, but no rain. Some darker clouds on the horizon. Erick biked to the marina office to turn in the key and asked for assistance to untie the lines from the buoy. The marina guy was there before we had completed our departure procedures. We left at 0614 and the city was quiet. Motored out and a tug cut behind us, we dodged a tanker at anchor and then had to cut behind an approaching car ferry. Finally we were out of the traffic pattern around Trieste. Dark clouds with rain formed behind us while some rain ahead of us moved off to the north. It is clearing just to the south of where we are heading. The course is 55.7 NM at 255°. It is cold and I have long pants and a jacket on. At 0840 we were approached by a Cabrini boat, which asked where we were headed, and where we departed from. As they didn't speak English, they just waived us on. By 0930 we had sunshine, with clouds in the blue sky. Later, the sky turned dark to the south, but it dissipated and we had no rain at all. Called the agent and said we would be in between 1530 and 1600. Reported to Venice Pilots and they gave permission to enter. As we entered Porto Lido, we passed a tug towing a barge. The traffic increased until it was hectic as we approached the Riva Sette Martiri. Ed was not there and we had to circle a couple of times in between the waterbuses and other traffic. He arrived by waterbus and directed us into a spot as the other area was taken by a couple of boats. We tied up alongside the quay at 1545. There are lots of waves from passing traffic that bounces the boat and causes wave slap. After we discussed things we walked forward to check out the dock and the other boats had left so we decided to move forward and take a spot directly behind a huge sailboat, Mamamouchi at 1620 (#7 Riva Sette Martiri). This left the other area open for the day-trippers. The wave slap and bouncing is no different, but we are closer to the cruisers. The only other alternative is to go between piles at Salute, but we might get kicked off on Saturday. So I guess it is here. We seem to be riding OK, and much of the time our fenders are not touching the quay. Heather went in search of a good restaurant to celebrate Paul's birthday, which is today. Went to dinner at Hostaria da Franz, which was fabulous. Then we returned to *ESCAPADE* and E&P walked to St Marks Square. It is still the scene!

Thursday, July 18, 2002 – Venice

Got up early and caught the 0700 waterbus to the train station. We arrived at 0730, just in time to get on the 0743 train for Torino, via Milano. We bought the ticket on the train with a 5 Euro penalty. The trip took 5 1/4 hours, arriving at 1300. Edith Robertson met us at the train station and we bought our return ticket and determined to take the 0907 tomorrow morning. We went to Parigi cafe on the sidewalk to have lunch. Then walked to the hotel- It was the one I have stayed at 4 or 5 times before! The Jolly Hotel Principi di Piemonte. We checked in and then the three of us took a walking tour of Torino. A highlight was the Palazzo Reale, which was the palace of the last king of Italy. It was incredibly luxurious with extreme use of gold foil. Then we walked to the Po River. It started to rain and we were running through the open areas between the arcades. Returned to the hotel to shower (Heather had a bath) and change. Went to The Robertson's apartment, just across from the hotel. It is very nice, with high ceilings; about 1700 square feet. Had dinner at Ristorante Montecarlo followed by a good, calm sleep.

Friday, July 19, 2002 – Torino

Had breakfast at the hotel, and then walked to the train station. Boarded the 0907 and it departed exactly on time. Another 5 hours on the train. Heather rested and Erick read. Had lunch of a sandwich, which we bought at the train station. Arrived back in Venice at 1400. Took the #1 waterbus to go down the Grand Canal. Called the agent and arranged for him to come at 1800 so I can pay him. The windlass deck switch stuck on. From underneath I let some air into the switch and it then worked OK. We then took the dinghy and wondered around in the small canals. It was interesting. Saw the old hospital entrance where I entered many years ago. There were workboats, small motorboats, water taxis, gondolas, and others in the canals. It was real "back street" type of thing. Walked a bit in the local's area. The agent came by and the bill was $1032 ($155 for pilots, $612 for berthing, and $235 for the agent.) Most expensive! Rested. Went to Al Covo restaurant, which was OK, but not great. H & E walked around, down to St Marks Square, and returned.

Saturday, July 20, 2002 – Venice

This is the day of the Redentore Fiesta (La festa del Redentore). It is the third Saturday of July and was established in 1576 as a votive fest to celebrate the end of a terrible epidemic of the back plague. The festivity reaches its climax toward midnight when a large number of exquisitely prepared boats gather in St. Mark's basin to watch the fireworks. The boats then head for the Lido, to wait the sunrise. We will see how it goes. We plan on departing by 0630 on Sunday morning. The day is bright, clear and with no clouds in the sky. E has diarrhea, maybe from Al Covo. Decided to do the engine service as we are at 3,822 hours, and the 250-hour service was due at 3,814 hours. Completed that and a few other checks as well. Boats keep coming to the quay we are on and the security guard shoes them away. I guess the money we paid may be worth it, or at least we do have privileges for it. E went to the maritime museum and then E&H had McDonalds for lunch. Walked St. Marks Square and the Rialto Bridge. Returned to *ESCAPADE* to rest, as it is very hot and sunny today. E walked ahead in case he needed the bathroom while H followed. Some how, she got lost and ended up on the opposite side of the island. Tempted to take the water taxi back, she nevertheless walked back which was probably quicker and was treated to a view of the front of the arsenal. There were two guys who were also misdirected as she kept running in to them until arsenal. After getting back to the boat, she made the marinade for the chicken then E set up the computer on the table so she could play. The boats started flowing in. There was a tug behind us who left; a fishing boat pulled up closer but still a smaller fishing boat squeezed in between us leaving only about 2 feet. Then a sailboat squeezed in in front of us and Mamamouchi. Ouch. Made us very nervous. We enjoyed watching all the boats jockeying for positions. A few sailboats tried to tie along side us but it was still bouncy so we used that as an excuse, not withstanding the fact that we paid $1,000 to be there. Two more fishing boats tied up to the one behind us. Later, huge boats crammed with people came up the canal. One ferry blasted his horn to get through. It seemed as if the canal was totally crossed with boats but there was a way through. H made dinner of Vietnamese chicken, rice and lime carrots proceeded by melon and ham. Later we saw that the ferry docked and had tables set up where cars usually are. Everything that floated passed us. In fact, about 100 kayaks paddled by, sporting bow lights and lighted headbands which looked like twinkling jewels coming down the canal. There were all types of boats- tugs, a barge, fishing boats, mega yachts, sailboats, square riggers, ferries, water taxis, waterbuses, small motorboats, workboats, RIBs, police boats, day tripper boats, etc. Lots of horns were being blown as boats cut in front of others making an exciting scene to watch. After dinner, E & H walked down to San Marco Square. The restaurants along the front put out as many tables as they had, and all were full. Some places that didn't look like restaurants had tables in front and were serving. The houses in front of us put out picnic tables and balloons and lanterns. The fishing boats put up tables and chairs and were barbequing off their sterns. Down by the Giardini taxi stop, the fishing boats were five deep. Some put the metal fences around an area near their boat to demark their party area. Some people sat on blankets; others had chairs. A marching band walked down the quay. All in all, the crowd was fairly well behaved, except for the screaming people who commandeered the bench right beside our boat. They kept up the hooting and hollering until after the fireworks. I hope they are hoarse tomorrow. P walked to the Square and said he could not cross the bridge where you see the Bridge of Sighs as it was chockablock with people and as far as he could see were people. We are so glad we had the roominess of our boat. The boats began anchoring (Eddie said they were not supposed to) and some rafted. They were lit up and a few had strobe lights and colored lights for their disco. We could not believe how many people were on each boat. The taxi boats continued to run but were empty later. The fireworks began at 2340 and continued until 0035. All the boats turned off their lights and music to watch as quiet descended except for the noises behind us. (They were so annoying.) The fireworks were amazing. We had never seen such a display and variety. The sky was filled with smoke, fortunately going away from us. Roof top terraces were opened and had oodles of people taking in the sight. After the fireworks, the boats immediately began exiting, the smaller ones first then the larger ones. E said I could go to bed but he and Paul stayed up until most of the traffic had gone to protect the boat. The sailboat in front of us stayed all night but the fishing boats behind us left quickly. E came to bed; he said it was about 0200. I couldn't sleep with the wave slap and went to the salon where it was quieter.

Sunday, July 21 - Venice to Port Garibaldi 57.6 NM

Dawn came much too early as someone called to us at 0545 to wake up. We knew we had to leave by 0630 as a cruise ship was coming in. We planned to leave early anyway as we had a 60 NM day. The day was slightly hazy but the sky is clear. First, the small boat ahead of us left, then we left and went up to the Grand Canal to poke our nose in. As we turned around, we saw the Festival cruise ship coming in. They were early. It was as large as Eddie said. We left the dock at 0600 and then passed our position heading out at 0615. After we got out it seemed so peaceful and devoid of people. We passed Mamamouchi and headed SE. At first, the wind showed promise, by it was never strong enough. Murray called, and they will not be able to visit us as we will be out of Italy by the time they get here. Had lunch of yesterday's leftovers. The water became very muddy from the river Po and there were many floating branches and logs that we had to keep a sharp eye out for. The depth is minimal, like 8 meters 10 NM from shore. H watched The Bachelor on the computer. As we approached the harbor, there was a huge mussel bed, stretching 5 or more miles. Went around it and entered the mouth of the river. Each side was lined with fishing boats, or weekend boaters. The beaches were crowded with umbrellas and people. Followed the bends to the Marina Degli Estensi. No one was around to direct us so we poked our nose onto a pontoon and tied up at 1453. Erick took the dinghy and went to the marina office. Although I made it clear the boat was 17 meters, the man directed me in the dinghy to a very tiny spot. As he couldn't speak a word of English, we returned to the office and when the woman got that it was 17, not 7, she put me into a 20-meter berth. He then had to walk the whole length of the marina to assist us in. All the electrical outlets were locked so I went back to marina reception and he had to walk out again. They don't seem to have a dinghy or handheld VHF. We had to back into a spot between poles and went stern to in space #O-9. There were lines on the poles we used as our bowlines. Paul washed the boat, including the hull just above the water line, as it had gotten very dirty in Venice. It became very hot in the bright sun and with no wind. Had the A/C on and Heather ironed the wash. Went to dinner at the restaurant overlooking the marina. Very nice food. Returned to *ESCAPADE* and watched the DVD MacArthur. Just as we went to bed there were a few fireworks. They were so minimal we didn't bather watching and we were very, very tired. H even went to bed before the end of the movie.

Monday, July 22, 2002 - Porto Garibaldi to Cesenatico, Onda Marina 31.2 NM

The night was so still it was as if we were on land. Except for the earlier fireworks, there wasn't a sound to be heard. We kept the A/C on all night. Slept till 0730. A light haze covered the sky but then cleared. Erick cleaned the water intake strainer that was full of grass. Got on line to send E-mails. Left at 0925. The GPS, although green when we were in port, turned red with no satellites acquired. It came back a little later with 6 of 7, and stayed that way. The canal was busy already with day-tripper boats leaving. Very shallow on this side of the coast. Half an hour later, a coast guard boat pulled us over. They tied along side and wanted to check our papers, mainly the insurance. We pulled out the multiple language form that specifies we have third party liability insurance and they said we were fine. They also said our horseshoe buoy was not legal in Italy. Very light wind; have main and yankee out along with engine. Went through a firing range but it was not active today. The coastline is very flat and uninteresting. The water is still murky with some of that floating crud (yellowy green/dirty white algae looking stuff) about. Passed between two oilrigs. One looked abandoned and the other had a raised boat/drilling platform. Maybe they intend to drill a new wellhead. The shellfish farm was not as located on the chart; it was farther east and larger. Tried calling the marina on the phone and the number was wrong. Tried calling on VHF and got no response. Saw the marina at Cervia through the binoculars and we decided to go there as it seems to be easier to get in and there was no bridge. Turned toward Cervia and entered new waypoints. Heather got through on the telephone but they said they were full without even asking the boat size. Maybe it is not good to call, as they can easily say no on the phone or radio. It is difficult to enter and then negotiate a space, but it is harder to deny you a space if there are some around. So we resumed going to Cesenatico and decided to just show up. Entered the canal and there were day-tripper and fishing boats tied along the walls. Turned right into the first basin, which is the Yacht Club. They seemed full. The bridge is a swing one, which was open as we approached, so we went into the second basin. There was a hammerhead pontoon that we tied to at 1427. Went in to the marina office and they worked on it awhile, and decided that they could move a small boat out of a 16.5 meter slot and we could have it. We waited as the marina man moved the small sailboat out of the slip and then came onboard *ESCAPADE* at 1455. I backed down and in between poles to a dock on an angle. We just fit in. We were secure at 1505 in space #C-198. Once again, it is very hot out of the wind. Just rested, away from the heat. Erick took a short walk, and then returned to get the bike out. Took a big ride around town, including the beach, a ride on the chain ferry, into the old part next to the river, the traditional boats displayed in an outdoor museum, and in the new part to find a large supermarket (with no success). As nearly all the restaurants were fish type, and the ones downtown were next to fishing boats, we decided to go for pizza, as there was a good Pizzeria Munchen near the marina. Went to the mini supermarket after. E&H walked into the old part of town and they had stalls set up along many of the walking streets. Returned and watched the Bachelor on DVD. It was quiet for sleeping.

Tuesday, July 23, 2002 - Cesenatico to Baia Vallugola 23.6 NM

Although it is only 23 NMs to the Marina, we decided to leave early, as this is a new marina, not in the pilot book or on the chart. It is in the Mediterranean Almanac complete with sketch, GPS waypoint, and telephone number. However, arriving early will be before they break for lunch, and give us time to go on if we can't get in. The sky was clear but there was a slight haze about. No specific clouds but the visibility was only about 5 miles. Left the dock at 0826 and had to pull up the dinghy and wait for the bridge to open. Went through at 0830. Fishing boat traffic in the canal. Outside, there was a swell coming from the NE. Possibly the remnants of a Bora in Trieste. Had to dodge around the shellfish farms, which are not where the chart shows them. The GPS went out after 1100 and returned at 1205. The GPS could not acquire any satellites most of the time. At least not enough for a fix. The handheld had the same problem- no fix. When the base GPS came back, so did the handheld. Must be something other than the units. Found the marina by dead reckoning and approached slowly as it is shallow. The land finally has some contour and there are hills behind the marina. Entered the first basin and a guy waved us into the large boat basin. There was one spot next to the wall which we backed in to at 1215, #D-32. There were some stern lines already there and we also tied to the wall to hold us. *ESCAPADE* was down in a "hole" as the quay was above us. They had power as well. Had lunch of salami and cheese sandwiches made of bread H baked in the morning. Went for a walk and paid the marina. It was built in 1994, so I don't understand why it is not in the pilot book. There were three restaurants along the beach and the beach itself is of small stones. The water did not look that inviting, and smelled of seaweed. But there were lounge chairs and umbrellas covering the beach and lots of people around. Relaxed on the boat. Heather cut Erick's hair while sitting on the dock. The wind increased from the east and the sky remained clear with very bright sun. Had dinner at Dalla Pia, a restaurant on the beach. Watched the video of Silicon Towers.

Wednesday, July 24, 2002 - Baia Vallugola to Numana 48.7 NM

It was a quiet night and it is a clear and bright morning. Departed at 0757 with no wind. Motored the whole way. We got some wind on the nose when we reached the point to turn south. The coast is more interesting and Ancona was a large town with a huge shipbuilding facility. Could not see the marina until we finally got around the corner. Then we discovered that you had to enter the south entrance, as the north opening was an exit only. As we went by we noted that there were no large boats, even though the Almanac said the marina could accommodate boats up to 25 meters. Decided to tie up alongside the side of the fuel dock, which is not really inside the marina. It is in the opening, exposed to the SE, from which the wind was blowing. A man motioned that it was OK to tie up. He went on a bike to get another man who could speak English. That man said we would have to stay where we are as there is no other space, and the depths are less than 2.0 meters outside of the main channel. Seems OK, and we were able to run the power cords to get some power. Our back up strategy if the wind gets up from the SE during the nigh is to go 90° around to the front of the fuel dock, in which case the bow would be into the wind. But the prevailing winds are from the north we are told. Paul found a large supermarket and some large Diet Coke bottles. We went there and found Frosties and other items. The only things they did not have were Cadburys and Wherthers. Italy has been redeemed! Went to dinner at the top of the hill at La Torre. Walked around the nice town at the top after dinner. It is picturesque and nice. The wind has died and the boat is peaceful. Should be a good nights sleep except there are lighting flashes to the north.

Thursday, July 25, 2002 - Numana to Porto San Giorgio 23.1 NM

It did rain lightly during the night, but no wind and the boat remained calm. All had a good sleep. Relaxed morning. There are quite a few clouds about, some quite dark. Left at 0855. Did not have to pay anything! It was blowing 12 to 20 knots from the NNW so we could sail. Just put up the yankee as the wind was directly astern. Could have gone faster with the yankee on a pole, but we would have had to jibe and the day was not that long. There were 1-2 meter swells from the north and we rolled a fair bit. The really dark clouds moved ahead of us and inland. The sky behind was blue, however. Had to dodge the oil platforms but it was a good run down the coast. The view was great as the land is interesting and pretty. There are old towns, castles and monasteries on the hill tops, there are fields of different greens, many houses with red tile roofs, new high rise buildings along the coast, and an endless stream of various color umbrellas on the beaches. Had lunch of fired-egg sandwiches. Entered the marina directly as it has an opening to the north (not good for this wind direction). Called them on VHF 14 and two guys came out waving their arms. They directed us into a spot and I went stern-to into the wind (blowing around 16 knots) quite well at 1310. But both bowlines broke when Paul tried pulling them in with the windlass. They were encrusted with many shellfish so they had not been used in a long while and were weak (and small as well). So they said we could go along side a long quay (#L-560), which we did at 1328. The wind is blowing us off so it should be comfortable. The bow was filthy from the black muck from the broken bowlines and the whole boat was dirty from the rain last night. Paul got out the hose and went to town. There are dark rain clouds to the north. We may get some rain tonight! E went to pay the marina, and found the office outside the front gate. Had to return after 1630, as the secretary could not handle the paperwork. The head guy was there when I returned and he personally filled out the form and took the credit card. He was aware that two lines had broken for us. This is a huge marina, quite well laid out. It is under utilized. The town proper is about a 15-minute walk north. Erick & Paul had dinner at the restaurant at the David Palace Hotel. Heather stayed on the boat and watched the video, Butch Cassidy and the Sundance Kid. The sky has cleared a bit, with only high altitude clouds.

Friday, July 26, 2002 - Porto San Giorgio to Pescara 47.7 NM

During the night there was a thunderstorm with lightening all around (per Heather). Woke to a steady rain. It is very heavy overcast all over. The wind is from the west so it might make a good sail, but a very wet one. Decisions, decisions. Should get to Pescara today. The rain subsided, and then stopped. We left at 0828 into a dull grey hazy day. Moist, but not really raining. The wind was 23 knots from the west so we set the main and yankee right away. Were doing up to 9 knots SOG. The only thing was there were large (1 to 2 meter) swells coming from the NE that made it interesting. A thunderstorm was south of us, with large lightening bolts. It seemed to be moving south as well, and out to sea. Per the radar, it was 12 miles away when we first looked at it. We slowly approached and even went to the west to avoid it. But then it suddenly started moving west, to our right in front of us. So we went back to track and it then slowly dissipated. The sky behind us was nice, with high-level clouds and some blue sky. Continued south, making good time. Turned on the engine once for 15 minutes when the wind dropped to below 8 knots. Had lunch of macaroni and cheese. Kept sailing well. In fact it turned out to be one our best sails since Antalya, although it was not a very pretty day. We averaged 7.21 knots and had only 15% engine usage. The swells from the NE were still large as we approached Pescara and they became larger as the bottom shoaled. Pulled into the fuel dock at 1505. Took on 302 liters of diesel, and it was the most expensive this year at 272 Euros or about $0.86 per liter. Left the dock at 1522 and followed a marina dinghy to our spot at A-17. Were tied up stern-to at 1530. It is on the outside wall, far from everything. The bowline appears to be strong enough. Took a long bike ride to the control tower to pay the marina. It is near the fuel dock but requires going around the whole marina. The weather forecast for tomorrow is for 25 to 30 knots from the NE and the man said that would create very high waves in the middle of the Adriatic. The sky has cleared somewhat but the wind is trending above 20 knots. Barry called from Rome and I told him where we are located. He will arrive early afternoon tomorrow. Maybe we will eat at a restaurant here as it is a long way to the marina entrance, then it is 1.5 km into the town. Ate at La Vela d'Oro at the Marina. Looked at the handicrafts exhibit, which had a large number of exhibitors covering a wide range of items from gold, wrought iron, ceramic, jewelry, wood carving, glass, musical instruments, paintings, cloths, etc. On the way back to ESCAPADE a sudden downpour drenched us. Went to bed early.

Saturday, July 27, 2002 – Pescara

The day started sunny with clouds around, some darker than others, especially to the west, but the wind remained unabated at 16 to 24 knots. The sea is churned up a lot, and we can see spray over the top of the fence. Not a good day to be sailing, and tomorrow may be no better. However, the wind is from the NNE, which is good for us. There were daytime fireworks over the beach to the north. Wonder why. Had lunch on board of BLT's. Watched a sailboat depart the marina and soon it returned, as it was very rough outside. Officials watched it intently. Barry and Sheena arrived around 1400 in a rental car. They stowed their stuff and we then went to the coast guard in town to get them put on the Cruising Permit and it took us nearly an hour, as they did not really know what to do and were consulting their manual and calling other people. Then we went to a great supermarket where we loaded up on provisions. After putting those away we decided to look around town for a restaurant, but as soon as we pulled out of the marina we were in a traffic jam that hardly moved. After a long time we finally got across the bridge into the main part of town and were still in heavy traffic. Eventually we worked our way to the coast street along side the beach. Saw a couple of Chinese restaurants and even though H & I had not showered and we were still in boat clothes, we decided to eat as it was so late and would have taken two hours to go back and return. After dinner, we found the Europcar location in town but you would have to leave the car on the street and there were no taxis. So we proceeded to the airport and determined they would leave the car there tomorrow if we go. The wind was swinging to the north and the seas were down considerably so everything looks favorable for tomorrow. After finding an ATM and getting petrol, we fought our way into the marina through the crowds attending the events. There were hundreds more than last night. Plus a carnival next to the marina was in full swing.

Sunday, July 28, 2002 - Pescara to Termoli 45.7 NM

The sky was overcast, though not very thick. The wind had shifted further to the NW and was at 16 to 20 knots. The sea at the entrance was nearly flat. Decided to go, but to our backup port, as wind from the NW would not be good for the anchorage on Isola San Domino. The GPS would not get a fix, even with the spare antenna, but it finally worked. Also the handheld did not get a fix for the longest time. Barry and Sheena took their car to the airport, and there was a drop box for the keys, but there were no taxies. So they took a bus to the train station and caught a taxi from there. They returned to the boat by 0900. We departed at 0912 and the seas were not too bad. Just headed in the right direction as soon as we cleared the marina entrance. The sail was great, with speeds often at 9 knots SOG. The waves were OK, but they occasionally reached 3 to 4 meters. A dark area ahead of us kept moving away, gradually dispersed and the remainder went inland. The day was then overcast with high clouds, but much lighter. To the north, behind us, there was blue sky and white clouds. The winds diminished somewhat and later the sky cleared and it became hot. Came into the harbor and the place where the pilot book said to tie up was occupied by fishing boats and a ferry. Saw two men on a small dock to the south waving so we went stern in to the somewhat rickety dock. But they have power. The wind was from off the bow and it took three tries to back down as the wind kept pushing the bow, but we got tied up at 1435. The man was nice, but the marina was expensive- first he wanted 100 Euros, then after convincing him ESCAPADE was 16.8 meters and not 18.2 meters he lowered it to 75 Euros. When I asked for a receipt, he later delivered it with some change so the final price was 60 Euros. All of us took a walk into town, primarily the old part but some of the new. It is very small, but we booked a table at a restaurant in the old part for 2030, when they open. Had cocktails and nibbles on the boat. Dinner was at San Carlos, which had no menu, and really no choice in the food (everyone got the same thing), and it was all fish. H did get prosciutto and melon. It had an interesting decor and atmosphere. Returned to ESCAPADE; B&S had coffee. The boat next to us has slapping halyards.

Monday, July 29, 2002 - Termoli to Trani 93.6 NM

The day was still grey when we awoke, and there was thin high cloud cover. Later the sun came out with partially a cloudy sky. Had winds of 24 knots when we departed at 0555. The seas were not bad and we were sailing at up to 10 knots SOG. A great sail on a broad reach. Did not need the pole. Passed another shellfish farm. Had lunch of ham & cheese sandwiches. The wind declined slowly till it was down to around 12 knots from behind. We turned on the engine while going around the corner of the "spur" of Italy and we took in all the sails as they were flapping too much. As we were motoring south the wind continued to decline until it was down to 3 knots and the seas became glassy; and the sun came out and it became hot. Finally saw the coast through the haze and then Trani, with the large cathedral near the outer harbor. Came right in and found a space at a Comune di Trani pontoon. Tied up at 1745 near the end of B pontoon on the north side. There was a friendly couple on a boat near us that provided information (he was English and she was from Trani). Learned that today was the end of a three-day fiesta and that St. Nicholas, the patron saint of Trani, would be leaving by fishing boat after fireworks tonight. Paul washed ESCAPADE. E replaced the bow thruster control head with a new one of a different design. Everyone was glad to be in early. All the streets near the harbor were being taken over by street stalls and vendors and all sorts of things were being sold. It was a very active place. Heather had taken a scouting trip to find a restaurant, and we checked out the two best. However, we first went to look at the cathedral, which was huge and had a very high ceiling. It was rather plain in appearance, but the size made it impressive. On the way we saw another restaurant at the Regis Hotel that looked nice. So we went there for dinner, which was a really good choice as the fireworks went off at 2200 and we had a great view from the restaurant. They lasted about 15 minutes and were quite good, but not up to the Venice level. We were also able to get the type of food we wanted, although they brought 5 shrimp starters when we ordered one. Returned to *ESCAPADE* through the street throngs. Went to sleep with the A/C on so as to keep all the hatches closed against the noise.

Tuesday, July 30, 2002 - Trani to Monopoli 46.0 NM

The day dawned with some high level clouds, but still. We had a good sleep after the music stopped and raising the dinghy that was banging against the dock due to waves. The town was cleaning up from last night. Heather went for bread, but did not find a bread store or a grocery but found an open-air market in a square. We departed at 0857 in calm weather. Out side, the sea was flat with wind of 5 knots or less. Motoring. Had to dodge some very strange structures in the sea, which appeared to be associated with fish farming. At first it was sunny, with high thin clouds, but as we went southeast, black clouds formed over the land behind us and to our starboard. There was lightening in the clouds, and it finally passed us but it remained over land. So we stayed dry. Had lunch of chicken salad sandwiches made from cooked chicken and baked bread, and gazpacho. Had radio call from Jioia. Came into the harbor, around the extended outer breakwater. Went first to the sailing club area in the NW part of the harbor, but there was no place for us to tie up and only very small boats were on small buoys. So we went to where the pilot book said, in the SE corner, behind the south breakwater. Tied up alongside the quay behind a French schooner at 1545. The woman on the schooner said the whole quay was taken up with fishing boats from around 1700, including the quay opposite, sometimes three deep. They unload their fish there. As there was no power anyway, there was no reason to stay and fight off the fishing boats. So we went back to the NW part of the harbor and anchored at 1610 in 3.9 meters of water. It is very quiet now, but we are in line with the harbor opening facing to the SE. Unfortunately the wind, what little of it there is, is from the SE. But we do not expect a big blow so it should be OK. Jioia, the boat we met in Trani, came in about an hour later and anchored ahead of us. Some local men from the sailing club came out and warned us not to go astern as it is shallow there. The good news is that they didn't say we couldn't anchor where we are located. We appear to be out of the way of the rest of the harbor and any fishing boat traffic. There is a mini tanker discharging oil to tanker trucks and a small coaster being unloaded of gravel in the SE corner as well. So we are well away from the noise. H & B played scrabble. P went to scope out the marina and talk with Jamie. The sky cleared except for one thunderhead in the south. Six fishing boats have come in but none have tied up at the quay where we were. By 1800 more than 12 fishing boats had come in and all empty quays were occupied and they all had laid lines to anchors to hold them off the quay. So they would not have appreciated us being there. In fact, one was along side the French boat as well. Paul stayed on *ESCAPADE* while we went into town to find a restaurant. We saw one at the top of the hill where we landed in the dinghy but thought we might do better. So we walked into the new part of the town, toward the large square. Saw none so we headed into the old town and went into the cathedral, which was prettier and more elaborate than Trani's. The burgundy and cream marble was gorgeous. Still could not find anywhere to eat except for a couple of tiny cafes. So we went back to the first one, Arena, and ate there. Actually it was quite good as they had an English menu, the waiter spoke English and we got what we ordered. Paul came in the dinghy and picked us up.

Wednesday, July 31, 2002 - Monopoli to Brindisi 39.2 NM

We had a very good sleep, as the harbor was very quiet. The morning was sunny but there are high thin clouds about. Jioia left at 0710, and all the fishing boats were already gone. We pulled up the anchor at 0840 and departed before one of the ships. The sea was calm, with slight wind from the North. Motored all the way. The sky turned dark behind us, over the land. Then a storm developed north of us, over the sea. As we approached Brindisi, the wind turned on the nose from the ESE and increased to 20 knots. The storm to the north began approaching us, and it had lightening and thunder in it. Slowed down before rounding the breakwater as there was a ferry coming out. Rounded the breakwater and we were then going with the wind. The sky grew darker and it seemed like a race to see if we would get docked before it rained. As we approached the middle moles, another ferry was picking up her anchor. Just as we went through the gap, two tugs came charging out as well. Then, for good measure, a ferry cat came out of the inner harbor. We dodged them all and went through the neck into the inner harbor and turned to the right. The wind seemed to increase for a while, and we considered anchoring until the storm passed. But we saw the Yacht Club (Lega Navale) ahead and we pushed on. A man did come out and indicated a position where we could dock and the wind dropped. We backed in and were attached by 1435 at space #B 42. It was not raining but there were drops here and there. We quickly connected power in case it rained hard and then put up the passerelle. It did not rain then. E replaced the port side dinghy davit spring. Glad I have a dozen spares as they break so often. Later, we paid the dockage fee. H, B & S went in search of the supermarket. We had Jamie and J over and we sat on the poop deck. Had dinner onboard of salad and veal plus baked potatoes. Very good. Went to bed early.

Thursday, Aug 1, 2002 - Brindisi to Santa Maria di Leuca 68.0 NM

The morning was mostly clear sky above us with some thin high clouds but there are lower ones on the horizon. Sheena said there was lightening all around us last night, but no rain. The water was on so we filled the tank. Departed at 0555. No wind in the harbor. There were no ferries in port, but two arrived as we were leaving. The wind is from the west at 10 to 12 knots so we have both the main and yankee out for assistance. But still motoring at 7.2 knots SOG. Had lunch of BLT's and melon for desert. The wind kept following us around as we first turned south, then SW. A large old gaff rigged schooner passed us, motoring faster than we were. Saw no Albanians jumping into the water to be "saved" (which we were warned against). The sky became totally clear with lots of sun and the temperature increased. Even 0.6 miles away we still could not see the marina. Finally we turned the last corner and there it was- with a very high breakwater of those giant "jacks". Two sailboats were approaching from the west but we cut in before them so we got first shot at docking. Went stern to at space #A16 and tied up at 1624. Before we got secured, our outboard caught the stanchions of the boat on our starboard side, but did no damage that we can see. That was because we had a cross wind with which to contend. In fact the wind is exactly in the wrong direction for the entrance to the harbor, and for our 70-mile trip tomorrow. What to do? Paul washed the boat. Paid the marina, and they said the weather report would be ready at 1800, then 2000, and then at 2115 they said it was not available. The man on the dock said force 2 to 3 from the SW, "always". Don't know if I believe him for tomorrow, but that is what it is now. Went to dinner at a pizza place near the harbor. Then took a long walk around town to find a post box. The boats, including ESCAPADE, are all rocking back and forth. Will rock us to sleep.

Friday, August 2, 2002 - Santa Maria di Leuca to Crotone 71.4 NM

We have finally left the Adriatic Sea and entered the Ionian Sea. The sky was completely clear and the sun rose bright and powerful. The wind had died, as well as the swells rocking the boat. The decks were wet with dew. We departed at 0555, just after another boat heading west. We soon passed a second boat heading west. Received the Greek weather forecast on Inmarsat-C and it said that the wind would shift "soon" to the NW in the "boot". That would be good but right now we are making 7.5 knots SOG on our course of 233° so things aren't too bad. Everyone is getting used to getting up early. Good thing as we have three more early days to go. The routes are nearly directly to Malta. The sea is calm and the ride is smooth. At this rate it we will arrive at approximately 1530.   Saw three sailboats motoring in the opposite direction. Had lunch of ham & cheese sandwiches. At 1.5 hours (14 NM) to go we still could not see the coast. It must be there! Land Ho was at 1445. Came straight in, directed by some guys in a dinghy at the entrance. Went to the east side where a new "marina" has been constructed. Stern-to with laid lines at 1605. All seems to be in place, including electrical boxes, water and permanent offices. However, the offices and rest rooms are empty and the power has not been turned on. They say "next year". Oh well. But they still want to charge 50 Euros. The GPS screen lost the bottom row of numbers. Guess I need to get a new screen. A large, old powerboat came next to us. His engine was loud and noisy. The generator is none to quiet as well. Have to see if it is disturbing. As we entered the wind was from the south, into the mouth of the harbor, and the direction we have to go tomorrow. It was very hot with no breeze to cool us in the harbor. Went to Casa di Rosa for dinner. Very good, and had meat dishes as well as fish. There was loud music coming from the area of the Yacht Club but we were able to sleep.

Saturday, August 3, 2002 - Crotone to Rocella Ionica 62.5 NM

Were awakened at 0400 by the large powerboat next to us starting their generator, then their engine and then leaving. The day was clear, with bright sun. There was next to no wind. Departed at 0650. Ran the generator upon leaving and Heather did a load of wash. Had lunch of open face cheese and tomato sandwiches on freshly made bread. The wind came up from the ESE at about 6 knots, but it helped us reach the high 7's SOG. The harbor today is small and still not finished. Hope we get in. The wind dropped and we pulled in the sails. Saw the harbor breakwater and turned in. Tried to keep well off but there were two flag buoys, one black and one red, and turned to avoid them and we went aground. The engine was in neutral, but we hit once and then bounced over a little bar then hit again. There was a small swell that kept banging us up and down. Tried to reverse out but that didn't work. So then brought the bow into the swells and we were able to power off the way we came in. We then anchored at 1554 and Paul and Barry took the dinghy in with the handheld depth gauge and with the help of some local people in small boats they determined the route in. It turns out that you should go around the buoys and then the minimum depth is around 11 feet. That means the flags should be green to indicate you should leave them to starboard and that they are not two fishing flags. Picked up the anchor at 1620 and followed Paul in the dinghy in and it was OK. We went bow in to a very short finger pontoon at 1635 so the generator would not reverb against the wall. Warrior and Tradewinds were there. We saw Warrior in Indonesia and Tradewinds in the Suez Canal. Small world. A Coast Guard guy came around and said we should take our papers to the Coast Guard office. So Heather & Erick walked there and filled in a form and then checked out the restaurant. Had some ice cream as it was very hot and there was not much breeze. There is no charge for tonight as the marina is not finished. Actually, it is done and all the power boxes are installed. They have just not turned on the power. Wonder why they don't? H ironed. Went to dinner at the marina restaurant and had pizza. It turned out to be a madhouse as it was Saturday night and all the tables were filled. There were several large groups. We got our order in early so it wasn't too bad. Ordered 1 meter of pizza in two styles, but we got four styles. Went to bed early.

Sunday, August 4, 2002 - Rocella Ionica to Siracusa (Sicily) 94.6 NM

Got up early and left by 0518. It was still dark and we had to use the running lights. Got out easily by following the curved track. No wind and the sea was glassy. Motored. Erick replaced Write Now and it's preferences on the computer because every time we shut down Write Now the computer would lock up. Strangely there was a hidden preferences file as well which had to be deleted. It was probably the cause of the problem. Seems to be OK now. After passing the toe of Italy, the wind went exactly on the bow (217°) and we kept tacking the staysail back and forth. Finally, around 1245, the wind clocked slightly west and gave us about 30° to starboard so we could set the sails better, and increased to 12 knots. Had lunch of smoked salmon and cream cheese on toasted open face sandwiches and a little left over pizza. The ride is quite smooth, but the seas are building in line with the increased wind. The good news is that the fetch will be reduced as we close on the coast. The sky was thinly overcast so the sun was not quite as hot as usual. About 1400 the wind switched back to port. Oh well, but we are now doing only 6.3 knots SOG. Continued to motor-sail. Had cheese and Ritz crackers. We entered the Grand Harbour and saw the marina, Marina Yachting, to the north and proceeded around the west end. They directed us immediately into a space on the pontoon on the west side. We were tied up by 1911. Had dinner onboard so we would not waste time finding a place to eat. Heather made shrimp with rice plus corn and carrots with peaches for desert. It seems quite secure here and we are protected a little from southern winds. At least we have two very strong lines and we have power. There were lots of other boats with people on them around us.

Monday, August 5, 2002 – Siracusa

Everyone slept in late. By 0715 many other boats had departed. We took a walk around the old town, which is in a state of decay. Although they are trying to fix many buildings, there is too much lost grandeur. But it must have been magnificent when they had so much power and wealth. Had lunch onboard of tuna salad sandwiches. It turned VERY hot, near 100° and we hid in the A/C comfort of *ESCAPADE*. There was no wind to cool the outside. At 1600 the wind started to blow from the south! Barry and Paul took the dinghy and went windsurfing in the west part of the bay. I went to checkout. The wind was like from a searing hot oven. Went first to Immigration and after waiting for two of the officers to return, they stamped our passports. Then went to the Capitaneria di Porto, which is in the Coast Guard building. They stamped our Cruising Log, but gave it back to me! I thought they would collect it as this is our last port in Italy. But I think I may be able to use it when we return in September so it may make it easier then. When I came out of the building, I could see *ESCAPADE* clearly and the wind was blowing from the North. Great! Talked to George Lyttleton, the owner of Oyster 55-20, Phaedra. He said that we should arrive in Malta by 1800 or otherwise we will have to go to the Grand Harbour to clear Customs and it was a lot more hassle. So we decided to leave at 0500 instead of 0600 tomorrow morning. We hung inside *ESCAPADE* until dinnertime. We first went by a small restaurant that E had seen earlier but it was closed. So we went to the Grand Hotel and had dinner at their rooftop restaurant. The menu was in English, the waiter spoke English, and we got what we ordered. Barry treated, as it was their 35th anniversary dinner. Went to bed early, but put away the passerelle first.

Tuesday, August 6, 2002 - Siracusa, Sicily, Italy to Valletta, Malta 83.1 NM

Got up and departed at 0450. It was very dark and we had to rely on the computer chart to get us out. It started to turn light at 0550. We motored the whole way, as the wind was too light, and often just off the nose. Barry even steered for a bit, but with the engine going felt it was too boring and gave the helm back to auto. Had lunch of hot dogs and beans. Called Valletta Port Control at 10 NM out (about 1.5 hours) and then at 1 NM out. Went directly to the customs dock near the Black Pearl ship restaurant. Our agent, Matthew Lowell from Central Med Yachting International met us at the dock. We were tied up stern-to with laid lines at 1644. Cleared Customs right there and got Barry & Sheena's passports stamped so they can exit the country tomorrow. We will have to get our passports stamped tomorrow. Matthew took me to an ATM and showed me where we will dock and where his office is. He arranged for a restaurant and taxi tonight. Went to San Giuliano restaurant, where we had been before, in 1997. It is along the north coast in a little bay that is just magical in appearance, especially at night. The food was excellent. Went to bed early.

Wednesday, August 7. 2002 – Valletta

A bright, sunny morning. A bit of wind, up to 16 knots came up when we wanted to move. Heather made eggs, sausage, and potato croquettes for breakfast. Matthew came around 0900 and we discussed various alternatives. He secured a place in the Msida Marina, much further in and on the opposite side rather than along the dock in Ta'Xbiex. It is #G7, where the Oyster 55 Phaedra docks. We departed at 0915 and were secured by 0928. The power is a little low, at just over 200 volts. The spot is remote from Gzira, but closer to the old city of Valletta. We don't have to use the anchor as there are two laid lines and it seems very well protected. There are toilet facilities close by. He took our passports to get stamped. He returned with the passports and key for the dock. He took Heather to the large supermarket and she walked back. If P takes the dinghy to the other side, the walk is only 5 minutes; otherwise walking around the bay is lengthy. The GPS manual says that if it doesn't acquire a position within 10 minutes the backup battery could be flat. The battery lasts only 2 years and we last replaced it 2.5 years ago. Maybe that is the problem. H brought back good bread and we had lunch of BLT's waiting for the inverter guy. Erick made a backup of the computer. Barry and Sheena left at 1445. The inverter man finally came and he believes the batteries are too sulfated. So we made arrangements for him to take the batteries to his shop and treat them. In fact, we disconnected one set of four so he can take them easily. We also "pickeled" the water maker. Went to dinner at Manhattan, which was a very nice casual restaurant. Confirmed our flight for tomorrow morning at 0805.

Thursday, August 8, 2002 - Valletta to London to Detroit by Air

Various- While we were away, there were many maintenance items which Paul handled. The bilge pump failed and was replaced with a new one. The forward head was leaking, which required a fix and re-seal. Some of the bimini stitching failed so it was re-sewn professionally. The non-skid paint around the mast was dirty so Paul repainted it. The icemaker failed and we gave up on it. Paul replaced the mast boot tape and repaired many little gel coat scratches. Added a seacock so we could bleed the refrigeration system easily. He cleaned and polished the bow, which was stained. Had the yankee and staysail removed and cleaned of all the sand from the Red Sea. He cleaned and rebuilt the winches, re-painted the anchor chain depth marks, cleaned and rebuilt the windlass, and replaced the toilet breather filters. The galley sink pump failed so he replaced the diaphragm. We had the outboard cover professionally repainted. Then we added *ESCAPADE* decals to it.

Wednesday, October 9, 2002 - To Valletta from London by Air

Arrived London on time from Detroit and transferred to the Air Malta flight to Valletta that left at 1130. Easy flight, but I was tired. Arrived Valletta at 1600 and got to *ESCAPADE* by 1630. All went fine, I got the bag and they did not question that I had no flight out of Malta. Paul was there and *ESCAPADE* looked great. Unpacked, which was all boat stuff. Called Heather before she went for the Doctors appointment. I was tired but we went to Manhattan by dinghy to have dinner. Went to bed early.

Thursday, October 10, 2002 – Valletta

Got up about 0800, and I felt great. The shower made me human. Decided to tackle the new TV, which is now a flat screen monitor (Samsung 17" multimedia) so we can play DVDs from the computer on it. The VCR is a Samsung World Wide one that converts the signals on the fly. So we receive PAL and play NTSC on the monitor. We can record PAL, NTSC, or SECAM on VHS tape or play any one of those to our monitor. Will work anywhere! The picture looks great as well. Paul had mounted it. A very tight fit but it is in there. Looks good. I just had to connect up the units permanently. Decided to use the AC adapter as the VCR has only AC input and the monitor requires 12 VDC (or AC). I bought a cable at a local chandlery. Found I could string the cable behind the nav station, without drilling any holes, to the AC distribution panel. There were three spare AC switches and I used one of those. I hard wired the units to the cable using a junction box behind the monitor. I had brought the cables for attaching to the computer under the radar. Looks very neat and professional. Still have to turn on the DC TV switch as it powers the antenna amplifier, along with the AC TV switch. But they work off of 240 VAC, so it is easy dockside and while underway we will just need the inverter. No transformer sound as it is 240 VAC. Had lunch at KFC. Got petrol for the dinghy. Stopped by the agent's office and ordered a car for Saturday thru Monday. I ordered water for tomorrow at 1500. Will get diesel after we depart, as the fuel barge is open 24 hours. The only problem is that we could not get the propane tanks filled as they only accept them on Wednesday. We hope we can go directly to the filling station on Monday. Had to re-calibrate the water computer as Paul had wiped most of the memory and I went into the calibrate mode which changed those settings. Switched to liters and had to draw 5 liters, one at a time, to do the calibration. Poured that water back into the tank via the water maker outlet. But the computer kept turning off the water pump. After several tries, and setting the date to tomorrow, I got it to stay on. (I had set a water limit, and turned it off, but it still must have thought it should be off.) Had dinner at Caffe Oasis, on the quayside just a few pontoons further into the harbour. A very nice meal, I had veal, but there was no one else there.

Friday, October 11, 2002 – Valletta

Got a good night sleep. It is partly overcast, but some sun. Warm. Took apart the GPS and cleaned the contacts to the screen. Also fixed the antenna connection and put in a new battery. Seems to work fine now. Tried the icemaker but it does not even run. No hope there. Matthew called and said the water would be here at 1300, but to move to the quay early so we get the spot. We moved there at 1105. The bow thruster was not working well. So Paul dived and found a lot of barnacles on the prop, in the thru hulls, and on the bow thruster.

He cleaned them fairly well but the water in the harbour in not very nice. Should clean the bottom before the Oyster event. I cleaned off the tar that was squeezed out of the toe rail- even after 6 years. Turned on the fax from Rome, but not much luck. The fresh water system is at least running. Navtext for Malta is working. The engine ran well, and quiet. Paul went and bought some small pizzas for lunch. A small cat came in beside us as he was assigned the place next to the quay. They are an English man and an American lady as a married couple. We talked quite a bit and then I showed them our new TV as he was thinking about what to buy. He then invited us on his boat. When I returned to *ESCAPADE* the phone was ringing and it was Heather (and one missed call). At 1430 the water truck finally came. It took only 15 minutes to fill up. Paul left for his dentist appointment at 1500. It started to rain and the wind got up to 22 knots from the SW end of the harbour. Not nice for returning to our slip. Noticed that a boat went into our slip at G-7. Talked with them and they claimed that the marina sent them there (wasn't so). We called Matthew and asked him to call the marina. Later the marina harbormaster stopped by and said we should go into space G-2, which was blocked by the boat beside us. We waited for the people in the cat beside us to return, and then they ate dinner. We decided to go into space G-2 and haul our stuff down the pontoon. So we left the quay at 1724 and got to the fuel barge at 1734. Filled up with 492 liters of diesel, at 125.96 Malta Lira, or about $315. This converts to $0.64 a liter. Left there at 1755 and were tied up at 1805. Came in rather nice and Paul had attached the bowline to the bow of the motorboat to windward so he could get it to the bow quickly. Overall a good docking with complements from the boat owners helping with the lines. We accomplished what we intended to do, but it took all day. The GPS worked perfectly all day long with no loss of numbers on the screen. Tried using the AsanteTalk adapter to run the printer but it didn't work. Maybe I need the local talk connectors. Will bring them next time. Sorted the paper charts for our next leg. Paul found out that if they filled our propane tank, they would fill it with butane. Guess we will have to buy a small butane tank as back up. After we tided up it was dark. Went to the Black Pearl for dinner by dinghy, but they said they were full. (But no one was there yet at 1955) so we went to the coffee shop in the hotel opposite. Had salmon, but it was dry and chewy; a very bad meal. Will get the car at 0900 tomorrow. It is noisier in this slip as we are closer to the road.

Saturday. October 12, 2002 - Valletta & Malta

Woke to the sound of rain. It was late, about 0820, and the car was delivered here at 0900. It is a Peugeot 206. Sun came out later. The local weather forecast is not so good- the wind in turning to the NW from the SW. Got on AOL and there was no message from Heather, this morning or last night. Paul left to do his laundry and I took the car to explore. The guy with the outboard cover and the shop with the Onan dealer, which has Camping Gaz, were closed. So I purchased some petrol and finally found the supermarket. It is one that we had been in the last time we were here, and has a very small garage under the building. Returned to the boat with some basic provisions. Will also go shopping on Monday with G&G to pick up things they need. Made a sandwich onboard. Paul returned and also had a sandwich. We then took a tour of the island, first driving East to Marsaxlokk, then to the West on the North shore to St. Paul's bay. It is where the tourist hotels are located. Returned via the coast road and St. Julians bay to the boat. Took a side trip to visit the Royal Malta Yacht Club in the old fort at the end of Manoel Island. Shortly after we were back onboard, there was heavy rain. Got the forward cabin ready for Grace and Graham. Relaxed while it rained. Will leave at 1930 to pick up G&G. Just received the weather forecast and it looks good for the passage. I was getting depressed with the cold rain today. Here is the summary from Commanders Weather:

Summary…Conditions improving the next couple days with lighter winds Mon/Tue!!! Looks good for departure on Tue. Light winds to start with increasing S-SW winds during week, which should make for pleasant sailing conditions. May have to deal with a cold front as you approach Menorca on Friday!!! G&G's flight arrived 15 minutes early and they were through quickly. So we were on *ESCAPADE* by 2030. Then we went back to Caffe Oasis for dinner. As G&G had eaten on the plane only Paul & I ate. Got back to the boat by 2230. G&G unpacked. All went to bed.

Sunday, October 13, 2002 - Valletta & Malta

Got up late to sun and blue sky. Still windy from the NE. Sent an E-mail to CW to ask if it would be better to leave Monday night rather than Tuesday morning, and to put their recommendation in their final forecast due on the 14th. The water we bought turned out to be terrible, the worst tasting we had from all around the world. I don't know why we went through the expense and effort of getting tanker water as other cruisers have been using the water on the pontoon for washing and drinking. Paul stayed on the boat and we went sightseeing. Went first to Valletta and to Fort St. Elmo that was staging a reenactment with lots of period costumes and music. Very nice. Walked around the fort then drove along the side of the Grand Harbour. Proceeded to The Royal Malta Yacht Club to have a view Valletta. As it was already 1230, we had lunch there. It was very pleasant outside with the view in the background. Saw boats leaving and arriving into the harbour. Then drove west along the North shore, thru St. Julian's bay and all the way to the west coast from where we could see Gozo. Returned via the middle of the island. Tightened the starboard inner stay to help straighten the mast. This did not affect the curve of the mast top to the aft. Sat in the salon talking. Grace took a nap. Went to dinner at the Black Pearl and then drove to St. Julian's Bay. We walked around to view the sights and returned to *ESCAPADE* by 2220. G&G felt they had a good tour of Malta, and that one-day was sufficient. The wind has dropped all day long, as predicted.

Monday, October 14, 2002- Valletta

Woke to a bright beautiful day with no clouds, only deep blue sky. It became quite warm in the afternoon. Heard about the explosions killing nearly 200 Australians in Bali. Grace's son was scheduled to be at one of the resorts that were bombed, but he delayed his trip due to work commitments. After breakfast G&G and I took the car and went to the store to buy a small Camping Gaz cylinder and new hose. We assembled these to the new regulator. So we are ready to convert to butane if required. Went to see Matthew Lowell at Central Med Yachting International to pay off the bill. Used cash dollars at the bank exchange rate. Cost $2055.But overall reasonable. The berthing was only $15.78 per day for 70 days. Also paid for repairing the bimini, two loads of fresh water, taxi trips, gel coat repair, car hire for three days, Customs clearance, and the agency fee. The agency fee was $206.59, which was reasonable. We then went to the supermarket and completed our provisioning. Should be more than enough as we might only have three dinners onboard. The rest we will be eating out. Returned to the boat to store the stuff. Went to Burger King for lunch so we wouldn't use up our stores. I also used up all my remaining Malta money. When we returned the man was here to repaint the anti-skid and he had brought the outboard cover. Paul & Grace went to the Internet cafe. Matthew is due at 1500 to take me to customs for clearance out. We have up to 24 hours to leave so we can leave at our discretion. The day is a really pretty day. I only have to leave the car in the lot here with the key under the floor mat before 1800. So the only remaining issue is the recommendation of CW as to when we leave. Matthew finally came around 1520 and we went directly to clear out. It was very easy when using an agent. Got back to the boat and was told that Heather had called. While Matthew waited I got online and got the forecast from Commanders Weather. They recommended leaving earlier, so I said go! I gave Matthew the marina gate key and said goodbye. Called Heather and told her we were leaving. She sounded so great. She was much more alive and happy. So much so she started to tell me what to do on our passage. So I said yes ADMIRAL! Locked the car and we prepared the boat to leave. Grace did a little preparation for dinner before we left the dock. We actually left at 1650. It was very pretty leaving with the sun on the old town and the fort. We got to near Gozo before it got dark. There is a half moon out tonight and it glints on the water. Not going very fast- 5.5 to 5.9 knots SOG because of headwinds of about 10 to 12 knots. The wind seems to be diminishing, as predicted. By tomorrow morning it should be from the East. Graham took the 1800 to 2100 watch. I will take the 2100 to 2400. He is getting back into the *ESCAPADE* routine. At around 2000 we hit waypoint #7 and started our direct line to Menorca. (522 NM) After dark it became quite cool, but not really cold. The moon was very pretty, being about half (but increasing). The moonlight on the sea was pleasant. There is shipping traffic all around going both directions but they have all kept their distance from us. (At least one mile.)

Tuesday, October 15, 2002 - In passage from Malta to Mahon, Menorca 542.0 NM

I had the 0600 to 0900 watch. It was pitch black to start, the moon having set after 0300, but sunrise was at 0715. It was gorgeous with the big red ball slowly lifting over the sea, but some of it "sticking" until it broke free. Took a short nap, then a shower. Had lunch of ham and cheese sandwiches. The wind clocked to the NNE and with the main and staysail out we were doing 7.1 kts SOG, with the engine at 1800 RPM. Finally! Received a message from Heather on Stratos. She is much stronger and had Bickenbach's and Pek's visit and she made lasagna. Sent a return E-mail message. Everybody on *ESCAPADE* is getting into the routine nicely. The sea is becoming really flat. Had to take in the staysail. Called Heather on Iridium. She was surprised to hear from me. The sea turned glassy then at about 1700 the wind started to increase from the South and SE. Doing nicely, about 7.2 kts SOG with staysail back out. I had the 1500 to 1800 watch. At 1650, or 24 hours we had done 141.8 NM for an average of 5.91 knots. Dinner was steak (unknown cut) with mashed potatoes and cucumber/onion salad. It is still very pretty and light at 1820. Most of the ships seem to be passing south of us as they want to aim for the traffic separation schemes at Cap Bon and Cap Blanc on the Tunisia coast. I had a nap and when I woke at 2300 the wind was up to 12 knots from the SSE. Pulled out the yankee and eased the main and we started doing 8.9 knots SOG with the engine still going. Now we are making up for the lost time.

Wednesday, October 16, 2002 - In passage from Malta to Mahon, Menorca

I had the 0000 to 0300 watch. The speed had dropped to 7.0 then 6.5 kts SOG for a while. This is an area of banks so presumably there are a variety of currents in the area. Our boat speed remained fairly constant. It was a watch with a lot of activity. First, a cruise ship approached from the north, but it went behind us with all lights blazing. A ship, which appeared military, came within two miles off our starboard beam and paralleled us for a while before heading away. There were fishing boats all around. One, in particular, was off the starboard bow. He turned on red over red lights indicating no maneuverability. But these went out and then with only green showing, he went beside us towards our stern. It was a very large boat. He turned on a huge spotlight, aimed it at *ESCAPADE*, and then started heading toward us (I could see both green and red nav lights). I turned on the spreader lights and he then turned off the spotlight and resumed going behind us. We came close to several other fishing boats and Paul had to deviate around one on his watch. Received an E-mail from Heather which said she was fine, but that one of the flats in London suffered water damage. The sunrise was at 0740 this morning. Generally doing around 7.1 knots SOG. Will reach half way soon. The reason we continue to motor and push for speed is that the forecast predicts that by 1200 on Thursday the wind will turn against us with 20 to 30 knot winds in squalls as the next front approaches. That means we will have to beat into Mahon for the last 12 or so hours. That does not sound pleasant. It is a pretty day today, however, with a clear blue sky. At 1103 we achieved half way- 271 NM. Lunch was turkey and cheese sandwiches. The day continued hot and pleasant. In the afternoon the Italian station issued a gale warning for a SSE gale, force 7, around Corsica and the seas north of us. Does not fit with what we are seeing. The wind has been below 5 knots since noon and at 1700 it was 3.4 knots. I sent an E-mail to CW asking if the front has been delayed based upon our seeing lower winds. At 1640, or 48 hours, we had done 311.3 NM for a 6.49 knots average. For the last 24 hours it was 169.5 NM and an average of 7.06 knots. At the present rate we will reach Mahon around 0200 on Friday. The engine oil pressure seemed low so I stopped the engine and checked the oil. It was very thin but seemed to be full based on the bubbles on the dipstick. I had the 1800 to 2100 watch. Dinner was spaghetti Bolognese. No activity except a ferry going into Sardinia. At 2130 we had only 200 NM to go. Received the new forecast from CW. Two fronts will pass us in next 12 hours. First should pass overnight or early Thursday. Second will pass around 0900 UTC tomorrow. Winds will remain SSW before and after first front but shift to West and then NW after second. Both fronts may bring rainsqualls with winds up to 30 knots. However, right now, it is lovely out. The seas are nearly flat, the winds are 7 knots from the SSW and it is a clear moonlit night. Couldn't be better. It is hard to believe that we will be battered in 12 hours. Although I hope we will be spared some of the squalls as the clouds in the sky form a line to the north with us heading toward the southern end. We will see. The sky was grey and purple with the water a glassy grey at sunset. Quite dramatic. Saw a few dolphins today but they just swam by and did not stop to play. Two land birds made *ESCAPADE* their home. Both were very tired. One was sitting by my feet (1 inch away) on the cockpit cushion and the other was sitting on the pedestal. Saw a US Navy warship just North of us. They were questioning ships in our vicinity. It was stopped, then went parallel to us, then cut across our bow. Will get some sleep before by 0300 watch.

Thursday, October 17, 2002 - In passage from Malta to Mahon, Menorca

Woke at 0230 and found that the sky was still clear, the moon was still out and the stars are still visible. The wind is still only around 8 knots from the SSW and the sea state is still mild. We have 161 NM to go, and at the current speed of 7.4 knots SOG, it is only 22 hours to go. We are still on a tight tack. Lovely! Don't have to put on the wet weather gear now at least. No weather info on the Navtex from Spain, just local notices. We are West of Sardinia by about 50 NM and still 10 NM South. I had the 0300 to 0600 watch. The moon set at 0330. When I emerged after showering at 1000, it was still great. We were doing 7.5 to 8.5 knots most of the time, on track, with the wind still SW at 13 knots. The sun is out; there are thin high clouds but still a lot of blue sky. Not quite like the forecast! Did get some warnings on Spanish Navtex and they predict higher winds farther north. The forecast for Menorca is Westerly 3 to 5 becoming north near midnight. At 1035 we had 100 NM to go. Had lunch of sandwiches. The motion of the boat is bouncy, far more than would be expected with this wind. The swells are quite large and are from the SW. Don't know the cause of the swells. Actually it is quite a pretty day. We had sun until 1430 when a line of clouds passed over us. That must have been the front as the wind increased to 20+ knots and shifted to the West. As a result, our SOG has reduced considerably- to about 4.5 knots. The waves are still coming from the SW so it doesn't make much sense to fall off because we would then have to go directly into the waves. So I guess we grin and bare it. Talked to Heather on Iridium. Woke her up. She slept without the oxygen for the first time. Still getting used to it. Doesn't have any visitors today, which is probably good. The wind increased to 30 knots plus, and the seas increased accordingly- to about 10 feet but they were very short and steep. It was a near gale. They were also confused due to the changing wind directions. We were continuously pounding and poking our bow into the next wave. Our speed dropped further- to 3.0 to 3.5 knots SOG. Even at that speed we could not maintain course and had to fall off considerable- more than 90° from our course. We even considered going to Mallorca instead. However, the 30° change was not sufficient to make a large difference. It was very uncomfortable for nine hours and Grace became sick. Did not have dinner. The bad weather started on Paul's watch and continued on Graham's. There was even some rain in the mess. It was still going badly when my watch started at 2400. During the pounding the forward bed became wet with water entering the large hatch. I found that one of the dogs was not secured. I tightened it and it stopped leaking. As Grace was using the saloon as a berth, I let Graham sleep in my bed.

Friday, October 18, 2002 - In passage from Malta to Mahon, Menorca

I had the 0000 to 0300 watch. Was able to head toward Mahon, roughly, with the staysail backing occasionally. Were able to get into the upper 4-knot range SOG, which was better than before, and we were finally heading somewhat right. At one point I saw another yacht in the bounding sea apparently heading right at us. I shined a flashlight on them and called on the VHF but there was no response. I increased engine RPMs to pass in front of them. They may have been hove-to and sleeping or traveling at a slow rate with no engine. Shortly after 0300 the wind shifted to the NE, still in the 20 to 23 knot range. We were finally able to shut off the engine and start sailing. The sail went well, making good time until we got to within 10 NM of Mahon when the wind dropped to 13 knots and we shifted our course so the wind went aft, so Paul turned on the engine. I got up at 0430 and we approached the entrance on track. Slowly saw the buoys appear in the dark. Unfortunately the moon set just before our arrival. All seemed in order and our track was accurate between the outer buoys. Several fishing boats were coming out which added to the excitement. It was easy and we went up stream and found the anchorage quickly. Took two tries to set the anchor so we were out of any danger. Got the hook down at 0555. It was so quiet and peaceful it was unreal and amazing after what we went through. There was no sound from shore even. The water was calm and virtually no wind. Everyone collapsed into sleep. I awoke at 1030 and soon there was someone alongside saying that we if didn't leave the anchorage within 30 minutes we would be charged. It was sunny for all the day, with a few white clouds about. Paul dived on the boat and cleaned the water intake for the refrigeration, as we didn't have good water flow. He also brushed the green slime from the hull down about 4 feet so we would get good photos even if we were heeled. Got no response from the main docking place on VHF (Ribera del Puerto). So I called them on the telephone and the woman, who spoke good English, said we could not get onto the quay and we would have to go to one of the "islands", but that we should call on VHF when we were ready. Picked up the anchor at 1135 and tried calling them on VHF, with no answer. As we didn't like the idea of docking at an island, we called Sunseeker who has a base here. They said they could accommodate us so we started to head their way when a huge cruise liner came in so we had to circle while they turned around. Then, just as we were approaching Sunseeker, a ferry came in. When we finally could approach the quay in safety the man said we could either go between two power boats stern-to, which were very close together, or alongside their floating pontoon. Even though the stern-to position would be more protected, the powerboat rails would extend over our lifelines so we selected the pontoon. Were tied up by 1215. There is power and water on the pontoon. The only issue could be bouncing against the pontoon from the wake of passing boats. I paid Sunseeker 140 Euros for two nights. Paul got out the hose and washed down the boat. I headed off to clear us in. In a long series of miss information I finally did the task after walking continuously for 2 hours. I was directed to many buildings, all wrong. I never did visit the Captain of the Port, but saw the Port Police many times. Did finally find Aduana (Customs), which said that if I was the owner of the boat they didn't care. No forms to fill out. Then I found the Policia National in the upper city, which stamped my passport. They were closing at 1400 so the others would have to return at 1130 tomorrow to get stamped in. All seems relaxed and no one was prepared for formal clear-in procedures. The Port Captain, where I was directed, is only necessary if you need a docking space not controlled by one of the other groups. Returned to the boat by 1430 and had lunch of leftover spaghetti. Sent the laundry to get done. It will be returned tomorrow at 1200. Grace was still not feeling well but she and Graham went in search of an Internet cafe and restaurant for dinner. Paul returned after a walk around. The harbour is very pretty and seems friendly. Went to dinner at 1930 at El Bódforo. Typical Spain, had drinks at 1930, restaurant opened at 2000, ordered at 2030. Quite good. It became chilly and I dug out the bedspread for the bed.

Saturday, October 19, 2002 - Mahon, Menorca

Woke at 0830 to bright sunshine and clear blue skies. But I had put the bedspread on and it was warm and cozy overnight. It is necessary because Heather is not beside me. Getting quite cool at nights. Laid out the course to Cala d'Or. It is 63 NM so it will take us 9 to 10.5 hours. I called the marina and they said they have people there 24 hours so arriving Sunday night would not be a problem. Paul fixed the staysail. The luff cord had come loose (we thought that it had broken) in the gale. I put *ESCAPADE* decals on the repainted outboard motor cover. G,G and P went to get their passports stamped at 1130. They also went to a supermarket to pick up a few things. I waited for the laundry and then went to join them at the top of the stairs. We had lunch at a cafe in Miranda square. They returned to the boat while I walked around the town and took some pictures. After returning to the boat, I went east toward the Yacht Club. Paul & Graham finally returned after trying to find an open chandlery (no luck) and pulled down the yankee and checked it for wear. Added some tell tails. Grace did some ironing. A nice lazy afternoon. An Oyster 45 came into the harbor, which we did not recognize. Wonder if they will be at the Oyster event? Went to dinner at Jàgaro, a nice restaurant near the Yacht Club. It had a pleasant atmosphere; sort of nautical, but with lots of paintings on the walls. The food was good and the headwaiter spoke good English. Watched Top Gun after we returned to *ESCAPADE*. The quality of the picture on the monitor is excellent. Went to bed at 2330.

Sunday, October 20, 2002 - Mahon, Menorca to Cala d'Or, Mallorca 63.2

Got up at 0620. In the dark a large freighter passed by leaving the port. Got things organized to sail. It finally became light at 0740. We spent 40 minutes trying to fill the large water tank. Gave up and decided to leave. Pulled away at 0755. Although the sun was not up, we could see very well. The entrance is very pretty. There are homes and villas all along the shore. At the outer entrance there are ruins of extensive fortifications. They were huge. I doubt a sailing ship could get in without being destroyed in the early 1800's. The wind increased as we left the harbor, on our nose as we were heading SE. But after we rounded Isla del Aire off the SE corner of Menorca we were able to head on our long course of 242°. We then were able to sail very nicely on a broad reach. The wind climbed to 17 knots from the SE by 1000 and we were doing 8.2 knots SOG. Great sailing! It was about time. It is quiet and there is a pleasant motion. The sky is totally clear, with deep blue overhead and the water is also deep blue. The Med at it's best. Still a little cool and I have my fleece on, but it is not cold. At this rate we could arrive by 1600. Thinking about going to El Arenal tomorrow. That would be the place Paul joined *ESCAPADE* in 1998. Grace made chicken with risotto as we had to use the chicken up as we had taken it out of the freezer the day of the big blow. Ran the generator and the water maker and generated 53 Liters of water. Wanted to make sure all was OK before we pickle it for the winter. I only used the short-term solution when we left the boat in August. The sail was absolutely fantastic. It was one of the best in the Med this year. It looked worse that it was entering the Cala as the waves were directly into the entrance. However, there was no bar and the bottom was still 32 meters in the gap. Turned to port and the seas dropped. Slowly entered the marina through a series of channel buoys. We were directed all the way to the end, which has a lagoon with a pontoon in the middle. Tied up at 1615 with the help of a marina guy at berth #M-3. He took the payment right from his motor scooter. We averaged 7.59 knots and used the engine only 16% of the time. It is very pleasant here with lots of people in the restaurants and along the quays as we passed. Another boat, which entered just before us was wandering around aimlessly. Don't know what he was doing except getting in the way. Everyone spiffed up for going out. Walked both sides of the harbor. Had drinks at a Pub overlooking the harbor and then dinner at Restaurante Zócao. G&G really liked Cala d'Or and thought it was unique and nice. Watched the DVD Behind Enemy Lines, but got to bed by 2300. It was very still and quiet at night.

Monday, October 21, 2002 - Cala d'Or, Mallorca to El Arenal, Mallorca 38.9 NM

Got up at 0720 and we all prepared for departure. The forecast is wind Force 4 from the SW. That means that we will have to motor into it until we turn the corner and head NW. Left the berth at 0822. It was still and really no wind in the harbor. There was a swell left over from yesterday but not as bad as when we came in. After we got out the wind was from the West at force 2. Rolling a bit due to the swell from the SE, which was on our beam. The engine started dipping in speed. I thought that meant that the engine fuel filter needed cleaning so I stopped the engine. We continued to sail slowly, with a lot of rolling. Changed the fuel filter on the engine and switched over to the other Racor. Tried to bleed engine with the manual lifter pump handle, as usual, but it would not yield any fuel. Ran through a series of checks to see why we were not getting fuel. Blew backwards into the fuel tank from the tap and it was clear. Blew forward from the tap to the fuel lifter pump and it was clear. I took the outlet tube off fuel pump and manual pumping yielded no fuel. Concluded that the fuel lifter pump had failed. Confirmed that the old fuel pump was bad, as it would not create any suction on the inlet side. Replaced the pump with a new one. But had to rotate the upper casing, as the tube connections were not at the proper angle. In doing so I rotated it too far and reversed inlet and outlet positions. Also, the replacement pump did not come with a gasket so we used liquid gasket goo. After reassembling, obviously it did not work. Saw that it was on backwards so I reversed it. After much pumping (as we had forced air back toward the tank) we finally got fuel out of the outlet. We then started the bleeding process again. This time fuel was being forced toward the fuel filter. However, the fuel pump was leaking diesel. Took it apart again and then reassembled but the leak persisted. Then discovered the leak was at the outlet tube. Tried several times to get the tube seated properly to no avail. We then continued the bleeding process and finally got the engine to run. It ran nicely and smoothly. It was important to get the engine running, as we could not enter port without it or it would require someone for a tow. The leak was not too bad and we put a cup under the leak to catch the diesel. We decided to get to port this way. Then I examined the old pump and discovered that there is a rubber "O" ring in the seat of the output tube. Now we know why it is leaking. I cleaned the old casting, which was very dirty with hard crud. When we get to port I will put the old casting back on, but install the new diaphragm and flapper valves, so it is basically a new pump. Hopefully that will result in a complete fix. All of this took three hours as we shut the engine off at 0920 and we did not restart until 1220. It was a smelly and laborious operation while the boat was bouncing about but I was proud that I could diagnose and fix the problem while underway. Resumed our passage. Had lunch of chicken sandwiches. After 2 hours Graham emptied the jar of diesel, which was full. Looked at the old pump and the diaphragm appeared to be OK, but one of the flapper valves was stuck shut. After freeing the flapper, it doesn't seem to seat well. That was the cause of the problem. It is a dark overcast day. There was a brief bit of rain while we were working on the engine. Passed Point Blanco at 1500. As we arrived a charter boat went in before us and took three times of near dangerous reversing to get into a berth due to a cross wind. We did it with precision and no excitement- great! We tied up at 1655 at berth #38. After we were tied up we broke out the champagne and toasted Paul for his circumnavigation (3 bottles). I then did the route for tomorrow. As we are all feeling fine, we decided to finish repairing the pump tomorrow as we have only 6.8 NM to go. Then we went off to dinner at the Italian Pizzeria Pescaro Restaurant. Actually it was very good with everybody enjoying his or her meals. Got back to the boat at 2200. The sky has cleared up somewhat with stars visible. The wind has picked up a bit to 15 knots or so. The halyards on the boats beside us are slapping. Very annoying.

Tuesday, October 22, 2002 - El Arenal, Mallorca

There was wind noise all night. At 0730 the wind was 20 knots from the WSW. I am not sure I want to try to dock in Palma with such high wind, although they should have less being on the west side of the bay. The sky is clear and the moon is still visible. By 0810 the wind is 26 knots with gusts to 32 from the West. We can still wait until tomorrow. The local Navtex says force 7 winds will continue to 0900 tomorrow, the 23rd. Inmarsat-C says that this is due to a deep low of 969 over the North Atlantic moving towards England. Wonder how this is affecting Tom and Gretchen in Glass Slipper as they may still be in England trying to go south. I paid for two nights. The seas are breaking over the breakwater behind us. The waves are sweeping past the entrance and covering the north mole occasionally. (The pilot book warns that the entrance is dangerous in a southwesterly.) The waves in the bay are not too large but it would be rough out there. I took apart the fuel pump once again and used the old upper housing in combination with the new base, diaphragm and flapper valve assembly. This time the nipple did not bottom out and the outlet was tight and not leaking fuel. After bleeding, the engine ran well and there were no leaks. Put everything back together to make the boat shipshape. Completed the work at noon. I then took a shower to get ride of all the diesel smell as I was nearly bathing in the stuff. The smell inside the boat should diminish, as we no longer have pans of liquid diesel sloshing in the engine compartment. The wind just keeps up; still at 30 plus knots- the instruments say that it has been even higher in the last hour. Paul called Christina and told her to come to El Arenel. Her plane lands around 1300. Called Real Club Nautico in Palma and told them we were not going to arrive there today due to the winds. She said, yes, she understood, and that we better stay were we are. The TV showed a weather chart and the low is moving quickly to the NE but there are east/west isobars over the Balearics. The day is a pretty sunny day with clear blue sky. The air in the marina is filled with salt spray. Christina arrived at 1340. G&G went up to the yacht Club in hopes of finding a laundry machine. They did, and returned later with all the laundry done. I spiffed up our cabin and head. Washed all the walls down and stowed all the extra stuff. Looks pretty good. The wind is down a little at 1800, around 24 knots. Hope this is a general trend. Will eat at the Yacht Club tonight. G&G are watching Captain Ron. I thought that would be fun for them. Had drinks onboard before going to dinner. Had dinner at the Club, and after being in there I concluded we had eaten there before. The winds are still strong, between 16 and 20 at 2220. But they are far less than the 30 knots earlier and the forecast is for further decreasing by tomorrow. The low is moving to the East of Corsica.

Wednesday, October 23, 2002 - El Arenal, Mallorca

Had wind sounds all night, but at around 0820 the wind dropped to 8 knots. The seas dropped accordingly. We got excited and prepared to leave. Decided that we did not need to get fuel as the whole Oyster course is only around 100 NM. We have nearly 400 Liters in the tank. Do not want to make the boat heavier than necessary. At 0900 the wind started to increase and it hit 25 knots. So we decided to wait and the women went to the supermarket to get a few things. Graham make some business phone calls, as he is keeping up to date on a daily basis while he is here. The sun is out and there is a clear blue sky. The wind kept up all morning. Had lunch of sandwiches onboard. The wind declined very slowly to the 15-knot range but the swells have not decreased much. At 1400 we decided that it is too dangerous to leave the harbour. The depth, as we know from Monday is 3.5 m and there are 1.5 m or greater swells sweeping past the entrance. A local advised against it because the depth is really shallow just north of the entrance and you could easily be swept on the sand and then onto the beach. We could probably leave later, maybe around 1800 but then we would miss the check-in and briefing. We changed into our evening attire- ESCAPADE shirts and long pants. We took a taxi to Real Club Nautico to check in, attend the owners meeting, and the drinks party and dinner. It all went smoothly but when we got to the YC, there was not much wind and there were no waves. Sure didn't look like we couldn't get out of a harbour only 6 miles away. The briefing was delayed to 1730. Two other boats did not show yet. I thought that we might be the oldest boat there, but #55-1 came in so they take the oldest prize. ESCAPADE of London is also here so there are two ESCAPADEs. Graham & I attended the briefing. The drinks party included local Mallorcan dancing. The dinner was upstairs, where we had dinner once. It was a buffet and we left early to get back to the boat. Our taxi cab driver drove fast- 160 kph so it didn't take long to get home to ESCAPADE. Paul & Christine washed the boat down in the dark. Went to bed at 2315. It is still with hardly any wind now. The sky is clear with stars out. But I just want to get out of this harbour!

Thursday, October 24, 2002 - El Arenal, Mallorca to Palma, Mallorca, Club Nautico 6.8 NM

Race #1 Day around the Bay of Palma

Woke early to absolute quiet. Turned on instruments at 0720 and there was 0.7 knots of wind. Crushed my hand in the hatch when opening it, as it moved very freely. Departed at 0817 and it was smooth in the entrance. The depth was actually 3.0 meters. There was a residual swell, but minor. The sun rose and it will be a pretty day with blue sky with a few small clouds about. Arrived at Real Club Nautico and docked at the fuel dock at 0925. Decided to stay here until the race and when we return we will go to the proper mooring spot. Have power and water here. We will leave the dinghy with Paul's windsurfer here at the marina so that the photos will be good. Also storing the passerelle away, and will get rid of the fenders. At about 1045 Oyster Race Control asked all boats to remain at dock. One boat had left, but was asked to return. Doesn't look good for a race. I went and checked in to the Marina. They still had our records from 1998! Got a water adapter. They know that we will stay where we are until we leave for the race or until the race has been called off. Then we will go to where all the Oysters are, in front of the Clubhouse. We will leave the dinghy with the windsurfer at the dock when we go sailing. Tomorrow, we will need the dinghy with us to get ashore. I replaced the starboard dinghy davit spring. The bimini is also folded down. We look sleek and clean as a race boat. By 1130 there still was no word from Race Control. So we wait. Race control at 1150 said that boats could go out, but that they had not set a start line, or time. We departed at about 1240, just after lunch. We sailed around a bit and then they said the start would be at 1330 and use the Bravo course. We left the declaration of MPS stand. We did one run down the start line and then came back up. Just then two ferries were leaving the harbour so the race committee postponed the start to 1340. We went down and back up again. So we were going parallel to the line on starboard tack (right of way) for the start. We made a clean start but were soon mid-way in the field. The first mark was up wind and we did well. We stuck close to the west coast and did better than those who went further out. When we rounded the mark, there were six boats ahead of us. It was a downwind leg and we set the MPS on the pole. Did well and there were only five boats ahead of us at the mark. Hardened up and did a beat to the finish. Still only five boats ahead of us. I think they were all larger boats. We finished at 1646. The wind started very light at around 6 knots but increased to 11-12 knots so it was good fun. We all felt good about our performance. We were photographed from a helicopter and a powerboat. Hope they got some good pictures. The day started nice but became overcast. It was a little cool. Got into the end spot at the club dock. The dinner will begin by leaving the Club at 1915. The restaurant was called Parliament, in the Parliament building. It was very nice and the meal was good. We found out the results of the day. We crossed the finish line 6th, and first in our class (55' and under). However, after handicap, we came in 5th overall and 4th in our class. We beat the winner in our class by more than 23 minutes but by corrected time we were more than 16 minutes behind. Our handicap was 20% worse than the winner (Blue Beat, 406/17) but only 9% better than the best boat there (Sarita, 66/07). Oh well, that is the way the cookie crumbles. We got a prize of a binder and two white laser flashlights. Returned to the boat by 2310. Talked to Heather and she is doing well even without oxygen. Had to sleep with a mask because the lights around the YC are so bright.

Friday, October 25, 2002 - Palma, Mallorca to Isla Cabrara 29.3 NM

Race #2

Woke to bright sunshine and a clear blue sky, but no wind. It has been 0.0 knots on the instrument for the past half hour. We are supposed to meet the committee boat outside at 0930 for a 1000 start. The alternate plan is for the fleet to motor behind the committee boat until they decide to start the race, conditions permitting. Just received a message from Race Control that the time has been put back one half hour. Departed at 0958 and when we got out there was not enough wind to sail so we first got in line (like baby ducks) for a photo shoot. Then we motored toward Cabrara. When we were off Point Blanco they decided to start the race at 1225. We maneuvered well and were in a very good position to start when they called it off. The start was then set for 1240. This time we were early and had to tack twice before getting under way. Thus we started out nearly last. We first had to beat to windward as the committee boat went upwind and then it was a broad reach to Cabrara. The wind was between 8 and 12 knots. It was a good sail. We crossed the finish line at 1523. There were only four boats behind us, so there were 11 ahead of us. Picked up orange buoy #9 at 1540. The island is a nature reserve, but there are 10 other boats here as well, so it is quite populated. There are a few motley buildings ashore and a castle on the hill. Everyone relaxed onboard. It is nice and quiet here. Everyone took a nap. Ran the generator. The sun has declined over the hills and the harbour is covered in shadow. There is a so-so boat tied to the small dock. It may be the "restaurant ship Samba". Yes, probably is it. Went over in the dinghy. We did not do well in the results. We were second across the finish line in our division, but came in 6th on corrected time. I don't think that a 55 has a chance with the handicaps. The dinner was quite good, but there was not enough seating for everybody. Returned to *ESCAPADE* at 2130. There is phone coverage so I will send an E-mail to Heather.

Saturday, October 26, 2002 - Isla Cabrara to Andraitx, Mallorca 37.1 NM

Had a gentle swell rock us all night. It was pleasant. Woke at 0710 so I read in bed for some time. Not much wind, but it is predicted to come from the SE today. That would be better than a beat to windward. Everyone is sleeping late this morning. The harbor is still and quiet and has that special early morning feeling. The dew is heavy on the decks but the sky is clear so we should have bright sunshine as soon as the sun rises over the hills. The restaurant ship is gone, and people are beginning to be seen on the other boats. The rally is to meet out side at 1000. My hand is still swollen but it is better. Ran the generator, along with the refrigeration, charger and water maker. The rendezvous was put back to 1030. Left the buoy at 1020. All the Oysters lined up abreast inside the harbour for a photo shoot with the hills behind. Tricky handling as all the boats were drifting about. Outside it was decided that there was not enough wind to race so we all headed off toward Andraitx motoring. Christina made lunch of a Spanish omelet with salad. Shortly after 1400 it was decided to stop and heave-to and give the wind a chance to build. The engine went off at 1412. The wind didn't increase so we resumed motoring at 1504. The committee boat was taking on water so they tried to find smooth place to pump out. We all stopped again just south of Isla El Toro and the wind was still not enough. So race #3 was abandoned. We all motored on. It is only another 6 NM to go to Andraitx. We have stopped there before, but only for a lunch stop. It was after our overnight passage from Barcelona. We just anchored out in the bay, before proceeding on to Palma. This time we go to the Club de Vela. The coastline is spectacular with large rock faces near the entrance to the harbour. We were near the last boat coming into the harbour and there was a long line getting in. The Oysters were packed in, and we had to wait for a long time before we could dock. Finally we were told to go into one spot, which was quite narrow. We squeezed in, really tight, quite professionally. Tied up at 1730. Grace & Christina went shopping and bought a few groceries that we were out of. Paul went off to find a boat hook. He came back with a borrowed one. Will have to buy one in Palma. Had drinks at the Club de Vela then took a bus to Golf de Andraitx for dinner. Talked to the Pantaenius guy, as they sponsored today's event. He said they would insure an American flagged boat in the US. Strange dinner with three pasta courses, but good. As there was no race, they needed a way to award the five bottles of champagne. So they gave a verbal quiz. We won one of them! Returned to the boat at 0030 in the morning. But the clocks go back one hour tonight so we gain one hour of sleep.

Sunday, October 27, 2002 - Andraitx, Mallorca to Palma, Mallorca 20.1 NM

Another bright sunny morning with clear blue sky. Does not seem like much wind, however. The barometer is 1024, which is very high. In fact, there is a high sitting stationary over the western Med. My hand is still improving and it only feels tight when I squeeze my fist really tight. I guess we do not meet outside the harbour until 1200. But that will not give much time for the concourse judging at Real Club de Palma this afternoon. It is now 0810, new time, and everyone is still sleeping. Also quiet outside as well. It appears that many of the Oyster boats will be kept in Mallorca over the winter. Even though they set the timing of the event to permit boats to proceed to the ARC, at most one boat will do that. At 1000 the wind instruments were not even turning, but Paul said it looked like there was some wind outside the harbour. Exchanged cards with John Dietz, an American who has a new 53 named Paul Gerard. He is from California and will keep his boat in Malta over the winter. We departed at 1138 for a meeting outside at 1200. They decided to motor to off Isla El Toro so we started off. The wind was very light- around 4 knots. Had lunch of frankfurters. Waited around, then they decided to move to off the next point. Some people on other boats went swimming. Then it was decided there was enough wind (6 knots) to start a race in the Bay of Palma. The start line was between the committee boat and Eddie in a dinghy. Once again the start was called off at the last minute because the helicopter had not arrived yet. On the second start we did quite well, but at the down wind end. Maybe we were among the first three to cross (which will yield another bottle of champagne). We beat upwind then went downwind with MPS. First we had it on the bow, but then we had to put it on the pole as the wind shifted aft a bit and also because the committee boat did not go East at 90° as they said. We crossed the finish line but Paul could not pull the sock down over the MPS. So we had to drop it on the deck and re-pack it later. The race was shortened, so the second mark became the finish. We then motored back to Real Club Nautico de Palma. Took our usual space at 1745. We actually sailed 27.9 NM. Spiffed up the boat for the concourse inspection. Then we had a champagne toast with the bottle we won last night. Also toasted to Heather's health. The concourse inspectors arrived (Eddie and Mike Riches from Boatyard Palma). Will get some fuel tomorrow before we leave. The dinner at the Real Club Nautico was nice. We did not win any prizes. I don't think that with our handicap it was possible to win. Returned to *ESCAPADE* sad that Heather was not there. Had to sleep with an eyeshade because of the dock lights. Did not get to bed until 0045.

Monday, October 28, 2002 - Palma, Mallorca to Porto Colom, Mallorca 43.8 NM

Got up early at 0645 as I was worrying about all the things we have to do to put the boat up for the winter. It was a quiet and still morning. I hope we have two more good days to get to Alcudiamar. Want to get some diesel before we depart. Also want to get a boat hook at the chandlery here. Have to return the special water fitting and get our 30 Euros back. But want to leave by 1000 so as to arrive in Porto Colom by 1700, which is when it is beginning to get dark after the time change. So much to think about; need to plan on dumping and rinsing the holding tanks, etc. Graham and Grace packed up and were getting ready to leave. Said our goodbyes. They were so helpful and made the past two weeks possible and enjoyable. They also set the record for distance traveled for a couple on *ESCAPADE*. I went to the chandlery and bought a new boat hook and Spanish courtesy flag as the old one is small, faded and frayed again. G&G were still there when I returned so we helped them into the Yacht Club. The man at the desk arranged for a hotel. They were going to take a taxi to the hotel (they will spend one night in Palma and fly out tomorrow). Paul and I retrieved his windsurfer and put it back onboard. We departed at 0940 and tied up at the fuel dock at 0947. Christina went to the marina office to return the water fitting. But there was no one there so she had to wait. A sign said "Back in 15 minutes". Paul and I put in 300 liters of diesel in 10 minutes. It was self-service. After 35 minutes there was still no one in sight at the office. I complained to the dock staff near *ESCAPADE* so they finally gave me the 30 Euros. Paul borrowed a bike and went and picked Christina up. We finally departed the fuel dock at 1030. When we got out of the harbour the wind was 12 to 14 knots from the NNE. Where was this the last four days? Turned off the engine at 1040. It was a pleasant sail. Then the wind turned slightly against us so we turned on the engine but we left the main up. As we approached Punta Salinas the wind shifted to the east at 15 knots (Force 4) so we had to roll up the main as we headed East. Turning NE we had to motor into it with an apparent wind of 20 knots plus. Not too choppy, but I regret that we left a half hour late. Making only 5.3 knots SOG. Had lunch of sandwiches. Tried calling Phil Jones of Yachtnet but got no answer. So I sent him an E-mail saying I would like to meet him on Wednesday. Talked to Heather on the phone. Didn't wake her, but she was still in bed. She is a bit tired but she is having an active social life. It will not be long before I am home again. All is proceeding to plan except for the NE wind. The approach to Porto Colom is easy, even with an easterly swell as you are protected by a point of land extending south. So we had a straight shot into the harbor and the seas diminished as we got inside. Arrived before dark! Secured stern-to with laid lines at 1734 at space #22 at the Club Nautico. The town does not look very lively. Actually it is rather dull. The two pontoons described in the pilot book are gone. But the fixed dock, which we are secured to, has been modernized. Christina wanted to make dinner pasta, so we will not have to go out. It is very quiet and peaceful here. It was totally dark by 1815. The pasta was very good. Went to bed early, as I was tired from last night.

Tuesday, October 29, 2002 - Porto Colom, Mallorca to Alcudiamar, Mallorca 40.7 NM

Had a good nights sleep but it is getting cold at night. The days are really short as well. Daylight starts at a little after 0700 and ends around 1800. The first two nights back on *ESCAPADE* I had to use the A/C in order to sleep. Now its full blanket and double spread plus underwear. Only one more night on *ESCAPADE* this year! The day looks acceptable; the sky is basically clear although there are a few low small clouds about (probably condensation clouds). There is no wind here, and the forecast from last night was easterly 4 to 5 decreasing to 3 to 4 by noon. Should be OK to motor. The TV had lots of pictures of high wind damage in Europe in the last few days. The airports in England were closed a few days ago due to high winds. There have been Force 10/11 gales in the Channel and Bay of Biscay. Sure hope Tom & Gretchen are all right in Glass Slipper. Phil Jones from Yachtnet, the person who will take care of *ESCAPADE* over the winter wrote back an E-mail. We will meet tomorrow, Wednesday. So all is falling into place. We left at 0746 while the town slept. At least it was very quiet. Got outside and the sea is quite calm, much better than yesterday when we pulled in. Hope to beat the waves today. We are making 7.3 knots SOG and the wind is only 4 to 5 knots from the NNW. Heard from Kiko. They would like to see us if we are in England. At 1100 we were at the most eastern point and started heading NW. The wind switched to the SE so all is well. The sea remains very calm and our SOG is still 7.1 knots. It is the final stretch of 16 NM. We have been going close to land so the view very dramatic. Would not want to be this close if there was a large sea running. We will do the dinghy today, as we want it on the foredeck when the boat is hauled. Paul made lunch of toasted ham and cheese sandwiches. We can see Alcudia! Accomplished the first item on the list- logged out and turned off Inmarsat-C. Even if we didn't sail, it was a pretty and good day. Arrived at the fuel dock at 1330 but there was a motorboat there arguing about paying, as his credit card didn't work. Jockeyed back and forth until they pulled the boat around the corner. We docked at 1354. Took on 451 liters. Left there at 1412 and were stern-to in #T48 at 1417. We immediately started the decommissioning process. I checked into the office and all was set for tomorrow. The hard standing is concrete and looks good. I asked several people about damage to boats here last winter. There was none to boats on the hard, but a few boats in the marina were damaged due to faulty lines. At the next marina north of here (Puerto de Pollensa), 47 boats were sunk in the marina. Called Heather and said all was going according to plan, but the VISA card had been rejected twice. We removed the sails and Phillip Jones took them away (including the MPS). He also said that it never freezes here. It may snow in the mountains, but it does not freeze near the sea. Put the outboard on the push pit rail and the dinghy on the foredeck. Removed all lines and sheets. Took off the cockpit tray and cup holder. Cleaned the water maker filters and pickled it with 5 oz. of preservative solution. Went to find a hotel and have dinner. The hotel was harder than I thought as many were closed. We found one open but it was closing tomorrow. Found another one at which we made a reservation, and it is closing on the 3rd. Ate at Bistro Mar in the marina, which was nice. We stayed here in 1998 but I don't recall it. Overall, it is a very nice marina with lots of facilities and services. A still night.

Wednesday, October 30, 2002 – Alcudiamar

Woke to a sunny morning although there are thin high clouds around. That was the last night on *ESCAPADE* for quite a while. The hotel is a fair distance away, so we will have to get a taxi or arrange other means to get our major luggage there. Overnight stuff we can carry. Paul washed the lines in the cockpit. We flushed the holding tanks. Took the laundry in to be done. Signed all the forms and we moved into the travel lift slot at 0935. At 1000 they moved the travel lift to us, but then they took a coffee break. Not much sun so things are drying slowly. The man at the marina said in order to get the boat into bond I would have to take the forms to Palma. Bummer. Don't know if I want to go through the hassle. *ESCAPADE* is listing to port with a full tank of fuel and nearly empty water tanks. At 1040 things started to happen. However, it took to 1230 before they pulled the travel lift away from the boat. At 1200 we tried to get lunch at the local cantina, but they didn't start serving until 1230. So we got back to work by 1315. The boat has not been power washed yet, but as they have lunch between 1300 and 1500, it will not be done until 1500. The sun finally came out and is starting to dry things so we can stow them. *ESCAPADE* is located at the western end of the outer wall, inside of a powerboat. She is next to a plastic shed of a large old wooden sailboat that is being rebuilt. The hard standing is concrete so there shouldn't be must dust, and the supports will not tip. *ESCAPADE* is supported by wooden posts and a couple of metal supports. I guess it should be OK, given the concrete hard. The bottom is fine, with no damage. Finally got onboard and started to work again. The zincs are in remarkably good shape. Talked to the rigger and sailmaker and organized their work. They finally power washed the bottom. Sat with Phil and organized their work and watching the boat. Determined that I must go to Palma tomorrow (Friday is a holiday) to put the boat into bond. That will save hassle later. Will organize a car tonight as that is the easiest and cheapest to get to Palma and back. As soon as the sun goes down it gets cold. Will walk to the hotel with our overnight things. The laundry was done today and everything is already back. Walked to the hotel and checked in. It is the Viva Golf. It is actually quite nice, with a large pool and right on the beach. Had dinner of pizza. Watched a bit of Euro Sport on TV as that is the only English Channel.

Thursday, October 31, 2002 – Alcudia

Left the hotel at 0800 and as I was walking to pick up the car, it was thundering and sprinkling lightly. Got the car, a VW Polo, which was black. Unusual color for a hot place. I got airport drop-off rights for 15 Euros so it will save a 60 Euros taxi to the airport. Drove to the marina and Paul put our extra gas into the car as it is empty and we also wanted to get rid of the fuel. I will also drop off Paul's large bag as we are concerned whether we can get all of our luggage into the car plus three of us on Saturday. It will probably rain today but Paul can work on the inside. Will need tomorrow to complete everything, as I have to organize all my papers and records and back up the computer. I could have used an extra day in London, but I need to complete everything here first. Before leaving I bought some oil so Paul could change the engine oil. The drive to Palma started out in the rain, and the traffic was slow on the two-lane road. But then the rain stopped and I got on the expressway. It took about one hour to get to downtown Palma. Took a while to find a parking space. Then went to the building I was told to go to, but it was the wrong one. Customs (Aduanas) was in the building next door. I wandered around inside and found a man who must have been very senior as he had a very nice, large corner office. He explained the new rules for the EC (18 months inside EC, then one day out) and then took me down stairs to a man in a small office to get the forms. We returned to his office to fill them out and then back down stairs. All was quick and courteous and I got the important file number. The bottom line is that the clock stops while the boat is in bond, so it does not count toward the 18 months. I do not have to go back to Palma when we want to get *ESCAPADE* out, just fax a form to them. As I still had time on the parking meter I went to McDonalds for lunch. Walking down the walking street, it was beautiful and a nice temperature. There was a clear blue sky and the fountain was going. Wanted to call Heather, but it was too early and she might not appreciate it. After driving around to find the street of the hotel for P&C, I finally found it. Dropped off Paul's large bag. Found my way out of the city and returned to Alcudiamar. Actually got back at 1400 so no one was at work. Later, I gave a copy of the form to the marina and to Yachnet. Bought a battery charger for the generator battery as the old one failed in Antalya when I had loaned it. Backed up the primary computer for the trip home. Put the PC away and packed the other Macintosh G4 for the trip. The marina and all shops will be closed tomorrow, but we will still be able to get into the hardstand area. Guess that means I will not get the deposits back on the key card and water connector until next year. Took the steering wheel off. After all the workmen from next door departed we ran the engine and generator on fresh water and then we devised a means of running the refrigeration and A/C units on fresh water. We attached the hose to the bleeder connection for the refrigeration and inserted it into the large A/C hose with a foam surround to pressurize the system. It worked well. Put fresh water thru the aft toilet and emptied all the sinks. Flushed the bilge with fresh water. Went back to the hotel at 1915. Cleaned up quickly and P&C went to a travel agent and Paul bought a ticket to Barcelona. Went to dinner. The town is closing before our eyes. Each night there are fewer and fewer shops and restaurants open. It is becoming a ghost town. By Monday, after the holiday weekend it will be nearly closed. There may be only two hotels open (out of 20 to 30 in town). Fell asleep watching Euro Sport.

Friday, November 1, 2002 – Alcudia

Got to the boat at 0805. Very quiet in town. It is threatening rain so we must complete the outside items. But we need to get everything dry before we stow them. Will finish up today. If we have time I will try to install the battery charger. The sun came out later and it turned into a pretty day. Finished the engine, transmission, etc. Christine did the refrigerator and freezer. At the end of all that I went to empty the water tanks and there was only two inches of water in the sink when the main tank went dry. There was about one sink full in the small tank. So we really judged that right. Took the dodger off, and Paul put his windsurfer down below. The deck is clean now. There was nothing to be stolen or to create wind resistance. I packed up the aft cabin and then packed the bag. I was able to take some more of the old brochures. P & C took off to go to the beach and pool. Had lunch at the cafe by myself. Returned to ESCAPADE and Heather called. Sitting here by myself in ESCAPADE, sad once again to see the sailing year-end, but lonely for Heather. The season is over and it is time to move on. Paul is confident of returning next year, but he took nearly all of his stuff. Tried connecting the battery charger but at first it didn't work, and then I blew the fuse at the power box. Also, the terminal on the battery broke. Will start over next year. Think I will pack up and go to the hotel. I will have to return Saturday morning to drop off my toiletries.

Saturday, November 2, 2002 - Alcudia to London

Got up early and left the hotel by 0800. Took the stuff to ESCAPADE and made sure all was OK. Said goodbye to her. It was a lovely, sunny day. Quite warm. Drove P&C to their hotel in Palma. Paul had been onboard ESCAPADE for four years, all around the world, so it was sad for him to say goodbye. Then I went to the airport. Got there by 0940. I was told to leave the car on floor 4 of the parking structure. The only problem was that floor 4 was full and it was blocked off. I proceeded up to floor 6, but there was no way out without entering. I talked to someone and they gave me a ticket that permitted me to pass thru without paying. I returned to the ground and looked at the entrance to the rental car returns but my rental group was not among those listed. So I call the rental company and they said to leave it on floor 5. This I did and later called them to tell them exactly where (5 J/J). Checked in and the flight was at 1200. We were delayed by air traffic control on take off. The flight was fine, but I had to wait 45 minutes to get the bags. Further, we arrived at the Gatwick North terminal. So I went to the south terminal and found Left Luggage and checked in the big bag. Took the Gatwick express, which was also late by 10 minutes. Got to the London flat at 1540. It is a dark, rainy, and cold day in London. This is the end of the sailing diary for 2002.

In summary, during the year we visited 13 countries, traveled 9,007.4 NM, and were underway 1,289.9 hours, of which the engine was running 780.32 hours or 60.49% of the time. The average speed was 6.98 knots. There were 16 other people onboard ESCAPADE as crew. It was a most exciting and successful year.

CHAPTER 31

Memories *and* Experiences

A Random Collection of Interesting Cruising Events

The future belongs to those who believe in the beauty of their dreams.

ELEANOR ROOSEVELT

This is a collection of memories and experiences that stand out from my fifteen years of cruising. Actually, there was a story each day and these are some of the more memorable ones, in no particular order.

Entering St. Katharine's Dock in London England

This occurred when we still did not have a lot of experience. In fact, we had only been sailing for only about a month, and we had taken on a new 55' boat, handling it in tight quarters, with high tides, coping with customs requirements etc. We were in Ramsgate, England, and wanted to go to London and St. Katharine's Dock, which—since the Thames River is very tidal—is a marina behind a lock. In fact, they only open the lock when the Thames is at high tide to insure that the water in the marina does not drain out, and we knew that it would be best to ride the flood tide upstream. So we calculated a time for departure that would get us to St. Katharine's around high tide. We knew that—since we did not want to sail up the Thames—we would have to motor the whole trip. That particular day, the second high tide in London would be around 10:00 PM, which was after sunset. So that was our target.

We had a very pleasurable run up the Thames estuary and past the Thames Barrier. We then passed Greenwich,

which is zero longitude. In fact, since the Thames does a double bend as you pass Greenwich, you pass zero longitude three times. We continued upstream and it turned dark. Near the destination, we rounded a bend in the Thames, and saw the Tower Bridge all lit up. Located just beyond St. Katherine's Dock, it was a magnificent sight. We felt elated, as we had arrived in London in our own sailboat.

Unfortunately, the lock was closed, and it was not operating. After several radio calls, we learned that the lock opened at high tide, but only during normal business hours (9 to 5). It was a critical, but small detail. So there we were, in the dark, with the tide sweeping us toward the bridge, and it would be twelve hours before we could enter the marina on the next high tide.

There were a couple of mooring buoys for use by troubled sailors like us, but they were low to the water, with no line attached. I had to motor against the current and position the bow so my wife could slip a line into a ring on the buoy. It was dark, I could not see the buoy from the helm, and she had to lie on the deck so she could reach down, which meant I could not hear her. It took many attempts before we were secured, but then had an uneventful night before entering the marina in the morning. That was our first time in a lock with several other boats, which was

196   SAIL THE WORLD

nerve racking. But, once we were inside the marina, all was fine. I learned that it was critical to check the details of your plans in all aspects before you start out.

Chain wrap in Rhodes Greece

Rhodes, Greece, is a wonderful place to visit as it has old world charm and Greek ambiance. The island is easy to explore, and the city of Rhodes can be visited on foot. The harbor where private boats dock is where the ancient "Colossus of Rhodes" stood at the entrance, although there is nothing remaining now. Our first visit was in 1997, and docking was stern-in or Med moor. We were directed to tie up to the north/south quay on the east side, but fairly close to the east/west quay just north of us. During our several-day stay a fleet of sailboats arrived as part of a race from Athens. They Med moored to the east/west quay, which meant their anchor lines were at a right angle to our anchor chain.

We were walking around town on the day before our departure, and I noticed that a boat docked near us was having a lot of difficulty getting away, although I could not see why. The next day when we departed, we dropped the stern dock lines, and used the windlass to pull the boat forward so the bow was over our anchor. The windlass was straining a lot, and when the anchor finally got to the surface we found out why. There was a smaller chain and anchor from one of the race boats wrapped around our anchor. We were then effectively moored in the center of the harbor. So we dropped the dinghy, and tried to loosen the small chain from the dinghy. But when we raised the chain (in order to reach it), the small chain became taught and we could not unwrap it. It could only be unwrapped when our anchor was at the bottom of the harbor. There was no way possible for the smaller chain to wrap around our anchor by itself. Very perplexing!

Then things began to become clear. It was shouted from shore that there was a local diver who would undertake the job to free us for a fee. We also knew that it was illegal for a foreigner (non Greek) to dive in Greek waters without a Greek guide. This is to prevent people from stealing ancient artifacts. I was a certified scuba diver, and I had my equipment as well as my air tank aboard. But I knew that if I dived the local diver would call the police on me.

Then someone from one of the race boats called out, and told us that it was their anchor chain we were caught on. So I dinghied over to him. He claimed to be a Greek special services diver that could dive anywhere in Greece, but told me he had used his air tank up freeing another boat earlier that day. So I said he could use my air tank if he would dive and free the anchors. It did not take him long before we were free, and I gave him a bottle of booze for his work. It was clear that a local diver had found a clever way to make some money by wrapping chains at night, but we outfoxed him and avoided paying

him anything. We thanked the Greek sailor and finally departed several hours late.

On our next visit to Rhodes, we used an agent who found us a spot much closer to town that would have no wrapped-chain drama. Maybe by now the local diver stopped his evil ways. But do not miss Rhodes, as it is such a worthwhile, lively and lovely place.

Being Boarded

We were boarded three times by officials. The first was in 1998, off the coast of Morocco in the Atlantic—at night. We had just left the Mediterranean by the Strait of Gibraltar, and were heading toward the Spanish Canary Islands off the west coast of Africa. We were still in the territorial waters of Morocco; I was off duty, and sleeping. Note that things often happen when you least expect them. An experienced crewmember, however, was on watch. Although it was very dark, he said he sensed something. Suddenly, a bright spotlight was trained on us from the aft starboard side. It was a large cutter from the Moroccan Navy. They requested that ESCAPADE come alongside. As the seas were quite large, and such a maneuver would cause great damage to our boat, my crew suggested they come to ESCAPADE in a rib. The navy had one person, who could speak English on the cutter, but they agreed. They requested that we continue sailing, and said they would send a boarding party to us in a rib. At that point, I was awakened. As captain, I always requested that I be notified of any emergencies or unusual events. We continued to sail for 15 or 20 minutes with the cutter following behind, but then they said the rib could not keep up with us. We were asked to come back to them. That's when I concluded that the Moroccan Navy was not up to par. So we rolled up the sails and motored back. The rib finally arrived, and several navy personnel boarded. They had poor equipment, and none of them spoke English. So I had to communicate by VHF radio to the person on the cutter who would then translate for the Navy people on ESCAPADE. I believe that it was mostly a training exercise for the Navy, but they did look around ESCAPADE. At least they caused no damage, but it was a rather exciting experience.

The second boarding was by the US Coast Guard in international waters in 2000. We were sailing from Savannah, Georgia, to Panama and it happened in the gap that is west of Haiti and south of Cuba. We were sailing south, away from the US. Once again, it was at night, and a ship approached on the aft quarter. Again, a bright spotlight was trained on ESCAPADE and it remained on so as to blind us so that we could not see anything behind. The Coast Guard hailed us and requested to board. I questioned why they wanted to board in international waters. They said that if our boat was documented in the US they had the right to board us anywhere in the world. So I said, "Welcome." The US Coast Guard was much better prepared, and had all the equipment they needed. Again, I suspected it was a training exercise, as they need to practice on boats that were not a real threat. Maybe they have a quota as well. As we were sailing away from the US it would not seem likely that we were smuggling drugs. In any event, they went through the drill. They kept one person armed with an automatic weapon on the poop deck, and he would not speak to anyone. The others wanted to see the bilge first (to make sure we were not sinking), and then the engine compartment (to make sure we were not on fire). They requested to see the official documents, and then checked the required equipment. They found no problems. I demonstrated our navigation system, and they said the charting was better than they had. We were cleared quickly, they gave us a boarding receipt, and we never stopped sailing.

The third time was in 2008, also by the US Coast Guard, in Long Island Sound. It was a quick and efficient boarding, the same things as before were checked. Since it was daylight for a change, they did not need a person with an automatic weapon to board ESCAPADE. Again, we received a clean inspection and receipt. So it is always a good idea to have all your documents, flares, charts, fire extinguishers, etc., up to date.

Dolphins, Whales, Fish and Sea Life

One of the great pleasures about sailing is getting close to all forms of sea life. On a small boat you have the ability to enjoy many interactions and wonderful experiences. We encountered many dolphins from a variety of species—in all waters—and they always made the day more enjoyable. We would rush to the bow to look at them because that's

Lady Susan Reickert at Tracey Arm, Alaska, USA

PHOTO BY ERICK REICKERT

where the dolphins would often play around. My theory was that they preferred the fun of playing with a bow wave over swimming in the featureless ocean. In general, dolphins swim in pods. If the pod is swimming when crossing the boat's path, they often break off their course to play. They will dip and dive and cross over the bow, keeping just ahead of the boat. They often turn sideways to look up at you, but the playing generally lasts no longer than 10 minutes.

One cute example of family life occurred when one pod had played for a while at our bow, and then all of them—except for a younger one—continued on their course. The younger one was having too much fun, and ignored the pod. Finally, we could see one of the larger dolphins come out of the water and hit the waves with its flipper. The young one immediately stopped playing, and set off to join the pod. Evidently, even dolphins have to obey mother.

A very unusual behavior occurred when we were sailing between St. Augustine, Florida, and Charleston, SC. It was late afternoon turning into night, there were two waterspouts to our stern, and a storm was developing ahead of us. The sky was very dark with multiple lightening flashes. Suddenly, dolphins surrounded us. They did not play at the bow, but stayed on both sides of us near the cockpit. We could hear them splashing as they swam, and they made their little chirping noises. Since, it was dark, we couldn't really see them. But they kept up with us for over 30 minutes, until there was a break in the clouds above us, and the sky became lighter. About an hour later—as we approached the storm—it became darker again. Out of nowhere, the dolphins returned and resumed their vigil besides us. After another 30 minutes or so they departed. This was, by far, the longest time that dolphins had stayed with the boat. It was clear to us they were being protective and they stayed with us until we were out of danger.

We also encountered many whales. Most of these occurred in Alaska and British Columbia. In Tracy Arm we came upon a mother whale that was lying still on the surface with her baby whale on the other side of her. Maybe she thought the bottom of *ESCAPADE* looked like whale. In any event, she lay motionless—while protecting her baby—looked at us critically. She was at least 50 feet long—since she was no more than 20 feet away—we could judge her size accurately by comparing her to *ESCAPADE's* length. We stopped beside her, and floated that way for ten minutes before she moved on. It was a very bonding experience.

When sailing south of Glacier Bay National Park in Alaska we could see (and hear), the whales blowing. We were often close enough to smell the blows and even get a spray. There is no mistaking the smell, as it is a very heavy fish odor.

We also witnessed an unusual activity in the same area by killer whales. There were at least six of them, and they had located a school of fish. They used group action to achieve their objective. All but one or two of them swam in a circle around the school of fish emitting bubbles. This effectively contained the fish to inside the circle. Then the remaining whales swam up through the center of the circle with their mouths open at full speed to catch the fish. Then they switched positions so that all of them

Erick Reickert while at anchor at Belize

PHOTO BY BARRY HEDLEY

could eat. We could not see the fish, but we could see some of the whales swimming in a circle, and the bubbles that rose to the surface. We could also see the whales breaching the water in the center. It appeared to be very effective feeding technique for the whales.

When sailing from Panama to Ecuador we—literally—ran into a whale. In fact, we hit it. We knew it was a whale because we could see its tailfins rise into the air as it dove. We concluded that it had been asleep on the surface, and as we were sailing it had not heard our approach. I don't think we hurt the whale, and ESCAPADE wasn't damaged.

Fish generally abound—except in the Mediterranean—which is nearly a dead body of water. In the Sea of Cortez, the fish are so plentiful that they almost jump into the boat. At night, if you shine a flashlight into the water, it attracts so many fish that the water seethes and boils. We did not fish a lot on ESCAPADE, but a crewmember caught a yellow fin tuna in the Pacific and a salmon off the coast of Alaska. Off the coast of North Carolina we saw many stingray fish under the surface. They looked like pieces of a cardboard box floating under water.

On the passage to the Canary Islands, the Atlantic became so calm that it was like glass. We then noticed lumps on the horizon. When we got closer, it became evident the lumps were sea turtles. There were hundreds so we had to avoid them. We don't know if there are turtles around more frequently, but perhaps we just never noticed them because if the water has waves you cannot see the lumps.

We frequently saw jellyfish of all sizes. They always point into the current. We were very careful not to swim whenever they were present because some are quite poisonous, especially around Australia.

When crossing oceans you will encounter flying fish. They have little wings and they rise above the sea surface for many feet. They will often emerge from one wave, and then fly to another wave. Frequently, at night they are so plentiful that in the morning they litter the deck because they land there rather than back in the ocean. If you don't get rid of them, they will bake on deck and smell.

Venice, Italy

Venice is a wonderful city that is truly magical. I had been to Venice several times before, but I wanted to arrive on my own boat. The problem is that there is no good marina. There were a few docking locations, but ESCAPADE would not fit. So I contacted an agent to see if he could find a suitable location. He was able to get us in, but it was very expensive. Not only was there the agent's fee, but there was also the docking charge to the city, as well as a pilot's fee (but I never saw a pilot). The location, however, was perfect. It was alongside the main waterway

on the south side of the city, on Calle San Biagio. The only problem was that there was wash from the waterbus and the water taxies. And the quay, which was made of old stone, was very rough so there was always a possibility of damage to the boat. But, on the other hand, it was only a short walk to St. Mark's Square, and we were right in the middle of a beautiful, exciting city in July. It was perfect. I was able to take the dinghy around the small canals—carefully avoiding the gondolas—and was able to enjoy Venice from the water. The only restriction was that foreigners were not allowed on the Grand Canal.

Then we learned of the best part. The weekend we were there was going to be the Festa del Redentore, a celebration of the ending of the plague in 1576. It was a wonderful and exuberant experience, and everybody in Venice participated. A floating bridge to the church on San Giorgio Maggiore Island is built and there is one of the best fireworks displays you have ever seen. The fireworks are sent up from barges that are located in the water just off the shore. That put us, and ESCAPADE, in the best possible position because we had a ringside seat. In fact, we even put folding chairs out on the deck so we could watch the festivities in comfort. On the evening of the fireworks, the largest boat flotilla imaginable gathers for the event. There were literally hundreds of boats, all jockeying for position, and moving at the same time in the dark. Some boats anchored, which is not normally permitted. We did not see any collisions, but there must have been some. The boats ranged from huge ferry boats, large fishing boats, pleasure motor and sail boats, waterbuses, water taxis, gondolas, rowboats, kayaks with lights on the rowers head, dinghies, etc. In other words, anything that floated. The large ferries had all the cars removed, and the loading area fitted out as a disco with flashing lights and blasting out loud music. It was organized pandemonium, but everybody was well behaved and enjoying themselves. The fireworks lasted nearly an hour, and there were several types of displays that we had not seen before. It was a wonderful experience that we had not expected, so it was even more pleasurable.

Santorini, Greece Anchoring

Santorini (or Thera) is one of those picturesque Greek islands portrayed in travel brochures. A bright white church with blue dome against a dark blue sky is the classic image. The town of Fira is located on top of the hill with a near vertical cliff down to the sea. Tourists often ride donkeys up a steep and winding stone path to the town. In town there are narrow, winding streets lined with shops and tavernas. Views down to the Aegean Sea are breathtaking. It is a place not to be missed.

The challenge is how to go there with your own boat. The island is the remains of a volcano that had its center blown away. For that reason, the water is very deep inside the center area, and not suitable to anchor. (The east side of the island is actually quite low to the water, but is not the classic approach for tourists.) There was one large buoy that could be tied to that was located a short distance from the docks where the donkeys and cable car depart. This, however, was designed for multiple boats, and it is not advisable to leave your boat there unattended. Also, there did not seem to be a place to leave the dinghy ashore. We arrived in time for us to go up to the town, and we left our First Mate aboard to watch the boat. Later, we let him go up to see the town while we stayed onboard. Another boat came and tied to the buoy, which was large enough to walk on. In calm seas it was acceptable, and we stayed overnight. But the next day, the wind and seas increased, which bounced the boats and could have potentially caused damage. (The other boat was a light speedboat that moved differently to the waves.) It was also becoming uncomfortable. In fact, we did sustain some damage from the motorboat, and concluded that we had to either find another alternative or go to another island.

On the other side of the central water area is the island of Thirasia (little Thera). From the charts, it appeared to be a possible alternative, and it was definitely sheltered from the NW winds. So we motored over there, but found that the water—although shallower—was still too deep to anchor. The actual village is up the hill, but there is, however, a community at sea level. There were small private buoys along the shore, and we motored by them to see if there was any buoy we could tie to. There were several restaurants that extended into the sea, and it appeared to be laid back compared to the tourist frenzy of Santorini. At that point, a local fishing boat departed a small buoy, and we called out to ask if there were any buoys that we could use. They replied, "Yes"—we could use theirs, and tie our stern to the nearby restaurant. We did as directed, and then proceeded to visit the restaurant. We were welcomed as family, and they said we could remain tied up. We then patronized the restaurant for the next two days. Evidently, tourists from Santorini take a boat ride to Thirasia for a change of view and a more relaxed atmosphere during the day. At night, when all the tourists leave, the island becomes quiet and sort of private. We enjoyed our stay there, and it was a wonderful experience we hadn't expected. We were able to walk the island and enjoy the calm, so a bad situation turned into a truly memorable experience.

Fishing Boats

You will quickly learn the different types of fishing boats, and how they maneuver when fishing. Remember that fishing boats have the right of way when engaged in fishing operations. Further, when fishing, the fishermen are generally not paying attention to the other boats that are around them and at night they use high intensity lights to illuminate their decks. Because of that practice, the crew are blind to other boats.

There are a wide variety of fishing boats, and there is further variety between different parts of the world. But let me cover the ones that present the most issues to sailors. One of the most frequent fishing boats is the trawler. These pull a net—either from the stern or from outriggers—that attempts to catch fish. The net is often kept open by underwater "doors" that apply an outward force. Heavy steel cables often connect the net, and it is pulled into the boat when full. Trawlers generally motor at slow speeds (under 8 knots), and generally in a straight line—otherwise the net may collapse. The nets can extend quite a distance behind the trawler. Never go behind a trawler unless you leave plenty of clearance for the net.

We had one very unusual occurrence with a trawler in the Mediterranean off the coast of Spain. We were heading south, and a trawler was heading SW on a course that would intersect with ours. Based on a constant closing angle, it looked like we were on a collision course. I was deciding when and what course to change to so that we would go well astern of him, but just then the trawler started to go backwards at quite a speed. We could see the fishermen running around their deck as water was splashing over their stern and they were clearly not backing down as the cables to the net were still taught. There was only one explanation—that they had caught their net on a submarine, and the sub was pulling them backwards. They did not release the cables, probably because the net and cables are expensive gear. But the trawler quickly disappeared out of sight. I wondered how long it took for the sub to figure out that it was towing something. By the way, submarines are always a possibility. Off the coast of Turkey, we had a black submarine surface only a quarter mile away. It was quite a surprise!

Longliner fishing boats use a long line, sometimes up to 10 miles long, suspended from floats on the surface. They can adjust the depth of the line by the length of the vertical support lines. Along the length of the main line is a series of fishhooks. These can vary in distance between them. The ends of the longline are sometimes marked with small buoys, which sometimes have lights, or radio signals so the fishing boat can locate them. I emphasize sometimes, as I never found any consistency that you can depend upon. If you miss seeing the end buoys, then you might spot the floats in daylight—but not at night. Depending upon the depth the longline is set, it may be possible to sail over the line, but—depending upon the depth of your keel—I would be extremely cautious. You just have to keep a lookout for small floats in a line. If the fishing boat is hauling the line in, they will be proceeding in the direction of the line.

Drift nets are especially dangerous. These are vertical nets that are suspended from the surface of the water from floats. From your boat, the series of floats will appear similar to the floats of a longline. The nets can be more than a mile long, and (again) the ends may be poorly marked. It is not possible to sail over drift nets without getting entangled. What makes these even more dangerous is their deployment. When we were sailing down the west coast of Mexico, we were going parallel to the coast. But we came upon drift nets that were set perpendicular to shore, thus ensuring that we would run into them. The difficult part was trying to determine where the ends of the net were. Sometimes, there would be a very small fishing boat hovering around to protect their property, but trying to decide which direction to go to avoid the net was difficult. At night, it would be impossible to see the floats. Luckily, we never ran into one, but we did spot several nets and went around them.

We heard on our VHF radio one example of the difficulty that nets can cause. We were sailing between Gibraltar and Malta, and had to go around a cape of land in Tunisia. It was night and there was a small sea running. We were passing the Gulf of Tunis (which is outside of Tunis) when we heard a Dutch sailor radio for assistance from the Tunisian Coast Guard. I am not sure they even have a Coast Guard but someone on shore answered the request for help—even though they were not willing to send any boat for assistance. The communication was in English and I could tell that they were having issues understanding each other. The situation was that the Dutchman was on a sailboat with only his wife, who—since she did not speak English—she could not operate the radio. They were caught in a net. He had taken down his sails, and now they were drifting with the net. He had gone overboard into the dark waters with a knife and tried to cut away the net, which would have been a very tricky and exhausting operation. The person on shore—who was unwilling to

Escapade at anchor in Prideaux Haven, BC, Canada

PHOTO BY ERICK REICKERT

help—nevertheless kept calling the Dutchman every 15 minutes to get a progress report. As the wife could not answer the radio, he was forced to climb back onboard to answer stupid questions from the shore. He then had to go back down into the water to resume cutting the net. Finally, he was able to free himself from the net. We were still not close enough to provide assistance, and I was concerned about being caught in the net if we attempted to approach the Dutchman. But it all ended well, and we proceed to Malta.

Another type of fishing boat is a seiner, or purse seiner. These fishing boats drop large nets, generally when the fishing boat is stationary, and hopefully around a school of fish. The Net is then hauled back aboard. The purse is created by drawing a line around the bottom of the net to close it (this creates a sealed net), which prevents the fish from escaping. These fishing boats are the easiest to avoid, and present the least problems for the sailor.

It was possibly a seiner that caused us a problem when we were sailing between Crete in Greece to Salerno Italy. It was night and I was off watch and sleeping. A crewmember was on watch, and he saw a fishing boat in the distance to the north. He observed the navigation lights and tried to determine the direction the boat was going. He then kept altering our course to avoid the other boat. I was awakened when the motion of ESCAPADE changed, which indicated that we had changed direction. When I looked at our track on the computer, it was clear we were now sailing north rather than westerly. What happened was the fishing boat was stationary and not moving at all. They were, however rotating round their nets, which caused the navigation lights to indicate that they were changing direction. So, essentially, we had sailed around the fishing boat because the crewmember was concerned about approaching the fishing boat. When I resumed our westerly course the fishing boat disappeared astern. This was a case of confusion caused by the fishing boat as it spun around its nets.

An unusual case of fishing occurred when we entered the Gulf of Corinth on the way to Athens via the Corinth Canal. It was night, and we saw many bright lights right near the surface of the water off to our starboard. The radar showed a large number of targets in the form of dots ahead. The situation was very confusing, but as we approached slowly it became clearer. There was a larger "mother" fishing boat, surrounded by many men in rowboats that were pulling small nets in circles (similar to seiners). Inside each of the nets was a bright light on a small float to attract fish. Fortunately, we were able to deviate safely around the frantic activity.

Anchoring Issues

As mentioned in Chapter 22, anchoring issues are one of the most common risks for cruisers because they are always going into new and unfamiliar areas. Plus, they often subject themselves to risks they cannot control. We had several examples, even though we tried to follow proper procedures and test the holding power of the anchor every time we anchored. On the coast of Turkey, south of Marmaris, we entered an inlet and then a smaller circular bay where other boats were anchored. Their anchors were in the center of the bay and their sterns were tied to the shore behind. That area is very rocky, but the round inlet looked good on the chart. We dropped the anchor as close to the far side as we could get, and then backed down toward the shore behind. The anchor seemed dug-in, so—using the dinghy—the First Mate tied a stern line to a rock on shore. Since it was rather calm, we seemed safe and secure.

In the middle of the night, ESCAPADE'S engine started, which will immediately waken anyone sleeping in the aft cabin. The First Mate had started the engine knowing it would wake me up. As he slept forward, he heard the chain scraping and clunking, which meant the anchor was dragging. When he went to the cockpit, he realized that the stern was about to hit the rocks behind ESCAPADE. He was using the engine to pull away from shore. We decided that we would not attempt to re-anchor in the dark because other boats were close by, and there was the possibility that we might drag again. So we tossed the stern line overboard, and motored forward so we could haul up the anchor. After getting outside the small circular bay, the First Mate went back in the dinghy to retrieve the stern line. Since we were up and awake, we kept going to Marmaris. I was glad we did not hit the rocks due to the First Mate's awareness.

We were sailing from Marseille, France to Spain—and Port Roses in particular. Our objective was the marina in Port Roses, 121 NM away. It was only my wife and I, and we departed in the afternoon expecting to arrive the next afternoon. There was no wind to start, and so we motored SW across the Bay of Biscay. The wind started to increase from the NW, and soon we were sailing. But the wind kept increasing until it reached gale force. We had a hard time pointing our course, and the seas soon became large. The wind was a Mistral, which has a bad reputation, and can occur even in clear air. In any event, our progress slowed and the voyage became exhausting for the two of us. It was late in the afternoon when we approached the Spanish coastline. Because of the high winds we did not want to attempt to go into the marina. On the chart, we saw a little bay behind the headlands that would offer protection from the wind. There were some rocks in the bay, but we thought we could get between the rocks and the shore for an anchorage.

We anchored successfully and—as we were exhausted—felt very relieved. We seemed to be riding nicely, and the water was calm—even though some wind came over the headland. By using sightlines ashore, a check of our position indicated we were not dragging anchor. We went to bed expecting to sleep late in the morning.

For some reason, I awoke early. I immediately checked our position, and discovered that we were dangerously close to the rocks. So I had to re-anchor before we organized for the day. But don't expect your sixth sense to save you every time!

Take Me to Your Leader!

Off the west coast of Fiji, there are many islands—including the Yasawa group. The whole area has multiple reefs, and sailing requires navigating between those reefs. It is a challenging and beautiful area to sail, but one charter fleet ceased operation there because of the many boats that went onto reefs. One tradition in the Pacific is the drinking of Kava, which is derived from the Kava root. Tradition has

it that it was originally made by virgins chewing the root and spitting the juice into a bowl. Today, I think they grind the root before mixing it with water. (Not enough virgins?) It is said to have both sedative and anesthetic properties. We were told of the Kava tradition and we had bought several bunches of Kava root at a market in Fiji for future use.

Upon arriving at Waya Island, we anchored in the bay just off the beach. The island people consider their bay "their property," just like a backyard. So they expect any visitor to get permission before they stay. To comply, we took the dinghy ashore, and were met by some local children. It was the only time I said, "Take me to your leader." They led us to the Chief's hut and we had to wait an appropriate length of time after we requested a meeting with the Chief. We then entered the official room and the Chief was sitting cross-legged on the floor. I did the same

Escapade at anchor in Bahia de Conception, Mexico

PHOTO BY ERICK REICKERT

SAIL THE WORLD

facing him, and a translator conveyed our conversation. As advised, I placed the Kava root on the floor between us. If he picked it up, he was accepting our gift. It is bad form to hand the root to him as that forces him to take it, which may not be his choice. We were accepted by the chief, and permitted to stay anchored in the bay. We walked around the village, and everyone was very friendly. It was a true South Pacific island and village, and we truly enjoyed our time anchored in their "backyard."

The Evil Spirits of Bali

On Bali, Indonesia, people are very careful of evil spirits, and in front of homes there is often a little model of the actual house that is mounted on a pole. These are known as spirit houses. The home is generally surrounded by a high stone wall with an opening in it for the entrance. But that opening is blocked by a wall that forces any visitor to walk around the wall. The reason for this is that "evil spirits" can only go in a straight line, so the wall blocks them from entering the home. When fisherman in Bali go fishing in their small outrigger canoes they do not want evil spirits on their boats because that could prevent them from catching fish. These outrigger canoes have sails and can sail quite fast, and the fishermen often operate far from the island. So you often see the sailing outriggers far at sea.

When we sailed from Bali, Indonesia, to Singapore we departed late in the day, and were heading north along the east coast of Bali. It was a moonlit night, and the sailing was pleasant. But then a group of the sailing outriggers started to come toward us. They had no lights, but we could clearly see them. They then started to aim directly at us, only swerving at the last moment to avoid a collision. Some came so close to our bow that our nav lights illuminated them—first in red and then in green. They made no noise except for the sound of the waves from their bows. We later discovered that they were getting rid of their evil spirits. Since any evil spirits on their boats would continue in a straight line, by swerving around *ESCAPADE* at the last moment, they were transferring their evil spirits to our boat. Hopefully they had a day of successful fishing. We did not, however, detect any evil spirits on *ESCAPADE*.

Nighttime Sailing

Sailing at night is very different from sailing during daylight. It can be pleasing and soothing or it can be terrifying. Usually, it is a magical time when sailing in the ocean, far from land and other boats. If there is moonlight, visibility can be nearly as good as daylight. Your sense of sound is increased, and hearing the splashing as the boat bounds ahead is delightful. It is a wonderful and calming experience, away from the rest of civilization. The world is nearly perfect.

But if it is dark and the seas are heavier, it is somewhat disconcerting to be plunging ahead into a pitch-black void of nothingness. It might be frightening, but soon your fear disappears as this continues for hours on end, and you remain perfectly safe. One special delight is bioluminescence on a dark night. Sometimes in certain locations, the water contains microbes that generate light when shaken, similar to a firefly glow. We saw this effect several times. When this happens, the bow wave and the quarter wave sparkle with light, almost like when a jeweler sprinkles diamonds onto a black cloth. You can even see the cone of water left behind a swimming fish. It is truly magical. When closer to land and other ships, nighttime sailing can present other challenges and different hazards.

Friends and Fellow Sailors

One of the pleasures of sailing is that you can make so many friendships along the way. You meet many "locals," and these people add to your understanding of the countries you are visiting. But we have also become lifelong friends with other sailors. We did not sail in company with any other boat, although some cruisers do that as well. Often boats with kids aboard maintained contact, as the kids were often lonely.

Our route around the world was a fairly common one, so we would meet other cruisers at various ports and then see them again—later—at another port. It was always exciting to see a boat that you knew in a harbor or while sailing. In some ports—especially along the coast of Mexico—some cruisers run a VHF chat every morning. This is very informative, and gives the locations of restaurants, boat services, laundromats, etc. You can announce your arrival and tell when you are leaving. It gets you into the cruising community quickly. Sailors who cruise oceans are special people who can genuinely share and understand the things that you are experiencing.

Sailing Challenges

The actual act of sailing is probably the easiest thing, or should be, about cruising. It is a natural act, and should be so ingrained that it is essentially second nature. Beside the planning, legal, maintenance, provisioning, etc. issues there are the true sailing challenges. These can include sailing, or motoring, under a wide variety of conditions. I have covered weather in Chapters 19 and 20. Others challenges include fog, glacier waters, Gulf Stream, overfalls, tides, traffic, etc.

I learned to sail in the Great Lakes of the US where there are no tides. Luckily, the Mediterranean also has virtually no tides, but in the rest of the world there are tides. In general, these will only have a slight impact on your plans. But when tides reach 40 feet you know you really have to pay attention. In fact, for every sailing plan, I noted the state of tide at both the departure port and the destination port. On the 40-foot side, the marina at St Helier on Jersey, in the Channel Islands off France, is a perfect example. You can only go into the marina at high tide. There is a floating pontoon on the outside where you can wait. When entering, there is a tide gauge that shows the amount of water over the sill. When it is deep enough for your boat, you can enter. There are floating pontoons inside the marina because when the tide drops, the water level drops to the height of the sill, maybe an eight to ten foot drop. But then the water level continues to drop so that at low tide the water level in the harbor will be 30 feet below the sill. It seems like the whole marina is floating above the ocean.

When going up or down a coast, tides can have a flow that can help or hurt your SOG. These are generally not that critical, but can affect your elapsed time between ports. Tides can impact the conditions of entry into ports, like along the east coast of the US and Australia. If there is an ebb tide with onshore wind and seas, then the entrance can become impassable. The effect of wind over tide increases the height of the waves, and if the entrance is shallow it could mean that your boat will hit bottom. This is a problem for both arrivals and departures.

In Australia, the Coast Guard and the associated volunteer organizations provided a lot of help when we were going up the east coast. They encouraged sailors to notify the departure port of both their destination and expected arrival time, which was forwarded to the destination port. In addition, they provided detailed information about the condition of the entrances—such as wave height and depth of the channel, at the present time. This was most helpful.

Contrast this to our experience with the US Coast Guard. We were sailing south from Charleston, SC heading for St Augustine, Florida. The winds were from the NE, thus rolling into all entrances. I had been to St. Augustine several years before but I knew the channel is often moved based on the shifting sands. Also, the official NOAA chart said: "St. Augustine Inlet- The entrance channel is subject to frequent changes in depth and direction because of shifting shoals. Buoys are not charted because of frequent changes in position. Mariners are advised to seek local knowledge." I wanted to ascertain the condition of the entrance as well as the depth in the entrance, and I wanted to do it before we passed the St. Johns River entrance. This was important because if we could not enter St. Augustine, then St. Johns River was the best alternative, and I did not want to beat back north.

Calling the US Coast Guard was an act of frustration. They refused to provide any information on the depth or condition of the inlet, and they referred me to the chart. I presumed that this was because of liability concerns. They said I should call local services like Tow Boat US, and ask them. So I decided that I would have go to the entrance myself, and view the conditions visually. At least I could see the width of the channel, and determine if I could turn around should the depths become too shallow. Ironically, the Coast Guard would have to come and rescue us if we got into trouble in the inlet.

Before we arrived off the inlet I was able to talk to a towing service. He said the seas in the inlet were large at the moment, but when we would arrive it would be a flood tide, and the waves should be manageable. He also said that the depth was sufficient for a 7 foot draft if we stayed to the center of the inlet. He was very helpful and reassuring. No thanks to the Coast Guard, we entered later with no problems. In fact, in other regards as well, the US Coast Guard is not as good as the Canadian and English equivalents.

Traffic can also be a challenge. By traffic I mean many other boats and ships. The high traffic areas that we sailed included New York Harbor, English Channel, Strait of Gibraltar, around Singapore, parts of San Francisco Bay, Sydney Harbour, Panama Canal, and the Suez Canal. We added AIS to *ESCAPADE* late in the voyage, and it immensely improved confidence in high traffic areas. I would say that AIS is now a necessity. Leaving the Mediterranean by the Strait of Gibraltar we were on the north side of the shipping channels. That meant we had to cut across the channels between huge ships that were going 20 or so knots, and it was nighttime. I recall being concerned regarding when to make the turn into the shipping lanes. Although we crossed at a right angle, it is still exciting to be turning into the path of the next ship.

Fog is another challenge. We ran into fog several times, most notably in Maine, entering New York Harbor and the Chesapeake Bay. When you first encounter fog it is very threatening. And you never really get used to it. The best solution we had was a very accurate electronic chart. With that, at least you knew where you were. You will not, however, know of things like anchored boats, buoys, lobster trap floats, moving boats, etc. We had a loudhailer that could be set with the appropriate sound signal (underway, stopped, anchored etc.) and it also acted as a listening device between our signals. Sounds are very deceptive in fog, and since they often carry a long distance, it can often be hard to pinpoint the direction of specific sounds. Radar can be useful, but it takes years of practice to really understand a radar display. The settings are critical to the size of objects that are displayed. As radar is being displayed relative to your own boat, it is always moving. Thus, fixed objects—like land—move when you are underway. And, if a boat is also moving in the same direction and at the same speed that you are travelling, it will appear to be fixed.

In most situations, the fog was not expected. In some cases, you can experience a fog bank rolling over you so you know in advance that you will be entering fog. In other cases, it just sort of descends—and the visibility gets progressively worse and worse. We have also experienced a "marine layer," in which the fog is only on the surface of the water. Once we could see that the top of the mast was in sunlight, while at sea level it was dense fog. Only after we departed into fog—and as we expected—it turned out to be true that the fog was very local.

Off the east coast of the US, the Gulf Stream is a challenge. With wind from the north, the waves can become quite pointed and even larger than outside the Gulf Stream, which means it can be uncomfortable. We crossed the Gulf Stream many times, and it was never a problem for *ESCAPADE*. If it becomes uncomfortable, then simply get out of it as fast as possible. We always used the autopilot on "track," which automatically calculates a heading to maintain your desired course. In some cases, the heading was 30 to 45° off the desired course. Generally, the Gulf Stream is far enough off the coast to not present any issues when sailing north or south. It is closest at Cape Hatteras. As I never wanted to get too close to Cape Hatteras because of the shoals, we often clipped the edge of the Gulf Stream when rounding the Cape. Of course, if you are going north and there is a southerly wind, then riding the Gulf Stream north will make for a very fast passage. But don't let the Gulf Stream stop you from visiting the Bahamas.

Overfalls are a seldom-encountered phenomena that occurs as a result of the shape of the sea bottom, and it is exacerbated by tidal flows. We had encountered these symbols on charts in various places in the world, but they never affected us. We departed Wellington, New Zealand on the North Island to cross the Cook Strait for the South Island. As one would expect, there is a large flow of water between the islands. The chart indicated overfalls in one specific area, but (based on our prior experience) I ignored them, and plotted our course over them. We left after a gale had passed through, so the seas were moderate at around five feet. Suddenly, the seas rose to 10 feet, or more, and we were rocking sideways dramatically. We were on a reach, with the boom at about 45°, and for the first time ever the boom hit the water. That meant we were heeled over quite far. After enduring this "washing machine action" for some time, I looked at the horizon and noticed the water was much calmer only a quarter of a mile away on our beam. So a simple course change brought us to smoother water. That taught me the significance of overfalls!

At various places we actually had to run rapids in *ESCAPADE*. This was exciting and nerve racking, as you do not have total control over the boat. In British Columbia, Canada, we were heading north on the inside winding up various passages. Some of these had very high current flows due to the tides. The flows could exceed five knots, which meant we could not motor into them, and going with them meant you would be swept down

current and forced side to side. Although you would be going fast over the ground, the boat speed through the water was low, so it would be hard to maintain steerage. So the best time was to go through these at slack water, which requires careful planning to arrive at the critical point at the proper time. We successfully negotiated these rapids, but it did give us an adrenaline rush.

A strange occurrence happened in the Andaman Sea, when we were traveling between Phuket, Thailand, and Galle, Sri Lanka, and it was before we reached the Indian Ocean. The sea was quite calm with minor waves, and it was nighttime. In deep water we heard a rushing noise, like water tumbling down a rock path. The noise became louder and louder, before it started to diminish. So at one point in the middle of the sea the water was rushing around, but we did not go towards the noise to investigate. Later, I read that other people have experienced the same thing. As it is a volcanic region, I wonder if—perhaps—the rushing sound was created by gases that were coming to the surface

In French Polynesia, and the Tuamotus Islands, the islands are atolls—some of which have a complete ring of coral with a lagoon inside. One especially big one is Rangiroa. On the north side there are two passes into the lagoon that are narrow, and the tides create fast currents so it is treacherous to enter or depart. In fact, in one there was an abandoned sailboat that had gone on the rocks in the pass. We had tried to time our arrival to be at slack tide. But we soon discovered that predictions as to the state of the current were either very difficult or impossible—even for the locals, because it also related to the atmospheric pressures in the vicinity as well as the state of tide. So we had to fight our way into the lagoon slowly. Once inside, it was delightful because the water was calm, and it was quite shallow. In fact, you could anchor nearly anywhere you liked. Sailing inside the lagoon was nice, as long as you kept watch for "boomies," which were coral heads rising vertically from the floor of the lagoon to (almost) the water surface. There was a cultured pearl operation that was fascinating to visit.

Sailing with icebergs is interesting, and a bit of a challenge. We encountered many icebergs and smaller pieces of ice (called bergy bits), in British Columbia and Alaska. The icebergs often would be deep blue in color as a result of the ice being formed under pressure. It is advised not to sail too close to icebergs because they may suddenly turn over if they become top heavy due to the underwater part melting. In some areas, the water was so covered with pieces of ice that we actually had to push them aside as we motored forward. We even had one crewmember climb up the forestay so he could see forward enough to see clear water paths. He would point in the direction we should go. The water is very cold, near freezing. So it is extremely important that no one fall into the water. Death can occur from hypothermia within 15 to 30 minutes in near-freezing water. Even with water at 50° F (10° C), death can occur in one hour. But other reactions to cold shock can occur even more rapidly (some within two minutes) that can cause a person to become incapacitated or die. So we were very careful onboard and in the dinghy. After two months in northern waters we had no problems, and we completely enjoyed the experience.

Finding Marinas

We used all means to locate marinas—for one night, or to leave the boat for a month or more. The longer we wanted to leave *ESCAPADE*, the further in advance we attempted to make a reservation. We had to know there would be a place for *ESCAPADE* if we booked air flights out of the local airport. Most of these marinas were identified by using cruising guides. The guides have the basic information, but it often took a phone call to obtain details and make the booking. These days, many marinas have websites, so it is easier to get a feeling of what a marina will be like.

When cruising along a coast, we would try to book marinas a few days ahead by phone. In foreign countries language can play a role. When we were cruising south along the east coast of Italy, it was necessary to be in a marina every night because there are really no anchorages. At first, we tried calling marinas on the VHF to ask if they had space. The result was always a "no." So we changed tactics, simply entered the marina, and tied up at the most convenient spot—sometimes even at the fuel dock. Then I would go into the office, and ask for dockage. In general, they were very accommodating, and always found us somewhere to tie up. In several cases, they even moved boats around so we would fit. I concluded that if they did not speak good English, they did not want to expose this over the air on the VHF. So they either did not understand me, or simply found it easier to say "no."

In southern France, nearly all the marinas on the Mediterranean are very full and cannot accommodate transient boats. One time I even rented a car and drove south from Nice—checking out all the marinas along the way. It was not until I reached Port Grimaud near Saint Tropez that I found one that would accommodate *ESCAPADE* for a month. But that worked out well. The marinas were, in fact, full of boats. Another time we were looking for only a few nights and I wanted to get into Antibes because it is a large yachting center, and the walled town is very interesting. On the VHF radio they were turning all boats away. So again, I went in, and tied up to plead my case. After much discussion, I was given a berth for two nights between two huge boats.

On the French island of Porquerolles, the place I negotiated to tie up was the ferry dock. This meant we could only tie up after the last ferry left, and I had to promise to leave before the first ferry arrived in the morning. But the times were reasonable—like 6:00 pm and 8:00 am—and the town was small, so we saw it all even within the time constraints.

Cruising the Sea of Cortez

As we sailed north from La Paz, we entered a desert wilderness where the multi-colored rock walls continuously changed in appearance between sunrise and sunset. Very few boats were around, and there were few signs of habitation on shore. The sea life was extraordinarily abundant, and at night if you shined a light into the water it turned white with the froth of jumping fish. We found the Sea of Cortez fascinating, unique, and well worth a visit.

We had arrived in this magical area as part of our trip from Alaska to Maine via the Panama Canal. The timing was dictated by delaying our departure from San Diego to after the hurricane season, which is generally accepted to end around November 1st. As there is a local rally that departs around then, we set off two days earlier to avoid the mayhem. The rally is called the Baja Ha Ha, and they make two stops before Cabo San Lucas. So we sailed nonstop, and arrived about a week before they did.

The distance is 750 NM, and it took five days of easy sailing, never more than 50 NM off shore. Cabo San Lucas has very good marina facilities, and is a good port to clear into Mexico. It is, however, a brash tourist town with all the associated hotels, trinket stores, and other means to extract money from the "gringos" with a continuous fiesta-like atmosphere.

The easiest place to provision for the Sea of Cortez is at La Paz. It is a more typical Mexican town, and it's not overwhelmed by tourism. The marinas are good, and there are things to do in town. For example, we attended a symphony concert by a youth orchestra. And since there is an airport nearby, it is also a good place for crew changes.

To get from Cabo San Lucas to La Paz you have to go around the southern tip of Baja California. It is around 170 NM, so we broke that up into day sails and stopped at Cabo Los Frailes, Ensenada de los Muertos (Bay of the Dead), and at Isla Partida. The first two are really wide-open bays with protection from the north and west, but—otherwise—they are open to the ocean. There is nothing on shore at these anchorages, but the bottom is sand and the anchor dug nicely for a good night's sleep.

Mexico and the other Central American countries are some of the few places I did not trust the water. Since I did not want to contaminate our water tanks with bad water, I adopted the strategy of making water at sea so we could enter ports and anchorages with a full tank. That way knew we always had good, pure water to drink and cook.

*Kuna Indian Woman
in her house in
San Blas Islands,
Panama*

PHOTO BY ERICK REICKERT

sights that will remain in your mind forever, and helps you recall how wonderful it is to be cruising.

Puerto el Gato is another 37 NM north on the mainland. There is no port, only a sand beach that is set back from some protecting reefs. Puerto Escondido is another 39 NM north. The unique nature of this spot is that the inner harbor is basically completely enclosed, and is considered to be a good bad weather anchorage. There have been multiple attempts at building a marina, and some of the infrastructure has been completed (including a fuel dock). But when we were there, it was not a true marina. If you can get a ride, the town of Loreto is a half hour north. Alternatively, you can anchor off and dinghy into a breakwater protected tiny harbor to get provisions. I chose to go by road in the back of a pickup that I heard about on the VHF cruisers net that morning.

We also made stops at San Juanico and Punta Pulpito before reaching Conception Bay, which is a 21 NM long but narrow bay. This is a cruisers haven and it has many anchorages. The first one we tried was Playa Santispac, which had vacation homes called "palapas" spread along the very wide beach. There is a small town reachable by taxi, and there are a few businesses such as Ana's, a beach bar. We also anchored in Playa Coyote in Coyote Bay, which is another example of totally laid-back life in this world.

I found that both paper and electronic charts were not accurate in a number of the bays and anchorages because many have not been updated for more than 100 years. In several areas there are rocks around, so care has to be taken in eyeball navigation when close to shore. The cruising guides are most helpful in this regard.

There were very few other cruising boats around, and at most of the anchorages we were either the only boat or only one of a few. I am not sure of the reason for such few boats except we were there in November, which is early in the season. We enjoyed the solitude and peaceful ambiance, however, which made the cruising experience that much more special.

We anchored in The Hook bay of Isla San Francisco, which is a large, but nicely sheltered area 44 NM from La Paz. We climbed to the top of the south peak, and the view was dramatic in all directions. It is one of those

Summary

Cruising is very rewarding and enriching. It is also filled with many challenges and adventures, which is part of what makes it so special.

CHAPTER 32

Conclusion

Summary and Required Advanced-Planning Recommendations

*To confront the majesty of the sea is to contemplate
the beauty, mystery and power of the universe.*

LADY SUSAN WILLIS REICKERT

By now, you should believe that you could circumnavigate the world in your own boat. It is totally within your reach, yet few people have actually achieved the feat. The adventure and accomplishments will become a major element of your life, no matter what else you have achieved.

Sail the World has explained all the steps necessary to go world cruising, and to circumnavigate. It is fun, exciting, a learning experience, and sheer joy. There are risks, but these can be managed or mitigated if properly considered.

Good advance planning is required for all aspects of the adventure—from laying out your objectives, to selecting the right boat and equipment, and acquiring the necessary knowledge and skills. Then, planning and preparation are required for each part of the execution. Take each step deliberately, and by doing it one small bite at a time it will become manageable.

The sailing accomplishments that I achieved are presented as Exhibit 19. The major ports that we visited are listed on Exhibit 17. These, and more, can be yours.

Enjoy the adventure and the world.

May you have favorable winds and following seas.

Sailing into Sunrise

PHOTO BY ERICK REICKERT

EXHIBITS

EXHIBIT 1   Sailboat Requirements 212

EXHIBIT 2   Crew Agreement Yacht *ESCAPADE* 217

EXHIBIT 3   *ESCAPADE* Periodic Maintenance By System 219

EXHIBIT 4   *ESCAPADE* Maintenance Schedule By Time 224

EXHIBIT 5   *ESCAPADE* Passage Plan Form 226

EXHIBIT 6   *ESCAPADE* Passage Log Form 227

EXHIBIT 7   *ESCAPADE* Pacific Crossing Plan Example 228

EXHIBIT 8   *ESCAPADE* Pacific Crossing Log Example 229

EXHIBIT 9   Cruising Risk Chart 230

EXHIBIT 10   *ESCAPADE* Route Around the World 231

EXHIBIT 11   *ESCAPADE* Crew Suggestions Form .232

EXHIBIT 12   *ESCAPADE* Repair History 233

EXHIBIT 13   Sail Boat Data - 1995 247

EXHIBIT 14   Country Data 2006/7 248

EXHIBIT 15   *ESCAPADE* Spares List 249

EXHIBIT 16   *ESCAPADE* Safety & Navigation Equipment 252

EXHIBIT 17   *ESCAPADE* Major Ports 255

EXHIBIT 18   *ESCAPADE* Maintenance Log 260

EXHIBIT 19   Sailing Accomplishments 264

EXHIBIT 20   *ESCAPADE* Departure List 268

EXHIBIT 21   *ESCAPADE* First Mate Duties & Requirements 269

EXHIBIT 22   *ESCAPADE* First Mate Salary Conditions 270

EXHIBIT 23   *ESCAPADE* Lay-Up & Commission Schedule Example 271

Exhibit 1 SAILBOAT REQUIREMENTS

By Erick Reickert

GENERAL / HULL

General / Hull	Best Boat so Far	Boat X
Center cockpit	Yes	
Recognized naval architect	Yes	
Large enough for the ocean (48' to 60'), but still capable of sailing by two people	Yes- LOA 48' 6" LWL 37'6"	
Modern, distinctive exterior appearance	Yes	
Beam sufficient for large interior & increased stability	Yes- 14' 0"	
Medium displacement	Yes- 37,550 lbs	
Capable of complete sailing from the cockpit	Yes	
Equipped for documentation in the USA, and suitable for international operations	Yes	
Fiberglass or aluminum hull properly strengthened:	Yes	
-No coring below the water line	Yes	
-No screws or fasteners through a cored area	Yes	
-Bulkheads and stringers fiberglassed to hull	Yes	
-Fiberglass, Kevlar or carbon mats, hand laid	Yes- Kevlar opt	
-Isophthalic resin in gel coat	Yes	
-Internal hull flange with bolted hull-to-deck joint	Yes	
-Insulation for aluminum boat (Spray-on or applied)		
-Hull should be "stiff" with little flexing in heavy seas	Yes	
-ABS certification	Lloyds std.	
-10 year hull warranty	No- 3 year	
Bow area separated from interior by watertight bulkhead	Yes	
Foreward compartment with watertight door	Yes-opt	
Bulb or winged keel, 6' or less draft:	Yes- 6'0" Bulb	
-Long enough for directional stability in heavy seas	Yes	
-Short enough for quick response & tight maneuvering	Yes	
-Lead, external with adequate bolting	Yes- 13,000 lbs	
Rudder with partial or full skeg	Yes	
Rudder reinforced with stainless steel rudder post	Yes	
Positive Stability range to 125°	Yes - 127°	
Antifouling paint	Yes	
Lightning conductor on hull or keel connected to mast	Yes	

Type of Operation

Type of Operation	Best Boat so Far	Boat X
Coastal, ocean sailing, plus Caribbean & Mediterranean	Yes	
Moderate to hot weather	Yes	
Safety and comfort are prime considerations	Yes	
Should be sufficiently fast with good upwind performance	Yes	
Must be suitable for extended living periods on board, both at and away from dock (light and open below)	Yes- Very open	

Rigging

- Cutter rig- permanent, with running backstays
- Maximum mast height (above water) of 64'6"
- Mast, boom and spreaders of aluminum (carbon fibre OK)
- Mast stepped on keel
- Roller furling on both foresails
- In mast furling on main, electric
- Sails of Dacron with UV protection:
    - -Main cut for roller furling
    - -Genoa at least 130% (Must pass inner forestay easily)
    - -Storm staysail
    - -Cruising chute
- Spinnaker rigging (no pole)
- Dacron color coded sheets, halyards and lines
- Self-tailing winches- main & jib sheets located near helm
    - -Power winches for sheets and jib furling (3)
- Rigid boom vang
- Stainless steel cable rigging
  -Continous rigging desired
    - -Insulated backstay for SSB radio
- Backstay adjuster, manual or self-contained hydraulic
- Lightning protection at mast head

Best Boat so Far	Boat X
Yes-opt	
Yes- 63'7"	
Yes	
Yes	
Yes	
Yes	
Yes	
Yes	
Yes-132%	
Yes-opt	
Yes-opt	
Yes-opt	
Yes	
Yes	
Yes-opt Harken	
Yes	
Yes	
Yes	
Yes-opt	
Yes-opt	
Yes-opt	

Topside Gear

- Power anchor windlass with reversing feature, electric
    - -Remote control at helm
- Double anchor roller platform (For 2 anchors at once)
- Anchor- Plow type- CQR
    - -At least 250' of anchor chain for primary anchor
- Stern entry (with H & C shower, swim ladder, etc.)
- Dinghy davits over stern
- Strong stanchions, double lifelines (side & rear openings)
- Strong pullpit, seats on stern pushpit
- Side boarding ladders (2) mounted in side openings
- Safety jack line tiedowns
- Safety harness attachments in cockpit (4)
- Aluminum toe rail
- Table for eating in cockpit
- Teak decking in cockpit
- Backrest at helm and in cockpit
- Bimini and dodger, plus side curtains to enclose cockpit
- Windows of high strength glass or Lexan
- Adequate ventilation for below deck
    - -Aluminum hatches
    - -Dorades- 4
- International running lights, + deck & anchor light
- Pedestal & wheel, high quality
    - -Cockpit light on pedestal
- Place for emergency life raft on deck (thru bolted)
- Adequate deck storage (watertight to rest of hull)

Best Boat so Far	Boat X
Yes	
Yes	
Yes-opt	
Yes- 60#	
Yes-opt 200' std.	
Yes-opt H&C	
Yes-opt	
Yes	
Yes- opt seats	
Yes-opt	
Yes	
Yes	
Yes-opt	
Yes- Full deck	
Yes	
Yes-opt	
Yes- Glass	
Yes	
Yes- Lewmar	
No- only 2	
Yes	
Yes- Whitlock 36" D	
Yes-opt	
Yes	
Yes	

Topside Gear (continued)

- Outside vented propane storage
- Rub rail with stainless steel striker
- Engine instruments- RPM, hours, temp., oil press.
- Single lever engine control, plus key switch
- Auto-pilot with cockpit control and wander lead
- Full instruments close to helm (also see electronics)
    - Wind, speed/log, depth, magnetic & steering compasses
    - Navdata, radar & chart plotter repeater
- Companionway washboards that can be secured in place
- Salt water wash down at bow

Best Boat so Far	Boat X
Yes	
No- opt	
Yes	
Yes	
Yes- Autohelm ST7000	
Yes	
Yes- Autohelm ST50Plus	
Yes-opt	
Yes	
Yes-opt	

Accomodations

- Good looking light wood interior
- High quality joinery
- Companionway capable of decending facing forward
- Main salon that is full width and spacious
    - Folding or fold-away dining table
    - Two individual lounge chairs in addition to bench seating
    - Ultra-suede seating surfaces
    - Large navigation station table and chair
    - Ice maker
    - Entertainment center with TV, VCR, CD player & AM/FM
    - TV capable of international operation (all formats)
    - CD Player with 10 CD changer
- Galley aft of companionway with:
    - Stove (3 or 4 burner) & oven, propane
    - Ability to use Butane
    - Refrigerator, front opening- 8 cu. feet min.
    - Freezer- 4 cu. feet min.
    - Microwave/convection combination oven
    - Double sink, stainless steel
    - Corian counter tops, with plenty of surface area
    - Plenty of storage for food, dishes, glasses, pans, etc.
    - Foot pump for fresh water (Flush- Whale)
    - Trash bin built-in
    - Exhaust ventilation over stove and oven
    - Water filtration system
- Owners cabin with:
    - Queen size bed and seating
    - Make-up table and mirror
    - Plenty of storage for clothes, including full height closet
    - Attached bath with separate shower area
    - Electric head
    - Safe inside a closet
- Guest cabin with:
    - Queen size bed
    - Attached bath with electric head
    - Good size

Best Boat so Far	Boat X
Yes-opt Oak	
Yes	
Yes-opt	
Yes	
Yes	
Yes	
Yes- Alcantara	
Yes	
Yes- opt	
Yes- opt	
Yes-opt	
Yes-opt	
Yes	
Yes-Force 10	
Yes	
Yes- Grunert	
Yes	
Yes- opt	
Yes	
Yes- opt	
Yes	
Yes-opt	
Yes	
Yes-opt	
Yes-opt	
Yes	
Seat & mirror	
Yes	
Yes	
Yes-opt	
Yes-opt	
Yes "V"	
Yes-opt	
Yes	

Accomodations (continued)

- Crew cabin with two bunks
- Positive catches on all cabinets and drawers
- Fans in all areas
- Lee cloths for all sleeping positions
- Washer and dryer
- Speakers in saloon, owners cabin and cockpit
- Adequate lighting throughout- direct Halogen
    - -Indirect in saloon and owners cabin
    - -Red lighting for night
- Stainless steel opening ports
- Shades and screens on windows, ports & hatches
- Easy and good access to engine compartment
- Inside panels attached with Velcro for easy access
- Locks on major cupboards and drawers

Best Boat so Far	Boat X
Yes	
Yes	
Yes-opt	
Yes	
Yes-opt	
Yes-opt	
Yes-Halogen	
Yes-opt	
No- Al Lewmar/Gebo	
Yes-opt	
Yes	
Yes	
Yes-opt	

Mechanical / Electrical

- Powerful diesel engine, capable of 10 knots (HP)
    - -Exhaust loop, waterlift, and muffler
    - -Cooling water anti-siphon valve & see-thru strainer
    - -Engine drip pan
- Diesel generator set with cover- minimum of 5kw (KW)
- Central air conditioning with reverse heating
    - -Digital controls in main saloon and owners cabin
- Engine compartment lights and blower
- Sound insulated engine compartment
- Dual Racor see-thru fuel filters with changeover valve
- Easy access to filters and inspection items
- Oil change pump out system
- Automatic fire extinguisher in engine compartment
- Two sets of Gel Cell batteries- interior & engine (AH)
    - -All batteries fully secured in cases
    - -One battery located high, and connected to radio
- Inverter- 2000W continous (W)
- Charger- "Smart"
- Large alternator on engine, or two (Amps)
- Electrical outlets in all cabins, saloon, and galley (GFI)
- Large water tank (gals.)
- Large fuel tank (gals.) Desire 1000 mile range
    - -Gauges for fuel & water tanks
- Holding tank and Y valves Desire 50 gals. total
    - -Gauges for holding tanks
    - -Pump out system, electric
- Shore connections for:
    - -120v, 60 Hertz and 240v, 50 or 60 Hertz
    - -Water with pressure regulator and valve
    - -TV and telephone
- Pressure hot and cold water system, with back-up pump
- Electric water maker- DC power (gals. per day)
- Hot water from both engine and AC electricity (gals.)
- Bilge pumps, dual electric and manual

Best Boat so Far	Boat X
88- Yanmar-opt	
Yes	
Yes	
Yes	
Yes	
Yes-opt 6kw Onan	
Yes-opt Marineair	
Digital-opt	
Yes	
Yes	
Yes-opt	
Yes	
Yes	
Yes-opt Halon	
No- Varta 460 AH	
Yes	
Yes-opt	
Yes-opt Mastervolt	
Yes-opt Mastervolt	
Yes- 40A@24V	
Yes-opt	
OK-GRP 145 Gals	
OK- GRP 200 gals	
Yes-opt Tank Tender	
Yes- 50 gals-opt	
Yes-opt	
Gravity	
Yes-opt	
Yes-opt	
Yes-opt	
Yes- but no backup	
Yes-opt Seafresh-AC	
Yes- 10 gal	
Yes- Dual	

Mechanical / Electrical (continued)

- Emergency bilge pump engine operated
- Bow thruster
- Propshaft thrust bearing (like Aquadrive)
- Maxprop 3 blade propeller with spurs on shaft
- Refrigeration system- hold-over plates in ref. & Freezer
    - -Refrigeration compressor AC driven
    - -Temperature guages on refrigerator and freezer

Best Boat so Far	Boat X
Yes-opt	
Yes-opt TX 8hp	
Yes- Aquadrive	
Yes-opt	
Yes -opt	
Yes-opt	
Yes-opt	
Yes	

Communications/Electronics

- VHF radio at helm and at nav. station (2)
- SSB long range radio
- Radar
- Weather Fax
- GPS, including helm readout
- Sattelite Inmarsat C
- Chart plotter and repeater
- Integrated instrument system such as Autohelm ST-50
- Wiring for regular telephone at Nav. station (when at dock)
- Loud Hailer with Speaker on mast
- Navtex (can be combined with Fax)

Yes-opt	
Yes-opt	
Yes-opt	
Yes-opt	
Yes-opt	
Yes-opt	
Yes-opt	
Yes	
Yes-opt	
Yes-opt	
Yes-opt	

Loose items

- Deck items - - - -
    - -Docking lines, 50' (6) 2 x 66'
    - -Fenders, solid foam (2)
    - -Fenders, air filled (4)
    - -Flag staff
    - -Emergency tiller (should attach at deck level)
    - -Cockpit cushions
    - -Winch handles
    - -Boat hook
- Crockery, glasses, & cutlery for 8

2 x 66'	
No	
Yes	
Yes	
Yes	
Yes-opt	
Yes-4	
Yes	
Yes	

Pricing

- Base Price
- Total price with above options

Purchase Separately

- Second anchor (Danforth) and 300' rope rode
- Shock leader and grab hook
- Stern anchor and 200' of rode
- Barbeque (gas) for aft deck
- Carpet for owners cabin
- Rug and paintings for Saloon
- Barometer and clock for Saloon
- Tools and spare parts
- Dinghy, inflatable- 11.5'
    - -Outboard- 10 hp min.
- Emergency distress radio- EPIRB 406
- Fender Board
- Emergency Life raft and equipment
- Cellular telephone at Nav Station plus antanna

No	
No	
No	
No	
No	
No	
No	
No	
No	
No	
No	
No	
No	
No	

Exhibit 2 CREW AGREEMENT *YACHT ESCAPADE*

© 2014 Erick Reickert April 24, 2014

Voyage from: _____ Toward: _____ Date: _____

INTENTIONS: This agreement is intended to clarify relations and understandings so that problems or issues will be avoided. It is designed to protect you and all parties concerned, so please read it carefully. It is also wise to inform someone at home of your plans.

Crewing on *ESCAPADE* works best when all are considered teammates – you will be consulted, when appropriate, as part of decision making, but you must also be willing to accept that the Captain has final authority. In completing this agreement you TAKE FULL RESPONSIBILITY FOR YOUR DECISION TO JOIN, and agree that you are willing to accept all risks associated with being onboard and you attest that there have been no inducements, promises, or considerations that are not described in this agreement.

The Captain hereby declares his belief that the yacht *ESCAPADE* is properly equipped and prepared for the planned voyage, and that he is competent to manage it, alone or with crew. He invites the crew to test this statement in any way they wish. When you sign this you agree that you have fully investigated and found that *ESCAPADE* is seaworthy and properly equipped and that the Captain is capable, fit, and competent.

CAPTAIN DETAILS: xxxx, born xxxx Passport #xxxx and expires on xxxx. Home address: xxxxx His wife is xxxx. Next of kin is xxxx. You understand and agree that xxxx is the Captain and that you must obey all lawful orders, especially in times of emergency or distress.

YACHTS DETAILS: The yacht *ESCAPADE* is owned by xxxx Ltd., a U.S. corporation, with offices at xxxx. xxxx is President and sole shareholder. *ESCAPADE* is documented in the U.S.A. with #xxxx. She is an Oyster 55 raised deck saloon, cutter rigged sailing yacht.

CREW'S DETAILS: Name_____ Nationality_____

Birth date/place_____ Passport #_____

Issue Place_____Issue date_____ Expiration_____

Home Address:_____

Next of Kin's name address _____

Next of Kin's telephone number _____

Alternative Contact_____

MEDICAL DETAILS: *ESCAPADE* has a well-equipped medical kit and radio equipment with which emergency help may be obtained. However, YOU must take full responsibility for any current or past medical conditions that might recur, or any medical or health problems that may occur during or as a result of this trip. Make sure you have ample medication for a period at least twice as long as the expected passage. YOU MUST INFORM THE CAPTAIN OF ANY POTENTIALLY SERIOUS CONDITIONS that could affect safety at sea. Give details below of any known drug allergies, conditions that might recur, and current medication:_____

Medical Insurance may help save your life. List details of your medical insurance, if any, and all contact details:_____

Seasickness: Apart from spoiling your trip and making it harder for others aboard, seasickness can be dangerous, even fatal. Unless you know from extensive experience that you will not be affected, you must have, and be willing to use, reputable seasickness treatment obtained prior to joining the boat. This is your responsibility. Discuss and give details:_____

Exhibit 2 CREW AGREEMENT *YACHT ESCAPADE*

You will be responsible for obtaining any necessary immunizations or malaria pills required for the areas that will be visited.

Environment & personal capabilities: You should be able to swim in salt water. If not, you must be willing to wear a life preserver at all times. *ESCAPADE* is a non-smoking yacht, and all crew and visitors are expected to abide by this rule. It is expected that everyone onboard will not drink alcohol while on passage and when in port only in moderation. If you have any special needs, or preferences, in your diet, declare these here:

_____

Visas and Repatriation: When you enter another country you may need to have a visa in advance, and be able to prove you can get yourself out of the country (other than by yacht) to another country to which you have full right of entry. The simplest way is to have an air ticket home, or to carry and retain sufficient cash to cover one. Credit cards are of no use in some countries. You are responsible for this. Discuss and give details: _____

_____

Responsibilities: Everyone aboard is expected to share in all work aboard the yacht. This includes standing watches, operation of the yacht under sail or power, in-port handling, cooking, domestic work, and maintenance work. Keeping a cruising boat in operation and in safe condition requires work, and this is an obligation shared by all those aboard. Good crew look for ways to help, and taking part will make you feel involved and provide a learning experience.

Costs: Food aboard will be provided. You may want to bring your own special dietary or refreshment requirements. You agree that any money you pay toward your own costs, and all costs that you incur on shore, and in getting to and from the boat, will be your responsibility and is not for any charter fee or passenger fee or for the benefit of the yacht or its owner or the Captain, but only for reimbursement of your own costs.

DECLARATIONS: I have completed the above details fully and honestly, and have volunteered any further information I am aware of that may affect the safety and enjoyment of the proposed voyage by all aboard. I do not have any illegal drugs or weapons in my possession, and will immediately inform the Captain if I become aware of any onboard, or anyone trying to bring such items aboard. I will declare, by written statement on this agreement, details of any legal conviction, in any country, for involvement with illegal drugs or weapons. I will not carry any packages for any third party on the boat without first requesting permission from the Captain. I accept that the Captain may change his plans, and will not hold him responsible for getting me to the original destination, should that not be reached by boat or at the estimated time. I am aware that there are risks that I face in this voyage, and take full responsibility for my decision to join the boat. I hereby agree that I will hold harmless the Captain or the owner of the yacht for any accident, injury or damage that may happen to me or my belongings while aboard.

I will make myself familiar with the location and operation of all safety equipment aboard the *ESCAPADE*. I will seek to learn all aspects of seamanship by reading manuals and books aboard, and by asking help from the Captain and others. The responsibility is fully mine to learn and to ask to be taught any skills I need for the safe operation of the boat and my personal safety. I will inform the Captain of any problems that I am aware of that may affect the safe operation of the boat. I will respond with appropriate actions in the event of emergencies or crew overboard situations, no matter what time of day. If there is anything happening onboard about which I am uncomfortable I will discuss it with those concerned as soon as possible in order to avoid irreversible issues that may spoil the atmosphere for all those aboard. If I transgress local laws or customs, I agree to fully reimburse any costs incurred; and to compensate the Captain for any delay my actions may cause. I take full responsibility for any requirements and costs relating to my entry and exit in countries to be visited by the yacht. I agree to share all work aboard, and to obey all orders given to me relating to the safe conduct of the yacht, at all times.

Skipper: _____ Crew: _____

Date and place: _____

Exhibit 3 *ESCAPADE* **PERIODIC MAINTENANCE BY SYSTEM**

ESCAPADE Periodic Maintenance by System	Frequency
Engine- Perkins M90 LD	
Oil and coolant levels- Check & top up	-daily
Record hours	-daily
Raw salt water strainer- Clean	-weekly or sooner if necessary
Racor fuel filter- Check for pressure, water & contaminants	-weekly
Belts- check & tighten as required	-2 weeks
Zinc, check	-2 weeks
Racor fuel filter- Replace	-4 months or 250 hours
Air filter- Clean	-4 months or 250 hours
Oil and oil filter- Change (9.2L)	-4 months or 250 hours
Engine fuel filter- Replace & bleed air	-4 months or 250 hours
Water impeller- Check	-yearly
Exhaust system- Check for leaks, tighten clips	-yearly
Engine mounts- Check	-yearly
Coolant- Confirm anti-freeze solution	-yearly
Generator- Onan 9MDKWB	
Coolant level- Check	-daily
Record hours	-daily
Oil level- Check	-weekly
Racor fuel filter- Check for water & contaminants	-weekly
Belts- Check & tighten as required	-2 weeks
Zinc, check	-monthly
Generator assembly- Clean inside housing	-6 months or 250 hours
Racor fuel filter- Replace	-6 months or 250 hours
Oil and oil filter- Change (4.7L)	-6 months or 250 hours
Brushes- Check by Service Technician	-6 months or 250 hours
Coolant- Confirm anti-freeze solution	-yearly
Water pump impeller- Check	-yearly
Exhaust system- Check for leaks, tighten clips	-yearly
Transmission- Hurth HBW 250	
Fluid level- Check	-6 months
ATF Fluid- Change (0.7L)	-yearly
Gear shift cables- Check & tighten nuts	-yearly

Propeller and Shaft

Prop shaft stuffing box- 1/2 turn of greaser -2 weeks
Max Prop 22" 3 blade- Check operation & grease -yearly at haul out
Cutlass bearing- Check for wear & wash -yearly at haul out
Rope cutter- Ambassador- Check -yearly at haul out
Shaft coupling- Check for tightness -yearly
Shaft alignment- Check for true (in water) -yearly

Fuel tank	
Check level	-daily
Check for sludge & clean pickup gauze filter	-2 years

ESCAPADE Periodic Maintenance by System | Frequency

Outboard- Honda 15HP Model BF

Fuel- Check level	-weekly
Oil- Check level	-monthly
Oil- Change	-yearly, or sooner if used a lot
Gear lube- Check level	-yearly
Grease fittings- Lube	-yearly
Gear lube- Change	-2 years

Standing rigging

Backstay- Check tension	-daily
Check for cracks, wear	-6 months
Tape on all fittings- Replace	-yearly
Professional check	-yearly

Lines-

Remove, wash & dry	-yearly

Halyards

Inspect for wear	-yearly

Blocks

Wash with fresh water	-weekly
Polish, replace plastic ties	-yearly

Jammers-

Spinlocks- Oil & confirm function	-6 months

Sails

Wash, dry, inspect & repair	-yearly or sooner if necessary

Bimini & Dodger-

Wash, inspect & repair	-yearly

Winches -Harken

Wash with fresh water	-weekly
Take apart & grease	-yearly

Windlass- Lewmar 2000

Wash with fresh water	-weekly
Take apart, grease & oil	-yearly

Topsides

Wash with cleaner & fresh water	-weekly or as required
Wax	-yearly

Deck

Rinse with fresh water	-weekly or as required

Stainless Steel and Brightwork

Clean & polish	-weekly or as required

Lifelines

Check & tighten	-6 months

Cockpit Cushions

Clean	-6 months

ESCAPADE Periodic Maintenance by System | Frequency

Fenders
Clean — -monthly

Fender Covers
Remove, wash, replace — -6 months

Horseshoe Buoy
Clean — -yearly or as required

Passarelle
Wash & polish — -monthly

Davits- Whittall ED
Check for attachment & operation — -6 months

Chain Locker
Flush with fresh water — -monthly or as required

Steering System
Rudder tube- 1/2 turn of greaser — -2 weeks
Cables- Check tightness — -monthly
Cables- grease — -yearly
Rudder bearings- Check for wear — -yearly at haul out

Dinghy- Avon 3.11 RIB
Check pressure and inflate if necessary — -monthly
Clean & check for damage — -6 months

Batteries- Engine, Generator, House (460 AH @ 24 V)
Check charge and consumption — -daily
Fully charge, if possible — -daily
Check electrolyte level — -weekly

Watermaker- Seafresh H206A
Run — -weekly
Water Pre-filters -Check, clean or replace — -monthly or as required
Drive belts- Check tension — -monthly
Pump sump- Check oil level — -6 months
Pickle, if not using — -as required

Bilge
Check level — -daily
Electric Pump- Confirm operation — -weekly
Flush with cleaner & fresh water — -monthly
Electric Pump- Test by filling bilge, check for debris — -monthly
Manual pumps (both)- Check operation — -monthly
Engine driven- Check operation — -monthly

Fresh Water Tank
Check level and consumption, fill if required — -daily
Use water from small tank — -monthly
In-line strainer filter- Check & clean — -6 months
Seagull filter- Change — -6 months or as required
Flush with fresh water & white vinegar solution — -yearly
Check inside — -yearly

ESCAPADE Periodic Maintenance by System   Frequency

Refrigeration
Run to 4° in refrigerator or -10° in freezer	-twice daily or as required
Raw salt-water strainer- Clean	-weekly or as required

A/C Systems- Marine Air
Confirm operation	-monthly

Sea Cocks
Operate all	-monthly

Bow Thruster- Sleipner 10HP
Check oil level (EP 90)	-6 months

Holding Tanks
Check level, empty if required	-weekly or as required
Empty & flush with fresh water	-6 months

Heads
Vacuflush- Flush with fresh water	-monthly
Manual, Par- Check pellet feeder	-monthly

Light Bulbs (including nav. lights)
Check & replace	-monthly or as required

Electronics & Instruments
Confirm operation	-daily
Record log mileage	-daily
Speedometer Sender- Remove & clean	-monthly

Handheld VHF and Spotlight
Charge	-weekly

Handheld GPS, Autohelm Compass, ITT Night scope
Check batteries	-monthly
Personal EPIRBs- Check	-6 months

Hatches & Ports
Open and let "breathe"	-weekly
Seals- Coat with Vaseline	-6 months

Interior
Wash surfaces with weak bleach solution to prevent mold	-6 months
Open lockers, lift mattresses, raise cushions & lift floorboards to permit air circulation	-yearly
Fire Extinguisher- Automatic- Firetrace- Check pressure	-monthly
Gas Detector System- Vetus- Confirm operation	-daily
Smoke Alarms- Check batteries	-6 months
Sea Anchor & Drogue- Check	-yearly
Anchor Chain- 7/16"- Paint chain marks	-yearly

Bottom
Power wash, Paint with anti-fouling	-yearly
Check for blisters	-yearly

ESCAPADE Periodic Maintenance by System   Frequency

Zincs

Main, propeller & bow thruster- Check & replace   -6 months at haul out
Life raft- Givens 6 person- Test by certified station   -yearly

Flares

Confirm dates   -yearly

Keel bolts

Tighten   -3 years

Bicycles

Check operation   -yearly Exhibit 4 Exhibit 4
Escapade Maintenance Schedule by Time
Daily

Exhibit 4 *ESCAPADE* MAINTENANCE SCHEDULE BY TIME

DAILY

- Engine- Perkins- Oil and coolant levels Check & top up, record hours
- Generator- Onan- Coolant level- Check, record hours
- Batteries- Check charge and consumption, Fully charge, if possible
- Fuel tank- Check level
- Water tanks- Check levels, consumption, fill if required
- Log- Record mileage
- Refrigeration- Run to 4° in refrigerator or -10° in freezer is reached
- Electronics & Instruments- Confirm operation
- Gas Detector system- Confirm operation
- Check backstay tension- set as required

WEEKLY

- Engine Raw salt-water strainer- Clean
- Refrigeration & A/C Raw salt water strainer- Clean
- Engine Racor fuel filter- Check for pressure, contaminants & water
- Generator Racor fuel filter- Check for contaminants & water
- Generator- Onan- Oil level- Check
- Batteries -Check electrolyte level
- Bilge- Check level, Confirm operation of electric pump
- Topsides- Wash with cleaner & fresh water
- Deck- Rinse with fresh water
- Stainless steel and brightwork- Clean & polish
- Blocks- Wash with fresh water
- Winches and Windlass- Wash with fresh water
- Handheld VHF- Charge
- Spotlight- Charge
- Water maker- Seafresh- Run, unless pickled
- Holding tanks- Check level, empty if necessary
- Hatches & Ports- Open and let "breathe"

TWO WEEKS

- Engine Belts- Check & tighten as required
- Generator Belts- Check & tighten as required
- Prop shaft stuffing box- 1/2 turn of greaser
- Rudder tube- 1/2 turn of greaser
- Outboard- Check fuel level

MONTHLY

- Outboard Oil- Check level
- Dinghy- Check air pressure, fill if necessary
- Passarelle- Wash & polish
- Fenders- Clean
- Chain locker- Flush with fresh water
- Steering Cables- Check tightness
- Speedometer Sender- Remove & clean
- Water maker Pre-filters- Check, clean or replace
- Water maker drive belts- Check tension
- Water tanks- Use water from small tank
- Bilge- Flush with cleaner & fresh water
- Bilge Electric Pump- Test by filling bilge, check for debris
- Bilge Manual Pumps (both)- Check operation
- Bilge Pump, Engine driven- Check operation
- Sea cocks- Operate all
- Head- Vacuflush- Flush with fresh water
- Head, Manual, Par- Check pellet feeder
- Handheld GPS, Compass & nightscope- Check batteries
- A/C Systems- Confirm operation
- Light bulbs (including nav. lights)- Check & replace
- Fire extinguisher, automatic- Firetrace- Check pressure

FOUR MONTHS OR 250 HOURS ON ENGINE

- Engine- Perkins- Racor fuel filter- Replace
- Engine Oil and oil filter- Change
- Engine fuel filter- Replace & bleed air
- Engine Air filter- Clean

SIX MONTHS OR 250 HOURS ON GENERATOR

- Generator- Onan- Racor fuel filter- Replace
- Generator- Oil and oil filter- Change
- Generator- Clean inside housing
- Generator- Check Brushes- By Service Technician

SIX MONTHS

- Transmission- Hurth- Fluid level- Check
- Standing Rigging- Check for cracks, wear
- Davits- Check for attachment & operation
- Lifelines- Check & tighten
- Jammers- Spinlock- Oil, confirm function
- Cockpit cushions- Clean
- Fender covers- Wash
- Dinghy- Clean & check for damage
- Fresh water In-line strainer filter- Check & clean
- Seagull filter- Change if required
- Bow Thruster- Check oil level (EP 90)
- Holding tanks- Empty & flush with fresh water
- Interior- Wash surfaces with weak bleach solution to prevent mold
- Hatches & Ports- Coat seals with Vaseline
- Water maker- Seafresh- Check pump sump oil level
- Smoke alarms- Check batteries
- Zincs- Main, propeller & bow thruster- Check & replace if necessary

YEARLY

- Engine- Perkins
- Water impeller- Check (or 1,000 hours)
- Exhaust system- Check for leaks, tighten clips
- Engine mounts- Check
- Coolant- Confirm anti-freeze solution
- Generator- Onan-
- Coolant- Confirm anti-freeze solution (or 500 hours)
- Water impeller- Check
- Exhaust system- Check for leaks
- Transmission- Hurth
- ATF Fluid- Change
- Gear shift cables- Check & tighten nuts
- Propeller and shaft
- Max Prop- Check operation & grease
- Cutlass bearing- Check for wear & wash
- Rope cutter- Check
- Shaft coupling- Check for tightness
- Shaft alignment- Check for true (in water)
- Outboard- Honda
- Oil- Change
- Gear lube- Check level
- Lube fittings- Lube
- Standing rigging

- Tape on all fittings- Replace
- Professional check
- Lines- Remove, wash & dry
- Halyards- Inspect for wear
- Blocks -Replace plastic ties & polish
- Sails- Wash, dry, inspect & repair
- Bimini & Dodger- Wash, inspect & repair
- Horseshoe- Clean
- Steering
- Cables- Grease
- Rudder bearings- Check for wear
- Winches- Take apart & grease
- Windlass- Take apart, grease & oil
- Chain- Paint chain marks
- Topsides- Wax
- Bottom- Power wash, Paint with anti-fouling, check for blisters
- Fresh water tank- Flush with fresh water & white vinegar solution, check inside, then fill
- Interior- Open lockers, lift mattresses, raise cushions, & lift floor boards to permit air
- circulation
- Sea anchor & drogue- Check
- Life raft- Test by certified station
- Flares- Confirm dates
- Bicycles- Check operation

TWO YEARS

- Fuel tank- Check for sludge & clean pickup gauze filter
- Outboard- Honda- Gear lube- Change

THREE YEARS

- Keel bolts- Tighten

LAY-UP

- See separate schedule (Exhibit 23)

Exhibit 5 *ESCAPADE* PASSAGE PLAN FORM

Date _____

From _____ To _____ page

Total miles=   Tide & other timing:

Time required: Target Start Time-
@ 5.0 kts-

@ 6.0 kts-   Act. Average Speed-Comp.-   Charts:

@ 7.0 kts-   GPS-

Waypoint Data

No.	Description	Latitude	Longitude	Direction	Distance
1					
2					
3					
4					
5					
6					
7					
8					
9					
10					
11					
12					
13					
14					
15					
16					
17					
18					
19					
20					

Data

	Start	End	Change	%
Engine Hours				
Generator Hours				
Fuel- Tank Tender inches			Buy Ltrs=	
Log- Nautical Miles (Trip/Total)				
GPS (Trip/Total)				
Water- Liters			Made=	
Battery Charge- Amp Hours				
Time- Leaving/Arriving				

Notes: (Oil, water added, maintaince, etc.)

9/26//06 EAR

Exhibit 6 *ESCAPADE* PASSAGE LOG FORM

Date_____ From_____ To_____

Time (Local)	Position		GPS Data			Dist. W.P.	Trip Log	Course Steered		At Helm	Wind		Weather			Engine or Sail	Fuel (T.T.)	Amp. Hours	Water (L.)	Notes
	Latitude	Longitude	SOG	COG	XTE			Auto Pilot	Compass		Direction	Force	Barometer	Sea	Sky					

Exhibit 7 *ESCAPADE* **PACIFIC CROSSING PLAN EXAMPLE**

ESCAPADE Passage Plan

Date ___3-27-00___

~~3015~~
Total miles= 3004

From ___SANTA CRUZ___ To ___HIVA OA___ *FATU-HIVA* page *1*
___GALAPAGOS___ ___MARQUESAS___

Tide & other timing:

Time required:
@ 5.0 kts-
@ 6.0 kts-
@ 7.0 kts-

Target Start Time-

Act. Average Speed-Comp.- *6.93*   Charts:

GPS- *6.94*

Waypoint Data

No.	Description	Latitude	Longitude	Direction	Distance	
1	Anchorage	0° 45.00 S	90° 18.40	119	1.0	
2	Outside Bay	0° 45.50 S	90° 17.50	323	33.3	
3	Bet Isabela &	1° 10.00 S	90° 40.00	228	347	
4	Suggested	5° 00.00 S	95° 00.00	258	305	
5	"	6° 00.00	100° 00.00	262	1233	
6	"	8° 23.32	120° 34.28	264	1085	523
7	_____	9° 50.00	138° 50.00	273	11.4	
8	Off harbor	9° 49.40	139° 01.56	335	0.8	
9	Off Point	9° 48.65	139° 01.92	13	0.4	
10	Off Pier	9° 48.23	139° 01.74	—		
11						
7 / 12	Intermediate	9° 12.00	129° 21.74	262	542	
8 / 13	N of Reef	10° 17.32	138° 27.15	247	12.2	
9 / 14	N of Fatu-Hiva	10° 22.16	138° 38.53	232	4.6	
10 / 15	NW of " "	10° 35.01	138° 42.24	178	1.9	
11 / 16	W of Bay	10° 26.95	138° 42.16	115	2.3	21.0
12 / 17	Anchorage	10° 27.93	138° 40.00	—	—	
18						
19	At Anchor	10° 27.88	138° 40.06			
20						

GPS - Total 5884.1
    TRIP 3010.0

Data

	Start	End	Change	%
Engine Hours	2037ᴴ30'	2160ᴴ30'	123ᴴ0'	28
Generator Hours	901.9	997.4	95.5	
Fuel- Tank Tender inches	23.5	12.0	Buy Ltrs=	0
Log- Nautical Miles (Trip/Total)	0 / 8893.8	2518.7/11412.5		
GPS (Trip/Total)	0 /(2) 2874.1	3010.0 /(2) 5884.1		
Water- Liters	207	208	Made=	711
Battery Charge- Amp Hours	445	465		
Time- Leaving/Arriving	1540 (-6)	1415 (-9)	433ᴰ35'	

Notes: (Oil, water added, maintaince, etc.) on 3/27   on 4/14   433.58

11/26/97 EAR

Exhibit 8 ESCAPADE PACIFIC CROSSING LOG EXAMPLE

Date 4-7-00 From SANTA CRUZ To HIVA OA

Time (Local)	Latitude	Longitude	SOG	COG	XTE	Dist. W.P.	Trip Log	Auto Pilot	Compass	At Helm	Wind Direction	Force	Barometer	Sea	Sky	Engine or Sail	Fuel (T.T.)	Amp. Hours	Water (gals)	Notes
0800	8°10.72	118°21.08	9.1	264	0.0	134	1504	257	255	APT	SE	6	1010	6-10'	OVERCAST	S	1	407	228	
1200	8°12.40	118°38.29	8.6	266	0.0	115.3/522	263	263	260	APT	ESE	6	1011	"	"	S		401	227	
1200	8°14.069	118°56.781	8.7	261	0.0	98	1536	258	255	APT	ESE	5	1010	"	"	S		392	224	203.6
1400	8°15.66	119°12.33	8.2	259	0.10	814/550	256	255	APT		SE	6	1009	"	4	S		463	241	204.6 MADE 336oz
1620	8°17.47	119°31.69	8.1	269	0.0	622/567	257	257	APT		ESE	6	1008	"	"	S		391	239	
1800	8°18.24	119°49.45	8.1	292	0.0	119.0	1578	255	259	APT	ESE	5	1008	"	"	S		281	235	203.2
2000	8°20.28	120°01.38	8.2	260	0.0	327	1592	253	250	APT	SE	6	1009	"	"	S		393	227	
2200	8°21.55	120°18.44	8.5	261	.00	155	1609	257	260°	APT	ESE	7	1010	ROLLY	P.C	S		394	213	
2400	8°23.36	120°34.58	8.6	263	.01	1085	1601	254°	255	APT	ESE	4	1010	ROLLY	O.C	S		390	213	W.P.@2400
					SAT. 8	APRIL	2000													
0200	8°25.12	120°51.56	8.8	266	-.01	1068	1635	258'	255'	APT	ESE	7	1009	ROLLY	O.C.	S		364	222	
0400	8°26.84	121°08.31	8.8	270	0.0	1051/1651	257	250	APT	ESE	7	1008	6C	S		373	221	202.1
0600	8°28.61	121°25.80	9.0	262	0.0	1534	1666	249	250	APT	ESE	7	1009	VERY ROLLY	OC	S		372	221	202.3
0800	8°30.35	121°42.98	8.4	266	.00	1017	1681	256	250	APT	ESE	6	1011	ROLLY	P.C	S		401	220	200.6
1000	8°32.00	121°59.28	7.7	264	.00	1000	1695	255	255	APT	ESE	6	1012	LIGHT ROLL	P.C.	S		376	219	199.8 2/3 WAY!
1200	8°33.53	122°14.71	7.9	263	.00	985	1708	250°	250'	APT	E	5	1011	"	CLR	S		391	217	
1400	8°35.20	122°31.20	8.2	268	0.0	968	1722	255	255	APT	ESE	7	1009	"	"	S		385	213	197.8
1606	8°36.93	122°48.94	9.1	260	0.0	951/1736	250	243	APT	ESE	7	1008	"	"	S		377	212	Made 44gal
1800	8°38.64	123°06.37	8.3	261	.02	934	1750	255	250	APT	ESE	6	1009	"	"	S		365	209	
2000	8°40.24	123°23.30	8.2	266	.01	917	1764	254	252	APT	E	6	1010	"	"	S		376	211	200.6
2200	8°41.90	123°40.31	7.7	268	0.0	900.3	1778	257	254	APT	E	6	1011	slight	"	S		385	210	200.7
2400	8°43.47	123°56.84	8.5	262	0.0	883.8/1792	246	253	APT	ESE	6	1011	"	"	S	18P	390	210	
			9	APRIL	2000	SUNDAY														
0200	8°45.05	124°13.46	9.3	265°	.01	867	1805	254°	250°	APT	ESE	6	1009	MOD	H.C.C	S		377	210	200.6
0400	8°46.66	124°30.44	7.0	252	6.6	850	1819	254	250	APT	ESE	6	1008	LIGHT ROLL	P.C.	S		360	228	ENG INE ON 4 05:14
0600	8°48.00	124°45.00	6.9	261	0.0	836.1	1831	257	250	APT	ESE	6	1010	"	Cloudy	E		370	238	Start eng 0630
0800	8°48.43	125°01.30	8.6	257	1.1	819.1	1845	245	250	AP	SE	6	1011	MOD	"	E		397	237	197.4 Engine off 0830
1000	8°51.26	125°20.11	9.2	265°	0.01	801.2/1860	252°	260°	APT	ESE	6	1012	MOD	Cloudy	S		394	228	199.5.

Exhibit 9 CRUISING RISK CHART

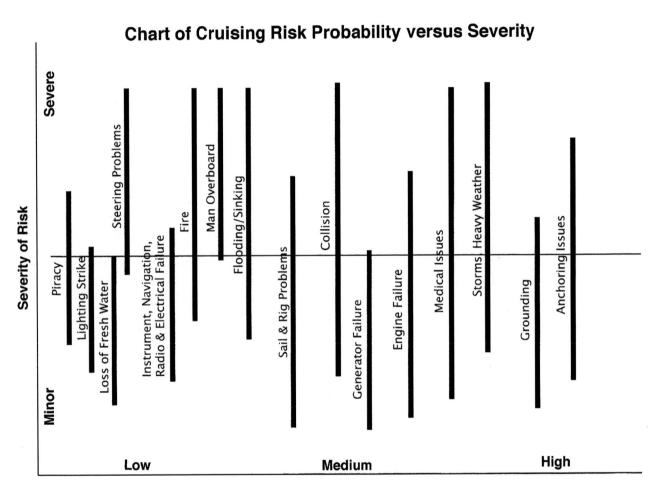

Chart of Cruising Risk Probability versus Severity

Probability of Risk

© Erick Reickert
December 2, 2008

Exhibit 10 *ESCAPADE* ROUND THE WORLD

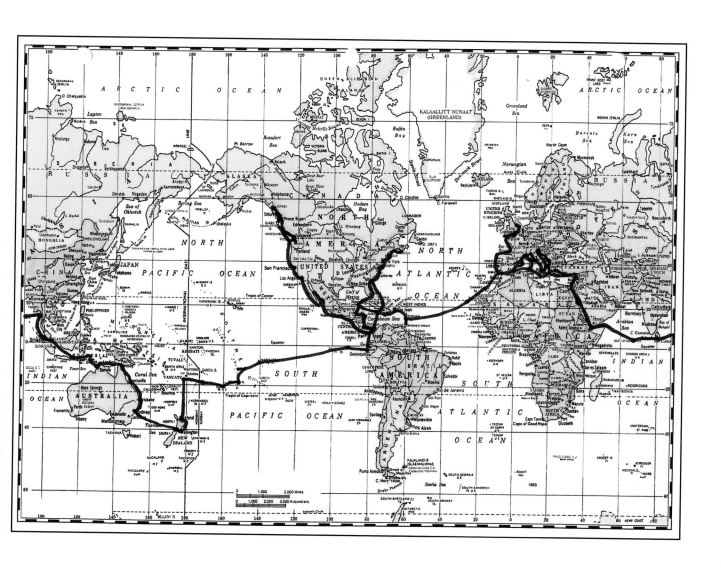

Exhibit 11 *ESCAPADE* CREW SUGGESTIONS FORM

Please bring the following:

- Passport with any necessary visas (discuss beforehand, need at least 6 months to expiry)
- Clothing for all conditions, preferably layered (cool, warm, hot, wet, sunny, touring, nice casual for dinner, etc.)
- Rain gear and/or umbrella for on shore use (It sometimes rains in paradise)
- Boat shoes with soft rubber soles that don't mark and are water resistant. These should be separate from any shoes that you intend to use on shore
- Sun protection lotions, cover-ups and sun hat with strap (with alligator clip)
- Sunglasses, with strap
- Extra glasses or extra contact lenses as spares
- Medicines and seasickness remedies, as required
- Personal toiletries
    - Books, games, VHS video tapes, and CD disks to your liking (we have some
    - CD's and video tapes, but bring what appeals to you)
- Sleeping mask and earplugs if you think you will need them
- Special foods or dietary requirements
- Camera, film, etc.

Other information:

- The basic voltage on Escapade is 230 VAC, 50 or 60 Hertz. (Depending on the location) (We can arrange for charging of cell phones etc. on 115 VAC)
- Do not assume that you will be able to buy any of the above items after you arrive.
- Use soft/foldable bags to carry your gear (There is no storage space for hard suitcases.)
- Carry your passport and legal documents on your person when traveling.
- The best, and easiest, source of local currency is to use ATM machines.

We will provide:

- Sheets, linens, pillows, blankets, towels, beach towels
- Life preserver (inflatable PFD) with built-in harness, tether and light
- Binoculars, compass, Handheld VHF
- Simple foul weather gear (mainly rain protection) good only for warm weather
- Hair dryer (operates only when we have shore power or when the generator is running)
- Snorkel gear

Exhibit 12 *ESCAPADE* REPAIR HISTORY

1996

- Boom toggle broke- Replaced by Hood
- Engine heat exchanger leaked- Replaced by Perkins
- Bent spinnaker pole- Replaced
- In-mast furling motor failed- Replaced
- Boom car stop broke-Replaced
- Windvane sender unit failed- Replaced by Autohelm
- Steering pedestal grab rail became loose - Whitlock epoxied
- **96/99** Replaced many refrigeration motors

1997

- Dinghy see-thru bottom fell out- Reglued
- Wiring wrong with leakage voltage- Rewired
- Battens missing- Replaced with battens with holes
- **97/99** Replaced many dinghy davit springs
- In-mast furling control box- Replaced with switch design
- **6/7/97** Generator water pump leaking-Replaced with new pump
- Generator failed- Replaced stator & rotor
- Weatherfax failed- Repaired and converted to 12 VDC
- Firetrace fire extinguisher lost pressure- Replaced
- Windlass friction washer broke- Replaced
- **11/1/97 6/7/97** Generator water pump leaking- Replaced with new pump
- Pulpit & lifelines damaged- Pulpit repaired & lifeline replaced
- Loudhailer bracket broke- Replaced w SS one
- Fresh water pump plastic connectors broke- Replaced
- **97-98** Galley sink pump diaphragm broke- Replaced

1998

- Dinghy see-thru bottom fell out- Strap added & reglued
- Engine water seal failed- Replaced
- GPS failed- Reconnected after starting w new antenna
- ST-80 Instrument lost contrast- Replaced by Autohelm

- Alternator bracket broke- Re-welded
- Windlass buttons failed- Replaced
- Hand toilet pump failed-Replaced
- Main sheet winch missing seal- Installed
- Stereo speaker failed- Replaced
- Windlass failed- Rebuilt at Palma
- **98/99** Halogen lights failed frequently- Replaced some w dropper
- Lazarette handle broke- Replaced
- Lazarette drain blocked- Drilled out
- Generator Battery failed- Replaced
- Dinghy see-thru bottom fell out- Screwed & re-glued
- Compass lights failed due to short- Replaced & re-wired
- **11/15/98** Refrigeration cooling water air lock problem- Oyster added vent tube
- **11/15/98** VHF Handset cable broke- Replaced

1999

- Limber hole chain broke- Can't replace
- **1/26/99** Hand toilet pump failed- Replaced
- **2/05/99** Bow thruster failed- Re-installed screws
- **4/07/99** Auto pilot ram failed- Replaced
- **5/21/99 6/7/97** Generator water pump leaking- Replaced with rebuilt pump
- **6/10/99** Refrigeration needed charging- Added Freon
- **7/11/99** Inverter failed- Replaced switch
- **8/24/99** Bow thruster failed- Tapped hub & reinstalled screws
- **8/24/99** Aft shower bracket failed- Replaced with new design
- Vacuflush toilet lost vacuum- Replaced seals & duck bill valves
- Bilge pump bottom- Replaced with new flapper valve
- **10/11/99** Hatch shade fwd broke- Replaced with new design
- Outhaul & mainsheet worn- Replaced
- **10/13/99** Port rub rail & toe rail damaged -Repaired **1/27/00**

2000

- **2/01/00** Dodger & Bimini worn- Replaced
- **2/01/00** Cockpit cushions worn- Replaced
- **2/01/00** Digital barometer failed - Replaced with new design
- **2/01/00** GPS input buttons cracked - Replaced cover
- **2/01/00** Replaced house & engine batteries- 4 years old
- **2/01/00** Bolt on main zinc broke due to over tightening- Used temp. fix
- **2/01/00** Drawer latch broke- Replaced
- **2/01/00** Icemaker failed- Major rebuild
- **2/05/00** Vacuflush pump seized- replaced
- **2/08/00** Showerhead broke- Replaced
- **2/09/00** Outhaul broke, threaded incorrectly- Replaced
- **2/16/00** Outboard propeller slips- Replaced
- **2/19/00** Spinnaker torn- Fixed
- **2/20/00** Generator heat exchanger leaking - Re-soldered
- **3/10/00** Stitching on leather grab bar broke - Re-sewed
- **3/20/00** Lazarette handle broke- Replaced
- **4/09/00** Hand toilet pump failed- Replaced
- **4/09/00** Fwd shower temperature valve not proper- Cleaned screens
- **3/20/00** Fresh water pump diaphragm failed- Replaced w larger pump head
- **4/13/00** Spinnaker halyard broke, opening plate missing
- **4/17/00** Fresh water pump plate failed- Replaced w smaller plate
- **4/18/00** Refrigeration temperature sensors failed-
- **4/20/00** Windlass broke into pieces- Replaced with Lofrans
- **4/21/00** Spinnaker ripped- Fixed
- **4/24/00** Loudhailer housing broke- Epoxied, reinstalled
- **4/24/00** Davit spring, port broke- Replaced
- **4/24/00** Cupboard latch broke- Replaced
- **4/24/00** Staysail roller- metal part Epoxied
- **4/24/00** Firetrace fire extinguisher lost pressure
- **4/28/00** DC house voltage cut out- Tightened nut on cable at shunt
- **4/29/00** Fresh water Pump leaked- Replaced w smaller size new pump
- **4/29/00** Pressure relief valve on water heater leaked- Tested & sealed tube
- **4/29/00** Max prop zinc eroded- Replaced
- **4/29/00** Mast furling foil crack- OK, as it is design
- **4/29/00** Filled gouge in gel coat in transom
- **6/03/00** Install new Lofrans Windlass
- **6/05/00** Replace water pressure relief valve
- **6/05/00** Install new light bulbs in Perkins instrument Panel
- **6/05/00** Replace halyard entry bracket for port spinnaker; Re-string halyard
- **6/05/00** Checked A/C wiring in Generator- Some overload found in switch panel
- **6/10/00** Loudhailer speaker broke on mast-
- **6/10/00** Generator hard to start
- **6/11/00** Generator over speed, would not stop- Injector pump failed- Replaced pump
- **6/12/00** Trim on staysail furler peeled up- Tied down with plastic tie, then pop rivet
- **6/12/00** Replaced davit spring
- **6/15/00** Generator water pump leaks- Replaced with new pump
- **6/16/00** Fix deck joint caulk in several areas
- **6/17/00** Leak at bottom of Fwd Head pump- Tighten clamps/screws
- **7/08/00** Vacuflush won't stop- Replace vacuum switch
- **7/11/00** Water maker developed leaks at ends of pressure vessel
- **7/12/00** Fwd shower volume valve leaking- broken tab- Can not fix, need new part
- **7/17/00** Generator heat exchanger using coolant- Replaced heat exchanger w new
- **7/22/00** Generator stopped-Alternator froze, belt broke-Fix by removing bad bearing
- **7/31/00** Speaker in cockpit broken-Replaced with new one
- **8/10/00** Generator belt broke, alternator froze- Replaced with new Alternator & Belt
- **8/19/00** Generator battery failed- Replaced with new (but too small)
- **8/21/00** Put in FirstStar anchor light at 12 V
- **8/26/00** Install new generator battery, drill air holes in battery box
- **8/28/00** Main furling top sleeve broke- Moved cover up & put piece in bottom
- **8/28/00** Yankee furling top bearings worn- Oiling improved- Wrote Oyster

- **8/28/00** Top of Yankee torn- Had sail maker repair
- **8/28/00** One main batten warn- replaced with new
- **9/02/00** Removed "fishooks" from dinghy davit cable; fixed one carbide
- **9/09/00** Fwd A/C water pump failed- Replaced
- **9/12/00** Fwd cabin small hatch screen broke- Repaired
- **9/20/00** Dinghy davit wire frayed-Reversed
- **10/01/00** Water pump hose fittings broke- Fixed with hose connections
- **10/04/00** Gas locker solenoid valve hot- Replaced
- **10/07/00** Water volume valve in fwd shower control leaked- Replaced
- **10/07/00** Leather in openings under dodger deteriorated-Replaced
- **10/10/00** Autopilot says low battery voltage- Voltage OK, Replaced computer
- **10/10/00** Fwd drain pump ring broke- Replaced Whale Gulper pump
- **10/13/00** Fwd cabin small hatch screen broke- Repaired
- **10/21/00** Dinghy cover torn by wind-Paul sewed
- **10/21/00** Bimini torn by wind-Repaired and clips added
- **10/21/00** Dorade scoop lost-Replaced
- **10/21/00** VHF Radio turns itself off- Outside handset took water, Replaced
- **10/21/00** VHF Radio outside speaker not operating- Took water- Replaced on 2/3/01
- **10/21/00** Generator shows hot exhaust alarm- Believed due to excessive heel-OK
- **10/21/00** Fresh water pump does not shut off- Due to heel?- OK
- **10/21/00** UV strips on staysail & yankee torn by wind-Replaced by sail maker
- **10/21/00** Crewsaver Life Vest inflated itself due to water- Replaced cylinder & bobbin
- **10/21/00** Wind instrument ceases to operate, but returns- Seems OK, no action
- **11/01/00** Dinghy davit wires replaced

2001

- **2/01/01** Anchor chain rusting-Re-galvanized
- **2/01/01** Upper Yankee Furling head replaced with new unit
- **2/01/01** Windlass fwd deck switches did not work- repaired wire in chain locker
- **2/01/01** Wind instrument ceases to operate, but intermittent- Replaced with new

- **2/02/01** Refrigeration pump failed- Replaced
- **2/02/01** Automatic fire extinguisher lost pressure- Replaced with Fireboy system
- **2/02/01** SSB antenna lead too short- Replaced with new, thicker conductor
- **2/02/01** Loudhailer speaker keeps breaking-Added SS wire enclosure on mast
- **2/02/01** Mainsheet too thick- Replaced with new metric size
- **2/03/01** VHF cockpit speaker failed-Replaced with new one
- **2/03/01** Ceiling light fixtures rusted- Replaced 3 (Fwd head, fwd cabin, aft shower)
- **2/04/01** Dinghy see-thru bottom frame came off- Screwed and bolted
- **2/11/01** Spring on TV cabinet door broke- Replaced
- **2/12/01** Gebo stb port in saloon broke-Replaced with new knob by drilling thru rod
- **2/18/01** Engine water pipe to transmission leaked- Cut pipe, used longer hose
- **2/23/01** Wind gauge stopped working-Replaced with new head unit
- **2/23/01** Stb staysail; deck block broke due to high load-Replaced with new
- **2/27/01** Installed SS bars in salon port light areas
- **2/27/01** Wire cover for port side solar panel came loose-Stuck on with tape
- **3/04/01** Generator impeller failed (slips)-Replaced (1254 hrs)
- **3/09/01** Trimble Galaxy failed to send/receive messages-Replaced antenna
- **3/10/01** Mainsheet car broke due to jibe-Replaced with new
- **3/10/01** Windvane pointer flew off-Replaced with new bracket & Windex
- **3/12/01** Compass lights not working-Replaced with new bulbs with upper connection
- **3/19/01** Bled water system to reduce green light flashing on water computer-DNW
- **3/19/01** Mainsail stitching near middle batten pocket-Re-stitched by sail maker
- **3/20/01** Companionway sides scratched-Sanded and varnished
- **3/20/01** Cockpit table & cup rack warn-Sanded and varnished
- **3/20/01** Bimini bracket bent due to jibe-Bent to original shape
- **3/26/01** Staysail head straps broke-Sail resewed by sail maker

- **3/27/01** Furling line block broke due to high load-Replaced with new
- **3/27/01** Deck locker latch broke-Replaced with new
- **3/27/01** Drawer, flatware latch broke-Replaced with new
- **3/27/01** Staysail foot latch broke-Replaced with new
- **3/28/01** Autopilot lost direction-Seems OK after restart; Due to too much heel
- **4/05/01** Vacuflush toilet looses vacuum-Replaced ball and seals
- **4/05/01** Seagull filter hose leaking-Replaced hose clamp
- **4/05/01** Anti-siphon valve leaking-Replaced with new plastic one with hose
- **4/24/01** Gulper pump for galley failed-Replaced with new unit
- **4/24/01** Windlass plain springs rusting-Replaced with new
- **5/10/01** Water computer sensor-Replaced with new- Fixed problem
- **5/10/01** Plug mounted for Anchorwatch system under DC panel
- **5/12/01** Washing machine trips breaker, blew fuse-Ran on 50 hertz
- **5/14/01** Transmission does not engage forward-Adjusted shift cable (at sea)-DNW
- **5/15/01** Engine seems to be running hot-Replaced impeller-DNW
- **5/15/01** Refrigeration will not operate-Bled cooling water system-OK
- **5/16/01** Windvane bent-bird flew into it-Replace with new
- **5/16/01** Connected auto adapter for G4 Computer
- **5/16/01** Installed new nav. computer mounting board
- **5/19/01** GPS Remote instrument light out-Fixed itself-7/13/01
- **5/20/01** Aft cabin door latch spring weak-Replace with new
- **5/20/01** Mast furling unit leaking oil-
- **5/20/01** Avon inflatable fender leaking-Filled with latex
- **5/29/01** Windlass loose-Tightened bolts
- **5/29/01** Transmission not engaging properly-Rebuilt with new thrust washer
- **6/12/01** Yankee sheet donut became loose-Re-attached

- **6/15/01** Anchor light failed-Replaced with normal 12 Volt bulb
- **6/15/01** Generator made only 190 VAC-Re-started and seems OK
- **6/16/01** Outboard did not start-Replaced sparkplug-OK
- **6/18/01** Outboard will not retract to down position-Used WD-40, added string
- **6/19/01** Engine runs hot-New thermostat installed, @2,890 check cam & wear plate
- **6/19/01** E went up mast to install 12V bulb and broke tricolor holder-Epoxied
- **6/20/01** Bimini torn at port, forward-Resowed
- **6/24/01** Engine tachometer reading low, fluxuating-Tightened spade lug on alt-OK
- **6/26/01** Main furling countershaft seal-Replaced with new-OK
- **6/27/01** Generator brushes replaced (1,318 hours)-OK
- **6/27/01** Outboard spark plugs replaced, re-balanced mixture-Let idle before shutting
- **6/29/01** Engine heat exchanger-Cleaned. Resolved heat problem
- **7/09/01** Watertight door handle lost roll pin-Replaced w carter pin, then new roll pin
- **7/19/01** Fwd head Gebo port knob frozen-Replaced with new after cutting off old one
- **7/24/01** Bimini-Added full width center support tube and zipper
- **7/24/01** Steiner Binoculars have rubber melting-
- **7/24/01** Staysail and baby stays-Shortened to reduce floppiness by rigger
- **8/10/01** Seal mast boot with Sicaflex
- **8/10/01** Windlass switch at bow lost cover-Replaced with old switch cover
- **8/10/01** Dinghy developed small leak-Repaired with patch
- **8/10/01** Rusted items in engine compartment-Cleaned and painted
- **8/10/01** Yankee sheet leather covers out of position-Redone
- **8/10/01** Aft shower & fwd head needs recaulking-Recaulked
- **8/18/01** Fwd head shower pump & galley pump diaphragms failed-Replaced
- **8/21/01** Engine heat exchanger & oil cooler core replaced with new-Works great
- **8/22/01** Replaced generator zinc- completely gone at 1,372 hours

- **8/22/01** Bike tires need replacement-Bought new tires
- **8/22/01** Replaced anchor light with Mark-II version- OK
- **8/22/01** Washing Machine-Trips CB in pump cycle after replacing controller
- **8/24/01** Yankee sheet car rubber pieces failed-Replaced with new
- **8/27/01** Tank Tender diesel gauge failed-Removed tube, used tube for #3 water tank
- **8/31/01** 100 amp Alternator failed-Changed wires to small alt for temp measure
- **9/01/01** Electronic Barometer failed-Replaced batteries (AAA-) OK
- **9/20/01** Replaced engine zinc-completely gone after 1 month
- **9/21/01** All Tank Tender tubes failed- Broken under nav seat
- **10/01/01** Washing machine water pump-Replaced-working OK
- **10/01/01** Large alternator- Replaced- OK
- **10/02/01** Washing machine-Sealed tub joint with Marine-Tex to stop leak
- **10/02/01** Steering wheel-Had stitching replaced
- **10/03/01** Tank tender-Replace tubing for diesel-OK
- **10/08/01** Transmission clunked when going into forward- Did not repeat
- **10/08/01** Fwd A/C trips circuit breaker-Reprogrammed CFD to 1-Seems OK
- **10/20/01** Hit coral-Chipped rudder, etc.- Repaired
- **10/20/01** A/C Panel- Shorted on feed to A/C switches-Replaced with larger wires
- **10/22/01** Engine start batteries dry-Apparently a short in one of them

2002

- **1/21/02** Engine start batteries boiling-Replaced with new ones
- **1/21/02** Fresh water pump inlet port broke-Replaced with new one
- **1/21/02** Engine raw water impeller torn vane-Replaced with new one
- **1/21/02** Generator raw water impeller warn vanes-Replaced with new one
- **1/22/02** PC Computer battery dead, won't charge-
- **1/23/02** Fresh water pump pressure switch failed-Replaced with new Micro switch
- **1/23/02** Port dinghy davit spring broke-Replaced with new one
- **1/13/02** TV won't react to remote control-

- **2/01/02** Bilge Pump won't pump-Replaced impeller
- **2/01/02** Bilge Pump leaks water-Replaced shaft seal
- **2/01/02** Steering Rams noise-Checked; port slightly stiff, Stb making clicking sounds
- **2/01/02** Generator DC circuit cuts out-Aired out so over temperature switches are OK
- **2/02/02** Generator won't start-Battery terminal bad condition-cleaned
- **2/04/02** Autopilot-Replaced computer; eliminated clunking noise; ram noise louder
- **2/07/02** Water heater pressure valve released-Replaced pressure Micro switch
- **2/08/02** Cleaned water filters in system and two shower filters
- **2/12/02** Chips in stern gelcoat-Fix
- **2/12/02** Fwd small hatch screen-Replace with new
- **2/14/02** Generator start battery using water-Replaced with new
- **2/15/02** Generator would not start-Charged new battery, cleaned contacts, add oil
- **2/23/02** Vacuflush would not pump-Bad motor-Replaced
- **2/24/02** Water maker filters dirty-Replaced
- **2/26/02** Starboard davit spring broke-Replaced
- **2/28/02** Windlass top seal rusting-
- **2/28/02** Sink drain pump not working-Blew blockage from pipe
- **3/05/02** Port cockpit speaker broken ribs-
- **3/07/02** Stereo not shuffling on 2-Tried various things, now seems to work
- **3/09/02** Autopilot failed; no steering-Stbd ram failed & fitting on port ram; swapped fittings and disconnected stbd ram; seems OK; Replaced stb ram
- **3/14/02** Fwd head froze-Cleaned of calcium deposits and rebuilt
- **3/14/02** Fwd drain pump made noise-Replaced with new
- **3/14/02** Aft compartment under seat in aft cabin had water-Emptied
- **3/14/02** Seagull filter lost pressure-Replaced with cartridge
- **3/17/02** Autopilot port ram failed-Disconnected & use new port ram
- **3/21/02** Generator water pump leaking water-Replaced with new
- **3/27/02** Autopilot failed-Pin dropped out of shaft arm- replaced

- **3/30/02** Water coming from hose when bilge pump running-
- **4/01/02** Deck organizer for outhaul has cracked pulley
- **4/07/02** Water leak over icemaker-
- **4/10/02** Dodger stitching on base coming off-Resowen at marina
- **4/20/02** Dinghy strap for seat re-attached
- **5/10/02** New outboard plastic fuel tank- 22 L
- **5/10/02** Replaced fwd head outlet hose with new
- **5/10/02** Cockpit table & mug rack-Re-varnished
- **5/10/02** Cockpit speaker-Glued in bars
- **5/10/02** Autopilot-Installed larger split pin on top ram
- **5/10/02** Fuel tank inspection ports-Replaced with new
- **5/30/02** Installed new Autopilot ram on port side-Adjusted, now really quiet
- **5/31/02** Installed new Spinlock deck organizer for outhaul
- **5/31/02** TV had new CHIP installed, but won't work on DC & quits periodically
- **6/16/02** Inverter fails when large load applied-Fix & replaced 10/7/02
- **6/17/02** Windlass top seal rusting-Replaced with new
- **6/19/02** Gebo pelican hook on port side lower lifeline broke-Replaced with new
- **6/20/02** Damage to aft stbd Gebo Thru-hull-Sealed top and gelcoat
- **6/20/02** Fwd head pressure buildup-Cleaned out pressure relief & flushed tanks
- **6/24/02** Refrigeration inlet hose tube broke, Leaking water-Pushed hose on further
- **6/28/02** Transmission sometimes will not engage fwd, mainly when hot-No action
- **7/06/02** Bow Thruster control fell apart; would not shut off-Cur clip failed-Used wire
- **7/06/02** Bow Thruster switch failed when shutting off-By passed switch
- **7/08/02** Refrigeration pump hose connector replaced with new
- **7/13/02** GPS lost position-Tried spare antenna, no better; Handheld also-Now, OK
- **7/19/02** Windlass switch stuck-Let air in to stop vacuum-OK
- **7/23/02** GPS lost position for 1 hour; Handheld also-Resumed OK
- **7/28/02** GPS did not start up until 30 minutes later-Then started OK
- **7/29/02** Bow thruster-Replaced control head with new
- **7/31/02** Dinghy davit spring, port side broke-Replaced with new
- **8/02/02** GPS bottom row of numbers lacking bars-
- **8/15/02** Bilge pump failed-Replaced with new
- **8/25/02** Deck seal replaced in several places
- **8/25/02** Fwd head leaking-Resealed
- **8/25/02** Bimini stitching failed-Re-stitched
- **8/25/02** Paint on boom and mast flaking-Repainted by hand
- **8/25/02** Refrigeration hose breaking at end-Replaced with new
- **8/25/02** Refrigeration-Added seacock for bleeding
- **8/25/02** Batteries sulfated-Shock charged at battery dealer
- **8/25/02** Deck sealer loose-Repaired 3 spots
- **8/25/02** Overhead lights rusting-Replaced 16 with new
- **8/25/02** Dorade vents-Cleaned inside vents
- **8/25/02** Hull stained at bow-Cleaned and polished
- **9/20/02** Clean Yankee & Staysail to remove sand
- **9/20/02** Seal around fuel inlet tube
- **9/21/02** Winches-Cleaned and rebuilt
- **9/23/02** Replaced toilet breather filters (both) & resealed panels
- **9/23/02** Main traveler squeaking-Replaced torlon balls
- **9/23/02** Anchor chain-Remarked depth marks
- **9/23/02** Windlass-Cleaned and rebuilt; cleaned rusting dish spring
- **9/23/02** TV faulty-Replaced with new system-Flat screen monitor & WW VCR
- **10/05/02** Mast boot tape-Replaced
- **10/05/02** Gel coat-Repaired many small spots
- **10/05/02** Cockpit speaker bars broken-Replaced
- **10/05/02** Non-skid paint around mast & hatch-Repainted
- **10/05/02** Ice maker failed, no noise at all-Did nothing
- **10/10/02** GPS-Replaced battery
- **10/10/02** Water computer-Recalibrated to 815 liters
- **10/11/02** GPS-Removed screen & cleaned contacts, reassembled, fixed antenna lead
- **10/12/02** Repainted outboard motor cover; added Escapade decals

- **10/18/02** Galley sink pump not working-Replaced diaphragm
- **10/19/02** Staysail luff cord came loose-Attached and put patches over warn spots
- **10/19/02** Personal EPIRB receiver not working-Fixed loose connection at plug
- **10/21/02** Engine stopped-Replaced fuel lifter pump with new, kept old upper housing
- **10/24/02** Stb Dinghy Davit spring broke-Replaced
- **10/26/02** Stereo did not turn on-Checked power, no avail-Worked OK next day
- **10/28/02** Freezer lid handle broke-Used wire to fix; don't risk removing

2003

- **5/23/03** Aft sink leaking-Reseal with silicon
- **5/24/03** Engine stopped-Blockage in fuel line between pump & fuel filter on engine
- **5/24/03** Racor switch not working-
- **5/25/03** TV Antenna not working-
- **5/29/03** Fwd Shower bracket broke-Replaced w new brackets
- **5/29/03** Repaired old Bikes
- **5/31/03** Generator running hot-Replaced impeller-Did not fix; Crud in connector-OK
- **5/31/03** Outboard stopped-Not idling smoothly
- **5/31/03** Aft cabin door latch spring replaced
- **5/31/03** Sheaves, fwd on boom-Removed and loosened, greased; OK
- **6/06/03** Windlass control at helm not working-Fuses in 24v power blown-Replaced
- **6/11/03** Washing machine won't rotate-Belt came off due to heavy load-Replaced
- **6/18/03** Completed connecting generator battery charger-Works well
- **6/19/03** Windlass dish washers rusted-Replaced
- **6/20/93** Mainsheet block bits replaced
- **7/10/93** Gas changed from Propane to Camping Gaz
- **7/10/03** Honda outboard serviced-Idle corrected, runs great, even at idle
- **7/13/93** Racor dual assy replaced with new assembly-Valve now works
- **7/17/03** Engine would not start-Battery low-Shorted house battery-Removed
- **7/22/03** Bow thruster seems weak after usage-Possible battery issue? No
- **7/23/03** Pelican Hook on port side opening pin lost-Replaced with new

- **7/23/03** Fan in fwd cabin failed-Replaced with new
- **7/23/03** Washing machine-Replaced belt with new
- **7/23/03** Batteries-House and Engine start-Replaced with new
- **7/25/03** Fuel tank- Did major cleaning & fuel polishing-Used 10 filters
- **7/30/03** Port side dinghy davit spring broke-Replaced
- **8/03/03** Replaced port side speaker in cockpit-Had broken grille and loose cone
- **8/15/03** Yankee furling gear stiff-Too many wraps-Bearings OK
- **8/16/03** Engine water pump leaking-Cleaned cover & housing, tightened with pliers
- **8/17/03** Engine surging-Replaced fuel filter on engine
- **8/20/03** Stb Backstay trimmer block broke free-Replaced w new jubilee clip
- **8/29/03** TV reception w antenna-Fixed by connecting antenna & intermittent in power
- **9/04/03** Scratch in starboard side gelcoat-Repaired temp with gelcoat filler
- **9/09/03** Hatch screen assy, Aft Cabin-Replaced w Ocean Air Screen MK 4
- **9/10/03** Fresh water pressure relief valve leaking-Replaced with new
- **9/16/03** VHF Handset in cockpit won't transmit-Replaced w new handset
- **9/18/03** MOM-8 brackets broke (H stood on it)-Replaced w new
- **9/20/03** Windlass up switch broke-Replace with old cover
- **9/30/03** Windlass up switch sticking-Resealed
- **9/30/03** Dinghy davit springs, both-Replaced with new
- **10/3/03** Outboard propeller slips after hitting rocks-Replaced with new
- **10/3/03** Generator shuts off due high coolant temp-Relieved pressure & added water
- **10/14/03** Water tank has growth-Cleaned
- **10/14/03** Fuel tank has sludge-Cleaned and emptied for winter

2004

- **3/31/04** Fwd head shower temp control leaked, screw broke out-Replace w bolt-OK
- **4/1/04** Aft head water feed pipe to toilet became separated-Reattached-OK

- **4/1/04** Transmission failed to engage forward immediately-Changed ATF, OK
- **4/5/04** Forward facing sonar has no display-Connection loose, now OK
- **4/5/04** Toilet seat cover in fwd head broke off screws-See 7/22
- **410/04** TV antenna does not work, better w/o power-Redid connector on top-OK
- **4/11/04** Sony Radio would not eject cassette-Broken teeth on eject gear-DNF
- **4/17/04** VHF Radio does not transmit (OK on receive) after being on-Repaired-OK
- **5/5/04** Fwd shower temperature control does not stop-Broken-Reassembled OK
- **5/6/04** Seagull filter hose leaking-Replaced hose clamp-OK
- **5/28/04** Salon A/C failed-Replaced water pump
- **5/30/04** Replaced windless switches with new ones
- **7/6/04** Stb Nav light broken on DYT ship-Replaced w new-OK
- **7/9/04** Stern light-Cracked inside-replaced w new-OK
- **7/16/04** Refrigeration has air lock-Bleed hose blocked-Cleared-OK
- **7/22/04** Toilet seat cover in fwd head-Replaced w new
- **7/22/04** Fuel tank inspection cover leaking-Removed & replaced, fixed w Super Glue
- **7/22/04** Galley drawer & cabinet latches broke-Replaced w new
- **7/22/04** Windlass switches sticking-Drilled air relief hole, now OK
- **7/22/04** Dinghy SS strap screws loose-Refitted with white mastic
- **7/31/04** Engine Exhaust Outlet developed leak-Repaired w Marine-Tax
- **8/3/04** Generator wouldn't start as DC circuit tripped-Reset, ran
- **8/5/04** Generator wouldn't start-Jumped, see below
- **8/6/04** Inverter failed-Replace switch which failed-OK
- **8/8/04** Generator-won't start-Cleaned cables, eliminated thru bolt feeds-Works fine
- **8/9/04** Windlass would not work-Circuit breaker shorted out-Replaced w new
- **8/11/04** Vacuflush-Pump does not shut off-Seems OK next day
- **8/12/04** Refrigeration still gets airlock-Refitted hose
- **8/13/04** Engine Exhaust Outlet-Replaced w new-OK
- **8/21/04** Vacuflush toilet-Replaced duck bill valves & vacuum switch-OK @ 40 sec
- **8/23/04** Changed from Camping Gaz (Butane) to Propane
- **8/25/04** Engine hour meter failed-Replaced with electrical one
- **8/25/04** Inmarsat Receiver-Kept waking us up-Covered sound hole with goop & tape
- **8/28/04** Stove-Added bracket to hold battery in place
- **9/3/04** Lazerette Lid-Glued corner back in place
- **9/5/04** No fresh water-Set screw on small pulley came loose, belt fell off-Tightened
- **9/9/04** Fwd head door sticking, noisy-Filed bottom of door, oiled hinges-OK
- **9/20/04** Deck locker latch handle broke-Replaced with new
- **9/23/04** Curtain rod over fwd companionway-Replaced w new

2005

- **3/18/05** Heater Installed
- **3/18/05** Companionway steps varnished
- **3/18/05** Gelcoat repaired on starboard side, stern, & bow
- **3/18/05** Engine hour meter replaced with new vibrator type
- **10/10/05** Cockpit table & cup holder varnished
- **10/10/05** Engine mounts painted black
- **10/10/05** Raw water manifold replaced with new, SS valves & SS housing

2006

- **4/23/06** Engine raw water impeller-Replaced with new
- **4/23/06** Bilge Pump not working- Replaced impeller
- **4/23/06** Generator battery-Replaced with new
- **4/23/06** Fire extinguishers-Replaced with new USCG approved with gauges
- **4/23/06** Propane system-Added pressure gauge
- **4/24/06** Heater not working-Repaired by fixing loose ground wire
- **4/24/06** Transmission did not engage-Worked back and forth until it engaged

- **4/24/06** Fwd toilet pellet feeder nipple broke-Replace with new
- **4/26/06** Fwd toilet worked hard-Replaced toilet and outlet hose with new
- **4/26/06** Fwd sink drain detached-Used new hose and adapter
- **4/26/06** Vacuflush toilet would not pump when flushed-Adjusted vacuum switch
- **4/26/06** Dodger sewing coming loose-Repaired by sail maker
- **4/27/06** Trans. heat exchanger cover plate cracked-Replace w new, plus longer bolt
- **4/27/06** Fresh water pump nipple broken-Replaced with new
- **4/27/06** Magnetronic not reading voltage-Can't find anything loose
- **4/27/06** Icom Handheld VHF not working-Burned up- had to replace
- **4/27/06** Eng Instrument cover latch broken-Replaced with new
- **4/27/06** Stanchion bolts missing/bent-Replaced with new
- **5/3/06** Aft cabin heater blower not working-Replaced with new fan
- **5/8/06** Aft Inboard fuel tank inspection cover cracked-Replaced with new
- **5/20/06** Stb Raw Water filter drain bolt broke-Repaired w hose clamp & rubber pad
- **5/30/06** Hose clamp on inside manual pump broke-Replaced w new
- **6/2/06** Outboard floods-Replaced fuel float needle valve
- **6/4/06** American Flag-Put on Backstay
- **6/8/06** Primary winch, port side, high speed switch DNW- Wiggled wires, now OK
- **7/5/06** Fwd head cabinet latch broke-Replaced w new
- **7/11/06** Fwd Center House Battery failed- center series- New set installed 8/24/06
- **7/12/06** Lazarette lid prop broke at ball joint-Replace w new ball joints
- **7/14/06** Wind instruments not reading right-Replaced w new
- **7/17/06** Outboard not idling well-Had carburetor cleaned by mechanic & new fuel
- **7/21/06** Gas locker lid handle broke-Replaced w new
- **7/21/06** Port Dinghy Davit spring broke-Replaced w new

- **7/21/06** Port Dinghy Davit wire wound on itself-Removed unit and untangled
- **7/30/06** Eng Inst. Panel-Replaced temperature bulb w new
- **8/2/06** Hot water tank discharging-Turned knob, let flow-Seems OK
- **8/2/06** Bilge pump switch not turning off-Turned screw ¾ turn-Now OK
- **8/2/06** Strap on cockpit table loose-Replaced w new
- **8/2/06** Stb speaker in cockpit lost cone-Replaced w new
- **8/9/06** Solar Panels not working-Replaced fuse
- **8/26/06** Refrigerator light switch broke-Replaced w new
- **9/6/06** Fresh water system fluctuating in pressure-Pumped up accumulator tank
- **9/9/06** Outboard flooding-Bent float in carburetor-Still did not fix it.
- **9/11/06** Fresh water pump not working-Replaced pressure switch
- **9/29/06** Replace companionway sill w teak & refinish wood under companionway
- **9/29/06** Repair bimini by stitching
- **10/1/06** Refrigerator light-Replaced switch w new
- **10/1/06** Lazarette lid-Replace ball joints w new
- **10/8/06** Replace cockpit speakers w new
- **10/9/06** Masthead wind transducer is not rotating-Replaced with repaired unit
- **10/10/06** Stern light bulb burned out-Replaced w new
- **10/4/06** Spinnaker block bungee cords weak-Replace w new
- **10/14/06** Exhaust hose leaking-Replaced w new
- **10/16/06** Boarding ladder rubber tip missing-Replaced set w new
- **10/16/06** Engine using more oil than previously-Check- Not so
- **10/18/06** Aft toilet-Clean water holes around rim to improve water flow
- **11/8/06** Hot water tank pressure relief valve-Replaced w new (old corroded)
- **11/8/06** Fresh water pump pressure switch-Replaced w micro-switch style
- **11/9/06** Aft Toilet-Cleaned bowl seal to prevent loss of vacuum-OK
- **11/10/06** Galley sink pump diaphragm broke-Replace w new + epoxied bolt
- **11/11/06** Mainsail fell down, luff rod swivel broke-Reassembled, added 3 screws

- **11/14/06** Yankee sheets warn-Replaced w new
- **11/22/06** Outboard leaking fuel-Take apart and rebuild, now is OK, again
- **11/24/06** Stb dinghy davit spring broke-Replaced w new
- **11/28/06** Aft toilet stuffed up-Finally cleared, flushed with water & tank cleaner
- **11/28/06** Dingy davit, Stb side, wire conduit came off-Replaced with new tape
- **12/1/06** Aft toilet-Replaced duckbill valves w new, cleaned all, flushed vacuum tank
- **12/2/06** Windlass-Replace dished springs & seal w new

2007

- **1/4/07** Aft toilet-Replaced pump and 2 duck bill valves, confirmed outlet clear
- **1/5/07** Latch in fwd head small compartment-Replaced w new
- **1/6/07** US Flag-Installed little block to hoist
- **1/8/07** Aft toilet-Replaced the vacuum switch w new
- **1/11/07** Aft toilet-Adjusted vacuum switch for 1 minute pump cycle (finally?)
- **1/11/07** Mast furling-Added 6 barrel headed screws to keep snap ring in place
- **1/13/07** Aft toilet-Finally adjusted vacuum switch timing to 45 to 60 seconds
- **1/14/07** Outboard-Replaced in-line fuel filter w new
- **1/14/07** Water maker salinity sensor-Dumps a lot-Clean sensor-OK
- **1/20/07** Steering cables at quadrant-Added SS cable clamps (old are rusty)
- **1/23/07** Aft toilet-Leaking at bowl seal-Replaced with new seals
- **1/27/07** Galley china cabinet door latch broke-Replaced w new
- **1/28/07** Fresh water pump kept running-Tightened setscrew on drive shaft
- **1/28/07** Salt water in bilge-Water taken into lazarette, drain plugged
- **1/29/07** VHF cockpit handset not working-Took apart, dried in sun, now OK
- **1/29/07** VHF cockpit speaker not working-Replaced w new
- **1/29/07** Cockpit table screws loose-Replaced w larger screws
- **2/1/07** Generator cutting out at 22 amp load-No solution, should take 30 amps
- **2/2/07** Bimini torn-Margaret sewed and applied sail tape
- **2/2/07** Generator has voltage fluctuations w no load-Replaced voltage regulator
- **2/4/07** Generator has no power output-Replaced voltage regulator w new
- **2/4/07** Yankee furling line broke-Replaced w new
- **2/4/07** Lazarette lid teak corner broke-
- **2/4/07** Engine fuel line developed crack-Fuel in bilge-Temp fix, replaced w new
- **2/6/07** Fwd Cabin light fixtures rusted-Replaced w new
- **2/6/07** VHF cockpit handset not working-Took apart, dried in sun, now OK
- **2/9/07** Engine panel lights-Oil & Generator not working-Replaced w new, burnt out
- **2/19/07** Bilge pump stopped-Circuit breaker tripped, replaced impellor w new
- **2/20/07** Wire conduit on stb davit came off-Stuck on w double-sided tape
- **2/23/07** Dive mask lens not secure-Silicone in place, now OK
- **2/27/07** Bilge pump not working well-Removed cable clamps & grunge from pipe
- **2/27/07** Aft A/C not working-Replaced water pump w new & new fitting
- **3/2/07** Bimini-New bimini to replace worn one
- **3/2/07** Sea Gull water filter low output-Replaced w new cartridge
- **3/7/07** Dinghy seat strap broke-
- **3/10/07** Water maker cutting out-Do to aeration from pounding?- OK in harbor.
- **3/10/07** Windlass foot switches not working-Fixed open wire in chain locker
- **3/12/07** Generator has unstable voltage-Then failed
- **3/15/07** Inverter drops in voltage occasionally-
- **3/15/07** Outboard stopped under full power-Cleaned carb, thermostat OK, New fuel
- **3/16/07** Power winches noisy-Took apart, greased
- **4/6/07** Screen in fwd large hatch torn-Replaced w new screen
- **4/7/07** Log did not work-Cleaned bottom of boat, OK, but 0.7 knots low
- **4/11/07** Port Nav light not working-Replaced with new
- **4/12/07** Microwave trips A/C circuit breaker on defrost-Changed to 20-amp breaker
- **4/12/07** Eyeball light in fwd cabin broken-Replaced w new

- **4/13/07** Wood molding on utility room door came off-Re-glued
- **4/24/07** Log is reading low-Missing paddle, Replaced w New 5/15/07
- **4/26/07** Engine overheated at 1900 RPM-Cut revs and appears OK
- **4/26/07** Stb yankee sheet car rubber piece destroyed-
- **4/29/07** Door to stb cabin sticking-Pried up and added Vaseline
- **5/2/07** Hot water pressure relief valve overflowing-Hit pressure switch, OK
- **5/4/07** Outboard-Bought new Honda 15HP outboard
- **5/11/07** Generator-Replaced stator, added diode & eliminated pot- OK
- **5/11/07** Dinghy-Repaired strap for seat
- **5/11/07** Hot water pressure relief valve-Removed and cleaned
- **5/11/07** Fresh water pump pulley off- Replaced and tightened
- **5/15/07** Engine-Mech. checked heat exchanger, flushed fresh water, new coolant
- **5/15/07** Generator-Replace exhaust tube w new
- **5/20/07** Generator-RPM's drop when under light load (below 20 amps)
- **5/21/07** Bilge Pump-Impellor disintegrated-Replaced w new
- **5/30/07** Generator-Replaced field circuit breaker w new-OK Finally? OK
- **6/2/07** Dinghy punctured by anchor of another boat-Repaired by professional-OK
- **6/3/07** Hot water tank is leaking-
- **6/10/07** Engine RPM drooping-Switched to new Racor, Engine maint 224 hours-OK
- **6/10/07** GPS Screen has blank spots on lower row-Took apart, cleaned contacts-OK
- **7/5/07** Transmission not engaging in 1st gear-Rebuild, replace thrust washers-OK
- **7/15/07** Refrigeration not getting enough water-Opened cross-over seacock-OK
- **7/18/07** Large hatch shades-Replaced w new shades
- **7/19/07** Cushion at Nav station-Replaced button w new tie-down
- **7/20/07** Power cable had exposed wires-Cut off 1" of wire
- **7/26/07** Hot water pressure relief releasing water-Took apart pressure switch-OK

- **8/3/07** Aft toilet-Did not start, moved plunger-OK
- **8/8/07** Galley drawer latch broken-Replaced w new
- **8/8/07** Nav Computer crashed-Hard drive failed, replaced w new & backed up
- **8/9/07** Aft Toilet leaking at bowl-Replaced seals, ball, & water valve w new
- **8/16/07** Aft Toilet leaking below bowl-Tightened hose clap and plastic rings
- **8/20/07** Oven broiler not lighting-Replaced burner, moved spark, DNW
- **8/24/07** Galley cabinet latch broken-Replaced w new
- **8/24/07** Freezer handle broken-Replaced wire
- **9/7/07** GPS screen problem-Replace w new screen-OK
- **9/9/07** Driveline vibration at 1700 RPM-Putting into reverse corrected issue temp.
- (Heavy growth on propeller blades and prop shaft)

2008

- **3/1/08** Replace propeller, cutlass bearings, and repack stuffing box
- **3/15/08** Straighten prop shaft & replace C/V joints
- **5/20/08** Anchor chain marks gone-Repainted
- **5/21/08** Fwd holding tank seacock stuck-Freed with PV Blaster
- **5/21/08** Mast furler lip seal rusted-Replaced & new ATF
- **5/21/08** Water heater hose stiff-Replaced
- **5/21/08** Lifesling line bad-Replaced
- **5/23/08** Outboard-Annual service and recall completed
- **5/23/08** Stb cockpit drain seacock broke in closed position-DNF
- **5/25/08** Noise in drive train-Took apart & reinstalled- Works perfectly
- **5/25/08** Engine heat exchanger leaking water-Replaced
- **5/26/08** Generator had no cooling water-Flushed heat exchanger, replaced water pump, hoses, connectors, & anti-siphon
- **5/27/08** Dodger & Bimini-Replaced with new
- **5/27/08** Mainsail outhaul line too big-Replaced w new high strength line
- **5/28/08** Windlass will not come apart
- **5/30/08** Outboard cover scratched-Replaced with new

- **6/12/08** GPS not getting position-Replaced battery-OK
- **6/13/08** Fwd head cabinet latch broken-Replaced
- **6/13/08** Engine driven bilge pump not working-Ordered parts
- **6/17/08** VHF does not work on US weather stations-Don't know why-Now OK
- **7/3/08** Fresh water pump not pumping-Belt came off, Replaced & realigned pulley
- **7/4/08** Galley drain pump not pumping-Removed coffee grounds from pump-OK
- **7/7/08** Fresh Water pressure switch not shutting off-Disassembled and cleaned-OK
- **7/22/08** Windlass serviced w new dish springs & lip seal-OK
- **7/25/08** Salon curtains replaced w new
- **7/25/08** Cleaned A/C unit filters-Aft ones were blocked
- **7/27/08** Small port winch sticky-Took apart, cleaned & greased both small-OK
- **7/29/08** VHF Radio "breaking up"-Radio checked OK, antenna missing-New one
- **8/15/08** Replaced A/C screens w new aluminum screen (Fwd & saloon)
- **8/15/08** Oven burner not enough flame-Checked valve, cleaned jet-Did not last
- **8/18/08** Oven burner-Replaced orifice with new one-OK
- **8/19/08** Galley fan will not work-Replace w new fan
- **8/26/08** Fresh Water pressure switch not shutting off-Disassembled and cleaned-OK
- **9/3/08** Yankee furling line got jammed-Un-jammed
- **9/3/08** Water flowing into bilge from unknown hose-Water stopped when not healed
- **9/4/08** Fresh Water pressure switch not shutting off-Disassembled and cleaned-OK
- **9/13/08** Aft Head cabinet door latch broken-Replaced
- **9/17/08** Galley sink pump diaphragm broke-Replaced w new
- **9/7/08** Watermaker hose leaking-Removed elements
- **11/15/08** Lazarette Hatch-Repair corners w new teak
- **11/15/08** Water Heater leaking-Replaced with new water heater
- **11/15/08** Cockpit drain seacock (Starboard)-Replace w new seacock
- **11/15/08** Max Prop-Clean & polish
- **11/15/08** Bottom-Sand and paint w Dark Blue Micron
- **11/15/08** Topsides-Clean around waterline
- **12/10/08** Raw water seacock, Refrig-Replace w new seacock & removable screen
- **12/10/08** Engine Driven Bilge Pump-Repair w new parts- Would not shut off

2009

- **1/15/09** Check & Lube all other seacocks
- **6/16/09** Rope cutter on prop shaft not in proper slot-Fixed
- **6/18/09** Galley drain pump failed-Replaced w new pump
- **6/20/09** Bilge pump switch could not be set-Attached tube to bottom fitting & adjusted
- **6/23/09** Yankee furling line short and wrong size-Replaced w new, cover removed
- **6/21/09** Watermaker hose leaking-Replace w new
- **6/23/09** MaxSea Electronic Charting-Update to 12.6 and add AIS capability
- **6/23/09** AIS unit added
- **6/24/09** Engine Driven Bilge Pump-Send to Jabsco for rebuild
- **6/27/09** Bilge pump impellor burned up-Replaced impellor
- **6/28/09** Bilge pump not working-Tightened new hose clamp at pump-Fixed
- **6/30/09** Spreader light, Port, not working-Replaced with new
- **7/1/09** Fresh water pump leaking-Replaced w new
- **7/3/09** LVR Blew up-Ordered new voltage regulator circuit board
- **7/10/09** Engine driven bilge pump-Replaced, works fine
- **7/13/09** LVR-Replaced voltage regulator circuit board- Works perfect
- **7/21/09** Adjusted switches on bilge pump & high water alarm-Tests OK
- **7/25/09** LVR failed under no load-
- **7/26/09** LVR would not start-Found to be cable problem
- **7/27/09** Black power cord-Something is wrong-Replaced w new white cord
- **7/27/09** 30 to 50 Adapter Cord-Not working with standard power cable-Rewired
- **7/28/09** Yellow power cord extension, female end burnt-Replaced w new plug

- **7/29/09** Seagull Filter running slow-Replaced w new filter
- **8/1/09** Salon A/C-Put insulation around compressor to reduce sound-OK
- **8/11/09** Water heater pressure relief valve overflowing-Took apart pressure switch-OK
- **8/11/09** Fwd holding tank overflowed into compartment-Pumped out and cleaned up
- **8/12/09** Refrigeration did not come on went temp climbed-Cleaned off ice-OK
- **8/18/09** Bilge pump switch-Replaced w new design
- **8/20/09** Aft A/C failed, no air-Left off and it returned to normal
- **8/26/09** Water heater pressure relief valve overflowing-Took apart pressure switch-OK
- **8/26/09** Rattle sound in aft cabin under bed, possibly shaft noise-
- **9/3/09** Prop shaft zinc-Replaced by diver
- **9/10/09** Gebo port fwd, port side knob broke off-Replaced w new
- **9/24/09** Fresh water pump pressure switch-Replace w new, and new design
- **9/25/09** Gebo port light, salon port, aft latch-Replaced w new (drilled pin)
- **9/28/09** Bilge pump not pumping-Replaced impellor w new
- **9/29/09** A/C raw water hose to pump-Replaced w new and added bleed valve
- **10/1/09** Rattle related to prop shaft RPM is present-
- **10/15/09** Galley sink pump not working-Replaced diaphragm
- **10/21/09** Prop shaft rattle fixed-Replaced plastic bearings w new on rope cutter-fixed
- **10/23/09** Heater stopped w "flame out" error message-Reset by turning off and on
- **10/29/09** Heater-Bled air from unit with bleed valve
- **11/4/09** Generator would not run; no water from exhaust-Replaced impellor w new
- **11/4/09** Autopilot makes loud noises-Replaced stb ram w new, connected clutch wires
- **11/14/09** GPS failed by cycling continuously-Took apart & reassembled- working OK

2010

- **5/22/10** Stove, poor flame distribution-Replaced 2 air baskets
- **5/22/10** Forward toilet blocked-Worked pump and finally it cleared

- **5/22/10** Filtered water running slow-Replaced Sea Gull filter
- **5/25/10** Outboard not starting-Had carburetor removed and cleaned, new gas
- **5/29/10** Bimini side curtain strap, snap broke-Replaced
- **5/29/10** VHF Handset wires exposed-Fixed by shortening cable
- **5/29/10** US Flag came down-Fixed cord
- **6/3/10** Green Nav. Light did not work-Sanded corrosion off lamp and contacts
- **6/4/10** Fwd shower hose, leaking and low pressure-Added washer, all improved
- **6/5/10** Mast Boot Tape, warn and cracked-Replaced with new tape & silicone
- **7/30/10** Nav system-No wind readings-Replaced wind instrument w ST60
- **7/30/10** No positions shown on chart-Solved by using AIS position data
- **7/30/10** Nav system not getting GPS data-Reconnected wires
- **7/30/10** Water Computer reading low-Recalibrated
- **7/30/10** Magnetronic DCC 4000 has no readout-Replaced w new unit
- **8/3/10** Tri-color & anchor light lens broken-Replaced w new
- **8/3/10** Anchor LED light bulb broken-Replaced with normal 12v bulb
- **8/4/10** AIS data not shown on MaxSea-Added NEMA data Bridge-Fixed
- **8/7/10** Solar Panel Controller clicks, analyze light flashing-Replace w new
- **8/8/10** VHF Radio has no speaker volume-Replaced w new Icom radio
- **8/12/10** Fwd. Head pump leaking-Did total rebuild of all valves
- **8/14/10** Microwave failed-Replaced w new, larger Kenmore unit
- **8/16/10** Ceiling light in fwd head rusted-Replaced w newer unit
- **8/16/10** Buttons popped of the seat cushions-
- **10/7/10** Bilge pump impellor lost all vanes-Replaced impellor
- **10/7/10** High water alarm sounder failed-Replaced with new
- **10/30/10** Heater fan in salon not working-Replaced w new
- **11/1/10** Bilge pump not actuating-Switch case not fully closed-Fixed

- **11/1/10** High water alarm activating too soon-Raised sensor tube-Fixed
- **11/2/10** Generator overheats and stops-Replaced fresh water pump-Fixed
- **11/2/10** Engine stopped w electrical problem-Wires shorted-Replaced connector-OK
- **11/12/10** Dinghy davit spring-Stb side broke-Replaced w new
- **11/13/10** Vinyl pealing away in starboard cabin-Re-glued
- **11/15/10** Horseshoe buoy bracket cracked-Replaced w new

2011

- **1/29/11** Generator engine stopped-Tried again and it works fine
- **2/13/11** Aft thermostat for heater failed-Replaced w new
- **2/22/11** Fwd. toilet hard to pump, tank full & not draining or pumping out
- **3/3/11** Fwd. holding tank cleaned of all deposits
- **3/4/11** Fwd toilet hose to holding tank replaced
- **5/11/11** Magnetronic digital readout lost bars-Back to normal OK
- **5/10/11** Fwd toilet treated with vinegar to remove calcium
- **5/20/11** Fwd toilet pellet feeder cracked-Temp fix of epoxy-Replaced with new
- **5/28/11** Aft hatch leaked-Tightened stb side latch-Removed old & put on new
- **5/29/11** Yankee port sheet block rubber snubber broke-
- **6/11/11** Aft cabin port reading light out-Replaced w new bulb

Exhibit 13 SAIL BOAT DATA - 1995

Boat	LOA	LWL	Beam	Draft	Displace (pounds)	Sail Area (sq. feet)	Auxiliary H.P.	Ballast (pounds)	Rig	Notes	Price (Base)
Oyster 485 cc	48' 6"	37' 6"	14' 0"	7'0"or 6'0"	37,550	1,224	82 Perkins	13,000	Cutter	English	$627,000
Oyster 55 cc	55' 3"	42' 11"	15' 9"	5'8" or 6'8"	50,000	1,597	80 Perkins	13,360	Cutter	English	$789,500
Hylas 49 cc	48' 10"	37' 9"	14' 3"	6'	32,000	1,051	62 Yanmar		Cutter	Taiwan- Queen Long	$339,000
Hylas 51 cc	50' 8"	40' 0"	15' 5"	6' 4"	37,480	1,385	78 Yanmar	15,430	Cutter	Taiwan- Queen Long	$389,000
Taswell 49 cc	48' 10"	34' 9"	15' 0"	6'9"or 5'10"	32,000	1,064	75 Yanmar		Cutter	Taiwan- Ta Shing	$440,000
Taswell 56 cc	55' 10"	46' 9"	16' 6"	6' 0"	48,500	1,389	110 Yanmar	17,750	Cutter	Taiwan- Ta Shing	$625,000

REJECTED

Boat	LOA	LWL	Beam	Draft	Displace (pounds)	Sail Area (sq. feet)	Auxiliary H.P.	Ballast (pounds)	Rig	Notes	Price (Base)
Alden 50cc	50' 4"	37' 1"	13' 6"	5'4"/10'1"	35,000	1,074			Sloop	Too Traditional- Too expensive	
Alden 52cc	52' 7"	41' 8"	14' 4"	5' 6" Board	42,500	1,170			Cutter	Too Traditional- Too expensive	
Baltic 47	47.74'	39'6"	14.4'	8.69'	24,692	1,168	62 Yanmar	10141	Sloop	Finnish- Poor Saloon- Expensive	$574,000
Baltic 52	52' 6"	43' 2"	15' 5"	9' 2"	32,000	1,310	88 Yanmar	13,228	Sloop	Finnish- Too Expensive	$828,000
Bavaria 47 Holiday	47' 0"	40' 5"	15" 0"	7' 11"	27,500	1,398	59 Volvo	12,320	Sloop	German, Not full width saloon	$260,000
Beneteau Oceanis 44cc	44' 7"	36' 9"	14' 0"	5' 9" wing	20,944	832		6,835	Sloop	Only 2 cabins, Helm forward	$240,000
Beneteau 50	49' 10"	44' 2"	14' 9"	5' 11"	28,000		80 ?	8,600	Sloop	New-Not built, Not full width saloon	$350,000
Beneteau 510	50' 3"	44' 6"	15' 7"	6' 0"	30,860	1,120		10,800	Sloop	French, no data, aft cockpit	$356,000
C&C 51 XL	51' 9"	43' 11"	15' 7"	10'4" or ?	33,900	1,343	85 Yanmar	15,800	Sloop	Canadian, cored hull, aft cockpit	
Cabo Rico Cambria 46	46' 0"	37' 2"	13' 5"	8'6"or 5'11"	29,400	943	62 Yanmar	12,300	Cutter	Costa Rica, Too small	$469,000
Cabo Rico Cambria 52	52' 6"	45' 9"	15' 2"	9'6" to 6'	28,000	1,434	62 Yanmar	10,500	Sloop	Costa Rica, Too expensive	$765,000
Caliber 47 LRC	52' 11"	39' 6"	13' 2"	5' 2"	32,000	1,014	75 Yanmar	13,000	Cutter	Florida, Only 2 cabins	$258,000
Cap Cod Mercer 44	44' 0"	30' 0"	11' 9"	4'3'/9'0"	27,000	885		8,600	Sloop	Too small	
Catalina 50	50' 5"	44' 3"	14' 9"	6'7"or 5'7"	36,000	1,108	75 Yanmar	13,250	Sloop	USA, no data, aft cockpit	$300,000
Crealock 44	44' 1"	33' 6"	12' 8"	6'3"or 5'3"	27,500	971	50 Yanmar	11,000	Cutter	Too small, traditional	$377,200
Dehler 43 cws	43.63'	34.78'	12.96'	6.56'	20,700			9,000	Sloop	Do not like layout, too small	
Endeavour 52 cc	52' 4"	42' 3"	15' 0"	5' 6" wing	35,000	1110	88 Yanmar	14,500	Cutter	US, But not built boats in 4 years	$350,000
Explorer 4850	48' 9"	42' 0"	14' 4"	5' 9"	34,000	1,083	88 Yanmar	13,600	Sloop	New- Not yet built	$389,000
Finngulf 44	43' 8"	36' 9"	12' 9"	7'3"or 5'11"	22,700	1,046	Volvo	9,000	Sloop	Too small	$295,000
Freedom 45cc	44' 6"	34' 5"	13' 6"	6'6"or 4'11"	27,500	873	75 Yanmar	9,500	Sloop	Feels too small	$350,000
Gozzard 44	50' 0"	37' 3"	13' 8"	5' 6"	29,850	1,152	82 Westerbe	11,800	Cutter	Wrong style	
Hallberg-Rassy 46	48' 3"	38' 0"	14' 3"	6' 2"	35,300	1,075	69 Volvo	14,100	Sloop	Swedish, Too small	
Hallberg-Rassy 53cc	54' 0"	43' 8"	15' 3"	7' 6"	50,700	1,460	145 Volvo	19,900	Cutter	Swedish, Too "cave like"	$515,000
Hans Christian 52	51' 6"	41' 2"	14' 0"	5' 11"	31,350	1,296	77 Yanmar		Cutter	Too Traditional	
Hinckley 51	51' 3"	37' 6"	14' 0"	9'4"	40,000	1,128		15,000	Cutter	Too Traditional- Too expensive	$780,000
Hoek 55	55' 1"		14' 11"	7' 10"	55,000	1,894	110 Yanmar		Cutter	Aluminum- Duch	
Hunter Legend 42cc	42' 6"	38' 0"	14' 0"	4' 11"	24,000	812	62 Yanmar	7,600	Sloop	Too small	$215,000
Hunter 430	42' 6"	38' 0"	14' 0"	4' 11"	23,800	839	50 Yanmar	7,600	Sloop	Too small	$184,500
Island Packet 44	44' 6"	37' 0"	13' 2"	4' 10"	27,900	1,082	62 Yanmar	12,500	Cutter	Too small	$260,000
J/160	52' 7"	46' 5"	14' 5"	8'8"or 6'9"	26,000	1,376	88 ?	11,000	Sloop	Too racing	
Jeanneau 47cc	47' 3"	38' 5"	14' 7"	6' 11"	27,560	1210	75 ?		Sloop	French, production & small	$329,000
Jeanneau 51	50' 5"	42' 4"	15' 11"	6' 7"	30,800	1342		9,900	Sloop	Not full width saloon	
Kanter 51 Pilot	51' 1"	41' 7"	14' 3"	7'0"or 6'6"	42,800	1,231	85 Perkins	20,000	Cutter	Aluminum, Canadian, seems small	$423,000
Kirie Feeling 446	45' 3"	35' 3"	14' 6"	6'7"or 5'3"	19,841	1,018		6,000	Sloop	French, Too small	
Kirie Feeling 486	47' 6"	35' 3"	14' 6"	6'7"or 5'3"	22,220	961	62 Yanmar	6,000	Sloop	French, Not full width saloon	$240,000
Kirie Feeling 546	55' 5"	43' 0"	17' 1"	6' 7"	39,683	1,591		12,800	Sloop	French, need data	
Lager 53										Custom Built, US design	$550,000
Little Harbor 46	45' 8"	36' 6"	13' 8"	5' 4"	37,500	968	69 Westerbe	13,800	Sloop	Too Traditional- Too Expensive	$900,000
Little Harbor 54	53' 11"	42' 2"	15' 1"	5' 8" Board	51,450	1278	100 Westerb	18,000	Cutter	Too Traditional- Too expensive	$1,250,000
Moody 44cc	43' 0"	36' 0"	13' 8"	6'6"or 4'11"	23,000	994	50 Penta	8,900	Sloop	English, Too small	$300,000
Morgan 45cc	45' 3"	37' 10"	13' 6"	6'6"or 5'7"	25,450	816	50 Yanmar	9,200	Sloop	Only 2 cabins	$213,000
Morris 44	44' 6"	35' 6"	13' 0"	5' 6"	23,500	879		8,630	Sloop	Too small	
Oyster 48	48' 0"	41' 8"	14' 4"	6' 3"	32,000	1,337		11,000	Sloop	English, Aft cockpit	
Oyster 49 pilot	48' 9"	41' 0"	14' 0"	7'0" or 5'9"	42,000	1,238	82 Perkins		Sloop	English, didn't like	$646,000
Passport 44cc	45' 6"	37' 4"	14' 2"	6'6"or 5'4"	25,611	924		10,200	Sloop	Taiwan/USA	$390,000
Passport 47 cc	47' 0"	37' 4"	14' 2"	6'6"or 5'4"	25,611	924		10,200	Sloop	Taiwan/USA, Only 2 cabins	$400,000
Sabre 425	42' 5"	34' 8"	12' 10"	6'10"or 5'0"	19,200	766	46 Westerbe	8,200	Sloop	Too Small	$227,000
Swan 46	47.12'	37.89'	14.47'	8.9'	31,300		53 Perkins	11,400		Finnish- Too Expenxsive	$1,100,000
Ta Chiao CT-48	48' 0"	37' 6"	14' 6"	6' 4"	40,000	954	85 Perkins	12,800	Cutter	Taiwan- "Junk" type	$348,000
Ta Chiao CT-56	55' 6"	44' 6"	15' 6"	6' 5"	61,500	1,563	135 Ford	19,750	Ketch	Taiwan- "Junk" Not two handed	$529,000
Tartan 4600	46' 2"	39' 7"	14' 4"	8'11"or 5'6"	24,000	1,014	62 ?	8,500	Sloop	Too small	$370,000
Ta Shing 43	42' 10"	35' 4"	13' 8"	6'3"or 5'3"	23,500	859		9,600	Cutter	Taiwan	
Ta-Yang Tayana 48cc	47' 0"	40' 3"	14' 6"	6'0"or 5' 3"	35,000	1,378	62 Yanmar	11,675	Cutter	Taiwan, Not strong enough	$293,500
Ta-Yang Tayana 52cc	52' 6"	42' 1"	15' 0"	6'6"or 5'8"	38,570	1,156	88 Yanmar	14,800	Cutter	Taiwan, Not strong enough	$355,000
Ta-Yang Tayana 55	55' 0"	45' 11"	16' 1"	5' 3" Board	48,400	1,345	140 Yanmar	17,600	Cutter	Taiwan, too large	$417,000
Valiant 42	42' 0"	34' 6"	12' 9"	6'0"or 5'6"	24,600	862		9,500	Cutter	Double ender, Too small	$219,000
Valiant 50	50' 0"	40 3"	13' 10"	6'3"or 5'6"	35,500	1,036	63 Westerbe	11,000	Cutter	Double ender, don't like	$326,000
X-442	44' 4"	36' 9"	13' 7"	7' 6"	21,300	1,033	59 Volvo	9,480	Sloop	Denmark, too small	
X-512	51.1'	41.5'	14.8'	9.1'	30,112	1,562		13,230	Sloop	Denmark, Narrow salon- Close	$500,000

Exhibit 14 COUNTRY DATA 2006/7

3/14/2006

Country	Clearance	immigration	Customs	Permits/Taxes	Other
Mexico	Crew lists in Span-6 In- Cabo San Lucas Out- Huatulco? In- Cozumal Out- Isla Mujeres	Tourist Card for all in advance No Visa	Temp. Import Permit $10 6 months Port Tax	Health Permit Req'd Fishing Lic. Req'd Can get in advance Tonnage Fee Radio License?	Malaria Carry passport & Tourist Card
El Salvador	In/Out- Barillas Marina	Tourist Card No Visa	No Fruit	Entrance & Exit Tax of 6 Colones	Insurance issue Malaria Dengue Fever
Costa Rica	In- Playa de Coco Out- Golfito Coco	No Visa	Temp. Import Permit 3 months	Fishing Lic. Req'd Maybe?	Malaria Dengue Fever
Panama	Use Agent In- Balboa YC Out- Porvenir	Tourist Cards for US No Visa	3 months	Cruising Permit Specify San Blas	Yellow fever Req'd
Columbia	Must Use Agrent In/Out- Providencia	No Visa		Cruising Permit? Obtain in Colon	Insurance Issue Travel Warning Yellow Fever Malaria
Guatemala	Rio Dulce Bar 2.2m Check Tide-VHF 68	Tourist Card No Visa	Need sticker 3 months		Insurance Issue Malaria
Belize	Crew Lists-4 Stores List-4 In- Punta Gorda Out- San Pedro	No Visa	All fresh produce Taken 6 months	Navigation charge	Avoid Belize City Use Cucumber Beach Marina Malaria Typhoid Hepatitis A Polio

Need Agent for Panama Canal

Exhibit 15 *ESCAPADE* SPARES LIST

1/8/2003

ENGINE (PERKINS)

- All periodic items for projected usage
  Oil filter, fuel filter, Racor filter, zincs, oil, raw water impeller, antifreeze
- Perkins spares kit
- Belts
- Liquid gasket
- Injectors
- Starter motor
- Heat exchanger
- Fuel lift pump
- Raw water pump
- Fresh water pump

GENERATOR (ONAN)

- All periodic items for projected usage
  Oil filter, Racor filter, oil, raw water impeller, brushes
- Alternator
- Belts
- Raw water pumps
- Fuel injection pump
- Heat exchanger

STEERING (RAYMARINE 7000)

- Course computer
- Steering ram
- Logic board for control head
- Steering cables

DECK AND ABOVE

- Lazarette lift handles
- Dinghy davit springs
- Nav light bulbs
- Compass light bulbs
- Engine cluster light bulbs
- Spinnaker halyard & block
- Yankee halyard
- Lifeline pelican hooks
- Tricolor light assembly
- Inflatable fenders
- Spare dock lines
- Spare anchor (Fortress) and rode

- Fender covers
- Mast paint
- Mast furling gearbox seal
- Mast furling motor
- Yankee sheet car rubber up stands
- Main sheet traveler
- Main sheet outhaul torlon balls (and feeder)
- Mast boot self-amalgaming tape
- Dorade scoops
- Spare line for a variety of uses
- Gelcoat repair kit
- Sail repair kit & stick-on sail patch tape
- Chafe tape
- US Flag
- Sicaflex for deck repair & special chisel
- Fairleads
- Cockpit stereo speakers
- Deck locker latches
- Battens (vertical)
- Yankee furling line blocks (attach to stanchions)
- Lifeline wire
- Staysail sheet turning block
- Leather for covering lifeline ends etc.
- Windlass" dish springs"
- Air horn canisters
- Bosuns chair
- Chafe guards
- Wire cutter
- Webbing, nylon 1"
- Inflatable PFD cartridges & bobbins
- "O" rings for fuel & water deck caps
- Loudhailer speaker
- Mast slot bracket

WINCHES

- Winch tools
- Parts kits
- Grease, lubricant
- Winch handle levers

INSTRUMENTS, RADIOS AND ELECTRONIC NAVIGATION

- Spare computer with electronic charts loaded
- Masthead wind instrument
- Masthead Windex
- GPS repeater
- Multi instrument
- Spare VHF radio (Shipmate) handset
- VHF emergency antenna
- Dynaplates
- Fax paper

GPS

- Antenna
- Cable
- Viewing screen
- Battery, lithium

INMARSAT-C

- Antenna

ELECTRICAL

- Circuit switch (Red)
- Extra wire, extra lugs
- Soldering iron, solder
- Halogen light fixtures
- All bulbs
- All fuses
- Large alternator (for house battery charging)
- Variety of shore connectors
- Wire for shore power extension
- Degausser for TV
- VHS player cleaner assembly
- Hydrometer for batteries
- Multimeter, digital

COOKER AND OVEN (FORCE 10)

- Jets & controls for both propane and butane
- Spares kit from Force 10
- Butane regulator (propane in use)

INSIDE

- Prop for opening forward windows
- Knobs & threaded shafts for Gebo ports
- Plunger assemblies for Oyster latches
- Bilge pump
- High water bilge alarm assembly
- Electric submersible bilge pump with plastic outlet hose reaching overboard
- Hatch screen assembly
- Smoke alarm
- Fan (Hella)

FUEL SYSTEM

- Fuel tank observation ports and gaskets
- Racor filter for "fuel polishing"
- Electric fuel pump (24 VDC) and hoses
- Baja filter
- Diesel additive

BOW THRUSTER

- Zincs, oil, bolts
- Shaft connection assembly
- Control switch assembly
- 3-point puller tool

REFRIGERATION AND AIR CONDITIONING

- Cooling pumps, A/C
- Refrigerant, if I could legally obtain it
- Digital temperature gauges

WATER MAKER

- Periodic maintenance
  Filter cartridges, storage solution powder, high pressure pump oil
- High pressure pump valve kit

WATER SYSTEM

- Pump complete
- Pump inlet/outlet connectors
- Microswiches for fresh water pump pressure regulator
- Seagull filters
- Shower control valve
- Water tank observation ports and seals
- Tubing for tank tender
- Water heater pressure relief valve

GRAY WATER SYSTEM
- Pumps
- Diaphragms

TOILETS
- Manual (Jabsco)
    Complete assembly
    Rebuild kit
- Vacuflush
    Vacuum pump complete
    Valves, duck bill
    Seals
    Ball assembly
    Holding tank gauge

OUTBOARD
- Pull rope
- Spark plugs
- Propeller
- Fresh water adapter

Exhibit 16 *ESCAPADE* SAFETY & NAVIGATION EQUIPMENT

1/14/2011

BASIC HULL AND DECK CONSTRUCTION

- Medium Displacement (50,000 pounds)
- Fiberglass construction with no coring in the hull (solid FRP), Lloyd's approved design
- Kevlar reinforcement below waterline from bow to keel
- Bulkheads and stringers fiber glassed to hull, heavily reinforced
- All fiberglass and Kevlar hand laid matting
- Internal hull flange with bolted hull-to-deck joint
- Fuel and water tanks are integral FRP which form a "double bottom", 200 gal each
- No screws or fasteners through a cored area of the deck
- Isophthalic resin in gel coat
- Bow chain locker is a self-contained watertight compartment, self-draining
- Forward cabin is constructed to be watertight with a sealed door
- Aft lazerette is isolated from the aft cabin
- The keel is external lead, 14,000 pounds
- The rudder has a full skeg with bronze bottom shoe
- The positive stability range is up to 126°
- Small center cockpit with large drains and no cockpit hatches
- Large and easy access to the engine
- Bow thruster, 10HP Sleipner tunnel type
- Stern entry with platform and boarding ladder
- Perkins Range 4M.90 diesel engine, 82 HP

RIGGING

- Capable of complete sailing from the cockpit
- Cutter rig with roller furling on both yankee and staysail
- Three forestays-- forestay, cutter stay, and baby stay
- Two backstays-- permanent backstay and running backstays for storm operation
- Continuous rigging
- Electric in-mast furling for the main sail
- Mast stepped on keel
- Lightning protection- "No-strike" dissipater; the mast and stays are grounded to the keel
- Rigid boom vang
- Preventer to prevent accidental jibes
- Powered yankee and main sheet winches
- Electric anchor windlass with controls in cockpit
- Granny bars at mast

OTHER EQUIPMENT

- Primary anchor is 75# CQR with 300' of 7/16" chain
- Two other anchors carried- 44# Bruce and 33# Fortress (500' and 300' rodes)
- Companionway washboards that can be fastened in place
- Safety harness attachments in cockpit (4) and Safety jack lines from bow to stern

- Automatic fire extinguisher in engine compartment
- Seafresh Water Maker, 25 gallons per hour
- Rope-cutter on prop shaft, Ambassador AM 15 "stripper"
- Loudhailer and foghorn, Raytheon 430
- Guardrail- double SS wires, 28" high
- Red interior lighting for night sailing
- Inflatable Avon dingy, 10', mounted on dinghy davits at stern (15 HP Honda outboard)
- Forward Facing Sonar

REDUNDANT SYSTEMS
- Five bilge pumps- 2 electric, 2 manual, and emergency engine driven, Jabsco 3,000 gal/hr
- Three sets of batteries-- engine, house, and generator
- Battery charging from engine alternator, generator, or shore power
- Manual foot pump for fresh water in addition to the electric pump
- Two see-thru fuel filters with change over valve on engine
- Two see-thru engine cooling water strainers with cross over emergency valve
- Three VHF radios (one integrated, and two handheld- ICOM IC-M1)
- Three GPS units (one integrated, one handheld, and MaxSea)
- Four hand fire extinguishers

NAVIGATION & COMMUNICATION EQUIPMENT
- Icom IC-M504 VHF Radio with DSC and GMDSS SOS capability
- Phillips AP Mark 9 GPS
- Raytheon R40XX Radar, with antenna mounted on Questus leveling mount
- Furuno 207N Weather Fax with Navtex
- Icom IC-M710-05 SSB Radio
- Autohelm ST-50/ST-80 integrated instrument system
- Autohelm ST 7000 Autopilot
- Computer (IBM laptop) with electronic charting program, MaxSea Yacht
- Inmarsat-C/GPS System- Worldwide E-mail & safety-at-sea system
- Iridium satellite telephone and GSM cellular telephone with antenna on mast
- Sextant- Celestaire IIB

SAFETY GEAR
- Safety harnesses with inflatable vests and strobe/flash lights, Crewsaver- 6
- Life vests, Class I- 4
- Personal EPIRB's (3) and receiver
- Two low light binoculars- Steiner Commander III with compass
- Night scope- ITT generation 3
- Digital Barometer- (plus standard barometer)
- Scuba gear, including dry suit, for checking the hull
- Horseshoe Buoy, with strobe light
- Man overboard module, MOM-8
- Life sling, with strobe light and hoisting tackle
- Radar reflector on mast, Firdell Blipper #210-7
- Emergency distress radio-- EPIRB 406 MH, ARC Category II, model 2758

- Emergency distress radio-- EPIRB Class B, 125.5 MH
- Givens 6 person Deluxe Life Raft with dual stabilization chambers and double floor
- Medical kit, Coastal Cruising Pak, CCP-1; inflatable splints
- International Medical Guide for Ships- WHO Geneva
- Engine spares and tools including heavy duty wire cutter (up to 5/8")
- Cooking gas remote shutoff and "sniffer" alarms
- High bilge water alarm
- Loss of engine cooling water alarm
- Bosuns chair
- Sea anchor, Para-Tech 24'; and Drogue, Delta 114"
- Searchlight, handheld
- Air Horn, hand held and Brass Bell
- SOLAS flares, parachute and meteor
- Smoke signals, dye markers, and signaling mirror
- Hull repair kit, sail repair kit, wood thru hull plugs
- Emergency tiller
- Emergency VHF antenna
- Abandon Ship Bag

Exhibit 17 *ESCAPADE* MAJOR PORTS

6/19/2011

ENGLAND

London	7/12/96	51.30N	0.04W
Ipswich	6/19/96	51.57N	1.18E
Falmouth	6/22/96	50.10N	5.05W
Dartmouth	6/25/96	50.22N	3.35W
Cowes	7/3/96	50.46N	1.18W
Portsmouth	7/5/96	50.48N	1.07W
Ramsgate	7/9/96	51.20N	1.25E

FRANCE

Cherbourg	7/20/96	49.38N	1.37W
St. Malo	7/27/96	48.39N	2.02W
Brest	8/4/96	48.24N	4.26W
La Rochelle	8/17/96	46.09N	1.10W
Nice	7/21/98	43.42N	7.17E
St. Tropez	7/24/98 & 6/12/03	43.17N	6.38E
Marseille	8/1/98 & 6/2/03	43.18N	5.22E
Bonifacio, Corse	6/26/98 & 8/7/03	41.23N	9.10E

SPAIN

San Sebastian	8/26/96	43.19N	2.00W
La Coruna	9/4/96	43.22N	8.23W
Cadiz	9/28/96	36.33N	6.17W
Barcelona	8/9/98 & 5/24/03	41.23N	2.12E
Valencia	10/8/98	39.26N	0.20W
Marbella	10/24/98	36.29N	4.57W
Palma de Mallorca	8/13/98 & 10/24/02	39.34N	2.38E
Las Palmas, G. Canary	11/9/98	28.08N	15.26W
Mahon, Menorca	10/18/02	39.53N	4.16E

PORTUGAL

Lisbon	9/19/96	38.42N	9.12W
Leixoes	9/13/96	41.11N	8.42W
Lagos	9/25/96	37.06N	8.40W

MALTA	5/27/97 & 8/6/02	35.54N	14.30E
GIBRALTAR	10/1/96 & 10/27/98	36.09N	5.21W
JERSEY	7/22/96	49.11N	2.07W
GUERNSEY	6/20/96	49.28N	2.32W

GREECE

Athens	6/7/97 & 6/17/97	37.56N	23.39E
Mykonos	6/11/97	37.27N	25.20E
Hyrda	7/6/97	37.21N	23.28E
Rhodes	7/17/97 & 6/11/02	36.27N	28.14E
Simi	7/20/97 & 6/15/02	36.37N	27.50E
Patmos	7/25/97	37.19N	26.33E
Crete	5/24/98	35.11N	25.43E
Santorini	6/18/02	36.25N	25.26E
Corfu	6/28/02 & 9/22/03	39.39N	19.51E

TURKEY

Kusadasi	7/30/97 & 9/19/97	37.52N	27.16E
Canakkle	9/14/97	40.09N	26.24E
Bodrum	9/24/97	37.02N	27.26E
Marmaris	9/28; 10/14/97 & 6/9/02	36.51N	28.17E
Antalya	10/5/97 & 4/8/02	36.53N	30.42E

ITALY

Salerno	6/1/98	40.40N	14.45E
Capri	6/4/98	40.33N	14.14E
Elba	6/17/98	42.49N	10.20E
Porto Chervo, Sardinia	6/29/98 & 8/9/03	41.08N	9.32E
Portofino	7/27/03	44.18N	9.13E
San Remo	7/15/98 & 7/24/03	43.49N	7.47E
Trieste	7/15/02	45.39N	13.46E
Venice	7/19/02	45.26N	12.21E
Siracusa, Sicily	8/4/02	37.04N	15.17E
Palermo, Sicily	8/24/03	38.09N	13.22E

MONACO- MONTE CARLO

	7/19/98 & 7/19/03	43.44N	7.25E

MEXICO

Cancun, Isla Mujeres	5/3/99 & 4/19/07	21.16N	86.45W
Cabo San Lucas	11/3/06	22.53N	109.54W
Puerto Vallarta	12/6/06	20.40N	105.15W
Acapulco	1/15/07	16.50N	99.54W

USA

San Juan, PR	3/9/99	18.28N	66.06W
Key West, FL	5/9/99 & 4/26/07	24.34N	81.48W
Miami, FL	5/16/99	25.47N	80.11W
Ft. Lauderdale, FL	5/17/99, 5/26/04, 5/2/07	26.07N	80.07W
St. Augustine, FL**	6/1/99, 5/20/07, 11/9/09	29.54N	81.18W
Savannah, GA	6/9/99 & 11/6/99	32.02N	81.03W
Charleston, SC**	6/27/99, 5/26/07, 11/6/09	32.47N	79.57W
Norfolk, VA	7/10/99, 10/30/09	36.51N	76.18W
Annapolis, MD**	7/22+10/18/99, 6/11/07	38.59N	76.29W
Baltimore, MD**	7/26+10/17/99, 6/13/07	39.17N	76.36W
Atlantic City, NJ	8/5/99, 7/8/07, 8/16/09	39.23N	74.26W
New York, NY	8/11/99, 7/11/07, 8/7/09	40.45N	74.01W
Greenwich, CT	8/16/99, 6/26/08, 8/2/09	41.01N	73.37W

USA (continued)

Newport, RI**	9/14 &10/12/99, 8/3/07	41.29N	71.19W
Nantucket, MA	9/25/99	41.17N	70.06W
Boston, MA	10/2/99,8/13+9/6/07,7/19/08	42.22N	71.04W
Seattle, WA	9/6/04, 9/9/04 & 8/23/06	47.37N	122.21W
Ketchikan, AK	5/27/06	55.21N	131.41W
Juneau, AK	6/13/06	58.18N	134.25W
San Francisco, CA	9/7/06 & 10/4/06	37.47N	122.23W
San Diego, CA	10/25/06	32.43N	117.14W
Portsmouth, NH	8/17 & 9/4/07, 8/1 & 9/8/08	43.04N	70.44W
Portland, ME	8/21 & 9/3/07, 8/6 & 9/6/08	43.39N	70.15W
Bar Harbor, ME	8/27/07, 8/18/08, 9/3/08	44.23N	68.12W

ST. LUCIA

	12/9/98	14.05N	60.57W

GUADELOUPE

	2/1/99	16.13N	61.32W

ANTIGUA

	2/5/99	17.01N	61.46W

BVI'S- TORTOLA

	2/23/99	18.25N	64.37W

DOMINICAN REPUBLIC

	4/2/99	18.27N	69.38W

JAMAICA, MONTERO BAY

	4/9/99	18.28N	77.57W

GRAN CAYMAN

	4/15/99	19.18N	81.23W

PANAMA

Colon	2/17/00 & 2/17/07	9.21N	79.54W
Balboa	2/22/00 & 2/12/07	8.56N	79.33W
Bocas del Toro	3/4/07	9.20N	82.15W

ECUADOR

Salinas	3/3/00	2.12S	80.58W
Santa Cruz, Galapagos	3/21/00	0.45S	90.18W

FRENCH POLYNESIA

Hiva-Oa	4/16/00	9.48S	139.02W
Nuka-Hiva	4/22/00	8.55S	140.06W
Rangiroa	5/1/00/ & 6/7/00	14.58S	147.38W
Tahiti	5/4/00	17.32S	149.34W
Bora-Bora	7/10/00	16.29S	151.46W

PACIFIC ISLANDS

Rarotonga, Cook Is.	7/16/00	21.12S	159.47W
Niue	7/22/00	19.03S	169.55W
Vava'u, Tonga	7/26/00	18.39S	173.59W
Suva, Fiji	8/25/00	18.07S	178.25E
Musket Cove, Fiji	9/1/00	17.46S	177.12E

NEW ZEALAND

Opua	10/23/00	35.19S	174.07E
Auckland	2/14/01	36.51S	174.46E
Wellington	3/5/01	41.17S	174.47E
Nelson	3/12/01	41.64S	173.17E

AUSTRALIA

Sydney, NSW	3/29/01	33.52S	151.12E
Southport, Gold Coast	5/20/01	27.58S	153.25E
Whitsunday Island	6/13/01	20.16S	148.57E
Cairns, Queensland	6/26/01	16.55S	145.47E
Darwin, Queensland	7/18/01	12.27S	130.49E

INDONESIA

Kupang, Timor	8/26/01	10.10S	123.35E
Benoa, Bali	9/14/01	8.45S	115.13E
Nongsa Point, Batam	9/28/01	1.12N	104.06E

SINGAPORE

Raffles Marina	9/30/01	1.21N	103.38E

MALAYSIA

Port Dickson	10/8/01	2.29N	101.51E
Port Klang	10/10/01	3.00N	101.23E
Langkawi I.	10/16/01	6.18N	99.51E

THAILAND

Phi Phi Don	10/20/01 & 1/28/02	7.44N	98.46E
Phuket, Boat Lagoon	10/21/01 & 1/21/02	7.58N	98.23E

SRI LANKA

Galle	2/7/02	6.02N	80.14E

MALDIVES

Male	2/18/02	4.11N	73.30E

DJIBOUTI

Djibouti	3/11/02	11.36N	43.08E

SUDAN

Port Sudan	3/20/02	19.37N	37.14E

EGYPT

Suez	3/31/02	29.57N	32.35E
Port Said	4/3/02	31.16N	32.19E

CYPRUS

Larnaca	4/4/02	34.55N	33.39E

CROATIA

Dubrovnik	7/2/02 & 9/25/03	42.39N	18.05E
Split	7/7/02	43.30N	16.26E

CANADA

Vancouver, BC	7/5/04, 7/21, 9/29; 5/5/06	49.18N	123.08W
Victoria, BC	9/2/04, 9/26/04; 5/1/06	48.25N	123.22W
Prince Rupert, BC	5/24/06, 7/20/06	54.19N	130.19W
Halifax, NS	8/26/08	44.39N	63.34W

EL SALVADOR

Jiquilisco	1/31/07	13.16N	88.29W

COSTA RICA

Golfito	2/6/07	8.37N	83.09W

COLOMBIA

Isla Providencia	3/10/07	13.22N	81.23W

BELIZE

Belize City	3/20/07	17.28N	88.15W

BAHAMAS

Port Lucaya	2/21/11	26.31N	78.39W

**

St. Augustine also 5/21/10, 11/8/10, 5/21/11
Charleston, SC also 5/24/10, 5/24/11
Annapolis also 9/28/09, 6/2/10, 6/1/11
Baltimore also 8/26/09, 7/31/10
Newport also 7/7/08, 9/12/08, 7/13/09

Exhibit 18 *ESCAPADE* MAINTENANCE LOG

Dates work performed

Item

Daily

Item			
Engine- When Oil Added			
Engine- When Coolant Added			
Generator- When Coolant Added			

Weekly

Item										
Engine- Raw Water Strainer- Cleaned										
Ref.- Raw Water Strainer- Cleaned										
Engine Racor Filter- Checked										
Generator Racor Filter- Checked										
Generator- When Oil Added										
Batteries- Electrolyte Checked										
Bilge- Checked, Pump Tested										
Topsides- Washed										
Deck- Rinsed										
SS- Cleaned & Polished										
Blocks- Washed										
Winches & Windlass- Washed										
Handheld VHF- Charged										
Spotlight- Charged										
Watermaker- Ran										
Holding Tanks- Emptied										
Hatches & Ports- Breathed										

Two Weeks

Item			
Engine Belts- Checked			
Generator Belts- Checked			
Prop Shaft- 1/2 Turn of Greaser			
Rudder Tube- 1/2 Turn of Greaser			
Outboard- Checked Fuel Level			
Radar- check operation			
Prop shaft seal- Checked			
Speedometer Sender- Cleaned			

Monthly

Outboard Oil Level Checked											
Dinghy- Washed, Pressure Checked											
Passerelle- Washed & Polished											
Chain Locker- Flushed with Fresh Water											
Steering Cables- Tightness Checked											
Watermaker Pre-filters- Cleaned											
Watermaker Drive Belts- Checked											
Water Tanks- Switched to Small Tank											
Bilge- Flushed with Fresh Water											
Bilge Pump, Electric- Tested											
Bilge Pumps, Manual- Tested											
Bilge Pump, Engine- Tested											
Sea Cocks- Operated All											
Head, Vacuflush- Flushed											
Head, Manual- Checked Pellet Feeder											
GPS, Compass, Nightscope- Checked											
A/C Systems- Ran											
Light Bulbs, All- Checked											
Fire Extinguisher, Auto- Checked											
Zinc, Engine- Checked/replaced											
Zinc, Generator- Checked/replaced											
Cooking Gas- Checked											

4 Months or 250 Hours HOURS-NEXT>

Engine- Racor Filter- Replaced		
Engine Oil- Changed		
Engine Oil Filter- Replaced		
Engine Fuel Filter- Replaced & Bled		
Engine Air Filter- Cleaned		

6 months or 250 hours HOURS-NEXT>

Generator Racor Filter- Replaced		
Generator Oil- Changed		
Generator Oil Filter- Replaced		
Generator Housing- Cleaned & Check		
Generator- Brushes Checked by Tech.		

Six Months

Transmission- Fluid Level Checked								
Standing Rigging- Checked								
Davits- Checked								
Lifelines- Checked & Tightened								
Jammers- Oiled and Checked								
Cockpit Cushions- Cleaned								
Fender Covers- Washed								
Dinghy- Cleaned & Checked								
Water In-line Strainer- Cleaned								
Seagull Filter- Changed if required								
Bow Thruster- Oil level Checked								
Holding Tanks- Flushed								
Interior- Washed with Bleach								
Hatches & Ports- Coated with Vaseline								
Watermaker- Oil Level Checked								
Smoke Alarms- Batteries Checked								

Yearly

Engine Water Impeller- Checked								
Engine Exhaust System- Checked								
Engine Mounts- Checked								
Engine Coolant- Confirmed Anti-Freeze								
Generator Coolant- Confirmed Anti-Fr								
Generator Impeller- Checked								
Generator Exhaust System- Checked								
Transmission ATF Fluid- Changed								
Gear Shift Cables- Checked								
Max Prop- Greased & Checked								
Cutlass Bearing- Checked & Washed								
Rope Cutter- Checked								
Shaft Coupling Tightness- Checked								
Shaft Alignment- Checked								
Outboard Oil- Changed								
Outboard Gear Lube- Level Checked								
Outboard Lube Fittings- Lubed								
Outboard- Check plugs								

Yearly Cont'd

Item									
Standing Rigging Tape- Replaced									
Standing Rigging- Checked by Pro.									
Lines- Washed									
Halyards- Inspected for Wear									
Blocks- Polished & Replaced Ties									
Sails- Washed, Inspected & Repaired									
Bimini & Dodger- Washed, Inspected									
Horseshoe- Cleaned									
Steering Cables- Greased									
Rudder Bearings- Checked									
Winches- Disassembled & Greased									
Windlass- Disassembled & Greased									
Anchor Chain- Painted Marks									
Topsides- Waxed & Polished									
Bottom- Powerwashed									
Bottom- Painted & Checked Blisters									
Water Tank- Flushed & Checked									
Interior- Permit Air Circulation									
Sea Anchor & Drouge- Checked									
Liferaft- Tested by Certified Station									
Flares- Checked Dates									
Bicycles- Checked									

Two Years

Item		
Fuel Tank- Checked & Filter Cleaned		
Outboard Gear Lube- Changed		

Three Years

Item		
Keel bolts- Tightened		

Haul Out

Item		
Flushed Systems with Fresh Water		
See Separate Schedule		

Other Items

Exhibit 19 SAILING ACCOMPLISHMENTS

6/19/2011

ERICK A. REICKERT
(1996 thru 2011)

Sailed 73,211 nautical miles (NM) on Escapade; started June 19, 1996, ended June 13, 2011

Lived on-board nearly 6 years or 72.6 months (2,179 days)

Sailed for 11,459 hours = 477 days [6.39 knots average]

Had 135 different people on board, many multiple times

Circumnavigated world- October 6, 1997 to April 8, 2002 from/to Antalya, Turkey- 4.5 years

Crossed the Atlantic Ocean- A passage of 17 days and 2,714 miles (2,792 sailed) in 1998

Crossed the Pacific Ocean- A passage of 18 days and 3,004 miles (3,010 sailed) in 2000

Crossed the Indian Ocean- Three passages of 20.5 days & 3,490 miles (3,494 sailed) in 2002

Visited 39 Countries- England, France, Spain, Portugal, Gibraltar, Malta, Greece, Turkey, Italy, Dominican Republic, Jamaica, Mexico, USA, Panama, Ecuador, French Polynesia, Cook I., Niue, Tonga, Fiji, NZ, Australia, Indonesia, Singapore, Malaysia, Thailand, Sri Lanka, Maldives, Djibouti, Sudan, Egypt, Cyprus, Croatia, Canada, El Salvador, Costa Rica, Columbia, Belize & Bahamas

Visited 73 Islands- Jersey, Guernsey, Corsica, Sardinia, Mallorca, Menorca, Ibiza, Formentera, Lanzarote, Gran Canaria, St. Lucia, Martinique, Dominica, Gudalaoupe, Antigua, Nevis, St. Kitts, St. Eustatius, St. Barts, St. Martin, British Virgin Islands, St. John, St. Thomas, Puerto Rico, Gran Cayman, 8 San Blas, 2 Galapagos, 5 Marquesas, 2 Tuamotus, 5 Society, 1 Cook, Niue, 5 Tonga, 11 Fiji, 6 Maldives, Sicily, Isla Providencia

Encountered 16 foreign languages: French, Spanish, Portuguese, Turkish, Greek, Italian, Dutch, Indonesian, Malaysian, Thailand, Sri Lanka, Maldives, Sudanese, Egyptian, Croatian, Maltese

Achieved 214 miles sailing in 24 hours; 1,200 miles in 6 days in the Pacific Ocean

Entered 918 ports (1,155 entrances in all); Entered 20 ports at night

Hauled boat 12 times- Gibraltar, twice; Marmaris, Turkey; Savannah, USA; Gulf Harbour, NZ; Phuket, Thailand; Alcudia, Mallorca, Spain; Zadar, Croatia; Richmond, BC, Canada, Portsmouth, RI, USA (twice), Palm Beach, FL, Annapolis, MD

Went through locks, gates, and opening bridges (5,1,91)

Went through Panama Canal (twice), Suez Canal, Corinth Canal, C & D Canal (four times), Cape Cod Canal (six times)

Used all methods of securing: (1,301 times all told)
- Anchor (316 times)
- Along side (282 times)
- Stern-to or bow-to (248 times)
- Finger pontoon (206 times)
- Pontoon, hammerhead (94 times)
- On buoy (41 times)
- Quay, along side (27 times)
- Raft on other boats (23 times)
- Between poles (13 times)
- Anchor, line to shore (13 times)
- Travelift (12 times)
- Between two buoys (5 times)
- Hang on wall, tidal (4 times)
- Anchor, bow & stern (2 times)
- Onboard Ship- (2 times)
- Pile berth (1 time)

Crossed English Channel three times

Major reef areas- San Blas, Tuamotus, Fiji, Indonesia, Thailand, Maldives and the Red Sea

Shallow area- Bahamas

High tidal ranges- Channel Islands, St. Malo, Queensland coast, Australia

High current areas- Treguier River, Thames River, Alderney Race, Woods Hole, Hell Gate, Bali Strait, Dodd Narrows, Yuculta Rapids, Dent Rapids, Race Passage, Portsmouth, NH

High traffic areas- Strait of Gibraltar, English Channel, Intercoastal Waterway (ICW), Port of Singapore, Suez Canal, Strait of Messina, New York Harbor

Maneuvering in Ice at Glacier Bay National Park, Tracy Arm, Endicott Arm

Areas of interest- Atlantic, Bay of Biscay, Channel du Four, Alderney Race, Cape Finnesterre, Strait of Gibraltar, Gulf du Leon, Cape Hatteras, Cape Fear, Cook Strait; French Pass, NZ; Tasman Sea, Strait of Mallaca, Red Sea, Gulf of Aden, Nahwitti Bar, Capes Scott & Cook, Hudson River

43 Passages (In addition to crossing the Atlantic and Pacific)
- Passage of 11.2 days- (1,976 miles)- Male, Maldives to Djibouti, Djibouti
- Passage of 9 days (1,528 miles)- Savannah, GA, USA to San Blas, Panama
- Passage of 7.5 days (1,264 miles)- Gibraltar to Malta
- Passage of 7.5 days (1,166 miles)- Nelson, NZ to Sydney, Australia
- Passage of 6.8 days (1,095 miles)- Phuket, Thailand to Galle, Sri Lanka
- Passage of 6.8 days (1,077 miles)- Vuda Point, Fiji to Opua, New Zealand
- Passage of 5 days (826 miles)- Seattle, WA to San Francisco, CA
- Passage of 5 days (775 miles)- Nikolaos, Crete to Salerno, Italy
- Passage of 5 days (749 miles)- San Diego, CA to Cabo San Lucas, Mexico
- Passage of 4.2 days (673 miles)- Bawean I., Indonesia to Nongsa Point, Indonesia
- Passage of 4 days (676 miles)- Balboa, Panama to Salinas, Ecuador
- Passage of 4 days (672 miles)- Gibraltar to Lanzarote

- Passage of 4 days (593 miles)- Rarotonga, Cook Islands to Niue
- Passage of 4 days (538 miles)- Bora-Bora, F.P. to Rarotonga, Cook Islands
- Passage of 4 days (521 miles)- Huatulco, Mexico to Bahia Jiquilisco, El Salvador
- Passage of 3.4 days (612 miles)- Obock, Djibouti to Port Sudan, Sudan
- Passage of 3 days (555 miles)- Malta to Greece
- Passage of 3.5 days (542 miles)- Valletta, Malta to Mahon, Menorca, Spain
- Passage of 3 days (540 miles)- Puerto Lucia, Ecuador to San Cristobol, Galapagos
- Passage of 3 days (514 miles)- Isla Providencia, Columbia to Punta Gorda, Belize
- Passage of 3 days (502 miles)- Nuku-Hiva, Marquesas to Ahe, Tuamotus
- Passage of 3 days (501 miles)- Boca Chica, D. R. to Montego Bay, Jamaica
- Passage of 3 days (500 miles)- Norfolk, VA to Savannah, GA
- Passage of 3.2 days (498 miles)- Port Sudan to Safaga, Egypt
- Passage of 3 days (470 miles)- Darwin, Australia to Kupang, Timor, Indonesia
- Passage of 3 days (464 miles)- Tauranga, NZ to Wellington, NZ
- Passage of 3 days (458 miles)- Bahia Jiquilisco, El Salvador to Golfito, Costa Rica
- Passage of 3 days (442 miles)- Vava'u, Tonga to Suva, Fiji
- Passage of 2.5 days (419 miles)- Galle, Sri Lanka to Male, Maldives
- Passage of 2.5 days (417 miles)- Charleston, SC to Hampton, VA
- Passage of 2.4 days (395 miles)- Gove, Australia to Cape Hotham, Australia
- Passage of 2.5 days (355 miles)- Isla Mujeres, Mexico to Key West, FL
- Passage of 2 days (355 miles)- Isla Mujeres, Mexico to Key West, FL
- Passage of 2 days (351 miles)- Horn I., Australia to Gove, Australia
- Passage of 2 days (349 miles)- Newport, RI to Baltimore, MD
- Passage of 2 days (336 miles)- Golfito, Costa Rica to Balboa, Panama
- Passage of 2 days (331 miles)- Gran Cayman to Isla Mujeres, Mexico
- Passage of 2 days (326 miles)- Porto d'Ischia, Italy to Savona, Italy
- Passage of 2 days (278 miles)- Sausalito, CA to Santa Rosa Island, CA
- Passage of 2 days (255 miles)- Bocas del Toro, Panama to Isla Providencia, Columbia
- Passage of 2 days (247 miles)- Niue to Neiafu, Vava'u, Tonga
- Passage of 2 days (240 miles)- Acapulco, Mexico to Huatulco, Mexico
- Passage of 1.5 days (248 miles)- Beaufort, NC to York, VA

63 Overnights- Marmaris, Turkey to Nikolaos, Crete; Marseille, France to Roses Bay, Spain; Barcelona, Spain to Andraitx, Mallorca; Lanzarote to Gran Canaria; Ipswich, England to Guernsey; London, England to Cherbourg, France; Guernsey to Falmouth, England; Archeon, France to San Sebastian, Spain; Vilamoura, Portugal to Cadiz, Spain; Arecibo, Puerto Rico to Boca Chica, Dominican Republic; Montego Bay, Jamaica to Gran Cayman; Beaufort, NC to Norfolk, VA; Rangiroa, Tuamotus to Tahiti, French Polynesia- 3 times; Tahiti, F.P. to Huanine, French Polynesia; Ahe, Tuamotus to Rangiroa, Tuamotus; Kangean I., Indonesia to Bawean I., Indonesia; Port Stevens, Australia to Coffs Harbour, Australia; Kupang, Timor, Indonesia to Flores, Indonesia; Bali, Indonesia to Kangean I., Indonesia; Port Klang, Malaysia to Lumut, Malaysia; Endeavour Harbour, Egypt to Suez, Egypt; Port Said, Egypt to Larnaca, Cyprus; Larnaca, Cyprus to Antalya, Turkey; Thirasia, Greece to Porto Kayio, Greece; Corfu, Greece to Dubrovnik, Croatia- 2 times; Catania, Sicily, Italy to Argostoli, Cephalonia, Greece; Villasimius, Sardinia, Italy to Favignana, Sicily, Italy; Ampuriabrava, Spain to Marseille, France; Crotone, Italy to Vibo Valentia, Italy; Vis, Croatia to Brindisi, Italy; Vibo Valentia, Italy to Porto d'Ischia, Italy; Brindisi, Italy to Crotone, Italy; Zadar, Croatia to Vis, Croatia; Los Muertos, Mexico to Mazatlan, Mexico; Rose Harbour, BC, Canada to Port Hardy, BC, Canada; Charleston, SC to Beaufort, NC; Belize City, Belize to Puerto Aventuras, Mexico; West Palm Beach, FL to St. Augustine, FL; Puerto Navidad, Mexico to Ixtapa, Mexico; Key West, FL to Ft. Lauderdale, FL;

St. Augustine, FL to Hilton Head, SC; Shelter Bay, Panama to Bocas del Toro, Panama; Nuevo Vallarta, Mexico to Laguna Navidad, Mexico; Zihuanejo, Mexico to Acapulco, Mexico; Hilton Head, SC to Charleston, SC; Bar Harbor, ME to Shelburne, NS; Lockeport, NS to Bar Harbor, ME; Norfolk, VA to Beaufort, NC: Beaufort, NC to Charleston, SC; Charleston, SC to St. Augustine, FL; St. Augustine, FL to West Palm Beach, FL; Lantana, FL to St. Augustine, FL; St. Augustine, FL to Charleston, SC; Charleston, SC to Beaufort, NC; Beaufort, NC to Hampton, VA; Crisfield, MD to Beaufort, NC; Beaufort, NC to St. Augustine, FL; St. Augustine FL to West Palm Beach, FL; West Palm Beach, FL to St. Augustine, FL; St. Augustine, FL to Charleston, SC

Encountered Fog 14 times in several areas of the World

Encountered 2 sand storms entering ports in the Red Sea

Many gales and one storm- 45 to 60 knot winds with steep breaking seas- In Pacific

---

Substantial seas- 30 feet plus (In storm and in Tasman Sea)

Major overfalls- Cook Strait

Rode out Hurricane Floyd in port at Newport, RI

Avoided Maine lobster pot buoys

Crossed Gulf Stream four times

Exhibit 20 *ESCAPADE* DEPARTURE LIST

BELOW DECKS

- Review weather information
- Close all hatches, windows and ports
- Shut off propane gas switch
- Stow all loose items, including all galley items and pictures/plaques
- Empty water from sinks and shower trays
- Confirm bilge is empty
- Turn on salt-water pump if at anchor
- Confirm all engine and generator checks have been made (oil, water, fuel)
- If required, have life vests, tethers, and fowl weather gear ready
- Turn off the LVR (Line Voltage Regulator)
- Turn on DC electrics for engine, winches, bow thruster & mainsail furling
- Turn on all appropriate 24 VDC switches
- Turn on all electronics, confirm operation
- Confirm GPS waypoint data is entered
- Turn on navigation computer; turn on course tracking before departing
- Confirm AIS system is operating
- Enter all data in log and sail plan form, including departure time
- Prepare meals in advance, if possible

ABOVE DECKS

- Fill water tank, stow hose in lazerette
- Remove locks from deck lockers
- Stow companionway washboards in deck locker
- Remove all instrument covers and stow below
- Put binoculars, charts, pilot book, and hand compass on deck
- Put winch handles in place
- Attach cockpit VHF unit and turn on VHF to Channel 16
- Release steering wheel lock
- Lower dodger, if appropriate
- Put fender on deck for roving
- Put boat hook on cabin top
- Disconnect shore power, and stow cable in deck locker

- Stow Passerelle
- Confirm dinghy is raised and secured with straps
- Prepare sheets and lines for sailing
- Lock lazerette (leave lazerette key near companionway)
- Reduce shore lines to "slip release" configuration
- Start engine and confirm flow of water from exhaust, check oil pressure

AFTER DEPARTURE

- Stow fenders and dock lines
- Stow boat hook
- Secure anchor on deck
- Set sails and running rigging
- Do deck check of everything
- Confirm prop shaft is not turning after engine is shut down
- Empty holding tanks when far enough from land

IF GOING OFFSHORE- *PRIOR TO DEPARTURE*

- Confirm full tank of fuel
- Confirm full tank of fresh water
- Attach sea anchor & drogue to anchor lines
- Put outboard on rail
- Put cover on dinghy
- Attach jack lines
- Set up personal EPIRB receiver, confirm operation

NEW CREW ONBOARD

- Identify non-swimmers and have them wear life jackets
- Clarify second-in-command
- Identify location and explain use of safety and MOB equipment
- (MOM-8, Lifesling, MOB buttons, heaving line, fire extinguishers, flares, life raft, horn,
- First aid kit, VHF and SSB radios)
- Identify Mayday and Pan Pan procedures
- Discuss safety issues and procedures
- Discuss the process of leaving the dock, assign responsibilities

Exhibit 21 *S/V ESCAPADE* FIRST MATE DUTIES & REQUIREMENTS

DUTIES:

- Act as Captain in the absence or incapacity of the Owner.
- Act as First Mate at all times and assist with all sailing and boat handling activities, including standing watches and when docking or anchoring.
- Keep the boat in a high-class spic & span appearance. Wash the boat after each day's sailing, if water is available. Polish and clean as required. (Polish SS, clean & polish fiberglass, clean waterline, clean dinghy, etc.)
- Provide guests with a pleasant and comfortable experience. Share forward head with guests so they are not inconvenienced. Accommodation will be starboard cabin.
- Stay with the boat while the Owner is away, if required. Responsible for it's safekeeping.
- Perform preventative maintenance work, if required. (Change oil, check & fill batteries, check & clean raw water filters, etc.) Assist in all other maintenance activities.
- Occasional drinks preparation and meal preparation.
- Share in all other work including domestic clean up.
- Assist in putting the boat into the water at the beginning of the season and hauling the boat out at the end of the season.

QUALIFICATIONS:

- Qualifications at RYA Yachtmaster Ocean level or equivalent.
- Sailboat oriented. Experience on sailboats between 45' and 70' in various conditions.
- A US citizen or have a US B1/B2 Visa.

CHARACTERISTICS:

- No smoking or excessive drinking, no drugs.
- Cheerful & pleasant. Initiates duties without direction. Professional demeanor.

ADDITIONAL:

- There will be free time to go ashore, after work is accomplished.
- If *ESCAPADE* meals are taken ashore, you are welcome to join.

Exhibit 22 *ESCAPADE* FIRST MATE SALARY CONDITIONS

CONDITIONS

The salary package will consist of the following:

1. Pay will be by US dollar check, monthly, at the end of the month.

2. Travel to and from *ESCAPADE*, tourist or economy class, will be discussed. *ESCAPADE* is currently near Newport, Rhode Island, USA.

3. All food on board is provided. Meals ashore, if part of an *ESCAPADE* group, will also be provided.

4. Crew insurance is carried but this only covers major accidents. No medical coverage is provided.

5. Hotel and other costs ashore, while *ESCAPADE* is out of the water, will be provided.

6. Signing a Crew Agreement will be required. Termination can be at either party's initiation but a two-month notice will be required.

TIME PERIOD

Arrival at Newport, RI, USA should be on Sunday, May 18, 2008. It is planned to launch *ESCAPADE* into the water on May 21, 2008. *ESCAPADE* will be lifted from the water on September 18, 2008. The employment will be completed by Sunday, September 21, 2008.

CRUISING AREA

All cruising will between New York City and Canada, including Long Island Sound, Cape Cod, Boston, and Maine. Essentially all sailing will be day sails, thus being in port at night.

SALARY

The actual amount of salary will depend upon the skill level and experience of the person.

Exhibit 23 *ESCAPADE* LAY-UP & COMMISSION SCHEDULE

LAY-UP	FOR LAUNCH
ENGINE	
Engine- Perkins (6623 hours, oil changed at 6623)	Run engine
Racor fuel filter-change	Check
Replace engine fuel filter & bleed air	-
Replace oil filter-	-
Check zinc, drain water	Check
Change oil-	Check color
Clean air filter-	-
Check belts-	Check
Raw salt-water strainer- Clean	**Confirm strainer & fittings**
Water impeller-Remove & inspect	**Check,** Check water flow
Exhaust system- Check for leaks, tighten clips	Check
Engine mounts- Check	-
Flush with fresh water	-
Fresh water system- Check coolant (3.9 gal @ 50%)	Check
GENERATOR	
Generator- Onan (2280 hours, oil changed at 2250)	Run engine, check operation
Check oil-	Check color
Replace oil filter-	-
Clean inside housing	-
Replace Racor fuel filter-	Check
Flush with fresh water	-
Water impeller-	-
Check zinc	-
Check belts	Check
Fresh water system- Check coolant- OK	Check
Exhaust system- Check for leaks, tighten clips	Check
FUEL TANK	
Fill with diesel & conditioner	-
Fuel Taps- Turn off	**Turn on**
Fuel Breather- cover with tape	**Remove tape**
TRANSMISSION	
Transmission- Hurth (401 hours since rebuild at 6222 Eng. Hours)	
Gearshift cable- Check- OK	**Check**
ATF- Replace with new ATF	**Check ATF**
PROPELLER & SHAFT	
Max Prop- Check-	**Check- Grease**
Cutlass bearing- Check-	**Check**
Shaft coupling- Check-	**Check for tightness**
Rope cutter- Check- Not installed properly	**Check- Fix installation**
Stuffing Box- Check-	Check

*Items listed in Bold- Do prior to launching

LAY-UP	FOR LAUNCH

OUTBOARD
Honda (18 hours est.; 6 since service)

Put into lazarette-	**Put on rail**
Change oil-	Put on dinghy
Flush with fresh water-	Check
Drain Carburetor and run dry	-
Change gear lube if required-	Run
Lube fittings if required-	-
Fuel tank- Empty & let evaporate	-
	Fill

SONAR Forward Facing-Clean (do not paint)	**Check (for no paint)**

GPS-Turn off	Check
Personal EPIRB transmitters- turn off; receiver	Check

STANDING RIGGING

Check	Wash & Check
Slack off backstay	Tighten after launch

RUNNING RIGGING

	Rig Passerelle lift
Lines- Remove, wash & dry	Install
Blocks- Remove	Install (polish if required)
Cut off all ties	Add ties to all fittings
Halyards- Inspect for wear (especially spinnaker)	Check
Mast Boot Tape-Check	Check

WINCHES- Install covers	Remove, wash & store
Disassemble, grease & lube-	Check operation

FENDERS- Clean & store (4 in lazarette)	**Put on deck**

SAILS

Wash/let dry- (will be washed by sailmaker)	Get sails from sail maker
Staysail- remove and give to valet- 39#	Put up
Yankee- remove and give to valet- 98#	Put up
Main- remove and give to valet- 63#	Put up
MPS-remove and give to valet- 57#	Put in lazerette
Install flute stopper	**Remove flute stopper**

BIMINI & DODGER- Remove & store	Install, check

LIFE SLING- Remove, store forward	Install, add strobe light
MOM-8- Remove, store forward	Install
HORSESHOE- Remove, clean	Replace, Check name
SEA ANCHOR & DROGUE- Check	Check and air out

SPEEDOMETER SENDER- Remove & Clean	Replace, after launch

JAMMERS- Spinlocks- Oil	Oil, confirm function

LAY-UP	FOR LAUNCH

STEERING

Wheel- Remove	**Replace**
Cables- check	Grease
Rudder tube- 1/2 turn of greaser	**Check- Add grease**
Rudder bearings- Check for wear	**Check rudder for movement**
Auto pilot rams sound check-	Test underway

ZINCS

Main- Check-	-
Max Prop-Needs replacing	**Remove** (use Locktite)
-Bow thruster- Needs replacing	**Remove** (use Locktite)
-Prop shaft- (1.5") Gone! Needs replacing	**Remove** (use Locktite)
Prepare for moist, cold climate	
-Install three Damp-Rid containers	**Remove**

DINGHY

Wash	**Wash**
Deflate	**Inflate**
Put on deck & lock	Take off deck & launch
Name -Check	Check
Dinghy straps (on davits)- Remove	Replace
Passerelle- Wash, polish & stow	Check
Bottom- Power wash, remove all growth	**Paint with anti-fouling**

TOPSIDES

Mark strap points on outside of toe rail-	**Wash, polish, & wax**
	-

DECK

DECK	Clean
BOOM	Check & oil toggle
LIFELINES- check	Check and tighten
Stainless steel and bright work	Clean & polish
CHAIN LOCKER- Flush with fresh water	Check
ANCHOR CHAIN- Check-	**Check paint marks**

HEATER- Replace over winter	Check new installation
Turn off heater hoses at engine	Turn on at engine

WINDLASS

Slack off tension	Check operation
Rinse with fresh water	-
Inner parts-	Take apart, grease & oil, replace
	Take apart, grease & oil dish springs

BATTERIES

Fill and turn off all switches- house batteries	**Check, fill**
Engine battery- Disconnect	**Check, fill, charge, connect**
Generator battery- Disconnect & charge	**Check, charge, connect**

WATER MAKER-Seafresh

Pickle with 5 oz solution & Glycerin [2 L per 25 L]	-
Pre-filters- Clean-	Check visually
Check pump sump oil level-	Check
Check drive belts-	Check

LAY-UP	FOR LAUNCH

BILGE

Flush with fresh water & cleaner	-
Empty	Check High water alarm
Turn off bilge pump	**Check**
Electric Pump	**Test by filling bilge**
Electric Pump- Check for debris	Check
Manual pumps (both)	Check operation
Engine driven- Fix w new parts	Check operation

FRESH WATER TANK

Empty, add Anti-freeze [8 gal aft, 2 gal fwd, 1 gal heater]	Flush with water, fill
In-line strainer filter-Clean-	Clean
Seagull filter- Remove	Replace
Draw Anti-freeze thru system	Flush with fresh water

REFRIGERATION & A/C SYSTEMS

Run and check	Open seacock-Run & check
Clean raw salt-water strainer	**Confirm strainer & fittings**
Flush with fresh water	-
Clean out refrigerator & freezer & defrost	-
Blow out water from lines	-
	-

RAW WATER FILTERS-Cleaned — **Check tightness**

BOW THRUSTER- Clean propellors — **Check oil level/**Check operation

SALT WATER SYSTEM- Empty — Check operation

SEA COCKS- Operate and spray with WD-40 — **Operate & spray with WD-40**
Replace stb cockpit, engine intake, fwd head — **Confirm operation & check**

HOLDING TANKS- Empty & flush with fresh water & cleaner — **Close seacocks**

COCKPIT CUSHIONS- Clean — Check & Install

GAS LOCKER- Propane tank- close valve at tank — Check system, open valves
Fill second bottle

HEADS

Vacuflush- Flush with fresh water	Operate & check
Manual, Par- Flush with salt-water	Operate & check
Pellet feeder	Add pellet-Confirm blue water

LIGHT BULBS- including nav. lights-Check — Check & replace as required
Check port spreader light

ELECTRONICS — Turn on and check

ELECTRIC PANELS

DC Panel	Activate
DC Major Switch Panel	Activate
AC Panel	Check

DIGITAL BAROMETER- — Check, battery

LAY-UP	FOR LAUNCH
DOORS/LATCHES	Check
HATCHES & PORTS	
Open and let "breathe"	Open and let "breath"
Add Vaseline to seals	Add Vaseline to seals
Remove screens	Install screens as required
INTERIOR	
Open lockers, lift mattresses, raise cushions, & lift floorboards to permit air circulation	Sort out galley
Wash surfaces with weak bleach solution to prevent mold	Completely clean
GAS DETECTOR SYSTEM-Check	Check
SMOKE ALARMS	Check
CO DETECTOR	Check
FIRE EXTINGUISHERS	Check gages
LIFE RAFT- Lock locker	Confirm condition
LIFE VESTS- Wash	Inspect-Test blow up by mouth
FLARES	Inspect, check dates
BICYCLES- Stow forward	Check, ride, put in lazarette
STERN LADDER	Check leather
BEDSPREADS, & LINEN- Wash, pack	Install
GALAXY INMARSAT C- Log out, turn off	Log-in
HAND HELD EQUIPMENT- Hide	
VHF handsets (3)& Binocular [Aft cabin, under bed & seat]	Check
Spotlight [usual place]	Charge, check
GPS [Go bag]	Change batteries
Drill [usual place]	Charge both batteries
Handheld compass [fwd cabin, center upper port cabinet]	Check Battery
Headphones [under armrest]	Check operation
ITT Nightscope [aft cabin]	Check batteries
Handheld Depth finder [in bottom drawer]	Check operation
406 EPIRB- Buy new one	Check operation
Handheld VHF (2)- [Aft cabin]	Check, charge

MEMO:

Items to arrange and track:

    Painting bottom- Dark blue Micron CSC (Do not paint sonar)

    Waxing & polishing topsides

    Sails- Main, Yankee, staysail, & MPS- Check, repair & store

Other items-

    Give Key to Yard 9/17/08

    Get Key from office

    Load computer with new charts

Made in the USA
Middletown, DE
21 September 2017